New Trends in Stochastic Processes, Probability and Statistics

New Trends in Stochastic Processes, Probability and Statistics

Guest Editors

Alexander Tikhomirov
Vladimir Ulyanov
Elena Yarovaya

MDPI

Basel • Beijing • Wuhan • Barcelona • Belgrade • Novi Sad • Cluj • Manchester

Guest Editors

Alexander Tikhomirov
Institute of Physics and Mathematics
Komi Science Center of Ural Division of the Russian Academy of Sciences
Syktyvkar
Russia

Vladimir Ulyanov
Faculty of Computational Mathematics and Cybernetics
Lomonosov Moscow State University
Moscow
Russia

Elena Yarovaya
Faculty of Mechanics and Mathematics
Lomonosov Moscow State University
Moscow
Russia

Editorial Office

MDPI AG
Grosspeteranlage 5
4052 Basel, Switzerland

This is a reprint of the Special Issue, published open access by the journal *Mathematics* (ISSN 2227-7390), freely accessible at: https://www.mdpi.com/si/mathematics/Stoch_Processes_Probab_Stat.

For citation purposes, cite each article independently as indicated on the article page online and as indicated below:

Lastname, A.A.; Lastname, B.B. Article Title. *Journal Name* **Year**, *Volume Number*, Page Range.

ISBN 978-3-7258-4549-1 (Hbk)
ISBN 978-3-7258-4550-7 (PDF)
https://doi.org/10.3390/books978-3-7258-4550-7

Contents

About the Editors

Alexander Tikhomirov

Alexander Tikhomirov has been a professor at the Institute of Physics and Mathematics, Komi Science Center of Ural Division of the Russian Academy of Sciences, Russia, since 2008. Professor Tikhomirov received his Ph.D. degree in Mathematics from St. Petersburg State University, Russia, in 1977 and his Habilitation (Doctor of Sciences) from the St. Petersburg Department of the Steklov Mathematical Institute of the Russian Academy of Sciences, Russia, in 1996. From 1977 to 2002, he worked at the Faculty of Mathematics at Syktyvkar State University, where he became a full professor in 1998. His research focuses on random matrices, strong mixing conditions, limit theorems, and circular law.

Vladimir Ulyanov

Vladimir Ulyanov is currently a professor at the Faculty of Computational Mathematics and Cybernetics, Lomonosov Moscow State University, Russia, and a professor at the Faculty of Social Sciences, National Research University—Higher School of Economics, Russia. He received his Ph.D. degree from Lomonosov Moscow State University in 1978 and his Habilitation (Doctor of Sciences) from Steklov Mathematical Institute of the Russian Academy of Sciences in 1994. He was awarded the State Prize of the USSR for Young Scientists in 1987. He worked as an Alexander von Humboldt Research Fellow in Germany from 1991 to 1993 and a JSPS Research Fellow in Japan in 1999 and 2004, respectively. He has worked as a visiting professor/researcher at Bielefeld University, Germany; the University of Leiden; the University de Paris V; the University of Hong Kong; the Institute of Statistical Mathematics in Tokyo; the National University of Singapore; the University of Melbourne; Shandong University, China, etc. He is currently a Member of the Bernoulli Society. His research interests include limit theorems of probability theory, vector-valued random variables, weak limit theorems, Gaussian processes, approximation in statistics, and transforms of probability distributions.

Elena Yarovaya

Elena Yarovaya is currently a professor in the Faculty of Mechanics and Mathematics, Lomonosov Moscow State University, Russia. She received her Ph.D. from Lomonosov Moscow State University in 1999 and her Habilitation (Doctor of Sciences) in 2013. She is currently a Member of the Bernoulli Society and an elected Member of the International Statistical Institute (ISI) and the Society of Mathematical Biology. Her research interests lie in the limit theorems of probability theory, random processes, mathematical statistics, the application of probabilistic–statistical methods, and models in biomedical research.

Preface

This reprint focuses on contemporary trends in the theory of stochastic processes and mathematical statistics. Particular attention is paid to processes that allow us to study the evolution of particle systems in which each particle that is born, dies, and can move in space in various environments follows rules that take into account a random factor. Such processes are used in various fields, from statistical physics to population dynamics. One of the key issues in analyzing such systems is the limiting behavior of the set of characteristics describing their evolution. Despite the rigor of the theoretical results, their practical interpretation is required for numerous applications. The development of new methods for studying stochastic processes, combining martingale techniques and spectral approaches to analyze the spectrum of high-dimensional random matrices, is also a topic covered in this collection. At the same time, issues related to the modeling and statistical analysis of such systems in various applications are considered. This Special Issue is devoted to an important aspect of modern applied statistics, the identification of random process parameters and the development of non-parametric statistical methods. This reprint consists of ten articles—one review article and nine research papers—which are discussed below

An overview of various models of continuous-time branching random walks, which can be described in terms of the birth, death, and transport of particles on multidimensional lattices, can be found in the reprint of E. Yarovaya's "Space Structure of Branching Random Walks", Moscow: MCCME (Moscow Center for Continuous Mathematical Education), 2024 (in Russian). Such models have a wide class of applications in population dynamics—see, for example, the papers of S. Molchanov and coauthors. In branching random walks, lattice points where particle births and deaths can occur are known as sources of branching, and the motion of particles on lattices is described by random walks. The behavior of the moments of the numbers of particles is largely determined by the structure of the spectrum of the evolution operator of the mean number of particles. In contrast to previous studies, in Contribution 1, the authors consider a branching random walk on a one-dimensional lattice in a random non-homogeneous environment. The process starts with a single particle. This particle can either walk on the lattice or disappear with a random intensity until it reaches a certain point, which the authors call the reproduction source. At the source, the particle can split into two offspring or jump out of the source. The offspring of the initial particle evolve according to the same law, independently of each other and the entire prehistory. The aim of this paper is to study the conditions required for the presence of exponential growth in the average number of particles at every lattice point. For this purpose, the authors investigate the spectrum of the random evolution operator of the average particle number and derive the condition under which exponential growth has a probability of one. Moreover, the authors study the processes under the violation of this condition and present the lower and upper estimates for the probability of exponential growth.

In Contribution 2, Alexander Bulinski investigates the forward selection of relevant factors by means of an MDR-EFE method. Based on the MDR-EFE algorithm, the suboptimal procedure under consideration provides a sequential selection of relevant factors affecting the studied, in general, non-binary random response. The model is not assumed to be linear; the joint distribution of the factor vector and response is unknown. A set of relevant factors has specified cardinality. It is proved that, under certain conditions, the mentioned forward selection procedure asymptotically gives a random set of factors (with the probability tending to one as the number of observations grows to infinity) that coincides with the "oracle" set. This means that the random set obtained with this algorithm approximates the feature collection that would be identified if the joint distribution of the feature vector and response were known. For this purpose, the statistical estimators of the prediction error function of the studied response are proposed, which involve a new version of regularization. This permits the author to guarantee not only the central limit theorem for normalized estimators, but also to find the convergence rate of their first two moments to the corresponding moments of the limiting Gaussian variable.

Contribution 3, authored by Kalanka P. Jayalath, makes Bayesian inferences for the two-parameter Birnbaum–Saunders (BS) distribution in the presence of right-censored data. A flexible Gibbs sampler handles the censored BS data in this Bayesian work that relies on Jeffrey's and Achcar's reference priors. A comprehensive simulation study is conducted to compare estimates under various parameter settings, sample sizes, and levels of censoring, and further comparisons are drawn with real-world examples involving Type-II, progressively Type-II, and randomly right-censored data. The study concludes that the suggested Gibbs sampler enhances the accuracy of Bayesian inferences, and the amount of censoring and the sample size are identified as influential factors in such analyses.

In Contribution 4, Yufeng Shi and Jinghan Wang consider general mean-field backward doubly stochastic differential equations (mean-field BDSDEs), whose generator, f, can be discontinuous in y. They prove the existence of solutions to the theorem under stochastic linear growth conditions, obtaining the related comparison theorem. Naturally, they present these results under the linear growth condition, a special case of the stochastic condition. Finally, a financial claim sale problem is discussed, demonstrating the application of general mean-field BDSDEs in finance.

The Black–Scholes formula is essential for pricing a contingent claim in complete financial markets. This formula can be obtained assuming that the investor's strategy is carried out according to a self-financing criterion. Hence, a set of self-financing portfolios arises, corresponding to different contingent claims. In light of this, the following natural questions arise: If an investor invests according to self-financing portfolios in the financial market, what are the maximal and minimal distributions of the investor's wealth on some specific interval at the terminal time? Furthermore, how can the corresponding optimal portfolios be constructed if such distributions exist? In Contribution 5, Shuhui Liu applies backward stochastic differential equations theory to obtain affirmative answers to the above questions. The explicit formulations for the maximal and minimal distributions of wealth when adopting self-financing strategies are derived, and the corresponding optimal (self-financing) portfolios are constructed. Furthermore, this contribution verifies the benefits of diversified portfolios in financial markets, issuing a clear conclusion: do not put all your eggs in the same basket.

In Contribution 6, Huaijin Liang, Jin Ma, Wei Wang, and Xiaodong Yan demystify the two-armed futurity bandit's unfairness and apparent fairness—while a gambler may occasionally win, continuous gambling inevitably results in a net loss to the casino. This study experimentally demonstrates the profitability of a particularly deceptive casino game: a two-armed antique Mills Futurity slot machine. The main findings clearly show that both non-random and random two-arm strategies, predetermined by the player and repeated without interruption, are always profitable for the casino, despite the gambler refunding two coins for every two consecutive losses. The paper theoretically explores the cyclical nature of slot machine strategies and speculates on the impact of the frequency of switching strategies on casino returns. The obtained results not only assist casino owners in developing and improving casino designs, but also guide gamblers to participate in gambling more cautiously.

The most read article in the Special Issue is Contribution 7, a review by Vladimir V. Ulyanov. In 1733, de Moivre, investigating the limit distribution of the binomial distribution, was the first to discover the existence of the normal distribution and the central limit theorem (CLT). In this review article, the author briefly recalls the history of classical CLT and martingale CLT before introducing new directions for CLT, namely Peng's nonlinear CLT and Chen–Epstein's nonlinear CLT, as well as Chen–Epstein's nonlinear normal distribution function. The article first reviews the nearly four-hundred-year history of the CLT, with particular emphasis on the CLT under the axiomatic framework of nonlinear expectation and Shige Peng and Zengjing Chen's work establishing the CLT within this new axiomatic system. In particular, Chen's work on the new nonlinear normal distribution and the nonlinear CLT represents major discoveries in this field. The relationship between the axiomatic framework of nonlinear expectation and Kolmogorov's classical axiomatic system can be compared to the relationship between Euclidean and non-Euclidean geometry. Therefore, under this new framework, the review concludes, the CLT and normal distribution can greatly enrich our understanding of the stochastic world.

Four major schools have emerged in the development of probability theory, stochastic processes, and financial mathematics: the Soviet "School of Probability", the Japanese "School of Stochastic Integration", the French "School of Martingale Theory", and the American "School of Rational Expectations". The works of Peng and Chen gave rise to China's "School of Nonlinear Expectations".

In Contribution 8, Siyu Liu, Xiequan Fan, Haijuan Hu, and Paul Doukhan, with some mild conditions, established sharp moderate deviations for a kernel density estimator, providing equivalents for the tail probabilities of this estimator.

Contribution 9 is devoted to the investigation of the second Borel–Cantelli lemma for capacity without assuming the independence of events, with the authors managing to obtain a sufficient condition under which the second Borel–Cantelli lemma for capacity holds. These results are natural extensions of the classical Borel–Cantelli lemma. However, the proof differs from that found in the literature.

Yuping Song, Ruiqiu Chen, Chunchun Cai, Yuetong Zhang, and Min Zhu coauthored Contribution 10: "Self-Weighted Quantile Estimation for Drift Coefficients of Ornstein–Uhlenbeck Processes with Jumps and Its Application to Statistical Arbitrage." The estimation of drift parameters in the Ornstein–Uhlenbeck (O-U) process with jumps primarily employs methods such as maximum likelihood estimation, least squares estimation, and least absolute deviation estimation. These methods generally assume specific error distributions and finite variances. However, with the increasing uncertainty in financial markets, asset prices exhibit characteristics such as skewness and heavy tails, which lead to biases in traditional estimators. In this contribution the authors propose a self-weighted quantile estimator for the drift parameters of the O-U process with jumps, and verify its asymptotic normality in cases of large samples, given certain assumptions. Furthermore, through Monte Carlo simulations, the proposed self-weighted quantile estimator is compared with least squares, quantile, and power variation estimators, with estimation performance evaluated using metrics such as mean, standard deviation, and mean squared error (MSE). The simulation results show that the self-weighted quantile estimator proposed in the paper performs well across different metrics. Finally, the proposed estimator is applied to the inter-period statistical arbitrage of the CSI 300 Index Futures. The backtesting results indicate that the self-weighted quantile method proposed in the paper performs well in empirical applications.

In summary, this Special Issue proposes and develops new mathematical methods and approaches, new algorithms and research frameworks, and examines their applications to solve various nontrivial practical problems. We strongly believe that the selected topics and results will be attractive and useful to the international scientific community and will contribute to further research in the fields of probability theory and mathematical statistics.

Acknowledgments: The research activity of the Guest Editors was conducted within the framework of the HSE University Basic Research Programs and within the program of the Moscow Center for Fundamental and Applied Mathematics, Lomonosov Moscow State University.

Alexander Tikhomirov, Vladimir Ulyanov, and Elena Yarovaya
Guest Editors

mathematics

MDPI

Article

Branching Random Walks in a Random Killing Environment with a Single Reproduction Source

Vladimir Kutsenko [1,2], Stanislav Molchanov [3,4,*] and Elena Yarovaya [1,2]

1 Department of Probability Theory, Lomonosov Moscow State University, Moscow 119234, Russia; vlakutsenko@ya.ru (V.K.); yarovaya@mech.math.msu.su (E.Y.)
2 Department of Probability Theory and Mathematical Statistics, Steklov Mathematical Institute, Moscow 119991, Russia
3 Laboratory of Stochastic Analysis and Its Applications, National Research University Higher School of Economics, Moscow 101000, Russia
4 Department of Mathematics and Statistics, University of North Carolina at Charlotte, Charlotte, NC 28223, USA
* Correspondence: smolchan@uncc.edu

Abstract: We consider a continuous-time branching random walk on $\mathbb{Z}$ in a random non-homogeneous environment. The process starts with a single particle at initial time $t = 0$. This particle can walk on the lattice points or disappear with a random intensity until it reaches the certain point, which we call the reproduction source. At the source, the particle can split into two offspring or jump out of the source. The offspring of the initial particle evolves according to the same law, independently of each other and the entire prehistory. The aim of this paper is to study the conditions for the presence of exponential growth of the average number of particles at every lattice point. For this purpose, we investigate the spectrum of the random evolution operator of the average particle numbers. We derive the condition under which there is exponential growth with probability one. We also study the process under the violation of this condition and present the lower and upper estimates for the probability of exponential growth.

Keywords: branching processes; random walks; branching random walks; random environments

MSC: 60J27; 60J80; 05C81; 60J85

1. Introduction

In physical models with a random environment, phenomena can occur that differ substantially from what is usually encountered in statistical physics. In particular, the mean energy of the quantity under consideration can grow slower than the root of the mean square of this quantity, and both of these growth rates, in turn, are larger than the growth rate of a typical realization of the quantity under study. Such a phenomenon has been called intermittency (see, e.g., [1,2]). An example of such behavior is considered, in particular, in [3], where a model of particle population is considered. The intensity of particles splitting was assumed to be stationary in time and random in the spatial variables, with its mean value equal to zero. In addition, particle diffusion was included in the model.

The processes considered in papers [2,3] can be regarded as a special case of a branching random walk (BRW) in a random environment, which apparently was first presented in [1]. The authors introduced basic concepts for BRWs in a random environment and developed approaches to BRW analysis. The model studied in this work coincides with the previously introduced the parabolic Anderson model [4], where paper [1] itself is recognized as fundamental and has sparked active research on applications of the Anderson model in various fields [5].

The phenomenon of intermittency in the case of BRWs in random environments required the study of the asymptotic behavior of particle number moments averaged over the environment. In particular, it was required to study the regularity of the growth of such moments. The required asymptotics were obtained in [6] under the assumption of an asymptotically Weibull distribution of the right tail of the random potential, i.e., the difference between the splitting rate and the death rate. For the same potential but for a non-homogeneous model, similar results were obtained in [7]. For the case of a random subexponential potential results were obtained in [8,9]. The case of the Pareto potential was studied in [10]. Thus, the general question of the existence of intermittency in the BRW model has been practically fully investigated.

Further investigations focused on the non-averaged characteristics of BRWs, e.g., non-averaged moments in [11] or survival probability in [12]. These characteristics are more difficult to study, but they provide an opportunity to describe not only the qualitative but also the quantitative behavior of individual realizations of the process. One of the main tools for studying such problems is the study of the spectrum of the corresponding random operator.

The present paper extends the study of the spectrum of a random operator to a model of the BRW in a non-homogeneous random environment. We investigate the simplest characteristic of a random spectrum, the spectral bifurcation, consisting of the existence and non-existence of a positive eigenvalue. We also investigate the conditions for the occurrence of this bifurcation and estimate its probabilistic characteristics. Note that some of the results for this model are announced in [13].

The BRW model is in demand in various natural sciences and humanities, at least in demography, where branching processes are often considered to demonstrate a realistic model for the distribution of people, despite its obvious simplicity, and in biology in similar problems (see, e.g., [14–18]). The introduction of a random environment into the BRW model expands the range of biological problems that can be modeled [19].

We consider a BRW as a model of a population process rather than a physical model. A simple but extremely important characteristic of such a process is the criticality of the growth rate of the particle population. It is known that in the case of a random environment the particle population can be exponentially decreasing or exponentially increasing [20]. Exponential growth of the particle population entails the presence of a positive eigenvalue in the spectrum of the evolution operator for the average number of the particles. Therefore, we consider the spectral bifurcation study as a tool for qualitative assessment of changes in process behavior rather than as the purpose of this paper.

We note separately that many authors have considered the branching process in a random environment; see, e.g., [21–23]. In such processes there is no spatial structure, so the developed research methods are not suitable for the study of our problem. We also note the early work [24], where a BRW in a random medium in discrete time was considered. However, this model has no connection with the parabolic Anderson model, and, thus, is far from the BRW model under consideration.

2. Model Description

Let us consider a branching random walk (BRW) on a one-dimensional lattice $\mathbb{Z}$ with continuous time. On the lattice we define a field of independent identically distributed random variables $\mathcal{M} = \{\mu(x,\cdot), x \in \mathbb{Z}\backslash\{0\}\}$, which are defined on some probability space $(\Omega, \mathcal{F}, \mathbb{P})$. We assume that each random variable $\mu(x,\cdot)$ takes values from the closed interval $[0,c]$ with $c \geqslant 0$ and is a mixture of discrete and absolutely continuous random variables (r.v.). Also, we assume that the continuous component of $\mu(x,\cdot)$ has a positive density on $[0,c]$. The field $\mathcal{M}$ forms on $\mathbb{Z}$ a "random killing environment" that determines the intensity of particle death in the BRW. In addition, we introduce the parameter $\Lambda \geqslant 0$, which is responsible for the intensity of particle multiplication at zero, and parameter $\varkappa > 0$, which controls the intensity of particle walking on the lattice.

Suppose that at time $t = 0$ there is a realization of the $\mathcal{M}$ field denoted by $\mathcal{M}(\omega) = \{\mu(x,\omega), x \in \mathbb{Z}\backslash\{0\}, \omega \in \Omega\}$. Also, assume that the process at time $t = 0$ starts with a single particle at some point $x \in \mathbb{Z}$. The further evolution proceeds as follows. Suppose the particle is at zero, then in time $h \to 0$ it can split into two particles with probability $\Lambda h + o(h)$, move equally likely to one of the neighboring points with probability $\varkappa h + o(h)$, and remain in place with probability $1 - \Lambda h - \varkappa h + o(h)$. Suppose the particle is at the point $x \neq 0$, then in time $h \to 0$ it can disappear with probability $\mu(x,\omega)h + o(h)$, move equally likely to one of the neighboring points with probability $\varkappa h + o(h)$, and remain in place with probability $1 - \mu(x,\omega)h - \varkappa h + o(h)$. The new particles evolve according to the same law independently of each other and of all prehistory.

The introduced process is Markovian, and can be described in terms of a set of exponential and polynomial variables. This description may be more convenient for the perception of the model. Let us introduce the average waiting time $\tau(x)$ at an arbitrary point $x \in \mathbb{Z}$:

$$\tau(x) = \begin{cases} (\varkappa + \Lambda)^{-1}, & \text{if } x = 0; \\ (\varkappa + \mu(x,\omega))^{-1}, & \text{if } x \neq 0. \end{cases}$$

The evolution of a particle located at point x is as follows. If the particle is at zero, it waits for an exponentially distributed time with parameter $\tau(0)^{-1}$, and then instantly splits in two or moves equiprobably to one of the neighboring lattice points. The choice between these two events is made with corresponding probabilities $\Lambda\tau(0)$ and $\varkappa\tau(0)$. If the particle is at a point x outside zero, it also waits an exponentially distributed time with parameter $\tau(x)^{-1}$ and then vanishes instantaneously or moves equiprobably to one of the neighboring lattice points. The choice between these two events is made with corresponding probabilities $\mu(x,\omega)\tau(x)$ and $\varkappa\tau(x)$. The evolution of particles occurs independently of each other and of all prehistory.

We will show later on that the branching process of particles at the point $x \in \mathbb{Z}$ can be conveniently described by the potential $V(x,\omega)$, which reflects the criticality of the branching process at each point:

$$V(x,\omega) = \begin{cases} \Lambda, & x = 0; \\ -\mu(x,\omega), & x \neq 0 \end{cases}$$

or

$$V(x,\omega) = \Lambda\delta_0(x) - \mu(x,\omega)(1 - \delta_0(x)).$$

The BRW at time t due to the Markov property can be completely described by the set of particle numbers at time t at the points $y \in \mathbb{Z}$ denoted by $N_t(y,\omega)$. However, $N_t(y,\omega)$ is a random variable and hence is difficult to investigate. Therefore, it is common to consider the average particle number [1,6]:

$$m_1(t,x,y,\omega) = \mathbb{E}_x N_t(y,\omega),$$

where $\mathbb{E}_x$ is the mathematical expectation under the condition that at time $t = 0$ there is one particle at point x.

By F_μ we further denote the distribution function of $\mu(x)$. In this paper, we are interested in the probability $P(\Lambda,\varkappa,F_\mu)$ of the realization of an environment in which there is an exponential growth of $m_1(t,x,y,\omega)$ for given parameters Λ, $\varkappa$, and F_μ. We will refer to such exponential growth as "supercriticality". The formal definition is as follows:

$$P(\Lambda,\varkappa,F_\mu) = \mathbb{P}\left\{\omega \in \Omega : \exists \lambda, C(x,y) > 0 : \lim_{t\to\infty} \frac{m_1(t,x,y,\omega)}{C(x,y)e^{\lambda t}} = 1, \quad \forall x,y \in \mathbb{Z}\right\},$$

where $C(x,y) = C(x,y,\omega,\Lambda,\varkappa,F_\mu)$, $\lambda = \lambda(\omega,\Lambda,\varkappa,F_\mu)$. Note that we require exponential growth of the average particle population simultaneously in all points of the lattice. However, further we will show that this condition is equivalent to exponential growth at least in one point. Intuitively speaking, the exponential growth at one point "is spread"over the whole lattice with the help of random walk.

The purpose of this paper is to estimate $P(\Lambda, \varkappa, F_\mu)$ as a function of Λ, $\varkappa$, and F_μ. To achieve this, we first use the standard approach described, e.g., in [6,7,25], and write the Cauchy problem for $m_1(t,x,y,\omega)$:

$$\begin{aligned} \frac{\partial m_1(t,x,y,\omega)}{\partial t} &= (\varkappa\Delta m_1)(t,x,y,\omega) + V(x,\omega)m_1(t,x,y,\omega), \\ m_1(0,x,y) &= \delta_y(x), \end{aligned} \tag{1}$$

where $\varkappa\Delta f(x) = \frac{\varkappa}{2}\sum_{|x'-x|=1}(f(x') - f(x))$ is the discrete Laplace operator on $\mathbb{Z}$, and the sign $|\cdot|$ denotes the lattice distance on the l_1 norm. Here and below we assume that all operators are defined on $l_2(\mathbb{Z})$.

Let us introduce a random self-adjoint operator $H(\omega) = \varkappa\Delta + V(x,\omega)$ to rewrite the problem (1) in a simpler form:

$$\begin{aligned} \frac{\partial m_1(t,x,y,\omega)}{\partial t} &= H(\omega)m_1(t,x,y,\omega), \\ m_1(0,x,y) &= \delta_y(x). \end{aligned} \tag{2}$$

In problems of this kind, the behavior of $m_1(t,x,y,\omega)$ depends on the spectrum structure of the random operator $H(\omega)$. Therefore, the present work is mainly devoted to the study of the spectrum of the $H(\omega)$. In Sections 3 and 4, it is shown that the spectrum of $\sigma(H(\omega))$ consists of a non-positive non-random part and can contain a positive random eigenvalue; in Section 5 we derive the condition under which $P(\Lambda, \varkappa, F_\mu) = 1$; we address violation of this condition in Sections 6 and 7, where we present the lower and upper estimates for $P(\Lambda, \varkappa, F_\mu)$. The main proofs are given in the text of the paper after the corresponding statements, while the auxiliary proofs are placed in Section 9.

3. The Non-Random Part of the Spectrum of the Evolutionary Operator

We obtained the results of this and the next section using the technique described in [20]. In these sections, we prove the results for the Cauchy problem in arbitrary dimension $d \in \mathbb{N}$, although the case $d = 1$ is sufficient to study our model. Consider the following Cauchy problem for $m_1(t,x,y,\omega)$:

$$\begin{aligned} \frac{\partial m_1(t,x,y,\omega)}{\partial t} &= (\varkappa\Delta m_1)(t,x,y,\omega) + V(x,\omega)m_1(t,x,y,\omega), \\ m_1(0,x,y) &= \delta_y(x), \end{aligned} \tag{3}$$

where $\varkappa\Delta f(x) = \frac{\varkappa}{2d}\sum_{|x'-x|=1}(f(x') - f(x))$ is the discrete Laplace operator on $\mathbb{Z}^d$, and the sign $|\cdot|$ denotes the lattice distance on the l_1 norm.

For convenience of reasoning, let us introduce the averaging operator:

$$(\varkappa\bar{\Delta}f)(x) = \frac{\varkappa}{2d}\sum_{|x'-x|=1} f(x'),$$

where $\varkappa\bar{\Delta}f(x) = \frac{\varkappa}{2d}\sum_{|x'-x|=1} f(x')$. The Laplace operator $\varkappa\Delta$ can be represented as the difference of the averaging operator and the multiplication operator:

$$(\varkappa\Delta f)(x) = \varkappa\bar{\Delta}f(x) - \varkappa f(x).$$

Consider an auxiliary operator $H_\mu(\omega)$ for which the splitting intensity at zero is absent and the death intensity at zero $\mu(0,\omega)$ is defined in the same way as $\mu(x,\omega)$ for $x \in \mathbb{Z}\backslash\{0\}$.

$$H_\mu(\omega) = \varkappa\Delta - \mu(x,\omega) = \varkappa\bar{\Delta} - \varkappa - \mu(x,\omega).$$

The operator $H(\omega)$ can be viewed as a random one-point perturbation of the operator $H_\mu(\omega)$ at zero. Therefore, the essential spectra of these operators coincide [26]:

$$\sigma_{ess}(H(\omega)) = \sigma_{ess}(H_\mu(\omega)).$$

Furthermore, a single-point perturbation can only produce at most one positive eigenvalue. Thus, the first problem is to investigate the essential spectrum of the operator $H_\mu(\omega)$.

For convenience, we give the formulations of the lemmas from the works of [26,27], which will be needed to study the spectrum of the operator $H_\mu(\omega)$.

Lemma 1 (see, e.g., [26]). *The number λ belongs to the essential spectrum of the operator H_μ if we can construct a sequence of "almost eigenfunctions", i.e.,*

$$\exists\Big\{ f_n \in l_2(\mathbb{Z}^d) : \quad \|f_n\| = 1, \quad (f_n, f_m) = \delta(n,m), \ \|H_\mu f_n - \lambda f_n\| \to 0, \quad n \to \infty \Big\}. \tag{4}$$

Lemma 2 (see, e.g., [27]). *The spectrum of the operator $\varkappa\Delta$ is equal to $[-2\varkappa;0]$. For an eigenvalue $\lambda \in [-2\varkappa;0]$, there exists a representation*

$$\lambda = \frac{\varkappa}{d}\sum_{i=1}^{d}\cos(\phi_i) - \varkappa,$$

for some $\overrightarrow{\phi} = (\phi_1, \ldots, \phi_d)$, $\phi_i \in [-\pi,\pi]$. The corresponding function $\psi_\lambda(x) = \exp\{i(\overrightarrow{\phi}, x)\}$ is an eigenfunction for λ. As a consequence, the spectrum of the operator $\varkappa\bar{\Delta}$ is equal to $[-\varkappa;\varkappa]$.

Using these lemmas and the proof scheme from [20], we obtain the following result.

Lemma 3. *The spectrum of the operator $H_\mu(\omega)$ almost surely consists of only the essential part, which is equal to the interval $[-2\varkappa - c;0]$.*

Proof. The operator $H_\mu(\omega)$ is the sum of the averaging operator $\varkappa\bar{\Delta}$ and the multiplication by the function $-\mu(x,\omega) - \varkappa$. Due to Lemma 2, the operator $\varkappa\bar{\Delta}$ has a spectrum equal to $[-\varkappa;\varkappa]$ and a norm equal to $\varkappa$. In turn, the spectrum of the operator of the multiplication by the $-\mu(x,\omega)$ is equal to the closure of the set of values of this function. For almost sure (a.s.) any ω, this closure is equal to the interval $[-c;0]$ by virtue of the definition of $\mu(x,\omega)$. Therefore, the spectrum of the combined operator $-\mu(x,\omega) - \varkappa$ is equal to $[-\varkappa - c; -\varkappa]$.

The operator $H_\mu(\omega)$ can be considered as a perturbation of the self-adjoint operator $-\mu(x,\omega) - \varkappa$ by the self-adjoint operator $\varkappa\bar{\Delta}$. In such a case, according to perturbation theory [28], the spectrum of the operator H_μ will differ from the interval $[-\varkappa - c, -\varkappa]$ by at most $\varkappa$, leading to the following inclusion:

$$\sigma(H_\mu) \subseteq [-2\varkappa - c;0]. \tag{5}$$

To show the inverse inclusion, we use Lemma 1, and for each $\lambda \in [-2\varkappa - c;0]$ we will construct a sequence of "almost eigenfunctions" $\{f_n(x)\}$, $f_i(x) \in l_2(\mathbb{Z}^d)$. Note that we construct a sequence function for each fixed ω, i.e., $\{f_n(x)\} = \{f_n(x,\omega)\}$.

Let us represent λ as $\lambda = a + b$, $a \in [-2\varkappa;0]$ $b \in [-c;0]$. We need to construct f_n such that the approximations $\varkappa\Delta f_n \approx a f_n$ and $-\mu(x,\omega) f_n \approx b f_n$ are true in some sense because then,

$$(\varkappa\Delta - \mu(x,\omega)) f_n \approx (a+b) f_n = \lambda f_n.$$

The condition $\varkappa\Delta f_n \approx a f_n$ requires that the function be "almost everywhere", similar to $\exp\{i(\overrightarrow{\phi}, x)\}$ of Lemma 2 with a suitable $\overrightarrow{\phi}$. The condition $-\mu(x,\omega) f_n \approx b f_n$ requires that the function be non-zero only on the region where $-\mu(x,\omega) \approx b$.

The functions satisfying both conditions are indicators of the balls on which $-\mu(x,\omega) \in [b-\varepsilon; b+\varepsilon]$ for sufficiently small $\varepsilon > 0$. Therefore, $-\mu(x,\omega) \approx b$ and the multiplication operator will act "almost eigen-like". The diffusion operator $\varkappa\Delta$ will act "almost eigen-like" inside and outside such balls, but not at the boundary. Therefore, the radius of the balls must increase to infinity so that the "non-eigen" action of $\varkappa\Delta$ tends to zero. The exact construction of the system of functions $\{f_n\}$ and the proof they are "almost eigenfunctions" is given in Section 9.1.

In summary, for any $\lambda \in [-2\varkappa - c; 0]$ we can construct a sequence of "almost eigenfunctions" $\{f_n\}$, and hence

$$\sigma(H_\mu) \supseteq [-2\varkappa - c; 0]. \tag{6}$$

Inclusions (5) and (6) complete the proof of the lemma. □

Let us summarize the result of this chapter. The auxiliary operator $H_\mu(\omega)$ a.s. has an non-random essential spectrum $[-2\varkappa - c; 0]$.

4. The Random Part of the Spectrum of the Evolutionary Operator

Let us return to the operator $H(\omega) = \varkappa\Delta + V(x,\omega)$. As we have already mentioned, it can be viewed as a random one-point perturbation of the previously described operator H_μ with an essential spectrum $\sigma(H_\mu) = [-2\varkappa - c; 0]$. By the Weyl criterion [26], under compact perturbation the essential spectrum of the operator does not change, while one positive eigenvalue may appear, which we will denote by $\lambda(\omega)$:

$$\sigma(H(\omega)) = [-2\varkappa - c; 0] \cup \lambda(\omega).$$

As we mentioned, under Equation (2) the structure of the $\sigma(H(\omega))$ defines the behavior of BRW. In particular, if $\lambda(\omega) > 0$, an exponential growth of the average particle number is observed; see, e.g., [27]. Thus, the study of the probability of exponential growth is reduced to the study of the probability of the appearance of a positive eigenvalue:

$$P(\Lambda, \varkappa, F_\mu) = \mathbb{P}\{\omega : \exists\, \lambda(\omega) \in \sigma(H(\omega)) : \lambda(\omega) > 0\}.$$

Let us formulate the problem of finding the eigenvalue of $\lambda(\omega)$ with the corresponding eigenfunction $u(x)$. Note that from $u(0) = 0$ it follows that $u(x) \equiv 0$. Therefore, without restricting generality, let $u(0) = 1$:

$$\begin{aligned} &(\varkappa\Delta + V(x,\omega))u(x) = \lambda u(x), \\ &u(0) = 1. \end{aligned} \tag{7}$$

For convenience, Equation (7) can be decomposed into two equations. When $x = 0$ it takes the following form:

$$\begin{aligned} &(\varkappa\Delta + \Lambda - \lambda)u(0) = 0, \\ &u(0) = 1. \end{aligned} \tag{8}$$

When $x \neq 0$, it takes the following form:

$$\begin{aligned} &(\varkappa\Delta - \mu(x,\omega) - \lambda)u(x) = 0, \\ &u(0) = 1. \end{aligned} \tag{9}$$

For simplicity of the formulas, we introduce the following notations:

$$E = \varkappa + \lambda.$$

Due to this notation, Equation (9) takes the following form:

$$\begin{aligned} &(\varkappa\bar{\Delta} - (\mu(x,\omega) + E))u(x) = 0, \quad x \neq 0, \\ &u(0) = 1. \end{aligned} \tag{10}$$

Let us move on to finding the solution to this system of equations.

Lemma 4. *The solution to Equation (10) is given by the following formula:*

$$u(x) = \sum_{\gamma : x \rightsquigarrow 0} \prod_{z \in \gamma} \left(\frac{\varkappa/2d}{\mu(z,\omega) + E} \right), \tag{11}$$

where by $\gamma : a \rightsquigarrow b = \{a = x_1, \dots x_n \neq b\}$ we denote the path from point a to point b through the neighboring points of the lattice and a) the path does not intersect 0 and b) point b is considered to be excluded from the path γ. The solution given by Formula (11) makes sense for any $\lambda > 0$ in any dimension $d \in \mathbb{N}$.

The first part of the lemma is verified by directly substituting Formula (11) into the problem (10). The correct definiteness of the expression (11) for any $\lambda > 0$ in dimension is checked by combinatorial reasoning and asymptotic methods. The full proof of Lemma 4 is given in Section 9.2.

Remark 1. *Lemma 4 is a special case of the popular (especially in the physics literature) path expansion of the resolvent, but it is usually applied to the λ from an essential Laplacian spectrum, i.e., $\lambda < 0$ in our case. For such λ formula, (11) is incorrect due to the small denominators. Therefore, one has to study complex λ and later pass to the limit $\operatorname{Im} \lambda \to 0$; see details, e.g., in Lecture 6 of [20] or in [29].*

Our goal is to understand under what conditions there exists an isolated positive eigenvalue λ_0 of the operator H_μ, perturbed by the reproduction potential $(\Lambda - \mu)\delta_0(x)$. In such a case (11) is well defined and Lemma 4 is probably new. Let us stress that $u(x)$ is the resolvent kernel of H_μ with some normalization. In fact, $u(x) = \frac{R_\lambda(0,x)}{R_\lambda(0,0)}$ for $\lambda > 0$.

Remark 2. *The essential spectrum is the non-random support of the random spectral measure of $H_\mu(\omega)$. Under the condition that r.v. $\mu(x)$ has absolutely continuous distribution, it follows from the general theory of one-dimensional random Schrödinger operator on $l_2(\mathbb{Z})$ that the spectral measure is pure point and eigenfunctions are almost surely exponentially decreasing (exponential localization).*

This result is very old (see details in [20,29–31]), and we will not discuss this topic. Our case is the analysis of the spectral bifurcation: existence and non-existence of the positive eigenvalue.

5. Condition for Almost Certainly Supercritical BRW Behavior

Let us calculate the environment-independent interval in which the eigenvalue of the problem (7) lies. For this purpose, let us consider the "best" and the "worst" realizations of the environments. Namely, by setting $\mu = 0$ at all points, then setting $\mu = c$ at all points, we can obtain the following result.

Theorem 1. *The value $P(\Lambda, \varkappa, F_\mu)$ is equal to one if and only if the following condition is satisfied:*

$$\Lambda \geqslant \sqrt{(\varkappa + c)^2 - \varkappa^2} - c. \tag{12}$$

If the condition (12) is satisfied, then for any realization of the environments ω, the eigenvalue of $\lambda(\omega)$ lies in the interval

$$\lambda(\omega) \in \left[\sqrt{(\Lambda + c)^2 + \varkappa^2} - (\varkappa + c); \sqrt{\Lambda^2 + \varkappa^2} - \varkappa\right].$$

Proof. Consider Equation (8):

$$\begin{aligned} &(\varkappa\Delta + \Lambda - \lambda)u(0) = 0, \\ &u(0) = 1. \end{aligned} \tag{13}$$

Given the notation $E = \varkappa + \lambda$, it can be rewritten as follows:

$$(\varkappa\bar{\Delta}u)(0) + \Lambda - E = 0. \tag{14}$$

In dimension $d = 1$, the expression (14) takes a simpler form:

$$\frac{\varkappa}{2}(u(1) + u(-1)) + \Lambda = E.$$

Moreover, if μ is equal to some constant at all points, then $u(1) = u(-1)$ and the expression is further simplified:

$$\varkappa u(1) + \Lambda = E. \tag{15}$$

Note that for arbitrary environment ω, the solution $u(1)$ is bounded above and below by the solutions for the environments in which $\mu \equiv 0$ and $\mu \equiv c$. Let us find these estimates.

Let $\mu(x, \omega)$ be equal to some constant c_1 at all points. In this case, $u(1)$ is defined using Equation (11) as follows:

$$u(1) = \sum_{\gamma:1\to 0} \prod_{z\in\gamma} \left(\frac{\varkappa/2}{\mu(z,\omega) + E}\right) = \sum_{\gamma:1\to 0} \prod_{z\in\gamma} \left(\frac{\varkappa/2}{E + c_1}\right) = \sum_{\gamma:1\to 0} \prod_{z\in\gamma} \left(\frac{\varkappa/2}{E_1}\right), \tag{16}$$

where $E_1 = E + c_1$.

Reasoning using the reflection principle as in the proof of Lemma 4 (see Section 9.2) allows us to write out the series in the expression (16) exactly. First, let us compute $L(1,0,n)$, that is, the number of paths that start at 1, end at 0, contain n points, and do not intersect 0. Note that $L(1,0,1) = 1$, and for the remaining odd n according to reasoning (37) in Section 9.2 the following is true:

$$L(1,0,n) = C_{n-1}^{\frac{n-1}{2}} - C_{n-1}^{\frac{n+1}{2}} = \frac{2}{n+1} C_{n-1}^{\frac{n-1}{2}}, \quad n = 3, 5, \ldots.$$

Thus, let us write out $u(1)$ from the expression (16):

$$\begin{aligned} u(1) &= \sum_{\gamma:1\to 0} \prod_{z\in\gamma} \left(\frac{\varkappa/2}{E_1}\right) = \sum_{n=1,3,\ldots} L(1,0,n) \cdot \left(\frac{\varkappa/2}{E_1}\right)^n \\ &= \sum_{n=1,3,\ldots} \frac{2}{n+1} C_{n-1}^{\frac{n-1}{2}} \cdot \left(\frac{\varkappa/2}{E_1}\right)^n = \sum_{m=0,2,\ldots} \frac{2}{m+2} C_m^{m/2} \cdot \left(\frac{\varkappa/2}{E_1}\right)^{m+1} \\ &= \frac{\varkappa/2}{E_1} \sum_{k=0}^{\infty} \left(\frac{C_{2k}^k}{1+k}\right) \cdot \left(\frac{\varkappa/2}{E_1}\right)^{2k}. \end{aligned} \tag{17}$$

For convenience, we denote $\frac{\varkappa/2}{E_1}$ by a. The coefficient $\frac{C_{2k}^k}{1+k}$ is the Catalan number, so the series (17) can be calculated exactly; see, e.g., [32]:

$$\begin{aligned} u(1) &= a \sum_{k=0}^{\infty} \left(\frac{C_{2k}^k}{1+k}\right) \cdot a^{2k} = a \frac{1 - \sqrt{1 - 4a^2}}{2a^2} \\ &= \frac{1}{2a} - \sqrt{\frac{1}{4a^2} - 1} = \frac{E_1}{\varkappa} - \sqrt{\left(\frac{E_1}{\varkappa}\right)^2 - 1}. \end{aligned} \tag{18}$$

After substituting (18), the expression (15) takes the following form:

$$E = \Lambda + E_1 - \sqrt{{E_1}^2 - \varkappa^2}.$$

Since $E_1 = E + c_1$, the expression takes the form

$$E = \Lambda + (E + c_1) - \sqrt{(E + c_1)^2 - \varkappa^2}.$$

From here, we can calculate that

$$\Lambda + c_1 = \sqrt{(E + c_1)^2 - \varkappa^2}$$

or, finally,

$$\lambda = \sqrt{(\Lambda + c_1)^2 + \varkappa^2} - (c_1 + \varkappa).$$

Substituting $c_1 = 0$ and $c_1 = c$ completes the proof of the lemma. □

6. Upper Estimate for $P(\Lambda, \varkappa, F_\mu)$

In the previous section, we found that under the condition $\Lambda \geqslant \sqrt{(\varkappa + c)^2 - \varkappa^2} - c$ the BRW is a.s. supercritical, i.e., $P(\Lambda, \varkappa, F_\mu) = 1$. The goal of this and the next section is to give estimates for $P(\Lambda, \varkappa, F_\mu)$ when this condition is violated.

To obtain an estimate from above, let us fix a non-random "poor" environment and find out when it does not generate a positive eigenvalue. The poorer environments also do not generate an eigenvalue. If the probability of generating a family of poor environments is P_1, then $P(\Lambda, \varkappa, F_\mu) < 1 - P_1$. In this paper, we consider the simplest case: an environment that takes some negative values at points neighboring zero.

Lemma 5. *Consider an environment ω_1 in which points neighboring from zero have killing intensities equal to μ_1 and μ_{-1}. A positive eigenvalue in this environment exists if and only if the following condition is met:*

$$\Lambda > \frac{\mu_1 + \mu_{-1} + 2\sigma\mu_1\mu_{-1}}{(1 + \sigma\mu_1)(1 + \sigma\mu_{-1})}, \tag{19}$$

where $\sigma = \frac{1}{\varkappa/2}$ for $z \in \mathbb{R}$.

Let us give the general idea of the proof. The eigenvalue problem for the considered environment has the following form:

$$\begin{aligned} &(\varkappa\Delta + V(x, \omega))u(x) = \lambda u(x), \\ &u(0) = 1, \end{aligned} \tag{20}$$

where

$$V(x, \omega) = \begin{cases} \Lambda, & x = 0; \\ -\mu_1, & x = 1; \\ -\mu_{-1}, & x = -1; \\ 0, & |x| \geqslant 2. \end{cases}$$

In the appendix, we show that $u(x)$ must have the following form:

$$u(x) = \begin{cases} 1, & x = 0; \\ C_1 e^{-kx}, & x \geqslant 1; \\ C_{-1} e^{kx}, & x \leqslant 1, \end{cases} \tag{21}$$

where $C_{\pm 1}$ and k are some positive constants.

Then, we substitute (21) into (20) and derive the condition that is equivalent to the existence of positive eigenvalue λ with corresponding eigenfunction ψ_λ. It turns out that this is the condition (20), which completes the proof of the lemma. The proof is quite technical and is given in Section 9.3.

Now consider the general set of environments

$$\Omega_1 = \{\omega \in \Omega : \mu(1,\omega) = \mu_1, \mu(-1,\omega) = \mu_{-1}\}.$$

Note that the average number of particles in the non-random environment ω_1 is a.s. greater than the average number of particles in a population in any environment from Ω_1. Suppose that the condition (19) is satisfied for ω_1. In such a case, nothing can be said about the eigenvalues of the environments from Ω_1. Suppose that the condition (19) is not satisfied for ω_1. Then, according to the previous Lemma 5, there is no positive eigenvalue for ω_1 and hence there is no positive eigenvalue for all environments from Ω_1.

Let us denote the event "condition (19) is met" by A and write the previous reasoning more formally:

$$\begin{aligned} P(\Lambda, \varkappa, F_\mu) = \mathbb{P}\{\exists\, \lambda(\omega) > 0\} &= \mathbb{P}\{\exists\, \lambda(\omega) > 0|A\}\mathbb{P}(A) + \mathbb{P}\{\exists\, \lambda(\omega) > 0|\bar{A}\}\mathbb{P}(\bar{A}) \\ &= \mathbb{P}\{\exists\, \lambda(\omega) > 0|A\}\mathbb{P}(A) + 0 \cdot \mathbb{P}(\bar{A}) \leqslant \mathbb{P}(A). \end{aligned} \quad (22)$$

The event "condition (19) is met" for a random environment is written as follows:

$$\mathbb{P}(A) = \mathbb{P}\left\{\Lambda > \frac{\xi_1 + \xi_2 + 2\sigma\xi_1\xi_2}{(1+\sigma\xi_1)(1+\sigma\xi_2)}\right\},$$

where ξ_i are independent copies $\mu(x,\omega)$. Thus, we obtain the following theorem.

Theorem 2. *The following upper bound estimate is true:*

$$P(\Lambda, \varkappa, F_\mu) \leqslant \mathbb{P}\left\{\Lambda > \frac{\xi_1 + \xi_2 + 2\sigma\xi_1\xi_2}{(1+\sigma\xi_1)(1+\sigma\xi_2)}\right\},$$

where ξ_i are independent copies $\mu(x,\omega)$.

7. Lower Estimate for $P(\Lambda, \varkappa, F_\mu)$

The first method for obtaining a lower estimate for $P(\Lambda, \varkappa, F_\mu)$ is to consider some convenient function $\psi(x)$ and examine the quadratic form $(H(\omega)\psi, \psi)$. If for some $a > 0$ the quadratic form $(H(\omega)\psi, \psi)$ is positive with probability p_a, then the operator $H(\omega)$ has a positive eigenvalue with probability p_a at least. We have chosen the simple function $\psi(x) = 2^{-a|x|}, x \in \mathbb{Z}$ and this reasoning leads to the following theorem.

Theorem 3. *The following estimate from below is true:*

$$P(\Lambda, \varkappa, F_\mu) \geqslant \max_{a \in (0;\infty)} \mathbb{P}\left(\omega : \Lambda > \varkappa \frac{(2^a - 1)}{(2^a + 1)} + \sum_{\substack{x=-\infty; \\ x \neq 0}}^{\infty} \frac{\mu(x,\omega)}{4^{a|x|}}\right).$$

In particular, for $a = 1$:

$$P(\Lambda, \varkappa, F_\mu) \geqslant \mathbb{P}\left(\omega : \Lambda > \frac{\varkappa}{3} + \sum_{\substack{x=-\infty; \\ x \neq 0}}^{\infty} \frac{\mu(x,\omega)}{4^{|x|}}\right).$$

The proof of the theorem requires direct investigation of the quadratic form $(H(\omega)\psi, \psi)$ for the function $\psi(x) = 2^{-a|x|}, x \in \mathbb{Z}$, which is a technical task, and so the proof is placed in Section 9.4.

The second way to obtain an upper estimate of $P(\Lambda, \varkappa, F_\mu)$ uses the idea of Lemma 5. We consider a non-random killing environment of simplified form that can form "islands" around zero without killing. For this environment, we study the eigenvalue problem and then generalize the conclusion to all environments that are "better" than the one under consideration.

First, let us denote $P(\mu(x,\omega)) = 0$ by p. Random variables $\mu(x,\omega)$ can form an "island" around zero with probability p^{2l}. Let us denote such a case by Ω_l:

$$\Omega_l = \{\omega \in \Omega : \mu(i,\omega) = 0, \forall i \in -l,\dots,l\}.$$

Let us use an idea from Lemma 5 and consider a non-random environment ω_l of the following form:

$$\mu(x,\omega_l) = \begin{cases} 0 & \text{for } x \in -l,\dots,l; \\ c & \text{for } x \notin -l,\dots,l. \end{cases}$$

The environment ω_l admits a direct calculation of the condition on the positivity of the eigenvalue of the corresponding operator, which is presented by the following lemma. The proof of the lemma is technical and is therefore placed in Section 9.5.

Lemma 6. *If a positive eigenvalue exists for all $\omega \in \Omega_l$, then it is bounded from below by a solution with respect to λ of the following equation:*

$$\frac{2\alpha\varkappa}{1+\sqrt{1-4\alpha^2}} + \varkappa\alpha^{2l} \cdot R(\alpha,\beta) + \Lambda - \varkappa - \lambda = 0, \tag{23}$$

where $\alpha = \frac{\varkappa/2}{\varkappa+\lambda}$, $\beta = \frac{\varkappa/2}{c+\varkappa+\lambda}$, and the expression R is defined as

$$R(\alpha,\beta) = \sum_{k=0}^{\infty} \left(\beta^{2k+1} - \alpha^{2k+1}\right) C_{k+l}, \tag{24}$$

where C_n denotes the n-th Catalan number. If the series in Equation (24) does not converge then there exists a $\omega \in \Omega_l$ for which there is no positive eigenvalue.

Now, using Lemma 6 we find the smallest positive number $\hat{l}$ such that Equation (23) admits a positive solution. By the lemma, all environments of $\Omega_{\hat{l}}$ will have positive eigenvalues. Therefore the probability $P(\Lambda,\varkappa,F_\mu)$ is at least equal to the probability of generating an environment from $\Omega_{\hat{l}}$ or, equivalently, the probability of generating a $\hat{l}$-island. Finally, the probability of generating a $\hat{l}$-island is $p^{2\hat{l}} = (\mathbb{P}\{\mu(x,\omega) = 0\})^{2\hat{l}}$, which leads to the following theorem.

Theorem 4. *There is the following estimation from below:*

$$P(\Lambda,\varkappa,F_\mu) \geqslant (\mathbb{P}\{\mu(x,\omega) = 0\})^{2\hat{l}},$$

where $\hat{l} \in \mathbb{N}$ is the smallest number for which the expression described below admits a positive solution. If there is no such $\hat{l}$, then $P(\Lambda,\varkappa,F_\mu) = 0$.

$$\frac{2\alpha\varkappa}{1+\sqrt{1-4\alpha^2}} + \varkappa\alpha^{2l} \cdot R(\alpha,\beta) + \Lambda - \varkappa - \lambda = 0, \tag{25}$$

where $\alpha = \frac{\varkappa/2}{\varkappa+\lambda}$, $\beta = \frac{\varkappa/2}{c+\varkappa+\lambda}$, and the expression R is defined as follows:

$$R(\alpha,\beta) = \sum_{k=0}^{\infty} \left(\beta^{2k+1} - \alpha^{2k+1}\right) C_{k+l}, \tag{26}$$

where C_n denotes the Catalan number.

At first sight, Theorem 4 is useless due to its excessive complexity. However, unlike Theorem 3, it offers a concrete numerical algorithm for estimating $P(\Lambda, \varkappa, F_\mu)$ based on a non-Monte Carlo method. Moreover, this algorithm will run fast because of the exponentially fast convergence of the series used in the theorem.

8. Conclusions

We have studied a previously unconsidered model of branching random walk with a single branching source and a killing random environment. The introduction of a random environment into the BRW model expands the range of biological problems that can be modeled using BRWs. In the present work, we investigated the probability of the presence of supercritical BRW growth. The developed approaches made it possible to estimate the spectrum of the corresponding random evolution operator.

The generalization of the obtained results can be carried out in several directions. For example, in Theorem 2 one can consider not two but several points in the neighborhood of zero, and in Theorem 3 one can consider a function of a more general form. A rather interesting problem is the generalization of Theorem 4, in which instead of an "island" with zero killing intensity, one can consider an "island" consisting of points with small but non-zero positive killing intensity. Also, one of the directions of further research is the numerical evaluation of the accuracy of the estimates obtained in this paper.

9. Proofs

9.1. Continuation of the Proof of Lemma 3

Let us recall that we need to prove the inclusion $\sigma(H_\mu) \supseteq [-2\varkappa - c; 0]$.

Proof. Let us use Lemma 1, and for each $\lambda \in [-2\varkappa - c; 0]$ construct a sequence of "almost eigenfunctions" $\{f_n(x)\}$, $f_i(x) \in L_2(\mathbb{Z}^d)$. Note that we construct a sequence function for each fixed ω, i.e., $\{f_n(x)\} = \{f_n(x, \omega)\}$. Let us represent λ as $\lambda = a + b$, $a \in [-2\varkappa; 0]$ $b \in [-c; 0]$. Let us construct f_n such that in some sense $\varkappa\Delta f_n \approx a f_n$ and simultaneously $-\mu(x, \omega) f_n \approx b f_n$. Then,

$$(\varkappa\Delta - \mu(x, \omega)) f_n \approx (a + b) f_n = \lambda f_n.$$

The condition $\varkappa\Delta f_n \approx a f_n$ requires that the function be "almost everywhere", similar to $\exp\{i(\overrightarrow{\phi}, x)\}$ of Lemma 2 with a suitable $\overrightarrow{\phi}$. The condition $-\mu(x, \omega) f_n \approx b f_n$ requires that the function be non-zero only on the region where $-\mu(x, \omega) \approx b$.

A candidate function satisfying both conditions looks like this:

$$f_n(x) = f_n(x, \omega) = \frac{1}{\sqrt{|B_n(\omega)|}} \exp\Big\{i(\overrightarrow{\phi}, x)\Big\} I\{B_n(\omega)\},$$

where the random set $B_n(\omega) = B_n$ contains the points $x \in \mathbb{Z}^d$, such that $-\mu(x, \omega) \in \left[b - \frac{1}{n}, b + \frac{1}{n}\right]$, and the multiplier $1/\sqrt{|B_n|}$ is needed to normalize the function.

Lemma 1 additionally requires orthogonality of almost eigenfunctions. Hence, it should be required that $B_m \cap B_n = 0$ for $n \neq m$. Furthermore, it will turn out in the proof that it should be required in advance that $|B_n| \to \infty$.

Let us prove the existence of the required sets $\{B_n\}$. For this, we fix an arbitrary number n and recall that the density of $-\mu(x.\omega)$ is positive on the interval $[-c; 0]$. According to the Borel–Cantelli lemma, for an arbitrary realization of ω there exists a system of non-intersecting balls $\{C_i(n)\}_{i=1}^{\infty}$ consisting of lattice points $x \in \mathbb{Z}^d$ such that

$$\begin{aligned} &x \in C_i(n) \Rightarrow -\mu(x, \omega) \in \left[b - \frac{1}{n}, b + \frac{1}{n}\right], \\ &|C_i(n)| \to \infty \quad \text{for } i \to \infty. \end{aligned} \tag{27}$$

Now, the system of sets $\{B_n\}$ can be constructed by induction. Let the system $\{B_n\}$ be constructed up to the number k. Let us construct the system $\{C_i(k+1)\}$ described above. As the set B_{k+1}, we take any set of $\subset \{C_i(k+1)\}$ that is farther from zero than all points from $B_1, \ldots, B_n$. Thus, the induction is complete and the system $\{B_n\}$ is constructed.

Let us verify that the functions $\{f_n\}$ are almost eigenfunctions. First, consider the action of the operator $\varkappa\Delta$ on the function f_n:

$$\varkappa\Delta f_n = \frac{1}{\sqrt{|B_n|}}\varkappa\Delta \exp\{i(\overrightarrow{\phi}, x)\}I\{B_n\}.$$

If the points $x-1, x, x, x+1$ lie inside B_n, then the diffusion operator acts on its eigenfunction:

$$\varkappa\Delta f_n(x) = a\frac{1}{\sqrt{|B_n|}}\exp\{i(\overrightarrow{\phi}, x)\} = af_n(x).$$

If all points $x-1, x, x+1$ lie outside B_n, then the diffusion operator acts on the null function and also $\varkappa\Delta f_n(x) = 0 = af_n(x)$.

Let at least one of their points $x-1, x, x+1$ lie on the boundary of B_n. In this case, there remains a non-zero function f_n^{res} after applying the operator:

$$\varkappa\Delta f_n(x) = af_n(x) + f_n^{res}(x). \tag{28}$$

The function f_n^{res} reflects the "error" of the operator on the boundary of B_n with respect to the operator multiplying by a. This function is non-zero only at a finite number of points C_d, depending on the dimensionality but not on n. The norm f_n^{res} is bounded from above by $C_d/\sqrt{|B_n|}$, which tends to zero when $n \to \infty$.

Now consider the action of the operator $-\mu(x,\omega)$ on the function f_n. On the region $\{B_n\}$, the function $\mu(x,\omega)$ takes values in the interval $\left[b-\frac{1}{n}, b+\frac{1}{n}\right]$, so

$$\begin{aligned}-\mu(x,\omega)f_n(x) &= -\mu(x,\omega)\frac{1}{\sqrt{|B_n|}}\exp\{i(\overrightarrow{\phi}, x)\}I\{B_n\}\\ &= b\frac{1}{\sqrt{|B_n|}}\exp\{i(\overrightarrow{\phi}, x)\}I\{B_n\} + g_n^{res}(x) = bf_n(x) + g_n^{res}(x).\end{aligned} \tag{29}$$

The function g_n^{res} reflects the "error" of the operator on the area B_n with respect to the multiplication operator on b. The norm g_n^{res} is bounded from above by the value $1/n$, which tends to zero when $n \to \infty$.

Putting together the expressions (28) and (29), we obtain the following:

$$\|H_\mu f_n - \lambda f_n\| = \|(a+b)f_n - (a+b)f_n + f_n^{res} + g_n^{res}\| \to 0, \qquad n \to \infty.$$

Thus, $\{f_n\}$ is the desired sequence of almost eigenfunctions, and $\lambda \subset \sigma(H)$. The number λ was taken arbitrarily from the interval $[-2\varkappa - c, 0]$, hence

$$\sigma(H_\mu) \supseteq [-2\varkappa - c; 0], \tag{30}$$

which completes the proof of the lemma. □

9.2. *Proof of Lemma 4*

Let us recall the formulation of Lemma 4:

The solution to Equation (10) when $x \neq 0$ is given by the following formula:

$$u(x) = \sum_{\gamma: x \rightsquigarrow 0}\prod_{z\in\gamma}\left(\frac{\varkappa/2d}{\mu(z,\omega)+E}\right), \tag{31}$$

where $\gamma : a \rightsquigarrow b = \{a = x_1, \dots, x_n \neq b\}$ denotes the path from point a to point b through the neighboring points of the lattice, and a) the path does not intersect 0 and b) point b is considered to be excluded from the path γ. The solution given by formula (31) makes sense for any $\lambda > 0$ in any dimension $d \in \mathbb{N}$.

Proof. Note that, for a path $\gamma : x \rightsquigarrow 0$, the symbol $|\gamma|$ denotes the length of the path in the sense of "number of points in γ excluding zero" or "number of steps from x to 0" which are the same. For simplicity of notation, let us prove the lemma for the case of a one-dimensional lattice $d = 1$. Let us study the action of the operator $\varkappa\bar{\Delta}$ on the function $u(x)$ when $x \neq 0$:

$$\varkappa\bar{\Delta}u(x) = \frac{\varkappa}{2}(u(x+1) + u(x-1)), \tag{32}$$

Note that the set of paths $\gamma : x \rightsquigarrow 0$ included in $u(x)$ decomposes into two subsets: paths $\gamma_+ : x \rightsquigarrow x+1 \rightsquigarrow 0$ and paths $\gamma_- : x \rightsquigarrow x-1 \rightsquigarrow 0$. Thus,

$$u(x) = \sum_{\gamma}(\cdot) = \frac{\varkappa/2}{\mu(x,\omega)+E}\sum_{\gamma_+}(\cdot) + \frac{\varkappa/2}{\mu(x,\omega)+E}\sum_{\gamma_-}(\cdot)$$
$$= \frac{\varkappa/2}{\mu(x,\omega)+E}(u(x+1)+u(x-1)). \tag{33}$$

Or the following, which is the same thing:

$$u(x+1) + u(x-1) = \frac{\mu(x,\omega)+E}{\varkappa/2}u(x). \tag{34}$$

Combining (32) and (34) we obtain:

$$\varkappa\bar{\Delta}u(x) = \frac{\varkappa}{2}(u(x+1)+u(x-1)) = (\mu(x,\omega)+E)u(x). \tag{35}$$

By virtue of (35), the proof of the lemma in the one-dimensional case is complete:

$$(\varkappa\bar{\Delta} - (\mu(x,\omega)+E))u(x) = (\mu(x,\omega)+E)u(x) - (\mu(x,\omega)+E)u(x) = 0.$$

In the multidimensional case, the reasoning remains exactly the same, except that the expression (33) will contain paths on all lattice points neighboring x.

Now let us show the correctness of (31) for any $\lambda > 0$. For simplicity, we first consider the one-dimensional case $d = 1$. We investigate the convergence of the series (31). Note that the following upper bound estimate is true and achievable:

$$u(x) = \sum_{\gamma:x\rightsquigarrow 0}\prod_{z\in\gamma}\left(\frac{\varkappa/2}{\mu(z,\omega)+E}\right) \leqslant \sum_{\gamma:x\rightsquigarrow 0}\prod_{z\in\gamma}\left(\frac{\varkappa}{2E}\right) = \sum_{\substack{\gamma:x\rightsquigarrow 0,\\ |\gamma|=n}}\left(\frac{\varkappa}{2E}\right)^n L(x,0,n), \tag{36}$$

where $L(x,0,n)$ is the number of paths of the form $x \rightsquigarrow 0$ that contain n points. Note that if the parity of x and n does not coincide, then $L(x,0,n)$ converges to zero.

Without restricting generality, let us assume $x > 0$. Finding $L(a,b,k)$ is a standard problem for applying the reflection principle to discrete random walks; see, e.g., [33]. The answer is as follows:

$$L(a,b,k) = C_k^{\frac{k+b-a}{2}} - C_k^{\frac{k+b+a}{2}}, \qquad a,b,n > 0.$$

Therefore,

$$L(x,0,n) = L(x,1,n-1) = C_{n-1}^{\frac{n-x}{2}} - C_{n-1}^{\frac{n+x}{2}} = c_1 x^{c_2} 2^n, \qquad n \to \infty, \tag{37}$$

where c_1 and c_2 are positive constants.

Thus, the series in the (36) inequalities are geometric series:

$$\sum_{\substack{\gamma:x\rightsquigarrow 0,\\ |\gamma|=n}} \left(\frac{\varkappa}{2E}\right)^n L(x,0,n) < c_3 + c_4 \sum_{i=1}^{n} \left(\frac{\varkappa}{2E}\right)^n \cdot 2^n, \tag{38}$$

where c_3 and c_4 are positive constants.

The series (38) converges when $\varkappa/E < 1$. Which, given the notation $E = \varkappa + \lambda$, can be rewritten as follows:

$$\lambda > 0.$$

In the case $d > 1$, the estimation of (36) takes the following form:

$$u(x) = \sum_{\gamma:x\rightsquigarrow 0} \prod_{z\in\gamma} \left(\frac{\varkappa/2d}{\mu(z,\omega) + E}\right) \leqslant \sum_{\gamma:x\rightsquigarrow 0} \prod_{z\in\gamma} \left(\frac{\varkappa}{2dE}\right) = \sum_{\substack{\gamma:x\rightsquigarrow 0,\\ |\gamma|=n}} \left(\frac{\varkappa}{2dE}\right)^n L(x,0,n), \tag{39}$$

where again C_n is the number of γ paths of length n, where the length is counted with respect to zero and the conditions from Lemma 4 are imposed on the path.

Let us consider $n \gg x$, since the convergence of the series (39) depends on them alone. Note that when $n \gg x$, the number of trajectories $L(x,0,n) \sim L(0,0,n)$, $n \to \infty$. We denote by $L_0(0,0,n)$ the number of trajectories starting and ending at zero without the condition of non-intersection of zero. The event of a trajectory crossing the zero point in dimension $d > 1$ is rare, so $L(0,0,n) \sim L_0(0,0,n)$, $n \to \infty$.

Let us fix d movements "up" along each of the coordinates. Each path in $L_0(0,0,n)$ is defined by only $n/2$ steps, each of which can have one of the coordinate movements, i.e.,

$$L_0(0,0,n) = d^{n/2} C_n^{n/2} \sim \left(2\sqrt{d}\right)^n, \quad n \to \infty.$$

Proceeding as in the one-dimensional case, we obtain that the series in the estimaion of (39) is a geometric series:

$$\sum_{\substack{\gamma:x\rightsquigarrow 0,\\ |\gamma|=n}} \left(\frac{\varkappa}{2dE}\right)^n L(x,0,n) < c_5 + \sum_{i=1}^{n} \left(\frac{\varkappa}{2dE}\right)^n \cdot \left(2\sqrt{d}\right)^n, \tag{40}$$

where c_5 is a positive constant. The series (40) converges when $\varkappa/\sqrt{d}E < 1$. Which, given the notation $E = \varkappa + \lambda$, can be rewritten as follows:

$$\lambda > \varkappa\left(\frac{1}{\sqrt{d}} - 1\right).$$

Therefore, for $\lambda > 0$ the series converges, which completes the proof of the lemma. □

9.3. *Proof of Lemma 5*

Let us recall the formulation of Lemma 5:

Consider an environment ω_1 in which points neighboring from zero have killing intensities equal to μ_1 and μ_{-1}. A positive eigenvalue in this environment exists if and only if

$$\Lambda > \frac{\mu_1 + \mu_{-1} + 2\sigma\mu_1\mu_{-1}}{(1+\sigma\mu_1)(1+\sigma\mu_{-1})},$$

where $\sigma = \frac{1}{\varkappa/2}$ for $z \in \mathbb{R}$.

Proof. The eigenvalue problem for the considered environment is as follows:

$$\begin{aligned} &(\varkappa\Delta + V(x,\omega))u(x) = \lambda u(x), \\ &u(0) = 1, \end{aligned} \tag{41}$$

where

$$V(x,\omega) = \begin{cases} \Lambda, & x = 0; \\ -\mu_1, & x = 1; \\ -\mu_{-1}, & x = -1; \\ 0, & |x| \geqslant 2. \end{cases}$$

First, let us show how the eigenfunction for this problem looks in general form. We will use the forward and inverse discrete Fourier transforms; see, e.g., [27]. The Fourier transform of the function f is defined as follows:

$$\tilde{f}(\theta) = \sum_{x\in\mathbb{Z}} e^{i\theta x} f(x).$$

The inverse Fourier transform is defined as follows:

$$f(x) = \frac{1}{2\pi}\int_{-\pi}^{\pi} \tilde{f}(\theta) e^{-i\theta x} d\theta.$$

Let us write for the operator H the eigenvalue problem λ with the corresponding eigenfunction u:

$$\varkappa\Delta u(x) + \Lambda\delta_0(x)u(x) - \mu_{-1}\delta_{-1}(x)u(x) - \mu_1\delta_1(x)u(x) = \lambda u(x). \tag{42}$$

After applying the Fourier transform, the expression (42) takes the form

$$\varkappa(\cos(\theta) - 1)\tilde{u}(x) + \Lambda u(0) - \mu_{-1}u(-1)e^{-i\theta} - \mu_1 u(1)e^{i\theta} - \lambda\tilde{u}(x).$$

The Fourier transform of the eigenfunction $\tilde{u}(x)$ is as follows:

$$\tilde{u}(x) = \frac{\Lambda u(0) - \mu_{-1}u(-1)e^{-i\theta} - \mu_1 u(1)e^{i\theta}}{\lambda + \varkappa - \varkappa\cos\theta},$$

and, finally, the solution $u(x)$ can be represented as

$$u(x) = \frac{1}{2\pi}\int_{-\pi}^{\pi} \frac{\Lambda u(0) - \mu_{-1}u(-1)e^{-i\theta} - \mu_1 u(1)e^{i\theta}}{\lambda + \varkappa - \varkappa\cos\theta} e^{-i\theta x} d\theta.$$

Calculating here the integral for $x \geqslant 1$, we obtain

$$u(x) = -\mu_{-1}u(-1)\frac{w^{x-1}}{r} + \Lambda u(0)\frac{w^x}{r} - \mu_1 u(1)\frac{w^{x+1}}{r}, \tag{43}$$

where $r = \sqrt{\lambda(\lambda + 2\varkappa)}$ and $w = \frac{\lambda+\varkappa-r}{\varkappa}$.

The expression (43) can be rewritten in a more convenient form:

$$u(x) = w^x\left(-\mu_{-1}u(-1)\frac{1}{wr} + \Lambda u(0)\frac{1}{r} - \mu_1 u(1)\frac{w}{r}\right) = B_1 \cdot e^{-kx}, \tag{44}$$

where $B_1 = \left(-\mu_{-1}u(-1)\frac{1}{wr} + \Lambda u(0)\frac{1}{r} - \mu_1 u(1)\frac{w}{r}\right)$ and $e^{-k} = w$. Function w^x decreases as x tends to infinity, since $u \in L_2(\mathbb{Z})$, therefore $k > 0$.

Let us do exactly the same for $x \leqslant 1$ and put $f(0) = 1$ by normalization. We determine that the eigenfunction must have the following form:

$$\psi(x) = \begin{cases} 1, & x = 0; \\ C_1 e^{-kx}, & x \geqslant 1; \\ C_{-1} e^{kx}, & x \leqslant -1, \end{cases}$$

where $C_{\pm 1}$ and k are positive constants. Let us show that there is a positive eigenvalue for this function if and only if the lemma condition is satisfied.

Let us write the problem (41) for the point $x \in [2; \infty)$:

$$\frac{\varkappa}{2}\psi(x+1) + \frac{\varkappa}{2}\psi(x-1) - \varkappa\psi(x) = \lambda\psi(x);$$

from here we can calculate that

$$\lambda = \frac{\varkappa}{2}\left(e^{-k} + e^{k} - 2\right) = \varkappa(\cosh k - 1) = 2\varkappa \sinh^2(k/2) = k^2 + O(k^4), \quad k \to 0.$$

In particular, when $\lambda \to 0+$, it follows from the condition $k > 0$ that $k \to 0+$, that is

$$\lambda \to 0+ \quad \to \quad e^k \to 1+. \tag{45}$$

Now let us write the problem (41) for the point $x = 1$:

$$\frac{\varkappa}{2}\psi(2) + \frac{\varkappa}{2}\psi(0) - \varkappa\psi(1) - \mu\psi(1) = \lambda\psi(1).$$

From here, we can calculate that

$$C_1 = \frac{1}{1 + e^{-k}\frac{\mu_1}{\varkappa/2}}.$$

For simplicity we denote $\frac{1}{\varkappa/2}$ by σ. Let us perform similar reasoning for $x = -1$, obtaining

$$C_{\pm 1} = \frac{1}{1 + \sigma\mu_{\pm 1}e^{-|k|}}.$$

Finally, let us write the problem (41) for $x = 0$:

$$\frac{\varkappa}{2}\psi(1) + \frac{\varkappa}{2}\psi(-1) - \varkappa\psi(0) + \Lambda\psi(0) = \lambda\psi(0).$$

From here, we can calculate that

$$(C_1 + C_{-1} - 1)e^{-k} + \sigma\Lambda - e^k = 0$$

or, finally,

$$e^{2k} - \sigma\Lambda e^k - \left(\frac{1}{1+\sigma\mu_1 e^{-k}} + \frac{1}{1+\sigma\mu_{-1}e^{-k}} - 1\right) = 0.$$

First, for simplicity, let us make $\mu = \mu_{-1} = \mu_1$, also, denote e^k by z and obtain the following expression:

$$z^2 - \sigma\Lambda z - \frac{2}{1+\sigma\mu\frac{1}{z}} + 1 = 0$$

or

$$z^3 - z^2\sigma(\Lambda - \mu) - z(\sigma^2\Lambda\mu + 1) + \sigma\mu = 0. \tag{46}$$

The current problem is to write out conditions on Λ, μ, and σ that guarantee the positivity of λ. Let us use the expression (45) and note that (46) is a smooth function with respect to z, so we can make $z = 1$ to find the limit solution at $z \to 1+$:

$$1 - \sigma(\Lambda - \mu) - (\sigma^2 \Lambda \mu + 1) + \sigma \mu = 0 \Leftrightarrow \Lambda = \frac{2\mu}{1 + \sigma \mu}.$$

The eigenvalue $\lambda > 0$ exists when this condition is violated to the "supercritical side", i.e.,

$$\Lambda > \frac{2\mu}{1 + \sigma \mu}.$$

We obtain the conditions of the lemma under the assumption of $\mu_1 = \mu_{-1}$.

In the case of unequal μ_1 and μ_{-1}, the same solution method gives the condition of the lemma:

$$\Lambda > \frac{\mu_1 + \mu_{-1} + 2\sigma \mu_1 \mu_{-1}}{(1 + \sigma \mu_1)(1 + \sigma \mu_{-1})}.$$

□

9.4. Proof of Theorem 3

Let us recall the formulation of Theorem 3:
The following estimate from below is true:

$$P(\Lambda, \varkappa, F_\mu) \geqslant \max_{a \in (0;\infty)} \mathbb{P}\left(\omega : \Lambda > \varkappa \frac{(2^a - 1)}{(2^a + 1)} + \sum_{\substack{x=-\infty; \\ x \neq 0}}^{\infty} \frac{\mu(x,\omega)}{4^{a|x|}} \right).$$

In particular, for $a = 1$:

$$P(\Lambda, \varkappa, F_\mu) \geqslant \mathbb{P}\left(\omega : \Lambda > \frac{\varkappa}{3} + \sum_{\substack{x=-\infty; \\ x \neq 0}}^{\infty} \frac{\mu(x,\omega)}{4^{|x|}} \right).$$

Proof. Consider the function $\psi(x) = 2^{-a|x|}$. Let us denote $\varphi(x) = (H(\omega)\psi)(x)$ and directly calculate the quadratic form $(\varphi, \psi) = (\varphi(x,\omega), \psi(x))$. First, let us calculate the function $\varphi(x)$:

$$\begin{aligned} \varphi(x,\omega) &= \varkappa \Delta \psi(x) + \Lambda \delta_0(x) \psi(x) - (1 - \delta_0(x)) \mu(x,\omega) \psi(x) \\ &= \frac{\varkappa}{2}(\psi(x+1) + \psi(x-1) + 2\psi(x)) + \Lambda \delta_0(x) \psi(0) - (1 - \delta_0(x)) \mu(x,\omega) \psi(x). \end{aligned} \quad (47)$$

Let us substitute into (47) the expression for $\psi(x)$ and consider separately the points 0 and $x > 0$:

$$\varphi(0,\omega) = \frac{\varkappa}{2}(2^{-a} + 2^{-a} - 2) + \Lambda = \varkappa(2^{-a} - 1) + \Lambda; \quad (48)$$

$$\begin{aligned} \varphi(x,\omega) &= \frac{\varkappa}{2}(2^{-a} \cdot 2^{-ax} + 2^a \cdot 2^{-ax} - 2 \cdot 2^{-ax}) - \mu(x,\omega) 2^{-ax} \\ &= \frac{\varkappa}{2} 2^{-ax}(2^{-a} + 2^a - 2) - \mu(x,\omega) 2^{-ax}. \end{aligned} \quad (49)$$

Using (48) and (49), we calculate the required quadratic form:

$$
\begin{aligned}
(\varphi(x,\omega),\psi(x)) &= \sum_{\substack{x=-\infty;\\ x\neq 0}}^{\infty} \varphi(x)\psi(x) + \varphi(0)\psi(0) \\
&= \sum_{\substack{x=-\infty;\\ x\neq 0}}^{\infty} \left(\frac{\varkappa}{2}2^{-a|x|}(2^{-a}+2^{a}-2) - \mu(x,\omega)2^{-a|x|}\right)\cdot 2^{-a|x|} + \varkappa(2^{-a}-1) + \Lambda \\
&= \frac{\varkappa}{2}(2^{-a}+2^{a}-2)\sum_{\substack{x=-\infty;\\ x\neq 0}}^{\infty} 2^{-2a|x|} - \sum_{\substack{x=-\infty;\\ x\neq 0}}^{\infty} \frac{\mu(x,\omega)}{2^{2a|x|}} + \varkappa(2^{-a}-1) + \Lambda \\
&= -\varkappa\frac{2^{-a}-1}{(2^{-a}+1)2^{a}} + \varkappa(2^{-a}-1) + \Lambda - \sum_{\substack{x=-\infty;\\ x\neq 0}}^{\infty} \frac{\mu(x,\omega)}{2^{2a|x|}} \\
&= -\varkappa\frac{(2^{a}-1)}{(2^{a}+1)} + \Lambda - \sum_{\substack{x=-\infty;\\ x\neq 0}}^{\infty} \frac{\mu(x,\omega)}{2^{2a|x|}}. \qquad (50)
\end{aligned}
$$

If $(\varphi(x,\omega),\psi(x)) > 0$, then by virtue of Section 4, the operator $H(\omega)$ has a positive eigenvalue. Given the expression (50), the condition for the positivity of the quadratic form can be rewritten in the following form:

$$
\Lambda > \varkappa\frac{(2^{a}-1)}{(2^{a}+1)} + \sum_{\substack{x=-\infty;\\ x\neq 0}}^{\infty} \frac{\mu(x,\omega)}{2^{2a|x|}}.
$$

By substituting $a = 1$ we obtain:

$$
\Lambda > \frac{\varkappa}{3} + \sum_{\substack{x=-\infty;\\ x\neq 0}}^{\infty} \frac{\mu(x,\omega)}{4^{|x|}}.
$$

□

9.5. Proof of Lemma 6

Recall the formulation of Lemma 6:
Consider a set of Ω_l including environments that have l-islands around zero:

$$
\Omega_l = \{\omega \in \Omega : \mu(i,\omega) = 0,\ \forall i \in -l,\dots,l\}.
$$

If a positive eigenvalue exists for all $\omega \in \Omega_l$, then it is bounded from below by a solution with respect to λ of the following equation:

$$
\frac{2\alpha\varkappa}{1+\sqrt{1-4\alpha^2}} + \varkappa\alpha^{2l}\cdot R(\alpha,\beta) + \Lambda - \varkappa - \lambda = 0,
$$

where $\alpha = \frac{\varkappa/2}{\varkappa+\lambda}$, $\beta = \frac{\varkappa/2}{c+\varkappa+\lambda}$, and the expression R is defined as follows:

$$
R(\alpha,\beta) = \sum_{k=0}^{\infty}\left(\beta^{2k+1} - \alpha^{2k+1}\right)C_{k+l}, \qquad (51)
$$

where C_n denotes the Catalan number. If the series in Equation (51) does not converge then there exists a $\omega \in \Omega_l$ for which there is no positive eigenvalue.

Proof. For convenience in the proof, let us rewrite Formula (4) for $d = 1$:

$$u(x) = \sum_{\gamma: x \rightsquigarrow 0} \prod_{z \in \gamma} \left(\frac{\varkappa/2}{\mu(z,\omega) + E} \right). \tag{52}$$

By virtue of Equation (15), we are interested in the quantity $u(1)$, for which the paths from 1 to 0 are important. By the lemma condition, for any $\omega \in \Omega_l$ there exists an l-island around zero. Therefore, every trajectory from 1 to 0 of length less than $2l$ will not leave this island, and every trajectory of length greater than $2l$ must spend at least $2l$ steps in this island. We divide all trajectories into two families: trajectories of length less than or equal to $2l$ trajectories of length greater than $2l$. The contribution of each of the smaller trajectories to the sum (52) is exactly $\left(\frac{\varkappa/2}{0+E}\right)^{|\gamma|}$. The contribution of each of the large trajectories to the sum (52) is at least $\left(\frac{\varkappa/2}{0+E}\right)^{2l} \cdot \left(\frac{\varkappa/2}{c+E}\right)^{|\gamma|-2l}$. Thus,

$$\begin{aligned} u(1) &= \sum_{\gamma: 1 \to 0} \prod_{z \in \gamma} \left(\frac{\varkappa/2}{\mu(z,\omega_l) + E} \right) \\ &\geqslant \sum_{\substack{\gamma: 1 \to 0, \\ |\gamma| < 2l}} \left(\frac{\varkappa/2}{0+E} \right)^{|\gamma|} L(0,1,|\gamma|) + \sum_{\substack{\gamma: 1 \to 0, \\ |\gamma| \geqslant 2l}} \left(\frac{\varkappa/2}{0+E} \right)^{2l} \left(\frac{\varkappa/2}{c+E} \right)^{|\gamma|-2l} L(0,1,|\gamma|). \end{aligned} \tag{53}$$

Let us rewrite Equation (53) by introducing the notations $\alpha = \frac{\varkappa/2}{E}$, $\beta = \frac{\varkappa/2}{c+E}$:

$$u(1) \geqslant \sum_{\substack{\gamma: 1 \to 0, \\ |\gamma| < 2l}} \alpha^{|\gamma|} L(0,1,|\gamma|) + \sum_{\substack{\gamma: 1 \to 0, \\ |\gamma| \geqslant 2l}} \alpha^{2l} \beta^{|\gamma|-2l} L(0,1,|\gamma|). \tag{54}$$

Let us simplify Equation (54) in the way (17) does, yielding the following:

$$\begin{aligned} u(1) &\geqslant \sum_{k=0}^{l-1} \alpha^{2k+1} C_k + \alpha^{2l} \sum_{k=l}^{\infty} \beta^{2k+1-2l} C_k \\ &= \sum_{k=0}^{\infty} \alpha^{2k+1} C_k + \alpha^{2l} \sum_{k=l}^{\infty} \left(\beta^{2k+1-2l} - \alpha^{2k+1-2l} \right) C_k. \end{aligned} \tag{55}$$

Using (18) and (55) we obtain:

$$u(1) \geqslant \frac{2\alpha}{1 + \sqrt{1 - 4\alpha^2}} + \alpha^{2l} \sum_{k=0}^{\infty} \left(\beta^{2k+1} - \alpha^{2k+1} \right) C_{k+l}. \tag{56}$$

Substituting (56) into (15) completes the proof of the lemma. □

Author Contributions: Conceptualization, S.M. and E.Y.; methodology, S.M. and E.Y.; formal analysis, V.K.; writing—original draft preparation, V.K.; writing—review and editing, E.Y. All authors have read and agreed to the published version of the manuscript.

Funding: This study has been carried out at Steklov Mathematical Institute of Russian Academy of Sciences. The work was supported by the Russian Science Foundation, project no. 23-11-00375.

Data Availability Statement: Data are contained within the article.

Acknowledgments: The authors would like to thank N. Smorodina, E. Filichkina, and O. Ivlev for helpful discussions. The authors thank the anonymous reviewers for numerous valuable comments which, we hope, have substantially improved the presentation.

Conflicts of Interest: The authors declare no conflicts of interest.

Abbreviations

The following abbreviations are used in this manuscript:

BRW	Branching random walk
r.v.	Random variable
a.s.	Almost sure

References

1. Gärtner, J.; Molchanov, S.A. Parabolic problems for the Anderson model. I. Intermittency and related topics. *Comm. Math. Phys.* **1990**, *132*, 613–655. [CrossRef]
2. Zeldovich, Y.B.; Molchanov, S.A.; Ruzmaikin, A.A.; Sokolov, D.D. Intermittency in a random environment. *Uspekhi Fis. Nauk.* **1987**, *152*, 3–32. (In Russian) [CrossRef]
3. Zeldovich, Y.B.; Molchanov, S.A.; Ruzmaikin, A.A.; Sokolov, D.D. Intermittency of passive fields in random media. *J. Exp. Theor. Phys.* **1985**, *89*, 2061. (In Russian)
4. Anderson, P.W. Absence of diffusion in certain random lattices. *Phys. Rev.* **1958**, *109*, 1492. [CrossRef]
5. König, W. *The Parabolic Anderson Model, Random Walk in Random Potential*; (Pathways in Mathematics); Birkhäuser/Springer: Cham, Switzerland, 2016; pp. xi+192. [CrossRef]
6. Albeverio, S.; Bogachev, L.V.; Molchanov, S.A.; Yarovaya, E.B. Annealed moment Lyapunov exponents for a branching random walk in a homogeneous random branching environment. *Markov Process. Relat. Fields* **2000**, *6*, 473–516.
7. Yarovaya, E. Symmetric branching walks in homogeneous and non homogeneous random environments. *Commun. Stat. Simul. Comput.* **2012**, *41*, 1232–1249. [CrossRef]
8. Gün, O.; König, W.; Sekulović, O. Moment asymptotics for branching random walks in random environment. *Electron. J. Probab.* **2013**, *18*, 1–18. [CrossRef]
9. Gün, O.; König, W.; Sekulović, O. Moment asymptotics for multitype branching random walks in random environment. *J. Theor. Probab.* **2015**, *28*, 1726–1742. [CrossRef]
10. Ortgiese, M.; Roberts, M.I. Intermittency for branching random walk in Pareto environment. *Ann. Probab.* **2016**, *44*, 2198–2263. [CrossRef]
11. Molchanov, S.; Zhang, H. The parabolic Anderson model with long range basic Hamiltonian and Weibull type random potential. In *Probability in Complex Physical Systems*; (Springer Proceedings in Mathematics); Springer: Berlin/Heidelberg, Germany, 2012; Volume 11, pp. 13–31. [CrossRef]
12. Chernousova, E.; Hryniv, O.; Molchanov, S. Branching random walk in a random time-independent environment. *Math. Popul. Stud.* **2023**, *30*, 73–94. [CrossRef]
13. Kutsenko, V.A.; Molchanov, S.A.; Yarovaya, E.B. Supercriticality conditions for branching walks in a random killing medium with a single reproduction center. *Uspekhi Mat. Nauk* **2023**, *78*, 181–182. (In Russian) [CrossRef]
14. Dorman, K.S.; Sinsheimer, J.S.; Lange, K. In the garden of branching processes. *SIAM Rev.* **2004**, *46*, 202–229. [CrossRef]
15. Lambert, A. Population dynamics and random genealogies. *Stoch. Model.* **2008**, *24*, 45–163. [CrossRef]
16. Molchanov, S.; Whitmeyer, J. Spatial models of population processes. In *Proceedings of the Modern Problems of Stochastic Analysis and Statistics*; Springer Proceedings in Mathematics; Springer: Cham, Switzerland, 2017; Volume 208, pp. 435–454. [CrossRef]
17. Endo, A.; Abbott, S.; Kucharski, A.J.; Funk, S. Estimating the overdispersion in COVID-19 transmission using outbreak sizes outside China. *Wellcome Open Res.* **2020**, *5*, 67. [CrossRef]
18. Chernousova, E.; Hryniv, O.; Molchanov, S. Population model with immigration in continuous space. *Math. Popul. Stud.* **2020**, *27*, 199–215. [CrossRef]
19. König, W. Branching random walks in random environment. In *Probabilistic Structures in Evolution*; EMS Press: Berlin, Germany, 2021; pp. 23–41. [CrossRef]
20. Molchanov, S. Lectures on random media. In *Lectures on Probability Theory (Saint-Flour, 1992)*; Springer: Berlin/Heidelberg, Germany 1994; Volume 1581, pp. 242–411. [CrossRef]
21. Afanas'ev, V.I. A new limit theorem for a critical branching process in a random environment. *Diskret. Math.* **1997**, *9*, 52–67. [CrossRef]
22. Vatutin, V.; Dyakonova, E. Path to survival for the critical branching processes in a random environment. *J. Appl. Probab.* **2017**, *54*, 588–602. [CrossRef]
23. Vatutin, V.A.; D'yakonova, E.E. Properties of multitype subcritical branching processes in a random environment. *Diskret. Math.* **2020**, *32*, 3–23. [CrossRef]
24. Greven, A.; den Hollander, F. Branching random walk in random environment: Phase transitions for local and global growth rates. *Probab. Theory Relat. Fields* **1992**, *91*, 195–249. [CrossRef]
25. Den Hollander, F. *Large Deviations (Fields Institute Monographs), Volume 14*; AMS, American Mathematical Society: Providence, RI, USA, 2000.
26. Akhiezer, N.I.; Glazman, I.M. *Theory of Linear Operators in Hilbert Space*; Dover Publications, Inc.: New York, NY, USA, 1993; pp. xiv+147+iv+218.
27. Yarovaya, E.B. *Branching Random Walks in an Inhomogeneous Medium*; MSU, Faculty of Mechanics and Mathematics: Moscow, Russia, 2007; p. 104.

28. Kato, T. *Perturbation Theory for Linear Operators (Classics in Mathematics)*; Springer: Berlin/Heidelberg, Germany,1995; pp. xxii+619.
29. Aizenman, M.; Warzel, S. *Random Operators: Disorder Effects on Quantum Spectra and Dynamics (Graduate Studies in Mathematics)*; American Mathematical Society: Providence, RI, USA, 2015; Volume 168, pp. xiv+326. [CrossRef]
30. Kunz, H.; Souillard, B. Sur le spectre des opérateurs aux différences finies aléatoires. *Comm. Math. Phys.* **1980**, *78*, 201–246.
31. Carmona, R.; Lacroix, J. *Spectral Theory of Random Schrödinger Operators (Probability and Its Applications)*; Birkhäuser Boston, Inc.: Boston, MA, USA, 1990; pp. xxvi+587. [CrossRef]
32. Boyadzhiev, K.N. Series with central binomial coefficients, Catalan numbers, and harmonic numbers. *J. Integer Seq.* **2012**, *15*, 11.
33. Shiryaev, A.N. Probability 1. In *Graduate Texts in Mathematics*, 3rd ed.; Springer: New York, NY, USA, 2016; Volume 95, pp. xvii+486.

Σ mathematics

MDPI

Article

Forward Selection of Relevant Factors by Means of MDR-EFE Method

Alexander Bulinski

Faculty of Mathematics and Mechanics, Lomonosov Moscow State University, Leninskie Gory 1, 119991 Moscow, Russia; alexander.bulinski@math.msu.ru

Abstract: The suboptimal procedure under consideration, based on the MDR-EFE algorithm, provides sequential selection of relevant (in a sense) factors affecting the studied, in general, non-binary random response. The model is not assumed linear, the joint distribution of the factors vector and response is unknown. A set of relevant factors has specified cardinality. It is proved that under certain conditions the mentioned forward selection procedure gives a random set of factors that asymptotically (with probability tending to one as the number of observations grows to infinity) coincides with the "oracle" one. The latter means that the random set, obtained with this algorithm, approximates the features collection that would be identified, if the joint distribution of the features vector and response were known. For this purpose the statistical estimators of the prediction error functional of the studied response are proposed. They involve a new version of regularization. This permits to guarantee not only the central limit theorem for normalized estimators, but also to find the convergence rate of their first two moments to the corresponding moments of the limiting Gaussian variable.

Keywords: feature selection; relevant factors; MDR-EFE method; forward selection; suboptimal procedures; statistical estimators of error functional (of a response); regularized estimators; CLT; convergence of estimators moments

MSC: 62G20; 62H12; 62J02; 62L12

1. Introduction

This paper is dedicated to the eminent scientist Professor A.S. Holevo, academician of the Russian Academy of Sciences, on occasion of his remarkable birthday.

The classical problem of regression analysis consists in the search for deterministic function f, which, in a certain sense, "well" approximates the observed random variable (response) Y by the value $f(X)$, where $X = (X_1, \ldots, X_p)$ is a vector of factors influencing the behavior of Y. This approach was initiated by the works of A.-M. Legendre and K. Gauss. At that time it found application in the processing of astronomical observations. Nowadays one widely uses the methods involving the appropriate choice of unknown real coefficients $\beta_1, \ldots, \beta_p$ for a linear model of the form $Y = \sum_{i=1}^{p} \beta_i X_i + \varepsilon$, where ε describes a random error. Clearly, $X_0 = 1$ can be included in the collection of factors, then $Y = \beta_0 + \sum_{i=1}^{p} \beta_i X_i + \varepsilon$. For example, books [1,2] are devoted to regression. The close tasks also arise in observations classification, see, e.g., [3].

Since the end of the 20th century, stochastic models have been studied where the random response Y depended only on some subset of the factors in the set of $X_1, \ldots, X_p$. So, in article [4], the LASSO method (Least Absolute Shrinkage and Selection Operator) was introduced, using the idea of regularization (going back to A.N.Tikhonov), which allowed to find factors included with non-zero coefficients in a "sparse" linear model. Somewhat earlier, this approach was used by several authors for the treatment of geophysical data. Generalizations of the mentioned method are considered in monograph [5]. We emphasize that the idea of identifying some of the factors having a principle (in a certain sense) impact on a response is also intensely developing within the framework of nonlinear models. Such direction of modern mathematical statistics is called Feature Selection (FS), i.e., the choice of features (variables, factors). In this regard, we refer, e.g., to monographs [6–9] and also to reviews [10–14]. In [10] the authors consider filter, wrapper and embedded methods of FS. They concentrate on feature elimination and also demonstrate the application of FS technique on standard datasets. In [11] the modern mainstream dimensionality reduction methods are analyzed including ones for small samples and those based on deep learning. In [12] FS machinery is considered based on filtering methods for detecting the cyber attacks. Survey [13] is devoted to FS methods in machine learning (the structured information is contained in 20 tables). The authors of [14] concentrate on applications of FS to stock market prediction and applications of FS in the analysis of credit risks are considered, e.g., in [15]. Beyond financial mathematics the choice of relevant factors is very important in medicine and biology. For instance, in the field of genetic data analysis there is an extensive research area called GWAS (Genome-Wide Association Studies) aimed at studying the relationships between phenotypes and genotypes, see, e.g., [16,17]. The authors of [18] provide the survey of starting methods used by genetic algorithms. Review [19] is devoted to the FS methods for predicting the risk of diseases. Thus, research in the field of FS is not only of theoretical interest, but also admits various applications.

Note that there are a number of complementary methods for identifying relevant factors. Much attention is paid to those employing the basic concepts of information theory such as entropy, mutual information, conditional mutual information, interaction information, various divergences, etc. Here statistical estimation of information characteristics plays an important role. One can mention, e.g., works [20,21]. In this article, the accent is made on identifying a set of relevant factors in the framework of a certain stochastic model, when the quality of the response approximation is evaluated by means of some metric.

Recall that J.B. Herrick in 1910 described the Sickle cell anemia (HbS). Later it was discovered that all clinical manifestations of the presence of HbS are the consequences of the single change in the B-globin gene. This famous example shows that even the search of a single feature having impact on a disease is reasonable. Nowadays the researchers concentrate on complex diseases provoked by several disorders of the human genome. Even identification of two SNPs (single nucleotide polymorphisms) having impact on a certain disease is of interest, see, e.g., [22].

Now we turn to the description of the studied mathematical model. All the considered random variables are defined on a probability space $(\Omega, \mathcal{F}, \mathsf{P})$. Let a random variable Y map Ω to some finite set $\mathbb{Y}$. We assume that, for $k \in T := \{1, \dots, p\}$, a random variable $X_k : \Omega \to M_k$, where M_k is an arbitrary finite set. Then the vector $X = (X_1, \dots, X_p)$ takes the values in $\mathbb{X} = M_1 \times \dots \times M_p$. For a set $S = \{i_1, \dots, i_r\}$, where $1 \le i_1 < \dots < i_r \le p$, we put $X_S := (X_{i_1}, \dots, X_{i_r})$. Similarly, for $x \in \mathbb{X}$, x_S denotes a vector $(x_{i_1}, \dots, x_{i_r})$. A collection of indices $S \subset T$ (the symbol $\subset$ is everywhere understood as a non-strict inclusion) is called *relevant* if the following relation holds for any $x \in \mathbb{X}$ and $y \in \mathbb{Y}$:

$$\mathsf{P}(Y = y | X = x) = \mathsf{P}(Y = y | X_S = x_S), \tag{1}$$

whenever $\mathsf{P}(Y = y|X = x) \neq 0$. In this case, the set of factors X_S is called relevant as well. If (1) takes place for some $S = S_0$ then it will be obviously valid for any S containing S_0. Therefore, the natural desire is to identify a set S that satisfies (1) and has cardinality $r < p$ (if such a set other than T exists). Note that there are different definitions of the relevant factors collection, see, e.g., [23,24] and the references therein.

It is assumed that a collection of relevant factors has r elements ($1 \le r < p$), however, the set S itself, which appears in (1), is unknown and should be identified. We label this assumption as (A). There is no restriction that S satisfying (1) and containing r elements is unique. Usually the joint distribution of (X, Y) is also unknown. Therefore, a statistical estimator of S is constructed based on the first N observations $\xi_N := (\xi^{(1)}, \dots, \xi^{(N)})$ of a sequence $\xi^{(1)}, \xi^{(2)}, \dots$, consisting of i.i.d. random vectors, where, for $k \in \mathbb{N}$, $\xi^{(k)} := (X^{(k)}, Y^{(k)})$ has the same distribution as the vector (X, Y).

In 2001, the authors of [25] proposed a method for identifying relevant factors, called MDR (Multifactor Dimensionality Reduction). According to article [26], more than 800 publications were devoted to the development of this method and its applications in the period from 2001 to 2014. Research in this direction has continued over the last decade, see, e.g., [27–29]. In [30], for the binary response Y, a modification of the MDR method was introduced, namely, MDR-EFE (Error Function Estimation), based on statistical estimates of the error functional of the response prediction using the K-fold cross-validation procedure, see also [31]. Later this method was extended in [32] to study the non-binary response.

Recall how the MDR-EFE method is employed. Let a non-random function $f : \mathbb{X} \to \mathbb{Y}$ be used to predict the response Y by the values of the factors vector X. Further we exclude considering the trivial case when $Y = y_0$ with probability one for some $y_0 \in \mathbb{Y}$ (hence, X and Y are independent). The prediction quality is determined by applying the following *error functional*

$$\mathsf{Err}(f) := \mathsf{E}|Y - f(X)|\psi(Y), \tag{2}$$

where a penalty function $\psi : \mathbb{Y} \to \mathbb{R}_+$. The functional Err takes finite values for the discrete X and Y under consideration. The function ψ allows to take into account the importance of approximating a particular value of Y using $f(X)$.

In biomedical research, one often considers the binary response Y characterizing the patient's state of health, say, the value $Y = 1$ corresponds to illness, and $Y = -1$ means that the patient is healthy. In many situations it is more important to consider the disease detection, so the value of 1 is attributed more weight. Of interest is the situation when $\mathbb{Y} = \{-1, 0, 1\}$. Then the value 0 describes some intermediate state of uncertainty ("gray zone"). Following [32], we will consider a more general scheme when the set $\mathbb{Y} := \{-m, \ldots, 0, \ldots, m\}$ for some $m \in \mathbb{N}$. Lemma 1 in [32] describes for such model all optimal functions f_{opt} that deliver a minimum to the error functional (2). Note that we can suppose that the set of values of Y is strictly contained in $\{-m, \ldots, m\}$, i.e., some values are accepted with zero probability. For such y, we assume that $\psi(y) = 0$. Thus, it is possible to study Y taking values in an arbitrary finite subset of $\mathbb{Z}$. In order to simplify the notation, we further consider $\mathsf{P}(Y = y) > 0$ for all $y \in \mathbb{Y} = \{-m, \ldots, m\}$.

It is proved that in the framework of model (1) the relation $f_{opt} = f^S$ is valid, where, for $x \in \mathbb{X}$ and $U \subset T$, $f^U(x) = f(x_U)$ and a function f is constructed in a due way. At the same time, for any $U \subset T$ such that $\sharp U = \sharp S$ ($\sharp$ denotes the cardinality of a finite set) and S appearing in (1), the following inequality is true:

$$\mathsf{Err}(f^S) \leq \mathsf{Err}(f^U). \tag{3}$$

For $U \subset T$, the function f^U is introduced further. It depends on the joint distribution of (X, Y) which is usually unknown. Thus we use observations $\xi_N = \{(X^{(j)}, Y^{(j)}), j = 1, \ldots, N\}$ for statistical estimates of the functional $\mathsf{Err}(f^U)$, where $U \subset T$, and then select as an estimator of S the set U on which the minimum of the corresponding statistical estimate is attained. This approach is described in the next section of the article.

We underline that consideration of all subsets (of the set T) having the cardinality r in the mentioned comparison procedure (involving regularized estimators, as explained in Section 2) for statistical estimates of the error functional is practically unfeasible, when p is large and r is moderately large. Therefore, a number of suboptimal methods of sequential feature selection have emerged. Such methods are used in various approaches to identify sets of relevant factors.

Mainly, one aims either to sequentially add indexes at each step of the algorithm for constructing a statistical estimator of a set S appearing in (1), or to sequentially exclude features from the general set T. In [33], algorithms of forward selection, i.e., sequential addition of indexes to the initial set, based on information theory, are considered. The authors of [33] show that the various algorithms employed can be interpreted as procedures based on proper approximations of the certain objective function. In [34] the principle attention is paid to simple models describing the phenomenon of epistasis observed in genetics, when individual factors do not affect the response, and some combinations of them lead to essential effects (in statistics one says "synergy interaction" of factors). Besides we also demonstrated that a number of well-known algorithms, for instance, mRMR (Minimum Redundancy Maximum Relevance) using mutual information and/or interaction information with a sequential procedure for selecting relevant factors can lead to the identification of the desired set with probability which is negligibly small. In [35] a variant is proposed for sequential (forward) application of the MDR-EFE method within the binary response model involving the naive Bayesian classifier scheme. The latter means that, for any $y \in \{-1,1\}$ and all $x \in \mathbb{X}$, the following relation holds:

$$\mathsf{P}(X = x|Y = y) = \prod_{k=1}^{p} \mathsf{P}(X_k = x_k|Y = y). \tag{4}$$

In other words, the factors $X_1, \ldots, X_p$ are conditionally independent for a given response Y. In [35] the joint distribution of X and Y was assumed known.

The principle goal of our work is to derive, for a non-binary, in general, random response, the probability that a sequential selection of features based on the (forward) application of the MDR-EFE method, without assuming the validity of (4), leads to identifying a suboptimal set that would be constructed by means of the same method from observations with a known joint distribution of the response and the vector of factors.

This result builds on the central limit theorem (CLT) for statistical estimates of the prediction error functional for a possibly non-binary response, proved in [32], which extends the CLT for the binary response model studied by the author previously. In addition, for the purposes of this work, we found the convergence rate of the first two moments of the considered statistics to the corresponding moments of the limiting Gaussian variable as the number of observations tends to infinity.

The article has the following structure. Section 2 describes statistical estimates of the error functional (for a response prediction) based on the MDR-EFE method. We also introduce the regularized versions of these estimators. In Section 3, the convergence rate of the first two moments of the regularized estimators of the error functional to the corresponding moments of the limiting Gaussian variable is established. Section 4 contains the main result related to the forward selection of relevant factors. The concluding remarks are given in Section 5. The proof of elementary Lemma 2 is provided in Appendix A for completeness of exposition.

2. Error Functional Estimators

Consider, in general, a non-binary response, i.e., let $\mathbb{Y} := \{-m, \ldots, 0, \ldots, m\}$ for some $m \in \mathbb{N}$. In the framework of the introduced discrete model, Lemma 1 of [32] gives a complete description of the class of optimal functions f_{opt} providing the minimum error $\mathsf{Err}(f)$, determined by (2), in the class of all functions $f : \mathbb{X} \to \mathbb{Y}$. To define such a function (included in the optimal class) for $x \in \mathbb{X}$, we deal with a vector $w(x)$ having components

$$w_y(x) := \psi(y)\mathsf{P}(Y = y, X = x), \;\; y \in \mathbb{Y}.$$

It can be easily seen that

$$\mathsf{Err}(f) = \sum_{y,z \in \mathbb{Y}} |y - z|\psi(y)\mathsf{P}(Y = y, f(X) = z) = \sum_{z \in \mathbb{Y}} \sum_{x \in A_z} w^{\top}(x)q(z), \tag{5}$$

where $A_z := \{x \in \mathbb{X} : f(x) = z\}$, $q(z)$ is a column of $(2m+1) \times (2m+1)$ matrix Q having elements $q_{y,z} := |y - z|$ (the element $q_{-m,-m}$ is located in the upper left corner of the matrix Q), $\top$ stands for the transposition of column vectors. In other words, one employs in (5) the scalar product of the vectors $w(x)$ and $q(z)$. Thus, search for an optimal function f_{opt} means finding the partition of $\mathbb{X}$ into such sets A_z, $z \in \mathbb{Y}$, that provide the minimum value of the right-hand side of (5). Note also that, according to Formula (13) of [32], the error of response prediction can be written as follows:

$$\mathsf{Err}(f) = \sum_{i=0}^{2m-1} \sum_{i-m<|y|\le m} \psi(y)\mathsf{P}(Y=y, |f(X)-y|>i). \tag{6}$$

Let, for $y \in \mathbb{Y}$, the vector $\Delta(y)$ have the first $m+y$ components equal to 1, and the remaining $m-y+1$ components equal to (-1). For any $x \in \mathbb{X}$, we introduce a vector $L(x)$ with $2m$ components having the form

$$L_y(x) := w^\top(x)\Delta(y), \;\; y \in \mathbb{Y},\; y > -m. \tag{7}$$

According to formula (11) of [32] one infers that

$$f_{opt}(x) = y \Longleftrightarrow \begin{cases} L_{-m+1}(x) \ge 0, & y=-m, \\ L_{y+1}(x) \ge 0,\; L_y(x) < 0, & y \ne \pm m, \\ L_m(x) < 0, & y = m. \end{cases} \tag{8}$$

The joint distribution of (X, Y) is, in general, unknown. Therefore, the optimal function f_{opt} cannot be found in practice, so an algorithm is used to predict it, i.e., to approximate by means of specified statistical estimators. The response prediction algorithm is defined as a function $\widehat{f}_{PA} = \widehat{f}_{PA}(x, \xi(W))$ given for $x \in \mathbb{X}$ and a set of observations

$$\xi(W) := \{\xi^{(j)} = (X^{(j)}, Y^{(j)}), j \in W\}, \;\; W \subset \mathbb{N}, \;\; \sharp W < \infty. \tag{9}$$

The function $\widehat{f}_{PA}$ takes values in the set $\mathbb{Y}$. It is assumed that the value of $\widehat{f}_{PA}(x, \xi(W))$ becomes close, in a certain sense, to $f(x)$ for x in a specified subset of the set $\mathbb{X}$ when W is sufficiently "massive". More precisely, we consider a family of functions $\widehat{f}_{PA}$ that depend on sets $\xi(W)$ of different cardinalities, but we will not complicate the notation. Consider $M = \{x \in \mathbb{X} : \mathsf{P}(X = x) > 0\}$. For $x \in \mathbb{X}$, $U \subset T$ and $y \in \mathbb{Y}$, introduce a vector $w^U(x)$ with components

$$w_y^U(x) := \begin{cases} \psi(y)\mathsf{P}(Y=y, X_U = x_U), & x \in M, \\ 0, & x \notin M. \end{cases}$$

Set

$$L_y^U(x) := (w^U(x))^\top \Delta(y), \;\; y \in \mathbb{Y}, \;\; y > -m. \tag{10}$$

For $U \subset T$, let f^U be defined by means of a counterpart of formula (8), where $L_y^U(x)$ is now written instead of $L_y(x)$. Then, according to Section 5 of [32] (the notation α is used there instead of U), in the framework of model (1), the optimal function $f_{opt} = f^S$, where S appears in (1) and $\sharp S = r$. Therefore relation (3) is valid for f^U corresponding to any $U \subset T$ with $\sharp U = r$ (the assumption (A) holds).

To introduce an algorithm for predicting the function f^U, we employ statistical estimators of the penalty function ψ, as well as the values $L_y^U(x)$, where $x \in \mathbb{X}$, $y \in \mathbb{Y}$, $y > -m$. Consider

$$\psi(y) := 1/\mathsf{P}(Y=y), \;\; \text{where } \mathsf{P}(Y=y) > 0, \;\; y \in \mathbb{Y}. \tag{11}$$

In the case of a binary response, such a choice of the penalty function was proposed in [36], the justification for this choice is given in [31], see also Section 4 in [32]. For the specified function $\psi(y)$ and observations $\xi(W)$, where the finite set $W \subset \mathbb{N}$, we use

$$\widehat{\psi}(y, \xi(W)) := \begin{cases} \frac{1}{\widehat{P}(y,\xi(W))}, & \widehat{P}(y, \xi(W)) \ne 0, \\ 0, & \widehat{P}(y, \xi(W)) = 0, \end{cases} \tag{12}$$

where the frequency estimator of a probability $\mathsf{P}(Y = y)$ has the form

$$\widehat{P}(y, \xi(W)) := \frac{1}{\sharp W} \sum_{j \in W} \mathbb{I}\{Y^{(j)} = y\}, \quad y \in \mathbb{N}. \tag{13}$$

It is not difficult to see that the strong law of large numbers for arrays of random variables (see, e.g., [37]) entails for finite sets $W_N \subset \mathbb{N}$, such that $\sharp W_N \to \infty$, the relation

$$\widehat{\psi}(y, \xi(W_N)) \to \psi(y) \ \text{ a.s.}, \quad N \to \infty. \tag{14}$$

Let the prediction algorithm $\widehat{f}_{PA}^{U}(x, \xi(W_N))$ of a function $f^U(x)$ be constructed by means of formula (8) analogue, where, for $x \in \mathbb{X}, y \in \mathbb{Y}, y > -m$, and $W_N \subset \{1, \dots, N\}$, one uses now statistical estimators $\widehat{L}_y^{U,W_N}(x)$ of functions $L_y^U(x)$ introduced in (10). Namely, let us define the following random variables:

$$\widehat{w}_y^{U,W_N}(x) := \widehat{\psi}(y, \xi(W_N)) \frac{1}{\sharp W_N} \sum_{j \in W_N} \mathbb{I}\{Y^{(j)} = y, X_U^{(j)} = x_U\}, \quad y \in \mathbb{Y},$$

where $\widehat{\psi}(y, \xi(W_N))$ is an estimator of $\psi(y)$ appearing in (12). For $x \in \mathbb{X}, y \in \mathbb{Y}, y > -m$, set

$$\widehat{L}_y^{U,W_N}(x) := \widehat{w}_y^{U,W_N}(x)^\top \Delta(y).$$

Replace the value $L_y(x)$ in (8) by $\widehat{L}_y^{U,W_N}(x)$. Then one can claim that

$$\widehat{f}_{PA}^{U}(x, \xi(W_N)) = y \Longleftrightarrow \begin{cases} \widehat{L}_y^{U,W_N}(x) \geq 0, & y = -m, \\ \widehat{L}_{y+1}^{U,W_N}(x) \geq 0, \ \widehat{L}_y^{U,W_N}(x) < 0, & y \neq \pm m, \\ \widehat{L}_y^{U,W_N}(x) < 0, & y = m. \end{cases} \tag{15}$$

For $K \in \mathbb{N}, K > 1$, we take a partition of a set $\{1, \dots, N\}$ into subsets

$$D_k(N) := \{(k-1)[N/K] + 1, \dots, k[N/K]\mathbb{I}\{k < K\} + N\mathbb{I}\{K = N\}\}, \tag{16}$$

here $k = 1, \dots, K$, $[a]$ is an integer part of a number $a \in \mathbb{R}$, $\mathbb{I}\{A\}$ is an indicator of a set A. These sets are applied in the K-fold cross-validation procedure increasing the stability of statistical inference (cross-validation procedure is studied, e.g., in [38]). Following [32], the estimator of the functional $\mathrm{Err}(f^U)$, i.e., a statistical estimator of the prediction error functional for a function f^U and observations $\xi_N := \xi(\{1, \dots, N\})$, involving the K-fold cross-validation procedure, is given by the formula:

$$\begin{aligned} \widehat{Err}_{K,N}(f^U) := \sum_{i=0}^{2m-1} \sum_{i-m<|y|\leq m} \frac{1}{K} \sum_{k=1}^{K} \widehat{\psi}(y, \xi(D_k(N))) \\ \times \frac{1}{\sharp D_k(N)} \sum_{j \in D_k(N)} \mathbb{I}\{Y^{(j)} = y, |\widehat{f}_{PA}^{U}(X^{(j)}, \xi(\overline{D}_k(N))) - y| > i\}, \end{aligned} \tag{17}$$

where $\overline{D}_k(N) := \{1, \dots, N\} \setminus D_k(N)$ and $\widehat{\psi}(y, \xi(D_k(N)))$ are evaluated according to (12) for $W_N = D_k(N)$, $k = 1, \dots, K$. The estimator (17) is a natural statistical analogue of the error functional (2) written in the form (6) when one employs the K-cross-validation procedure. Namely, instead of $\psi(y)$ we apply its statistical estimator of the type (12) and instead of f we use its approximation by means of prediction algorithm based on the part $D_k(N)$ of observations. To obtain the statistical estimators of the probability appearing in Formula (6) we write the corresponding average of indicator functions. One employs also the averaging over different parts of observations.

By Theorem 2 of [32], if $S = \{i_1, \dots, i_r\}$ is a set of relevant factors, i.e., (1) holds, then, for each $\varepsilon > 0$ and any set $U = \{m_1, \dots, m_r\} \subset T$, the following inequality takes place almost sure for all N large enough:

$$\widehat{Err}_{K,N}(f^S) \leq \widehat{Err}_{K,N}(f^U) + \varepsilon. \tag{18}$$

Thus, it is natural to consider all subsets $U = \{m_1, \dots, m_r\} \subset T$ and choose as a statistical estimator of a relevant collection of indices $(i_1, \dots, i_r)$ a set U on which the minimum of $\widehat{Err}_{K,N}(f^U)$ is attained. Here we also note that, for the study of asymptotic properties of the error functional, the regularization of the prediction algorithm by means of a sequence of positive numbers $(\varepsilon_N)_{N \in \mathbb{N}}$ such that $\varepsilon_N \to 0$, as $N \to \infty$, plays an important role. Namely, for $W_N \subset \{1, \dots, N\}$, we define

$$\widehat{f}^U_{PA,\varepsilon_N}(x, \xi(W_N)) = y \iff \begin{cases} \widehat{L}^{U,W_N}_y(x) + \varepsilon_N \geq 0, & y = -m, \\ \widehat{L}^{U,W_N}_{y+1}(x) + \varepsilon_N \geq 0,\ \widehat{L}^{U,W_N}_y(x) + \varepsilon_N < 0, & y \neq \pm m, \\ \widehat{L}^{U,W_N}_y(x) + \varepsilon_N < 0, & y = m. \end{cases} \tag{19}$$

As in article [32], we assume that

$$\varepsilon_N \to 0+, \quad \sqrt{N}\varepsilon_N \to \infty, \quad N \to \infty. \tag{20}$$

Now we introduce a statistical estimator $\widehat{\mathsf{Err}}_{K,N,\varepsilon_N}(f^U)$ using an analogue of Formula (17), where one employs $\widehat{f}^U_{PA,\varepsilon_N}$ instead of $\widehat{f}^U_{PA}$. For the regularized statistical estimators, as mentioned in [32], the analogue of Formula (18) holds. In [32], for estimators $\widehat{f}^U_{PA,\varepsilon_N}$ constructed when condition (20) is met, the CLT is established. In the next section we apply a slightly different regularization for the error functional estimates, which will permit us to specify the convergence rate of the first two moments of these estimators to corresponding moments of the limiting Gaussian variable. This result is not only of independent interest, but is also applied in Section 4.

3. Asymptotic Behavior of the First Two Moments of Statistical Estimators of the Error Functional

As noted in Section 2, we will use the penalty function (11). Therefore, for $W_N = D_k(N)$, as a strongly consistent estimator $\widehat{\psi}(y, D_k(N))$ of $\psi(y)$ we will employ the variable appearing in (12), denoted below as $\widehat{\psi}_{N,k}(y)$, where $y \in \mathbb{Y}$, $k = 1, \dots, K$, $N \in \mathbb{N}$. Recall that the estimator $\widehat{\mathsf{Err}}_{K,N}(f^U)$ is defined by formula (2). If the regularized version $\widehat{f}_{PA,\varepsilon_N}$ is substituted into this estimator instead of $\widehat{f}^U_{PA}$, where $x \in \mathbb{X}$ and $N \in \mathbb{N}$, then the notation $\widehat{\mathsf{Err}}_{K,N,\varepsilon_N}(f^U)$ is used. We will apply the following Corollary 3 of [32] established in the framework of a model satisfying (1).

Theorem 1 ([32]). *Let U be an arbitrary subset of T having the cardinality r, the function f^U be defined after formula* (10), *$\widehat{f}^U_{PA,\varepsilon_N}$ appear in* (19) *for observations ξ_N, and the sequence $(\varepsilon_N)_{N \in \mathbb{N}}$ satisfy condition* (20). *Then*

$$\sqrt{N}\Big(\widehat{\mathsf{Err}}_{K,N,\varepsilon_N}(f^U) - \mathsf{Err}(f^U)\Big) \xrightarrow{\mathcal{D}} Z \sim N(0, \sigma^2(U)), \quad N \to \infty, \tag{21}$$

and in this case $\sigma^2(U)$ is the variance of a random variable

$$V(U) := \sum_{i=0}^{2m-1} \sum_{i-m<|y|\leq m} \frac{\mathbb{I}\{Y = y\}}{\mathsf{P}(Y = y)} (\mathbb{I}\{|f^U(X) - y| > i\} - \mathsf{P}(|f^U(X) - y| > i | Y = y)). \tag{22}$$

It is known that the convergence in distribution of random variables, in general, does not ensure the convergence of their moments even when the moments exist. We will manage to establish the convergence rate of the first two moments of the error functional statistical estimators to the corresponding moments of the limit random variable. For this purpose we slightly strength the condition of estimates regularization. We require that a sequence $(\varepsilon_N)_{N\in\mathbb{N}}$ satisfies the following condition:

$$\varepsilon_N \to 0+, \quad \frac{\varepsilon_N\sqrt{N}}{\sqrt{\log\frac{1}{\varepsilon_N}}} \to \infty, \quad N \to \infty. \tag{23}$$

Clearly, (23) implies the validity of (20). Relation (23) holds if one takes $\varepsilon_N = N^{-\delta}$, $N \in \mathbb{N}$, where $\delta \in (0, 1/2)$.

Lemma 1. *Let condition* (23) *be met. Then, for every* $K \in \mathbb{N}$, $K > 1$, *and any* $U \subset T$, *the statistical estimators* $\widehat{\mathsf{Err}}_{K,N,\varepsilon_N}(f^U)$ *satisfy the following relation:*

$$N\,\mathsf{E}(\widehat{\mathsf{Err}}_{K,N,\varepsilon_N}(f^U) - \mathsf{Err}(f^U))^2 \to \sigma^2(U), \quad N \to \infty, \tag{24}$$

where $\sigma^2(U) = \mathsf{var}\, V(U)$ *and* $V(U)$ *is introduced in formula* (22).

Proof of Lemma 1. Let us fix an arbitrary set $U \subset T$. For each $N \in \mathbb{N}$ one has

$$\begin{aligned}\mathbb{Z}_N &:= \sqrt{N}\Big(\widehat{\mathsf{Err}}_{K,N,\varepsilon_N}(f^U) - \mathsf{Err}(f^U)\Big) = \sqrt{N}(\widehat{\mathsf{Err}}_{K,N,\varepsilon_N}(f^U) - \widehat{T}_N(f^U)) \\ &+ \sqrt{N}(\widehat{T}_N(f^U) - T_N(f^U)) + \sqrt{N}(T_N(f^U) - \mathsf{Err}(f^U)),\end{aligned} \tag{25}$$

where

$$T_N(f^U) := \sum_{i=0}^{2m-1} \sum_{i-m<|y|\le m} \frac{1}{K}\sum_{k=1}^{K} \frac{\psi(y)}{\sharp D_k(N)} \sum_{j\in D_k(N)} \mathbb{I}\{Y^{(j)} = y, |f^U(X^{(j)}) - y| > i\}, \tag{26}$$

$$\widehat{T}_N(f^U) := \sum_{i=0}^{2m-1} \sum_{i-m<|y|\le m} \frac{1}{K}\sum_{k=1}^{K} \frac{\widehat{\psi}_{N,k}(y)}{\sharp D_k(N)} \sum_{j\in D_k(N)} \mathbb{I}\{Y^{(j)} = y, |f^U(X^{(j)}) - y| > i\}, \tag{27}$$

$\widehat{\psi}_{N,k}(y)$ are defined by means of (12) for $W_N = D_k(N)$, $k = 1, \ldots, K$, $N \in \mathbb{N}$. The proof is divided into several steps.

Step 1 . At first we consider

$$R_N := \sqrt{N}(\widehat{\mathsf{Err}}_{K,N,\varepsilon_N}(f^U) - \widehat{T}_N(f^U)), \quad N \in \mathbb{N}.$$

To simplify the notation, we do not write that R_N also depends on K, ξ_N and ε_N. Our aim is to show that if (23) holds then

$$\mathsf{E}R_N^2 \to 0 \text{ as } N \to \infty. \tag{28}$$

In the light of formula (71) of [32], under condition (20) the following relation is valid:

$$R_N \xrightarrow{\mathsf{P}} 0, \quad N \to \infty. \tag{29}$$

Taking into account (29), by Theorem 5.4 of [39], relation (28) holds if (and only if) the sequence $(R_N^2)_{N\in\mathbb{N}}$ is uniformly integrable. Due to theorem by De La Vallé - Poussin (see, e.g., Theorem 1.3.4 of [40]) it is sufficient to verify that

$$\sup_{N\in\mathbb{N}} \mathsf{E}(R_N^4) < \infty.$$

For $x \in \mathbb{X}$, $y \in \mathbb{Y}$, $i \in \mathbb{Z}_+$, $k = 1, \dots, K$ and $N \in \mathbb{N}$ we introduce the following random variables:

$$F_{N,k}^{(i)}(x,y) = \mathbb{I}\{|\widehat{f}_{PA,\varepsilon_N}^{U}(x,\xi(\overline{D}_{N,k})) - y| > i\} - \mathbb{I}\{|f^U(x) - y| > i\}, \tag{30}$$

$$\mathbb{S}_k(i,y) := \frac{1}{\sharp D_k(N)} \sum_{j \in D_k(N)} \mathbb{I}\{Y^{(j)} = y\} F_{N,k}^{(i)}(X^{(j)}, y), \tag{31}$$

where, for $W \subset \mathbb{N}$, $\xi(W)$ is defined by Formula (9). Write $R_N = U_{N,1} + U_{N,2}$, here

$$\begin{aligned} U_{N,1} &:= \sqrt{N}\left(\frac{1}{K}\sum_{k=1}^{K}\sum_{i=0}^{2m-1}\sum_{i-m<|y|\le m} \psi(y)\mathbb{S}_k(i,y)\right), \\ U_{N,2} &:= \sqrt{N}\left(\frac{1}{K}\sum_{k=1}^{K}\sum_{i=0}^{2m-1}\sum_{i-m<|y|\le m} (\widehat{\psi}_{N,k}(y) - \psi(y))\mathbb{S}_k(i,y)\right). \end{aligned}$$

Now note that, for any real numbers $a_1, \dots, a_v$, every $v \in \mathbb{N}$ and an arbitrary $\gamma > 1$, the Hölder inequality implies that

$$\left(\sum_{r=1}^{v} |a_r|\right)^{\gamma} \le v^{\gamma-1} \sum_{r=1}^{v} |a_r|^{\gamma}. \tag{32}$$

Evidently, (32) is true for $\gamma = 1$ as well. Consequently, we get

$$R_N^4 \le 8(U_{N,1}^4 + U_{N,2}^4), \quad N \in \mathbb{N}. \tag{33}$$

Clearly, for all $x \in \mathbb{X}$, $y \in \mathbb{Y}$, $W_N \subset \{1, \dots, N\}$ and $N \in \mathbb{N}$, one has

$$\widehat{L}_{y,\varepsilon_N}^{U,W_N}(x) := \widehat{L}_y^{U,W_N}(x) + \varepsilon_N = L_y^U(x) + (\widehat{w}_y^{U,W_N}(x) - w_y(x))^\top \Delta(y) + \varepsilon_N, \tag{34}$$

where the functions appearing in (34) were introduced in Section 2. For any $x \in \mathbb{X}$ and $y \in \mathbb{Y}$, the inequalities $L_y^U(x) \ge 0$, $L_{y+1}^U(x) < 0$ are satisfied if and only if, for arbitrary $\delta_N(x,y;U) > 0$ such that $\delta_N(x,y;U) \to 0$, as $N \to \infty$, and all sufficiently large $N \in \mathbb{N}$, the following inequalities are valid: $L_y^U(x) + \delta_N(x,y;U) > 0$, $L_{y+1}^U(x) + \delta_N(x,y;U) < 0$ (the analogous statement is true for inequalities corresponding to coordinates $y = m$ and $y = -m$ in Formula (19)). Obviously,

$$\begin{aligned} &|(\widehat{w}_y^{U,W_N}(x) - w_y(x))^\top \Delta(y)| \\ &\le |\widehat{\psi}(y,\xi(W_N)) - \psi(y)| + \psi(y)\left|\frac{1}{\sharp W_N}\sum_{q\in W_N}\mathbb{I}\{X_U^{(q)} = x_U, Y^{(q)} = y\} - \mathsf{P}(X_U = x_U, Y = y)\right|, \end{aligned}$$

where $\widehat{\psi}(y,\xi(W_N))$ is defined in (12). One has

$$\begin{aligned} &\sum_{x_U}\left(\frac{1}{\sharp W_N}\sum_{q\in W_N}\mathbb{I}\{X_U^{(q)} = x_U, Y^{(q)} = y\} - \mathsf{P}(X_U = x_U, Y = y)\right) \\ &= \frac{1}{\sharp W_N}\sum_{q\in W_N}\mathbb{I}\{Y^{(q)} = y\} - \mathsf{P}(Y = y) \\ &= \widehat{P}(y,\xi(W_N)) - \mathsf{P}(Y = y). \end{aligned} \tag{35}$$

For $x \in \mathbb{X}, y \in \mathbb{Y}, W_N \subset \{1, \ldots, N\}$ and $N \in \mathbb{N}$, consider the following event

$$A_{W_N}(x,y) = \left\{ \left| \frac{1}{\sharp W_N} \sum_{q \in W_N} \mathbb{I}\{X_U^{(q)} = x_U, Y^{(q)} = y\} - \mathsf{P}(X_U = x_U, Y = y) \right| \leq \frac{p_0^2 \varepsilon_N}{8\sharp\mathbb{X}} \right\}, \tag{36}$$

where $p_0 = \min_{y \in \mathbb{Y}} \mathsf{P}(Y = y)$ (we assumed that $\mathsf{P}(Y = y) > 0$ for $y \in \mathbb{Y}$). More precisely one can write $A_{W_N}(x,y) = A_{W_N}(x,y,U;\{(X^{(q)}, Y^{(q)}), q \in W_N\})$. We will not include a set U in the list of arguments since this set is fixed. Then, for $\omega \in A_{W_N}(x,y)$, in view of (35), we get

$$\left| \widehat{P}(y, \xi(W_N)) - \mathsf{P}(Y = y) \right| \leq \frac{p_0^2 \varepsilon_N}{8}. \tag{37}$$

Then by virtue of (37), for any $y \in \mathbb{Y}$ and all N large enough, i.e., for $N \geq N_0(\mathbb{Y}, (\varepsilon_N)_{N \in \mathbb{N}})$, one has

$$\widehat{P}(y, \xi(W_N)) \geq \mathsf{P}(Y = y) - \frac{p_0^2 \varepsilon_N}{8} \geq \mathsf{P}(Y = y) - \frac{\varepsilon_N}{8} > \frac{\mathsf{P}(Y = y)}{2} > 0,$$

and hence the following relation holds

$$|\widehat{\psi}(y, \xi(W_N)) - \psi(y)| = \frac{|\widehat{P}(y, \xi(W_N)) - \mathsf{P}(Y = y)|}{\widehat{P}(y, \xi(W_N))\mathsf{P}(Y = y)} \leq \frac{\frac{p_0^2 \varepsilon_N}{8}}{\frac{\mathsf{P}(Y=y)^2}{2}} \leq \frac{\varepsilon_N}{4}. \tag{38}$$

Thus if $\omega \in A_{W_N}(x,y)$, where $x \in \mathbb{X}$ and $y \in \mathbb{Y}$, then according to (36) and (38), for all N large enough, we can write

$$|(\widehat{w}_y^{U,W_N}(x) - w_y(x))^\top \Delta(y)| \leq \frac{\varepsilon_N}{4} + \left(\frac{1}{p_0}\right) \frac{p_0^2 \varepsilon_N}{8\sharp\mathbb{X}} \leq \frac{\varepsilon_N}{2}.$$

Taking into account that the sets $\mathbb{X}$ and $\mathbb{Y}$ have finite cardinalities, we ascertain that, for any $x \in \mathbb{X}, y \in \mathbb{Y}$ and all N large enough, for $\omega \in A_{W_N}(x,y)$, one has

$$\widehat{f}_{PA,\varepsilon_N}^{U,W_N}(x) = f^U(x). \tag{39}$$

Consequently, for any $x \in \mathbb{X}, y \in \mathbb{Y}, i = 0, 1, \ldots, 2m-1, \omega \in A_{W_N}(x,y)$, where $W_N = \overline{D}_k(N), k = 1, \ldots, K$, for all N large enough (i.e., $N \geq N_1$), the following inequality holds:

$$F_{N,k}^{(i)}(x,y)\mathbb{I}\{A_{\overline{D}_k(N)}(x,y)\} = 0. \tag{40}$$

Applying (32) we come to the inequality

$$|U_{N,1}|^4 \leq N^2 \frac{(2m)^6}{K} \sum_{k=1}^{K} \sum_{i=0}^{2m-1} \sum_{i-m<|y|\leq m} \psi(y)^4 \left(\frac{1}{\sharp D_k(N)} \sum_{j \in D_k(N)} \mathbb{I}\{Y^{(j)} = y\} F_{N,k}^{(i)}(X^{(j)}, y) \right)^4.$$

Let $\widetilde{\Sigma}$ denote the summation over all $x_j \in \mathbb{X}$ for $j \in D_k(N)$. For $N \geq N_1$ one has

$$\begin{aligned} &\mathsf{E}\left(\sum_{j \in D_k(N)} \mathbb{I}\{Y^{(j)} = y\} F_{N,k}^{(i)}(X^{(j)}, y) \right)^4 \\ = \; &\mathsf{E}\left(\widetilde{\Sigma} \left(\sum_{j \in D_k(N)} \mathbb{I}\{Y^{(j)} = y\} F_{N,k}^{(i)}(x_j, y) \right)^4 \mathbb{I}\left\{ \bigcap_{j \in D_k(N)} \{X^{(j)} = x_j\} \right\} \right) \end{aligned}$$

$$= \mathsf{E}\left(\widetilde{\Sigma}\left(\sum_{j\in D_k(N)} \mathbb{I}\{Y^{(j)}=y\}F^{(i)}_{N,k}(x_j,y)\mathbb{I}\{\overline{A}_{\overline{D}_k(N)}(x_j,y)\}\right)^4 \mathbb{I}\left\{\bigcap_{j\in D_k(N)}\{X^{(j)}=x_j\}\right\}\right)$$

$$= \mathsf{E}\left(\sum_{j\in D_k(N)} \mathbb{I}\{Y^{(j)}=y\}F^{(i)}_{N,k}(X^{(j)},y)\mathbb{I}\{\overline{A}_{\overline{D}_k(N)}(X^{(j)},y)\}\right)^4$$

$$\leq \mathsf{E}\left(\sum_{j\in D_k(N)} \mathbb{I}\{\overline{A}_{\overline{D}_k(N)}(X^{(j)},y)\}\right)^4,$$

here we employ (40) and take into account that $|F^{(i)}_{N,k}(x,y)|\leq 1$. We see that

$$|U_{N,1}|^4 \leq N^2\frac{(2m)^6}{K}\sum_{k=1}^{K}\sum_{i=0}^{2m-1}\sum_{i-m<|y|\leq m}\frac{\psi(y)^4}{(\sharp D_k(N))^4}\Big(\sum_{j\in D_k(N)}\mathbb{I}\{\overline{A}_{\overline{D}_N(k)}(X^{(j)},y)\}\Big)^4. \quad (41)$$

For $W_N\subset\{1,\dots,N\}$, $y\in\mathbb{Y}$ and $j=1,\dots,N$, introduce the functions

$$g_{W_N}(X^{(j)},y)=\mathbb{I}\{\overline{A}_{W_N}(X^{(j)},y)\}=\mathbb{I}\{\overline{A}_{W_N}(X^{(j)},y;\{(X^{(q)},Y^{(q)}),q\in W_N\})\}.$$

It is known (see, e.g., formula (15) in Chap. VI of [41]) that if a bounded Borel function $g:\mathbb{R}^n\times\mathbb{R}^m\to\mathbb{R}$, ξ and ζ are independent random vectors taking values in $\mathbb{R}^n$ and $\mathbb{R}^m$, respectively, then

$$\mathsf{E}(g(\xi,\zeta)|\zeta=z)=\mathsf{E}g(\xi,z),\ \ z\in\mathbb{R}^n.$$

Due to independence of $(X^{(j)},Y^{(j)})$, $j\in\mathbb{N}$, we can apply the lemma on grouping random vectors (see, e.g., [42], p. 28) to get the relation

$$\mathsf{E}\Big(\Big(\sum_{j\in D_k(N)} g_{\overline{D}_k(N)}(X^{(j)},y;(X^{(q)},Y^{(q)}),q\in\overline{D}_k(N)))\Big)^4\Big|(X^{(q)},Y^{(q)})=(x_q,y_q),q\in\overline{D}_k(N))\Big)$$

$$=\mathsf{E}\Big(\sum_{j\in D_k(N)} g_{\overline{D}_k(N)}(X^{(j)},y;(x_q,y_q)),q\in\overline{D}_N(k)))\Big)^4.$$

By the Rosenthal inequality (see, e.g., Theorem 2.9 of [43]), for independent centered random variables $Z_1,\dots,Z_v$, having $\mathsf{E}|Z_j|^t<\infty$ for some $t\in[2,\infty)$ and each $j=1,\dots,v$, one has

$$\mathsf{E}\Big|\sum_{j=1}^{v}Z_j\Big|^t\leq C(t)\Big(\sum_{j=1}^{v}\mathsf{E}|Z_j|^t+\Big(\sum_{j=1}^{v}\mathsf{E}Z_j^2\Big)^{\frac{t}{2}}\Big), \quad (42)$$

where $C(t)>0$ depends on t but does not depend on v and distributions of variables Z_j, $j=1,\dots,v$.

Set $\eta^{(j)}_{N,k}:=g_{\overline{D}_k(N)}(X^{(j)},y;\{(x_q,y_q)),q\in\overline{D}_N(k)\})$, $j\in\mathbb{N}$. Note that $0\leq\eta^{(j)}_{N,k}\leq 1$ for all $j\in D_N(k)$. Then according to (42) we come to the inequality

$$\mathsf{E}\left(\sum_{j\in D_k(N)}(\eta^{(j)}_{N,k}-\mathsf{E}\eta^{(j)}_{N,k})\right)^4\leq C(\sharp D_k(N))^2,$$

where $k=1,\dots,K$ and $C=2C(4)$. Hence, applying (32) for $\gamma=4$ and $v=2$, one has

$$\mathsf{E}\left(\sum_{j\in D_k(N)}\eta^{(j)}_{N,k}\right)^4\leq 8\left(C(\sharp D_k(N))^2+\left(\sum_{j\in D_k(N)}\mathsf{E}\eta^{(j)}_{N,k}\right)^4\right)$$

$$\leq 8C(\sharp D_k(N))^2 + 8(\sharp D_k(N))^4 \max_{j \in D_k(N)} (\mathsf{E}\eta_{N,k}^{(j)})^4.$$

Evidently, we can write

$$\mathsf{E}(\eta_{N,k}^{(j)}) = \mathsf{P}(\overline{A}_{\overline{D}_k(N)}(X^{(j)}, y; \{(x_q, y_q)\}, q \in \overline{D}_k(N)\}).$$

Let $M_k = \sharp\overline{D}_k(N)$, where $M_k = M_k(N)$, $k = 1, \ldots, K$. Set $\zeta_q = \mathbb{I}\{X_U^{(q)} = x_U, Y^{(q)} = y\}$, where $q \in \overline{D}_k(N)$, $\sigma_0^2 = \mathsf{var}\,\zeta_q$. Clearly, ζ_q depends on x_U, y and U. Random variables ζ_q are identically distributed for $q \in \mathbb{N}$. Therefore $\sigma_0^2 = \sigma_0^2(U, x, y)$, but does not depend on q. If $\sigma_0^2 = 0$, then the variables ζ_q are a.s. equal to some constant. According to (36), an event $\overline{A}_{\overline{D}_k(N)}(X^{(j)}, y; \{(x_q, y_q)\}, q \in \overline{D}_k(N)\})$ occurrence means that the variable which is equal to zero a.s. turns greater than $(p_0^2 \varepsilon_N)/(8\sharp\mathbb{X})$. Therefore, in the degenerate case one has

$$\mathsf{P}(\overline{A}_{\overline{D}_k(N)}(X^{(j)}, y; (x_q, y_q)), q \in \overline{D}_k(N))) = 0$$

and $\mathsf{E}\eta_{N,k}^{(j)} = 0$ for all $j = 1, \ldots, N$. Consider now the case when $\sigma_0^2 > 0$. Then we get

$$\mathsf{P}(\overline{A}_{\overline{D}_k(N)}(X^{(j)}, y; \{(x_q, y_q)\}, q \in \overline{D}_k(N)\}) = \mathsf{P}\left(\frac{\sum_{q \in \overline{D}_k(N)}(\zeta_q - \mathsf{E}\zeta_q)}{\sigma_0\sqrt{M_k}} > \frac{p_0^2\sqrt{M_k}\varepsilon_N}{8\sharp\mathbb{X}\sigma_0}\right),$$

where p_0 appeared in (36).

Now we employ the Berry-Esseen estimate of the convergence rate in CLT for i.i.d. random variables. Let $Z_1, \ldots, Z_v$ be i.i.d. random variables such that $\mathsf{E}Z_1 = 0$, $\mathsf{var}Z_1 = \sigma^2 \in (0, \infty)$, $\mathsf{E}|Z_1|^3 = \rho < \infty$. We write F for the distribution function of Z_1 and F_v stands for the distribution function of $(Z_1 + \ldots + Z_v)/(\sigma\sqrt{v})$. Then (see, e.g., Theorem 5.4 of [43]), for any $v \in \mathbb{N}$,

$$\sup_{u \in \mathbb{R}} |F_v(u) - \Phi(u)| \leq \frac{C_0\rho}{\sigma^3\sqrt{v}},$$

where $\Phi(u)$ is the distribution function of a standard normal random variable, C_0 is a positive constant (C_0 does not depend on distribution of Z_1 and v). According to [44] one has $C_0 \leq 0,4693$. Consequently, taking $Z \sim N(0,1)$, we have

$$\mathsf{P}\left(\left|\frac{\sum_{q \in \overline{D}_k(N)}(\zeta_q - \mathsf{E}\zeta_q)}{\sigma_0\sqrt{M_k}}\right| > \frac{p_0^2\sqrt{M_k}\varepsilon_N}{8\sharp\mathbb{X}\sigma_0}\right) \leq \mathsf{P}\left(|Z| > \frac{p_0^2\sqrt{M_k}\varepsilon_N}{8\sharp\mathbb{X}\sigma_0}\right) + \frac{2C_0}{\sigma_0^3\sqrt{M_k}} \tag{43}$$

since $\mathsf{E}|\zeta_q - \mathsf{E}\zeta_q|^3 \leq 1$ for $q \in \overline{D}_k(N)$, where $\zeta_q = \mathbb{I}\{X_U^{(q)} = x_U, Y^{(q)} = y\}$.

It is well-known (see, e.g., formula (29) of Chap. II of [41]), that, for $u > 0$, the following inequality is true:

$$\mathsf{P}(|Z| \geq u) \leq \frac{\sqrt{2/\pi}}{u} \exp\left\{-\frac{u^2}{2}\right\}.$$

Therefore, by virtue of an inequality $\sigma_0^2 \leq 1/4$ (which is valid for the indicator variance) and as

$$(K-1)[N/K] \leq M_k < N, \tag{44}$$

we can write under condition (23) that

$$\mathsf{P}\left(|Z| > \frac{p_0^2\sqrt{M_k}\varepsilon_N}{8\sharp\mathbb{X}\sigma_0}\right) \leq \frac{8\sharp\mathbb{X}\sqrt{2}\sigma_0}{p_0^2\sqrt{\pi M_k}\varepsilon_N} \exp\left\{-\frac{1}{2}\left(\frac{p_0^2\sqrt{M_k}\varepsilon_N}{8\sharp\mathbb{X}\sigma_0}\right)^2\right\}$$

$$\leq \frac{4\sqrt{2}\sharp\mathbb{X}}{p_0^2\sqrt{\pi M_k}\varepsilon_N}\exp\left\{-\frac{1}{32}\left(\frac{p_0^2\sqrt{M_k}\varepsilon_N}{\sharp\mathbb{X}}\right)^2\right\}$$

$$= \frac{4\sqrt{2}\sharp\mathbb{X}}{p_0^2\sqrt{\pi M_k}}\exp\left\{-\frac{1}{32}\left(\frac{p_0^2\sqrt{M_k}\varepsilon_N}{\sharp\mathbb{X}}\right)^2 + \log\left(\frac{1}{\varepsilon_N}\right)\right\} \leq \frac{C_1}{\sqrt{N}}, \quad N \in \mathbb{N},$$

and C_1 does not depend on N.

Introduce

$$\widetilde{\sigma}^2 := \min_{U\subset T, x\in\mathbb{X}, y\in\mathbb{Y}} \sigma_0^2(U,x,y),$$

where one considers only strictly positive $\sigma_0^2(U,x,y)$. Then obviously $\widetilde{\sigma}^2 > 0$, as there exists only a finite collection of different variants. Thus in view of (44), for all x, y and U under consideration, one has

$$\frac{2C_0}{\widetilde{\sigma}^3\sqrt{M_k}} \leq \frac{C_2}{\sqrt{N}}, \quad N \in \mathbb{N},$$

where C_0 appeared in (43) and C_2 does not depend on N.

Therefore, if condition (23) is satisfied then, for all $x \in \mathbb{X}$, $y \in \mathbb{Y}$, $k = 1,\dots,K$ and $j \in D_k(N)$, the following inequality holds:

$$\mathsf{E}\eta_{N,k}^{(j)} \leq \frac{C_3}{\sqrt{N}}, \quad N \in \mathbb{N}, \tag{45}$$

where C_3 does not depend on x, y, k and N. Hence, in view of (44) we come to the relation

$$\mathsf{E}\left(\sum_{j\in D_k(N)} g_{\overline{D}_k(N)}(X^{(j)}, y; \{(X^{(q)}, Y^{(q)}), q \in \overline{D}_k(N)\})\right)^4$$

$$\leq \left(8C(\sharp D_k(N))^2 + 8(\sharp D_k(N))^4\frac{C_3^4}{N^2}\right)\sum_{(x_q,y_q)),q\in\overline{D}_N(k)} \mathsf{P}((X^{(q)}, Y^{(q)}) = (x_q, y_q)) \leq C_4 N^2,$$

where C_4 does not depend on x, y, k and N. Thus according to (41), for all N large enough, we have proved the inequality

$$\mathsf{E}U_{N,1}^4 \leq C_5, \tag{46}$$

where C_5 does not depend on N.

In a similar way (taking into account (42) and (45)), for $i = 0,\dots,2m-1$, $y \in \mathbb{Y}$, $k = 1,\dots,K$, and all N large enough, we get

$$\mathsf{E}\mathbb{S}_k(i,y)^8 \leq C_6(\sharp D_N(k))^{-4}, \tag{47}$$

where $\mathbb{S}_k(i,y)$ is introduced in (31), and C_6 does not depend on N.

We will employ an elementary result for the Bernoulli scheme. Let $U_1, U_2, \dots,$ be a sequence of i.i.d. random variables such that $\mathsf{P}(U_1 = 1) = \mathsf{p}$ and $\mathsf{P}(U_1 = 0) = 1 - \mathsf{p}$, where $\mathsf{p} \in (0,1)$. Consider the following frequency estimator of a probability p:

$$\widehat{\mathsf{p}}_N := \frac{1}{N}\sum_{j=1}^N \mathbb{I}\{U_j = 1\}, \quad N \in \mathbb{N}.$$

Define

$$\widehat{\psi}_N := \begin{cases} \frac{1}{\widehat{\mathsf{p}}_N}, & \widehat{\mathsf{p}}_N \neq 0, \\ 0, & \widehat{\mathsf{p}}_N = 0. \end{cases} \tag{48}$$

Lemma 2. *For the Bernoulli scheme introduced above and the estimators $\widehat{\psi}_N$ provided by formula* (48), *for each $t \in \mathbb{N}$, the following relation holds:*

$$\mathsf{E}\left(\widehat{\psi}_N - \frac{1}{\mathsf{p}}\right)^t = O\left(\frac{1}{N}\right), \quad N \to \infty. \tag{49}$$

More precisely, the absolute value of the function in the left-hand side of (49)*, for all $N \in \mathbb{N}$, admits a bound c/N where $c = c(\mathsf{p}, t)$ for $\mathsf{p} \in (0,1)$ and $t \in \mathbb{N}$.*

For the sake of completeness the proof of this result is given in Appendix A.

Now we continue the proof corresponding to Step 1. For all considered k, i, y and any $N \in \mathbb{N}$, the Cauchy - Bunyakovsky - Schwarz inequality yields

$$\mathsf{E}((\widehat{\psi}_{N,k}(y) - \psi(y))\mathbb{S}_k(i,y))^4 \le \left(\mathsf{E}(\widehat{\psi}_{N,k}(y) - \psi(y))^8 \,\mathsf{E}\mathbb{S}_k(i,y))^8\right)^{\frac{1}{2}}.$$

Due to Lemma 2 one has $\mathsf{E}(\widehat{\psi}_{N,k}(y) - \psi(y))^8 = O\left(\frac{1}{N}\right)$, $N \to \infty$. Employing the Minkowski inequality (to take into account the summation over i, y, k), for all $N \in \mathbb{N}$, we come to the bound

$$\mathsf{E}U_{N,2}^4 \le N^2 C_7 \left(\left(\frac{1}{N}\right)\left(\frac{1}{N^4}\right)\right)^{\frac{1}{2}} = \frac{C_7}{\sqrt{N}}, \tag{50}$$

where C_7 does not depend on N.

Consequently, by virtue of (33), (46) and (50) the uniform integrability of a sequence $(R_N^2)_{N\in\mathbb{N}}$ is established. Thus (28) is verified.

Step 2. Now we study the asymptotic behavior of the variables $\sqrt{N}(\widehat{T}_N(f^{\mathsf{U}}) - T_N(f^{\mathsf{U}}))$, as $N \to \infty$, where $\widehat{T}_N(f^{\mathsf{U}})$ and $T_N(f^{\mathsf{U}})$ are given by Formulas (26) and (27), respectively. For $j \in \mathbb{N}$, $i = 0, \dots, 2m-1$, $y \in \mathbb{Y}$, we set $Z_i^{(j)}(y) = \mathbb{I}\{Y^{(j)} = y, |f(X^{(j)}) - y| > i\}$. One has

$$\sqrt{N}(\widehat{T}_N(f^{\mathsf{U}}) - T_N(f^{\mathsf{U}})) = \mathbb{W}_{N,1} + \mathbb{W}_{N,2},$$

where

$$\begin{aligned}
\mathbb{W}_{N,1} &= \frac{\sqrt{N}}{K}\sum_{k=1}^{K}\sum_{i=0}^{2m-1}\sum_{i-m<|y|\le m}\frac{(\widehat{\psi}_{N,k}(y) - \psi(y))}{\sharp D_k(N)}\sum_{j\in D_k(N)}(Z_i^{(j)}(y) - \mathsf{E}Z_i^{(j)}(y)),\\
\mathbb{W}_{N,2} &= \frac{\sqrt{N}}{K}\sum_{k=1}^{K}\sum_{i=0}^{2m-1}\sum_{i-m<|y|\le m}\frac{(\widehat{\psi}_{N,k}(y) - \psi(y))}{\sharp D_k(N)}\sum_{j\in D_k(N)}\mathsf{P}(Y^{(j)} = y, |f^{\mathsf{U}}(X^{(j)}) - y| > i)\\
&= \frac{\sqrt{N}}{K}\sum_{k=1}^{K}\sum_{i=0}^{2m-1}\sum_{i-m<|y|\le m}(\widehat{\psi}_{N,k}(y) - \psi(y))\mathsf{P}(Y = y, |f^{\mathsf{U}}(X) - y| > i).
\end{aligned} \tag{51}$$

The purpose of the second step is to prove that

$$\mathsf{E}\mathbb{W}_{N,1}^2 \to 0, \quad N \to \infty. \tag{52}$$

For $k = 1, \dots, K$, $i = 0, \dots, 2m-1$ and $y \in \mathbb{Y}$ introduce

$$\mathbb{G}_k(i,y) = \frac{1}{\sharp D_k(N)}\sum_{j\in D_k(N)}(Z_i^{(j)}(y) - \mathsf{E}Z_i^{(j)}(y)).$$

The Cauchy-Bunyakovsky-Schwarz inequality yields

$$\mathsf{E}((\widehat{\psi}_{N,k}(y) - \psi(y))\mathbb{G}_k(i,y))^2 \le \left(\mathsf{E}(\widehat{\psi}_{N,k}(y) - \psi(y))^4\right)^{\frac{1}{2}}\left(\mathsf{E}(\mathbb{G}_k(i,y))^4\right)^{\frac{1}{2}}.$$

For each considered N, y, i and k, the variables $\{Z_i^{(j)}(y), j \in D_k(N)\}$ are independent and $|Z_i^{(j)}(y) - \mathsf{E}Z_i^{(j)}(y)| \leq 1$, so by virtue of the Rosenthal inequality (42) we obtain

$$\mathsf{E}\left(\sum_{j \in D_k(N)} (Z_i^{(j)}(y) - \mathsf{E}Z_i^{(j)}(y))\right)^4 = O(\sharp D_k(N)^2).$$

Taking into account Lemma 2 for $t = 4$ and in view of (44), for each $k = 1, \ldots, K$, we get the relation

$$\mathsf{E}\mathbb{W}_{N,1}^2 = O\left(N^{-\frac{1}{2}}\right), \quad N \to \infty.$$

Therefore, the goal of the second step has been achieved.

Step 3. The implementation of steps 1 and 2 permits to reduce the study of the asymptotic behavior (as $N \to \infty$) of $\mathbb{Z}_N$ given by Formula (25) to the study of variables

$$\eta_N := \sqrt{N}(T_N(f^U) - \mathsf{Err}(f^U)) + \mathbb{W}_{N,2}, \quad N \in \mathbb{N},$$

where $\mathbb{W}_{N,2}$ is defined by Formula (51).

The aim of the third step is to prove that $\mathsf{E}(\eta_N)^2 \to \sigma^2(U)$, as $N \to \infty$, where $\sigma^2(U)$ is the variance of the random variable $V(U)$ appearing in Formula (22).

On this way, we will show that the sum of certain part of the terms in a specified representation of the variables η_N does not affect (in the sense of $L^2(\Omega, \mathcal{F}, \mathsf{P})$) the limit behavior of these variables for growing N. For $y \in \mathbb{Y}$ and $W_N \subset \{1, \ldots, N\}$, where $N \in \mathbb{N}$, we introduce the event

$$B_{W_N}(y) := \{\omega : \widehat{P}(y, \xi(W_N)) \neq 0\}, \tag{53}$$

where $\widehat{P}(y, \xi(W_N))$ is defined according to (13). Then, in view of the independence of observations $\xi^{(1)}, \xi^{(2)}, \ldots$ we have

$$\mathsf{P}(\overline{B}_{W_N}(y)) = \mathsf{P}\left(\bigcap_{j \in W_N} \{Y^{(j)} \neq y\}\right) = (1 - \mathsf{P}(Y = y))^{\sharp W_N}.$$

If $\omega \in \overline{B}_{W_N}(y)$ then $|\widehat{\psi}(y, \xi(W_N)) - \psi(y)| = \psi(y)$. Set

$$H_N := \frac{\sqrt{N}}{K} \sum_{k=1}^{K} \sum_{i=0}^{2m-1} \sum_{i-m<|y|\leq m} (\widehat{\psi}_{N,k}(y) - \psi(y)) \mathbb{I}\{B_{N,k}(y)\} \mathsf{P}(Y = y, |f(X) - y| > i),$$

where $B_{N,k}(y) := B_{D_k(N)}(y)$ and an event $B_{W_N}(y)$ is introduced by Formula (53). Then

$$\mathsf{E}(\mathbb{W}_{N,2} - H_N)^2 = \mathsf{E}\left(\frac{\sqrt{N}}{K} \sum_{k=1}^{K} \sum_{i=0}^{2m-1} \sum_{i-m<|y|\leq m} \frac{\mathbb{I}\{\overline{B}_{N,k}(y)\}}{\mathsf{P}(Y = y)} \mathsf{P}(Y = y, |f^U(X) - y| > i)\right)^2$$

$$\leq \frac{N(2m)^4}{p_0^2} \max_{y \in \mathbb{Y}} (1 - \mathsf{P}(Y = y))^{[N/K]} \to 0, \quad N \to \infty,$$

since $\sharp D_k(N) \geq [N/K]$ for $N \in \mathbb{N}$, $k = 1, \ldots, K$ and because all $\mathsf{P}(Y = y) > 0$ for each $y \in \mathbb{Y}$, $[\cdot]$ stands for an integer part of a number.

We verify that H_N for large N is approximated in the space $L^2(\Omega, \mathcal{F}, \mathsf{P})$ by the random variable

$$\widetilde{H}_N := \frac{\sqrt{N}}{K} \sum_{k=1}^{K} \sum_{i=0}^{2m-1} \sum_{i-m<|y|\leq m} \mathbb{I}\{B_{N,k}(y)\} \left(\frac{\mathsf{P}(Y = y) - \widehat{p}_{N,k}(y)}{\mathsf{P}(Y = y)^2}\right) \mathsf{P}(Y = y, |f^U(X) - y| > i),$$

where $\widehat{p}_{N,k}(y) := \widehat{P}(y, \xi(D_k(N)))$ and $\widehat{P}(y, \xi(W_N))$ was introduced by (13) for $y \in \mathbb{Y}$ and $W_N \subset \{1, \dots, N\}$. Evidently, $0 \le \mathsf{P}(Y = y, |f^{\mathsf{U}}(X) - y| > i) \le 1$ for all k, i, y and N under consideration. Consequently, it follows that

$$\begin{aligned}
\Delta_{N,k}(i,y) &:= \Bigg| \sqrt{N}\mathbb{I}\{B_{N,k}(y)\}\left(\frac{1}{\widehat{p}_{N,k}(y)} - \frac{1}{\mathsf{P}(Y=y)}\right)\mathsf{P}(Y=y, |f^{\mathsf{U}}(X)-y|>i) \\
&- \sqrt{N}\mathbb{I}\{B_{N,k}(y)\}\left(\frac{\mathsf{P}(Y=y)-\widehat{p}_{N,k}(y)}{\mathsf{P}(Y=y)^2}\right)\mathsf{P}(Y=y, |f^{\mathsf{U}}(X)-y|>i)\Bigg| \\
&\le \sqrt{N}\left|\frac{\mathsf{P}(Y=y)-\widehat{p}_{N,k}(y)}{\mathsf{P}(Y=y)}\right|\left|\widehat{\psi}_{N,k}(y) - \frac{1}{\mathsf{P}(Y=y)}\right| \\
&= \frac{\sqrt{N}}{\mathsf{P}(Y=y)\sqrt{\sharp D_k(N)}}\left|\widehat{\psi}_{N,k}(y) - \frac{1}{\mathsf{P}(Y=y)}\right|\mathbb{J}_N,
\end{aligned}$$

where

$$\mathbb{J}_N := \frac{1}{\sqrt{\sharp D_k(N)}} \sum_{j \in D_k(N)} (\mathbb{I}\{Y^{(j)} = y\} - \mathsf{P}(Y^{(j)} = y)).$$

For any considered k, i, y and N the Cauchy - Bunyakovsky - Schwarz inequality implies that

$$\mathsf{E}(\Delta_{N,k}(i,y))^2 \le \frac{N}{(\mathsf{P}(Y=y)^2 \sharp D_k(N)}\left(\mathsf{E}\mathbb{J}_N^4 \mathsf{E}\left(\widehat{\psi}_{N,k}(y) - \frac{1}{\mathsf{P}(Y=y)}\right)^4\right)^{\frac{1}{2}}.$$

The Rosenthal inequality (42) yields that $\mathsf{E}\mathbb{J}_N^4 \le 2C(4)$. By means of Lemma 2 (for $t = 4$ and multipliers $c(\mathsf{p}, t)$ with $\mathsf{p} = \mathsf{P}(Y = y)$), for all considered i, y, k and any $N \in \mathbb{N}$ we come to the bound

$$\mathsf{E}(\Delta_{N,k}(i,y))^2 \le \frac{N}{(\mathsf{P}(Y=y)^2 \sharp D_k(N)} \frac{(2C(4)c(\mathsf{P}(Y=y),4))^{\frac{1}{2}}}{\sqrt{N}}.$$

Therefore, $\mathsf{E}(H_N - \widetilde{H}_N)^2 \to 0$ as $N \to \infty$.

Let us define the variable G_N by formula similar to $\widetilde{H}_N$ but without the multiplier $\mathbb{I}\{B_{N,k}(y)\}$. In view of (44) it is easily seen that

$$\mathsf{E}(\widetilde{H}_N - G_N)^2 \le \frac{N(2m)^4}{p_0^4} \max_{y \in \mathbb{Y}}(1 - \mathsf{P}(Y=y))^{[N/K]}\left(\frac{1}{4}\right) \max_{k=1,\dots,K} \frac{1}{\sharp D_k(N)} \to 0, \quad N \to \infty.$$

Thus $\mathsf{E}(\eta_N - Q_N)^2 \to 0$ as $N \to \infty$, where

$$Q_N := \sqrt{N}(T_N(f^{\mathsf{U}}) - \mathsf{Err}(f^{\mathsf{U}})) + G_N, \quad N \in \mathbb{N}.$$

Taking into account Formula (6) for the function $f = f^{\mathsf{U}}$, we come to the relation

$$\begin{aligned}
Q_N = &\frac{\sqrt{N}}{K}\sum_{k=1}^{K}\sum_{i=0}^{2m-1}\sum_{i-m<|y|\le m}\frac{1}{\sharp D_k(N)}\sum_{j\in D_k(N)}\Bigg(\frac{\mathbb{I}\{Y^{(j)}=y, |f^{\mathsf{U}}(X^{(j)})-y|>i\}}{\mathsf{P}(Y=y)} \\
&- \frac{\mathsf{P}(Y=y, |f^{\mathsf{U}}(X)-y|>i)}{\mathsf{P}(Y=y)} + \frac{(\mathsf{P}(Y=y)-\mathbb{I}\{Y^{(j)}=y\})\mathsf{P}(Y=y, |f^{\mathsf{U}}(X)-y|>i)}{\mathsf{P}(Y=y)^2}\Bigg) \\
= &\frac{\sqrt{N}}{K}\sum_{k=1}^{K}\frac{1}{\sharp D_k(N)}\sum_{j\in D_k(N)} V^{(j)},
\end{aligned} \tag{54}$$

where, for $j \in \mathbb{N}$,

$$V^{(j)} := \sum_{i=0}^{2m-1} \sum_{i-m<|y|\leq m} \frac{\mathbb{I}\{Y^{(j)}=y\}}{\mathsf{P}(Y=y)} \Big(\mathbb{I}\{|f^{U}(X^{(j)}) - y| > i) - \mathsf{P}(|f^{U}(X) - y| > i|Y = y)\Big). \quad (55)$$

The variables $\{V^{(j)}, j \in \mathbb{N}\}$ are centered, i.i.d. and uniformly bounded for all j (clearly, $V^{(j)} = V^{(j)}(U)$). For each $j \in \mathbb{N}$, the distributions of $V^{(j)}$ and $V(U)$ coincide, where $V(U)$ is introduced in (22). Thus, one has

$$\mathsf{var}\, V^{(j)} = \mathsf{var}\, V(U) = \sigma^2(U), \quad j \in \mathbb{N}. \quad (56)$$

According to the lemma on grouping independent random variables, for each $N \in \mathbb{N}$, the variables $\sum_{j\in D_k(N)} V^{(j)}$, $k = 1, \dots, K$, are independent. Since $N/\sharp D_k(N) \to K$ as $N \to \infty$, for $k = 1, \dots, K$, we come to the relation

$$\mathsf{E}(Q_N^2) = \mathsf{var}\, Q_N = \frac{N}{K^2} \sum_{k=1}^{K} \frac{1}{(\sharp D_k(N))^2} \sum_{j\in D_k(N)} \mathsf{var}\, V^{(j)} = \sigma^2(U) \frac{1}{K^2} \sum_{k=1}^{K} \frac{N}{\sharp D_k(N)} \to \sigma^2(U),$$

as $N \to \infty$. Hence $\mathsf{E}\eta_N^2 \to \sigma^2(U)$, $N \to \infty$. The goal of the third step has been achieved.

In view of the above approximations (in $L^2(\Omega, \mathcal{F}, \mathsf{P})$) of the initial random variables $\mathbb{Z}_N$, introduced by (25), we conclude that $\mathsf{E}\mathbb{Z}_N^2 \to \sigma^2(U)$, as $N \to \infty$. Namely, we apply the following elementary statement: if $\mathsf{E}\alpha_N^2 \to 0$ and $\mathsf{E}\beta_N^2 \to \sigma^2$ then $\mathsf{E}(\alpha_N + \beta_N)^2 \to \sigma^2$, as $N \to \infty$. Therefore, (24) is established. The proof of Lemma 1 is complete. □

Further we will also employ a result that immediately follows from Theorem 1.

Corollary 1. *Let the conditions of Lemma 1 be satisfied. Then the following relations hold:*

$$\sqrt{N}\mathsf{E}\Big(\widehat{\mathsf{Err}}_{K,N,\varepsilon_N}(f^{U}) - \mathsf{Err}(f^{U})\Big) \to 0, \quad N \to \infty, \quad (57)$$

$$\mathsf{var}\,(\sqrt{N}\widehat{\mathsf{Err}}_{K,N,\varepsilon_N}(f^{U})) \to \sigma^2(U), \quad N \to \infty, \quad (58)$$

where $\sigma^2(U)$ *is a variance of the random variable* $V(U)$ *introduced in* (22).

Proof. Condition (23) implies (20). Thus, according to Theorem 1, we have

$$\mathbb{Z}_N \overset{\mathcal{D}}{\to} Z \sim N(0, \sigma^2(U)), \quad N \to \infty, \quad (59)$$

where $\mathbb{Z}_N$, $N \in \mathbb{N}$, are defined in (25). Due to Lemma 1 one has the uniform integrability of the sequence $(\mathbb{Z})_{N\in\mathbb{N}}$. Consequently, relation (59) implies (57), i.e., $\mathsf{E}\mathbb{Z}_N \to \mathsf{E}Z = 0$, as $N \to \infty$. Obviously,

$$\mathsf{var}\,(\sqrt{N}\widehat{\mathsf{Err}}_{K,N,\varepsilon_N}(f^{U}))$$
$$= \mathsf{E}\Big(\sqrt{N}(\widehat{\mathsf{Err}}_{K,N,\varepsilon_N}(f^{U}) - \mathsf{Err}(f^{U})\Big)^2 - \Big(\sqrt{N}\mathsf{E}(\widehat{\mathsf{Err}}_{K,N,\varepsilon_N}(f^{U}) - \mathsf{Err}(f^{U}))\Big)^2.$$

Therefore, to obtain (58), it is sufficient to use Lemma 1 and take into account (57). The proof is complete. □

Note that (59) can be obtained directly under conditions of Lemma 1. For each $N \in \mathbb{N}$ and any $k = 1, \dots, K$, according to Lindeberg's theorem applied to arrays $\{V^{(j)}, j \in D_k(N)\}$ of centered i.i.d. uniformly bounded summands, where a sequence $(V^{(j)})_{j\in\mathbb{N}}$ is introduced in (55), taking into account (56) one has

$$V_{N,k} := \frac{1}{\sqrt{\sharp D_k(N)}} \sum_{j\in D_k(N)} V^{(j)} \overset{\mathcal{D}}{\to} Z_k \sim N(0, \sigma^2(U)), \quad N \to \infty. \quad (60)$$

For every $N \in \mathbb{N}$, the random variables $V_{N,k}$, $k = 1, \ldots, K$, are independent and $\mathsf{var}\, V_{N,k} = \sigma^2(U)$. Since $N/\sharp D_k(N) \to K$ as $N \to \infty$, for $k = 1, \ldots, K$, by virtue of (60) we come to relation

$$Q_N \overset{\mathcal{D}}{\to} Z \sim N(0, \sigma^2(U)), \;\; N \to \infty, \tag{61}$$

where in view of (54) one has $Q_N = \frac{1}{K}\sum_{k=1}^{K}\sqrt{\frac{N}{\sharp D_k(N)}} V_{N,k}$, $N \in \mathbb{N}$. Applying (61) and Slutsky's lemma, we arrive at (59).

Also note that relation (29) can be easily derived from (36) and (39) without employment of [32].

4. Forward Selection of Relevant Factors

Now we can turn to the sequential selection of factors based on MDR-EFE method. At the first step one searches for $j_1 \in T$ a point where the function $\widehat{Err}_{K,N,\varepsilon_N}(f^{\{i\}})$ attains the minimum over all $i \in T$. If there are several such points, then we take, e.g., one with the smallest index value. Recall that according to (17) (more precisely, after regularization), the random variable $\widehat{Err}_{K,N,\varepsilon_N}(f^{\{i\}})$ is in fact a function of $\widehat{f}_{PA}^{\{i\}}$, which is a forecast of the function $f^{\{i\}}$. Then this procedure is repeated, namely, if at $(k-1)$-th step the set $S_{k-1} := \{j_1, \ldots, j_{k-1}\}$ is constructed, where $k \in \{2, \ldots, r\}$, then $j_k \in T \setminus S_{k-1}$ is selected at step k in such a way that given $j_1, \ldots, j_{k-1}$ the function $\widehat{Err}_{K,N,\varepsilon_N}(f^{\{S_{k-1},i\}})$ takes the minimum value over $i \in T \setminus S_{k-1}$ for $i = j_k$. It is convenient to assume that an empty set is taken at the zero step. Then at each next step one new element is added to the previously constructed sets. If at some step there are several minimum points of the considered function then we take only one of them, e.g., with the minimal index.

Thus, for each $N \in \mathbb{N}$ the random sets $S_k(N) = S_k(N, \omega) := \{j_1, \ldots, j_k\}$ arise, where $k = 1, \ldots, r$ and $j_m = j_m(N, \omega)$, $m = 1, \ldots, r$. By construction one can write

$$j_k(N,\omega) \in J_k(N,\omega) := \arg \min_{i \in T \setminus S_{k-1}(N,\omega)} \widehat{Err}_{K,N,\varepsilon_N}(f^{\{S_{k-1}(N,\omega),i\}}),$$

where $S_0 := \varnothing$ and $\{\varnothing, i\} := \{i\}$. In other words the choice $j_k(N,\omega)$ at step k means that, for $i \in T \setminus S_{k-1}(N,\omega)$,

$$\widehat{Err}_{K,N,\varepsilon_N}(f^{S_k(N,\omega)}) \le \widehat{Err}_{K,N,\varepsilon_N}(f^{\{S_{k-1}(N,\omega),i\}}), \tag{62}$$

moreover, $j_k(N,\omega) = \min\{i : i \in J_k(N,\omega)\}$, $k = 1, \ldots, r$. If the joint distribution of X and Y is known, then instead of the described scheme for constructing random sets, $S_k(N,\omega)$ we turn to considering the non-random "oracle" sets $T_k = \{i_1, \ldots, i_k\}$, where $k = 1, \ldots, r$,

$$i_k \in \arg \min_{i \in T \setminus T_{k-1}} \mathsf{Err}(f^{\{T_{k-1},i\}}), \tag{63}$$

$T_0 := \varnothing$, and the functional Err is introduced by formula (2). If there are several i_k satisfying (63) we take among them that one which has the minimal value.

For $k \in \{1, \ldots, r\}$ and $i \in T \setminus T_k$ introduce

$$C_{k,i} := \mathsf{Err}(f^{\{T_{k-1},i\}}) - \mathsf{Err}(f^{T_k}).$$

By construction of the sets T_k we have $C_{k,i} \ge 0$, where $k = 1, \ldots, r$ and $i \in T \setminus T_k$. We call a model, satisfying condition (1), *regular* whenever the following relation is true:

$$C_{k,i} > 0, \;\; k = 1, \ldots, r, \;\; i \in T \setminus T_k. \tag{64}$$

In other words, for each $k = 1,\dots,r$, a point i_k in (63) is determined uniquely. Further we employ the penalty function introduced in (11). We also use its strongly consistent estimate of type (48) with

$$\widehat{p}_N := \frac{1}{W_N} \sum_{j\in W_N} \mathbb{I}\{Y^{(j)} = y\}, \tag{65}$$

$W_N \subset \{1,\dots,N\}$ and $\sharp W_N \to \infty$ as $N \to \infty$.

Theorem 2. *Let the considered model* (1) *with a collection of relevant factors having cardinality $r < p$, be regular, i.e., let* (64) *take place. Then, for the random sets $S_r(N)$ introduced above, the following relation is valid*

$$\mathsf{P}(S_r(N) = T_r) \to 1, \quad N \to \infty, \tag{66}$$

where T_r is defined by means of (63) *for $k = 1,\dots,r$. In other words, with probability close to one, the described procedure of forward selection based on statistical estimates of the error functional leads to the "oracle" collection T_r, when N is large enough.*

Proof. For a random set $S_r(N,\omega) = \{j_1(N,\omega),\dots,j_r(N,\omega)\}$, where $j_k(N,\omega)$ is an element taken at k-th step, one has

$$\mathsf{P}(\omega : S_r(N,\omega) = T_r) \geq \mathsf{P}(\omega : j_1(N,\omega) = i_1,\dots,j_r(N,\omega) = i_r).$$

Note that

$$\mathsf{P}(\omega : j_1(N,\omega) = i_1,\dots,j_r(N,\omega) = i_r) \geq \mathsf{P}\left(\bigcap_{k=1}^{r} A_k(N)\right),$$

where

$$A_k(N) := \bigcap_{i\in T\setminus T_{k-1}} \left\{\widehat{Err}_{K,N,\varepsilon_N}(f^{T_k}) < \widehat{Err}_{K,N,\varepsilon_N}(f^{\{T_{k-1},i\}})\right\},$$

$k = 1,\dots,r$. Thus, we obtain:

$$\mathsf{P}\left(\bigcap_{k=1}^{r} A_k(N)\right) = 1 - \mathsf{P}\left(\bigcup_{k=1}^{r} \overline{A}_k(N)\right) \geq 1 - \sum_{k=1}^{r} \mathsf{P}(\overline{A}_k(N))$$

$$\geq 1 - \sum_{k=1}^{r} \sum_{i\in T\setminus T_{k-1}} \mathsf{P}\left(\widehat{Err}_{K,N,\varepsilon_N}(f^{T_k}) \geq \widehat{Err}_{K,N,\varepsilon_N}(f^{\{T_{k-1},i\}})\right), \tag{67}$$

where, as usual, $\overline{A} := \Omega \setminus A$ for $A \subset \Omega$. Then, for $k = 1,\dots,r$, $i \in T \setminus T_{k-1}$ and $N \in \mathbb{N}$, we get

$$\begin{aligned} \Delta_{k,i}(N) &:= \widehat{Err}_{K,N,\varepsilon_N}(f^{T_k}) - \widehat{Err}_{K,N,\varepsilon_N}(f^{\{T_{k-1},i\}}) \\ &= (\widehat{Err}_{K,N,\varepsilon_N}(f^{T_k}) - \mathsf{E}\widehat{Err}_{K,N,\varepsilon_N}(f^{T_k})) + (\mathsf{E}\widehat{Err}_{K,N,\varepsilon_N}(f^{T_k}) - \mathsf{Err}(f^{T_k})) \\ &+ (\mathsf{Err}(f^{T_k}) - \mathsf{Err}(f^{\{T_{k-1},i\}})) + (\mathsf{Err}(f^{\{T_{k-1},i\}}) - \mathsf{E}\widehat{Err}_{K,N,\varepsilon_N}(f^{\{T_{k-1},i\}})) \\ &+ (\mathsf{E}\widehat{Err}_{K,N,\varepsilon_N}(f^{\{T_{k-1},i\}}) - \widehat{Err}_{K,N,\varepsilon_N}(f^{\{T_{k-1},i\}})). \end{aligned} \tag{68}$$

For $U \subset T$, set

$$Z_N(U) := \widehat{Err}_{K,N,\varepsilon_N}(f^U) - \mathsf{E}\widehat{Err}_{K,N,\varepsilon_N}(f^U).$$

For any $k = 1,\dots,K$, $i \in T \setminus T_{k-1}$ and each $\delta \in (0,1)$ in light of formula (57) of Corollary 1, for all N large enough ($N \geq N_2(\delta,k,i)$) it holds

$$\mathsf{P}(\Delta_{k,i}(N) \geq 0) \leq \mathsf{P}(\sqrt{N}|Z_N(T_k(N))| + \sqrt{N}|Z_N(\{T_{k-1}(N),i\})| \geq \sqrt{N}C_{k,i} - \delta)$$

$$\leq \mathsf{P}\left(\sqrt{N}|Z_N(T_k(N))| \geq \frac{(1-\delta)\sqrt{N}C_{k,i}}{2}\right) + \mathsf{P}\left(|Z_N(\{T_{k-1}(N),i\})| \geq \frac{(1-\delta)\sqrt{N}C_{k,i}}{2}\right),$$

where $C_{k,i}$ are introduced in (66), $\Delta_{k,i}(N)$ is defined by (68).

Applying the Bienaymé - Chebyshev inequality and taking into account Formula (58) of Corollary 1, for each $U \subset T$ and any $c > 0$, we come, for a centered random variable $Z_N(U)$, to the relation

$$\mathsf{P}(\sqrt{N}|Z_N(U)| \geq c\sqrt{N}) \leq \frac{N \mathsf{var}\, Z_N(U)}{Nc^2} \sim \frac{\mathsf{var}\, V(U)}{Nc^2}, \quad N \to \infty, \tag{69}$$

where $V(U)$ is determined by Formula (22). According to (64), for $k \in \{1, \ldots, r\}$ and $i \in T \setminus T_k$, one has $C_{k,i} > 0$. Therefore, for all N large enough ($N \geq N_3(\delta, k, i)$), the following inequality takes place:

$$\mathsf{P}(\Delta_{k,i}(N) \geq 0) \leq \frac{4(\mathsf{var}\, V(T_k) + \mathsf{var}\, V(\{T_{k-1}, i\})}{N(1-\delta)^2 C_{k,i}^2}. \tag{70}$$

For a fixed $m \in \mathbb{N}$, one can change the summation order over i and y to write Formula (22) as follows:

$$V(U) = \sum_{y=-m}^{m} \frac{\mathbb{I}\{Y = y\}}{\mathsf{P}(Y = y)} W(y, U),$$

where

$$W(y, U) = \sum_{0 \leq i < |y| + m} \left(\mathbb{I}\{|f^U(X) - y| > i\} - \mathsf{P}(|f^U(X) - y| > i | Y = y)\right). \tag{71}$$

Thus, for any $U \subset T$, one has

$$|V(U)| \leq 2m \sum_{y=-m}^{m} \frac{\mathbb{I}\{Y = y\}}{\mathsf{P}(Y = y)}.$$

Consequently, we come to the inequality

$$\mathsf{var}\, V(U) \leq \mathsf{E}V^2(U) \leq 4m^2 \sum_{y=-m}^{m} \frac{1}{\mathsf{P}(Y = y)} =: a,$$

where $a = a(m, (\mathsf{P}(Y = y))_{y \in \mathbb{Y}})$. We see that $\mathsf{var}\, V(T_k) + \mathsf{var}\, V(\{T_{k-1}, i\}) \leq 2a$ for all $k \in \{1, \ldots, r\}$, $i \in T \setminus T_{k-1}$ and $N \in \mathbb{N}$. For each $\delta \in (0, 1)$, any $k \in \{1, \ldots, r\}$, $i \in T \setminus T_{k-1}$ and all N large enough, we get the following bound:

$$\mathsf{P}(\Delta_{k,i}(N) \geq 0) \leq \frac{8a}{N(1-\delta)^2 C_{k,i}^2}.$$

Hence, for each $\delta \in (0, 1)$ and all N large enough, by virtue of (67) the following inequality holds:

$$\mathsf{P}(S_r(N) = T_r) \geq 1 - \frac{8ar}{N(1-\delta)^2 C_0^2}\left(p + 1 - \frac{r+1}{2}\right), \tag{72}$$

where $C_0^2 := \min_{k=1,\ldots,r,\ i \in T \setminus T_{k-1}} C_{k,i}^2 > 0$ according to (64). Thus relation (72) implies the validity of (66). □

Now note that according to (69) the following relation is true:

$$\mathsf{P}(\sqrt{N}|Z_N(U)| \geq c\sqrt{N}) = O\left(\frac{1}{N}\right), \quad N \to \infty. \tag{73}$$

The question arises whether this probability decreases like C/N where C is a positive constant or more rapidly. The answer depends on the variance of the random variable $V(U)$ given by Formula (22). In view of (70) we will determine when the variable $V(U)$ is degenerate, i.e., equal to a constant a.s. This is also of independent interest for the CLT established in Section 6 of [32] and given above as Theorem 1. The following result provides a simple characterization of the $V(U)$ degeneracy.

Lemma 3. *For an arbitrary set $U \subset T$, the variance of the random variable $V(U)$, appearing in Formula (22), is zero if and only if, for every $y \in \mathbb{Y}$, there is $k_0(y) \in \{0, \dots, m + |y|\}$ such that*

$$\mathsf{P}(|f^{\mathrm{U}}(\mathrm{X}) - y| = k_0(y), Y = y) = \mathsf{P}(Y = y). \tag{74}$$

Thus, for each $y \in \mathbb{Y}$, on the set $\{Y = y\}$ the random variable $f^{\mathrm{U}}(\mathrm{X})$ does not necessarily take a constant value. Moreover, the values of $k_0(y)$ need not coincide for different y.

Proof. For $y = 0, \dots, m$ and a random variable $W(y, U)$, introduced by Formula (71), one can write

$$\begin{aligned}
W(y,U) &= \sum_{0 \leq i < y+m} \Big(\mathbb{I}\{|f^{\mathrm{U}}(\mathrm{X}) - y| > i\} - \mathsf{P}(|f^{\mathrm{U}}(\mathrm{X}) - y| > i | Y = y)\Big) \\
&= \sum_{0 \leq i < y+m} \; \sum_{i < k \leq m+y} \Big(\mathbb{I}\{|f^{\mathrm{U}}(\mathrm{X}) - y| = k\} - \mathsf{P}(|f^{\mathrm{U}}(\mathrm{X}) - y| = k | Y = y)\Big) \\
&= \sum_{k=1}^{m+y} \sum_{i=0}^{k-1} \Big(\mathbb{I}\{|f^{\mathrm{U}}(\mathrm{X}) - y| = k\} - \mathsf{P}(|f^{\mathrm{U}}(\mathrm{X}) - y| = k | Y = y)\Big) \\
&= \sum_{k=1}^{m+y} k(\mathbb{I}\{|f^{\mathrm{U}}(\mathrm{X}) - y| = k\} - \mathsf{P}(|f^{\mathrm{U}}(\mathrm{X}) - y| = k | Y = y)) \\
&= \sum_{k=1}^{m+y} k\mathbb{I}\{|f^{\mathrm{U}}(\mathrm{X}) - y| = k\} - \mathsf{E}(|f^{\mathrm{U}}(\mathrm{X}) - y| | Y = y).
\end{aligned}$$

In a similar way we consider $y = -m, \dots, -1$. Thus, for all $y \in \mathbb{Y}$, one gets

$$W(y,U) = \sum_{k=1}^{m+|y|} k\mathbb{I}\{|f^{\mathrm{U}}(\mathrm{X}) - y| = k\} - \mathsf{E}(|f^{\mathrm{U}}(\mathrm{X}) - y| | Y = y).$$

Recall that $\mathsf{P}(Y = y) > 0$ for all $y \in \mathbb{Y}$. If, for some $y, k, j \in \mathbb{Y}, k \neq j$, we have

$$\mathsf{P}(|f^{\mathrm{U}}(\mathrm{X}) - y| = k, Y = y) > 0, \;\; \mathsf{P}(|f^{\mathrm{U}}(\mathrm{X}) - y| = j, Y = y) > 0,$$

then on the events $\{|f^{\mathrm{U}}(\mathrm{X}) - y| = k, Y = y\}$ and $\{|f^{\mathrm{U}}(\mathrm{X}) - y| = j, Y = y\}$ the variable $W(y, U)$ takes different values. Therefore, $V(U)$ takes different values on these events. Hence $\mathsf{var}\, V(U) > 0$, if (74) is not valid. Thus (74) is a necessary condition to guarantee that $\mathsf{var}\, V(U) = 0$. Suppose now that, (74) holds. In this case we get

$$\mathsf{E}(|f^{\mathrm{U}}(\mathrm{X}) - y| | Y = y) = k_0(y), \;\; y \in \mathbb{Y}.$$

Clearly, $k_0(y)$ depends on U as well. We see that $V(U)$ on each set $\{Y = y\}$ takes (up to the set of measure zero) the value $\frac{1}{\mathsf{P}(Y=y)}(k_0(y) - k_0(y)) = 0$, $y \in \mathbb{Y}$. Therefore, $\mathsf{var}\, V(U) = 0$. Note that $k_0(y)$ need not coincide for different $y \in \mathbb{Y}$. The proof is complete. □

5. Concluding Remarks

The established asymptotical result (Theorem 2) is rather qualitative in nature, since relation (66) assumes increasing values of N. Relation (72) is more precise. However, (72) demonstrates that, loosely speaking, one has to employ $N >> rp$. As previously, we assume that assumption (A), introduced on page 2, is valid. Evidently, the sequential choice of relevant variables based on statistical estimators of the error functional (of response approximation), is attractive for implementation, although suboptimal. In this regard Theorem 2 shows that under certain conditions, forward (random) selection with a high probability leads to the same collection of factors, which is provided by the sequential procedure with known joint distribution of the vector of factors X and the response Y. In the future work, it would be reasonable to supplement the theoretical results by computer simulations (see, e.g., [45]).

Consideration of the proximity of the results of optimal and suboptimal procedures requires a separate study. In addition, we note that within the framework of linear models, estimates of the probability of correct identification of relevant factors are considered, e.g., in [46,47]. Theorem 2 does not assume the linearity of stochastic model. Presumably for the first time, in our work a forward selection of relevant factors affecting the non-binary random response is treated on the base of MDR-EFE method. It would be interesting to extend the conditions allowing to establish relation (66). Moreover, stability problems of FS deserve special attention, see, e.g., [48–50]. Algorithms stability for classification problems in the framework of random trees is treated in [51].

Finally, we emphasize that the problem of statistical estimation of the cardinality of a set of relevant factors appearing in definition (1) is very important and complex. Along with dealing with the deterministic number of selected factors, there is a research approach based on developing the rules for stopping the procedures used to identify the relevant set. In this regard, we indicate, e.g., article [52], dedicated to information methods for selecting relevant factors. The study of non-discrete stochastic models is also of undoubted interest, see, e.g., [53].

Further it would be interesting to study other functionals than (2) to measure the quality of a response approximation by means of functions defined on various collections of factors. One can also consider a random number of observations. In this regard we refer, e.g., to [27,54].

Funding: This research received no external funding.

Data Availability Statement: Data are contained within the article.

Acknowledgments: The author is very grateful to the Reviewers for careful reading the manuscript and making valuable remarks and suggestions. He would also like to thank Alexander Tikhomirov for invitation to present manuscript for this issue.

Conflicts of Interest: The author declares no conflict of interest.

Appendix A. Proof of Lemma 2

Proof. For any $t \in \mathbb{N}$ and $\mathsf{p} \in (0,1)$, one has

$$
\begin{aligned}
\mathsf{E}(\widehat{\psi}_N)^t &= N^t \sum_{j=1}^{N} \frac{1}{j^t} \binom{N}{j} \mathsf{p}^j (1-\mathsf{p})^{N-j} \\
&= \frac{N^t}{\mathsf{p}^t (N+1)\dots(N+t)} \sum_{j=1}^{N} \frac{(j+1)\dots(j+t)}{j^t} \binom{N+t}{j+t} \mathsf{p}^{j+t} (1-\mathsf{p})^{(N+t)-(j+t)} \\
&= \frac{1}{\mathsf{p}^t}(1+h_t(N)) \sum_{i=t+1}^{N+t} \left(1 + \frac{a_1}{i-t} + \dots + \frac{a_t}{(i-t)^t}\right) \binom{N+t}{i} \mathsf{p}^i (1-\mathsf{p})^{N+t-i},
\end{aligned}
$$

where $h_t(N) = O(1/N)$, as $N \to \infty$, and $a_1, \ldots, a_t \in \mathbb{N}$. We do not use the explicit formulas $a_1 = t(t+1)/2, \ldots, a_t = t!$. Note that

$$\sum_{i=t+1}^{N+t} \binom{N+t}{i} \mathsf{p}^i (1-\mathsf{p})^{N+t-i} = 1 - \sum_{i=0}^{t} \binom{N+t}{i} \mathsf{p}^i (1-\mathsf{p})^{N+t-i} = 1 - g_t(N),$$

where $g_t(N) := \sum_{i=0}^{t} g_{t,i}(N)$ and, for $i = t+1, \ldots, N+t$, one has

$$0 \le g_{t,i}(N) := \binom{N+t}{i} \mathsf{p}^i (1-\mathsf{p})^{N+t-i} \le (N+t)^t (1-\mathsf{p})^N = O(1/N), \quad N \to \infty.$$

For each $k = 1, \ldots, t$, introduce

$$q_{t,k}(N) := \sum_{i=t+1}^{N+t} \frac{1}{(i-t)^k} \binom{N+t}{i} \mathsf{p}^i (1-\mathsf{p})^{N+t-i}$$

$$= \frac{1}{\mathsf{p}^k (N+t+1) \ldots (N+t+k)} \sum_{i=t+1}^{N+t} \frac{(i+1) \ldots (i+k)}{(i-t)^k} \binom{N+t+k}{i+k} \mathsf{p}^{i+k} (1-\mathsf{p})^{(N+t+k)-(i+k)}.$$

Obviously, one can write $q_{t,k}(N) = O\left(1/N^k\right)$, as

$$(i+1) \ldots (i+k)(i-t)^{-k} \le (1+t+k)^k \le (1+2t)^t$$

for all $i \ge t+1$, $k = 1, \ldots, t$, and since

$$\sum_{i=t+1}^{N+t} \binom{N+t+k}{i+k} \mathsf{p}^{i+k} (1-\mathsf{p})^{(N+t+k)-(i+k)} \le 1.$$

Consequently, for any $t \in \mathbb{N}$, we get

$$\mathsf{E}(\widehat{\psi}_N)^t = \frac{1}{\mathsf{p}^t}(1 + h_t(N)) \left(1 - g_t(N) + \sum_{k=1}^{t} q_{t,k}(N)\right) = \frac{1}{\mathsf{p}^t} + R_t(N),$$

where $R_t(N) = O(1/N)$, as $N \to \infty$. Evidently, $\mathsf{E}(\widehat{\psi}_N)^0 = 1$ for $N \in \mathbb{N}$. For each $N \in \mathbb{N}$, set $R_0(N) = 0$. Thus, for $t \in \mathbb{N}$, one has

$$\mathsf{E}\left(\widehat{\psi}_N - \frac{1}{\mathsf{p}}\right)^t = \sum_{v=0}^{t} \binom{t}{v} \mathsf{E}(\widehat{\psi}_N)^v \left(-\frac{1}{\mathsf{p}}\right)^{t-v} = \sum_{v=0}^{t} \binom{t}{v} \left(\frac{1}{\mathsf{p}^v} + R_v(N)\right) \left(-\frac{1}{\mathsf{p}}\right)^{t-v} = O\left(\frac{1}{N}\right),$$

because

$$\sum_{v=0}^{t} \binom{t}{v} \left(\frac{1}{\mathsf{p}}\right)^v \left(-\frac{1}{\mathsf{p}}\right)^{t-v} = \left(\frac{1}{\mathsf{p}} - \frac{1}{\mathsf{p}}\right)^t = 0, \quad \sum_{v=0}^{t} \binom{t}{v} \left(\frac{1}{\mathsf{p}}\right)^{t-v} = \left(1 + \frac{1}{\mathsf{p}}\right)^t$$

and

$$\max_{v=0,\ldots,t} |R_v(N)| = O(1/N), \quad N \to \infty.$$

The proof of Lemma 2 is complete. □

References

1. Seber, G.A.F.; Lee, A.J. *Linear Regression Analysis*, 2nd ed.; J.Wiley and Sons Publication: Hoboken, NJ, USA, 2003.
2. Györfi, L.; Kohler, M.; Krzyżak, A.; Walk H. *A Distribution-Free Theory of Nonparametric Regression*; Springer: New York, NY, USA, 2002.
3. Matloff, N. *Statistical Regression and Classification. From Linear Models to Machine Learning*; CRC Press: Boca Raton, FL, USA, 2017.
4. Tibshirani, R. Regression shrinkage and selection via the lasso. *J. R. Stat. Soc. Ser. B Methodol.* **1996**, *58*, 267–288. [CrossRef]

5. Hastie, T.; Tibshirani, R.; Wainwrigth, R. *Statistical Learning with Sparsity. The Lasso and Generalizations*; CRC Press: Boca Raton, FL, USA, 2015.
6. Bolón-Candedo, V.; Alonso-Betanzos, A. *Recent Advances in Ensembles for Feature Selection*; Springer: Cham, Switzerland, 2018.
7. Giraud, C. *Introduction to High-Dimensional Statistics*; CRC Press: Boca Raton, FL, USA, 2015.
8. Stańczyk, U.; Zielosko, B.; Jain, L.C. (Eds.) *Advances in Feature Selection for Data and Pattern Recognition*; Springer International Publishing AG: Cham, Switzerland, 2018.
9. Kuhn, M.; Johnson, K. *Feature Engineering and Selection. A Practical Approach for Predictive Models*; CRC Press: Boca Raton, FL, USA, 2020.
10. Chandrashekar, G.; Sahin, F. A survey on feature selection methods. *Comput. Electr. Eng.* **2014**, *40*, 16–28. [CrossRef]
11. Jia, W.; Sun, M.; Lian, J.; Hou, S. Feature dimensionality reduction: A review. *Complex Intell. Syst.* **2022**, *8*, 2663–2693. [CrossRef]
12. Lyu, Y.; Feng, Y.; Sakurai, K. A survey on feature selection techniques based on filtering methods for cyber attack detection. *Information* **2023**, *14*, 191. [CrossRef]
13. Pradip, D.; Chandrashekhar, A. A comprehensive survey on feature selection in the various fields of machine learning. *Appl. Intell.* **2023**, *52*, 4543–4581.
14. Htun, H.H.; Biehl, M.; Petkov, N. Survey of feature selection and extraction techniques for stock market prediction. *Financ. Innov.* **2023**, *9*, 26. [CrossRef] [PubMed]
15. Laborda, J.; Ryoo, S. Feature Selection in a Credit Scoring Model. *Mathematics* **2021**, *9*, 746. [CrossRef]
16. Emily, M. A survey of statistical methods for gene-gene interaction in case-control genomewide association studies. *J. Société Fr. Stat.* **2018**, *159*, 27–67.
17. Tsunoda, T.; Tanaka, T.; Nakamura, Y. (Eds.). *Genome-Wide Association Studies*; Springer: Singapore, 2019.
18. Luque-Rodriguez, M.; Molina-Baena, J.; Jimenez-Vilchez, A.; Arauzo-Azofra A. Initialization of feature selection search for classification. *J. Artif. Intell. Res.* **2022**, *75*, 953–998. [CrossRef]
19. Pudjihartono, N.; Fadason, T.; Kempa-Liehr, A.W.; O'Sullivan, J.M. A review of feature selection methods for machine learning-based disease risk prediction. *Front. Bioinform.* **2022**, *2*, 927312. [CrossRef]
20. Coelho, F.; Braga, A.P.; Verleysen, M.A. Mutual information estimator for continuous and discrete variables applied to feature selection and classification problems. *Int. J. Comput. Intell. Syst.* **2016**, *9*, 726–733. [CrossRef]
21. Kozhevin, A.A. Feature selection based on statistical estimation of mutual information *Sib. Elektron. Mat. Izv.* **2021**, *18*, 720–728. [CrossRef]
22. Latt, K.Z.; Honda, K.; Thiri, M.; Hitomi, Y.; Omae, Y.; Sawai, H.; Kawai, Y.; Teraguchi, S.; Ueno, K.; Nagasaki, M.; et al. Identification of a two-SNP PLA2R1 haplotype and HLA-DRB1 alleles as primary risk associations in idiopathic membranous nephropathy. *Sci. Rep.* **2018**, *8*, 15576. [CrossRef] [PubMed]
23. Vergara, J.R.; Estévez, P.A. A review of feature selection methods based on mutual information. *Neural Comput. Applic* **2014**, *24*, 175–186. [CrossRef]
24. AlNuaimi, N.; Masud, M.M.; Serhani, M.A.; Zaki, N. Streaming feature selection algorithms for big data: A survey *Appl. Comput. Inform.* **2022**, *18*, 113–135. [CrossRef]
25. Ritchie, M.D.; Hahn, L.W.; Roodi, N.; Bailey, L.R.; Dupont, W.D.; Parl, F.F.; Moore J.H. Multifactor-dimensionality reduction reveals high-order interactions among estrogen-metabolism genes in sporadic breast cancer. *Am. J. Human Genet.* **2001**, *69*, 138–147. [CrossRef]
26. Gola, D.; John, J.M.M.; van Steen, K.; König, I.R. A roadmap to multifactor dimensionality reduction methods. *Briefings Bioinform.* **2016**, *17*, 293–308. [CrossRef]
27. Bulinski, A.; Kozhevin, A. New version of the MDR method for stratified samples. *Stat. Optim. Inf. Comput.* **2017**, *5*, 1–18. [CrossRef]
28. Abegaz, F.; van Lishout, F.; Mahachie, J.J.M.; Chiachoompu, K.; Bhardwaj A.; Duroux, D.; Gusareva, R.S.; Wei, Z.; Hakonarson, H.; Van Steen K. Performance of model-based multifactor dimensionality reduction methods for epistasis detection by controlling population structure. *BioData Min.* **2021**, *14*, 16. [CrossRef]
29. Yang, C.H.; Hou M.F.; Chuang L.Y.; Yang C.S.; Lin Y.D. Dimensionality reduction approach for many-objective epistasis analysis *Briefings Bioinform.* **2023**, *24*, bbac512. [CrossRef]
30. Bulinski, A.; Butkovsky, O.; Sadovnichy, V.; Shashkin, A.; Yaskov, P.; Balatskiy, A.; Samokhodskaya, L.; Tkachuk, V. Statistical Methods of SNP Data Analysis and Applications. *Open J. Stat.* **2012**, *2*, 73–87. [CrossRef]
31. Bulinski, A. On foundation of the dimensionality reduction method for explanatory variables. *J. Math. Sci.* **2014**, *199*, 113–122. [CrossRef]
32. Bulinski, A.V.; Rakitko, A.S. MDR method for nonbinary response variable. *J. Multivar. Anal.* **2015**, *135*, 25–42. [CrossRef]
33. Macedo, F.; Oliveira, M.R.; Pacheco, A.; Valadas, R. Theoretical Foundations of Forward Feature Selection Methods based on Mutual Information. *Neurocomputing* **2019**, *325*, 67–89. [CrossRef]
34. Bulinski, A.V. On relevant feature selection based on information theory. *Theory Probab. Its Appl.* **2023**, *68*, 392–410. [CrossRef]
35. Rakitko, A. MDR-EFE method with forward selection. In Proceedings of the The 5th International Conference on Stochastic Methods (ICSM-5), Moscow, Russia, 23–27 November 2020. . [CrossRef]

36. Velez, D.R.; White, B.C.; Motsinger, A.A.; Bush, W.S.; Ritchie, M.D.; Williams, S.M.; Moore, J.H. A balanced accuracy function for epistasis modeling in imbalanced datasets using multifactor dimensionality reduction. *Genet. Epidemiol.* **2007**, *31*, 306–315. [CrossRef] [PubMed]
37. Hu, T.-C.; Moricz, F.; Taylor, R. Strong laws of large numbers for arrays of rowwise independent random variables. *Acta Math. Hung.* **1989**, *54*, 153–162. [CrossRef]
38. Arlot, S.; Celisse, A. A survey of cross-validation procedures for model selection. *Stat. Surv.* **2010**, *4*, 40–79. [CrossRef]
39. Billingsley, P. *Convergence of Probability Measures*; John Wiley and Sons: New York, NY, USA, 1968.
40. Borkar, V.S. *Probability Theory: An Advanced Course*; Springer: New York, NY, USA, 1995.
41. Bulinski, A.V.; Shiryaev, A.N. *Theory of Stochastic Processes*, 2nd ed.; Fizmatlit: Moscow, Russia, 2005. (In Russian)
42. Kallenberg, O. *Foundations of Modern Probability*; Springer: New York, NY, USA, 1997.
43. Petrov, V.V. *Limit Theorems of Probability Theory: Sequences of Independent Random Variables*; Clarendon Press: Oxford, UK, 1995.
44. Shevtsova I.G. On absolute constants in the Berry-Esseen inequality and its structural and non-uniform refinements. *Informatics Its Appl.* **2013**, *7*, 124–125.
45. Bulinski, A.V.; Rakitko, A.S. Simulation and analytical approach to the identification of significant factors. *Commun. Stat.-Simul. Comput.* **2016**, *45*, 1430–1450. [CrossRef]
46. Shah, R.D.; Samworth, R.J. Variable selection with error control: another look at stablity selection *J.R. Statist. Soc. B.* **2012**, 74, 1-26. [CrossRef]
47. Beinrucker, A.; Dogan, U.; Blanchard, G. Extensions of stability selection using subsamples of observations and covariates. *Stat. Comput.* **2016**, *26*, 1059–1077. [CrossRef]
48. Nogueira, S.; Sechidis, K.; Brown, G. On the stability of feature selection algorithms. *J. Mach. Learn. Res.* **2018**, 18, 1-54.
49. Khaire, U.M.; Dhanalakshmi, R. Stability of feature selection algorithm: A review. *J. King Saud Univ.-Comput. Inf. Sci.* **2022**, *34*, 1060–1073. [CrossRef]
50. Bulinski, A. Stability properties of feature selection measures. *Theory Probab. Appl.* **2024**, *69*, 3–15.
51. Bénard, C.; Biau, G.; Da Veiga, S.; Scornet, E. SIRUS: Stable and Interpretable RUle Set for classification. *Electron. J. Statist.* **2021**, *15*, 427–505. [CrossRef]
52. Mielniczuk, J. Information theoretic methods for variable selection—A review. *Entropy* **2022**, *24*, 1079. [CrossRef]
53. Linke, Y.; Borisov, I.; Ruzankin, P.; Kutsenko, V.; Yarovaya, E.; Shalnova, S. Universal Local Linear Kernel Estimators in Nonparametric Regression. *Mathematics* **2022**, *10*, 2693. [CrossRef]
54. Rachev, S.T.; Klebanov, L.B.; Stoyanov, S.V.; Fabozzi, F.J. *The Methods of Distances in the Theory of Probability and Statistics*; Springer: New York, NY, USA, 2013.

mathematics

MDPI

Article

Improved Bayesian Inferences for Right-Censored Birnbaum–Saunders Data

Kalanka P. Jayalath

Department of Mathematics and Statistics, University of Houston—Clear Lake, Houston, TX 77058, USA; jayalath@uhcl.edu

Abstract: This work focuses on making Bayesian inferences for the two-parameter Birnbaum–Saunders (BS) distribution in the presence of right-censored data. A flexible Gibbs sampler is employed to handle the censored BS data in this Bayesian work that relies on Jeffrey's and Achcar's reference priors. A comprehensive simulation study is conducted to compare estimates under various parameter settings, sample sizes, and levels of censoring. Further comparisons are drawn with real-world examples involving Type-II, progressively Type-II, and randomly right-censored data. The study concludes that the suggested Gibbs sampler enhances the accuracy of Bayesian inferences, and both the amount of censoring and the sample size are identified as influential factors in such analyses.

Keywords: Bayesian inference; censoring; Gibbs sampler; Jeffrey's Prior; reference prior

MSC: 62F15; 62N02; 62M86

1. Introduction

The Birnbaum–Saunders (BS) distribution is a two-parameter lifetime distribution that was originally introduced by [1] to model the failure time due to the growth of a dominant crack that is subjected to cyclic stress, which causes a failure upon reaching the threshold level. The BS distribution has gone through various developments and generalizations and is found to be suitable for life testing applications. The distribution was originally derived to model the fatigue life of metals that are subject to periodic stress; this is sometimes referred to as the fatigue life distribution. Interestingly, it can also be obtained by using a monotone transformation on the standard normal distribution [2]. Moreover, as [3] indicated, the BS distribution can be viewed as an equal mixture of an inverse Gaussian (IG) distribution and its reciprocal. These relations are useful in deriving important properties of the BS distribution based on well-known properties of the normal and IG distributions. Ref. [4] showed that the BS distribution can be used as an approximation of the IG distribution. In practice, both the BS and IG distributions are often considered very competitive lifetime models for right-skewed data [5,6].

The distribution function of the BS failure time T with parameters α and β, denoted by $T \sim BS(\alpha, \beta)$, is given by

$$F_T(t) = \Phi\left[\frac{1}{\alpha}\left(\sqrt{\frac{t}{\beta}} - \sqrt{\frac{\beta}{t}}\right)\right], \quad (1)$$

where $0 < t < \infty$, and $\alpha > 0, \beta > 0$ are the shape and scale parameters, respectively. Here, $\Phi(\cdot)$ represents the distribution function of the standard normal distribution. Since $F_T(\beta) = \Phi(0) = 0.5$, the scale parameter β is the median of the BS distribution. The probability density function (pdf) of the $BS(\alpha, \beta)$ is given by

$$f_T(t) = \frac{1}{2\sqrt{2\pi}\alpha\beta}\left[\left(\frac{\beta}{t}\right)^{1/2} + \left(\frac{\beta}{t}\right)^{3/2}\right]\exp\left[-\frac{1}{2\alpha^2}\left(\frac{t}{\beta} + \frac{\beta}{t} - 2\right)\right] \tag{2}$$

It can be easily shown that $E(T) = \beta(1 + \alpha^2/2)$ and $Var(T) = (\alpha\beta)^2(1 + 5\alpha^2/4)$. Interestingly, Ref. [7] indicates that $T^{-1} \sim BS(\alpha, \beta^{-1})$, and therefore the reciprocal variable T^{-1} also belongs to the same family.

The parameter estimation for the BS distribution, including the maximum likelihood estimation (MLE), is largely discussed in its literature. For complete data, Ref. [8] derived the MLE's of the BS parameters. Ref. [9] introduced modified moment estimators (MMEs), a bias reduction method and a Jackknife technique to reduce the bias of both MMEs and MLEs. Ref. [10] introduced alternative estimators with a smaller bias compared to that for Ref. [9]. Point and interval estimations of the BS parameters under Type-II censoring are discussed in [11]. Ref. [12] suggested a modified censored moment estimation method to estimate its parameters under random censoring. Ref. [13] suggested using a fiducial inference on BS parameters for right-censored data.

Bayesian approaches have also been used to make inferences on the BS parameters. Ref. [14] used both Jeffrey's prior and a reference prior to derive marginal posteriors using Laplace's approximation; while [15] employed only the reference priors and considered an approximate Bayesian approach using Lindley's method. Ref. [16] justified that Jeffrey's reference prior results in an improper posterior for the scale parameter and suggested employing the reference priors that incorporate some partial information. In this situation, they suggested applying the slice sampling method to obtain a proper posterior for the case of censored data. A work by [17] adopted inverse-gamma priors for the shape and scale parameters and proposed an efficient sampling algorithm using the generalized ratio-of-uniforms method to compute Bayesian estimates. Ref. [18] also adapted the inverse-gamma priors for both the BS parameters and applied Markov Chain Monte Carlo (MCMC)-based conditional and joint sampling methods to handle censored data.

The censored data appear in life-time experiments due to various reasons; the nature of censoring plays a vital role in its analysis. In this study, we focus on the right-censored data that occurs when the test start time of each unit is known, but the test end time is unknown. This includes the random right, Type-II, and progressively Type-II censoring schemes. The progressively Type-II censoring scheme allows one to remove a pre-specified number of uncensored units from the remaining experimental units at the observed failure times [19]. As such, it is a more general form of Type-II censoring, where censoring takes place progressively in r stages. In this scheme, a total of n units are placed on a life-test, only r are completely observed until failure and the rest of $n - r$ units are rightly censored. However, at the time of the first failure, say $t_{(1)}$, R_1 of the $n - 1$ surviving units are randomly withdrawn from the experiment; at the time of the next failure, say $t_{(2)}$, R_2 of the $n - 2 - R_1$ surviving units are censored, and so on. At the time of the last (rth) failure, say $t_{(r)}$, all the remaining $R_r = n - r - \sum_{j=1}^{r-1} R_j$ surviving units are censored. Therefore, in progressively Type-II censoring experiments with pre-specified r and $\{R_1, R_2, ..., R_r\}$, the data will take the form $\{(t_{(1)}, R_1), (t_{(2)}, R_2), ..., (t_{(r)}, R_r)\}$.

In this work, we focus on estimating both BS parameters in the presence of right-censored units as well as the average remaining test time $\bar{T}$ of the censored units. For instance, let us consider n non-repairable units and assume we observe failures in r progressively censored stages with censored times $\mathbf{y}' = (t_{(1)}, t_{(2)}, ..., t_{(r)})$. If the experiment were to continue so that all $(n - r)$ -censored values could be observed, then we let $\tilde{\mathbf{y}}_i' = (t_{(i:1)}, t_{(i:2)}, ..., t_{(i:R_i)})$ be the set of true observed values of the censored values at the ith progressive stage. Then, the remaining total test time for these R_i censored elements is $\tilde{\mathbf{y}}_i'\mathbf{1} - t_{(i)}\mathbf{1}'\mathbf{1}$, where $\mathbf{1}$ is a column vector of 1's of length R_i. As such, the estimated and average remaining test time for all the censored units from all r progressive stages is

$$\bar{T} = \frac{1}{n-r}\sum_{i=1}^{r}\left(\tilde{\mathbf{y}}_i'\mathbf{1} - t_{(i)}\mathbf{1}'\mathbf{1}\right). \tag{3}$$

The rest of the article is organized as follows: In Section 2, we discuss the parameter estimation of the BS distribution using both the maximum likelihood method and the Bayesian method. Section 3 covers the Gibbs sampling procedure for handling censored data. In Section 4, we conduct a Monte-Carlo simulation study to compare the performance of the aforementioned methods. Illustrative examples are included in Section 5, and we conclude with remarks and recommendations in Section 6.

2. BS Parameter Estimation

In this section, we focus on the Bayesian parameter estimation with two different prior specifications: Jeffrey's and Achcar's priors for the BS parameters α and β. We discuss some of the practical challenges of these procedures while summarizing their methodological foundations.

On the other hand, the MLE of BS parameters, α and β, were heavily discussed in the literature; see [2,8] for details. Consider an experiment with n random failure times $\mathbf{T} = \{t_1, t_2, ..., t_n\}$ that follow the BS distribution. Then, its log-likelihood function, without the additive constant, becomes

$$l(\alpha,\beta|\mathbf{T}) = -n\ln(\alpha\beta) + \sum_{i=1}^{n}\ln\left[\left(\frac{\beta}{t_i}\right)^{1/2} + \left(\frac{\beta}{t_i}\right)^{3/2}\right] - \frac{1}{2\alpha^2}\sum_{i=1}^{n}\left(\frac{t_i}{\beta} + \frac{\beta}{t_i} - 2\right). \quad (4)$$

By differentiating Equation (4) with respect to α and solving it for zero, one can obtain

$$\alpha^2 = \left[\frac{s}{\beta} + \frac{\beta}{q} - 2\right], \quad (5)$$

where $s = \sum_{i=1}^{n} t_i/n$ and $q = \left[\sum_{i=1}^{n} t_i^{-1}/n\right]^{-1}$ are the sample arithmetic and harmonic means of the observed data. Next, when differentiating Equation (4) with respect to β and substituting α^2 from Equation (5), the following can be obtained to determine the MLE of β.

$$\beta^2 - \beta(2q + K(\beta)) + q(s + K(\beta)) = 0, \quad (6)$$

where $K(\beta) = \left[\sum_{i=1}^{n}(\beta + t_i)^{-1}/n\right]^{-1}$. The MLE $\hat{\beta}$ of β is the unique positive root of Equation (6), in which $q < \hat{\beta} < s$. With this estimate, the MLE of α becomes $\hat{\alpha} = \left[\frac{s}{\hat{\beta}} + \frac{\hat{\beta}}{q} - 2\right]^{1/2}$.

2.1. Bayesian Inference

Here, we consider the Bayesian work that was originally suggested by [14] by employing non-informative priors that include Jeffrey's and Achcar's reference priors. Jeffrey's prior density for α and β is given by

$$\pi(\alpha,\beta) \propto \sqrt{\det \boldsymbol{I}(\alpha,\beta)},$$

where $\boldsymbol{I}(\alpha,\beta) = \begin{pmatrix} \frac{2n}{\alpha^2} & 0 \\ 0 & \frac{n[1+\alpha g(\alpha)/\sqrt{2\pi}]}{\alpha^2\beta^2} \end{pmatrix}$ is the Fisher information matrix of the BS distribution, $g(\alpha) = \alpha\sqrt{\pi/2} - \pi\exp\{2/\alpha^2\}[1 - \Phi(2/\alpha)]$, and Φ is the standard normal distribution function.

Using the Laplace approximation, it can be shown that Jeffrey's prior takes the following form

$$\pi(\alpha,\beta) \propto \frac{1}{\alpha\beta}H(\alpha^2), \alpha > 0, \beta > 0,$$

where $H(\alpha^2) = \left(\frac{1}{\alpha^2} + \frac{1}{4}\right)$.

Assuming independence between α and β, [14] suggested a reference prior that takes the following form

$$\pi(\alpha, \beta) \propto \frac{1}{\alpha\beta}, \alpha > 0, \beta > 0.$$

In our discussion, we called this Achcar's reference prior.

2.2. Posterior Inference

For Jeffrey's prior, the joint posterior distribution of α and β becomes [14]

$$\pi(\alpha, \beta|\mathbf{T}) \propto \frac{\prod_{i=1}^{n}(\beta + t_i)\exp\{-Q(\beta)/\alpha^2\}}{\alpha^{n+1}\beta^{(n/2)+1}H(\alpha^2)}, \tag{7}$$

where $Q(\beta) = \frac{ns}{2\beta} + \frac{n\beta}{2q} - n$.

Then, using the Laplace approximation (see Appendix A), the approximate marginal posterior distributions of α and β for Jeffrey's prior can be written as

$$\pi(\alpha|\mathbf{T}) \propto \alpha^{-(n+1)}(4 + \alpha^2)^{1/2}\exp\left\{-\frac{n}{\alpha^2}(\sqrt{s/q} - 1)\right\}, \alpha > 0, \tag{8}$$

and

$$\pi(\beta|\mathbf{T}) \propto \frac{\prod_{i=1}^{n}(\beta + t_i)\{4 + [2n/(n+2)][s/(2\beta) + \beta/(2q) - 1]\}^{1/2}}{\beta^{(n/2)+1}\{s/(2\beta) + \beta/(2q) - 1\}^{(n+1)/2}}, \beta > 0, \tag{9}$$

respectively.

Then, for Achcar's reference prior, the joint posterior becomes the same as Equation (7) except where $H(\alpha^2) = 1$ and the approximate marginal posterior distributions of α and β become

$$\pi(\alpha|\mathbf{T}) \propto \alpha^{-n}\exp\left\{-\frac{n}{\alpha^2}(\sqrt{s/q} - 1)\right\}, \alpha > 0, \tag{10}$$

and

$$\pi(\beta|\mathbf{T}) \propto \frac{\prod_{i=1}^{n}(\beta + t_i)}{\beta^{(n/2)+1}\{s/(2\beta) + \beta/(2q) - 1\}^{n/2}}, \beta > 0, \tag{11}$$

respectively.

As both Jeffrey- and Achcar-based posteriors do not have closed-form distributions, the Bayes estimates of α and β cannot be obtained in an explicit form. However, [14] proposed that the mode of the corresponding posteriors may be used as the Bayes estimates for α and β.

The work by [16] has shown that the above Achcar's reference prior based posterior given in Equation (11) becomes improper when $\beta \to \infty$. In practice, both posteriors given in Equations (9) and (11) are numerically intractable for larger β and n values due to the increments of the products in their numerators. However, as $F_T(t, \alpha, \beta) = F_T(t/\beta, \alpha, 1)$, the parameter β in the BS distribution is solely a scale parameter which represents the median. Therefore, we suggest a simple and computationally efficient scaler transformation $t_{new} = t/\hat{\beta}$ to reduce this inflation and to avoid the situation that $\beta \to \infty$. As a result, the median of the transformed data and the posteriors of β will be centered around one.

3. Application of Gibbs Sampler

In this section, we introduce a Gibbs sampling procedure that can be used to estimate the parameters of the BS distribution in the presence of censored data. The procedure uses Markov Chain Monte Carlo (MCMC) techniques to generate data samples that replace the censored portion of the data set.

Here, we propose using Bayesian inference for BS parameters α and β, employing marginal posteriors obtained using both Jeffrey's and Achcar's priors via the Gibbs sampler. Moreover, upon sampling from a BS distribution for unknown realizations of censored units, the remaining average lifetime is also estimated.

The Gibbs sampler requires suitable initial values for α and β to achieve its convergence. Often the MLE's from the observed data given censoring are preferred for this purpose. Ignoring the additive constant, the BS log-likelihood function for the progressively Type-II-censored data of the form $\{(t_{(1)}, R_1), (t_{(2)}, R_2), ..., (t_{(r)}, R_r)\}$ can be written as

$$l(\alpha, \beta|\mathbf{T}) = \sum_{i=1}^{r} \Big\{ \ln f(t_{(i)}; \alpha, \beta) + R_i \ln \left(\Phi(-g(t_{(i)}; \alpha, \beta))\right) \Big\}, \tag{12}$$

where $f(\cdot)$ is the pdf of the BS distribution given in Equation (2), and $g(t; \alpha, \beta) = \frac{1}{\alpha}\left(\sqrt{\frac{t}{\beta}} - \sqrt{\frac{\beta}{t}}\right)$.

The MLEs of the BS parameters cannot be obtained in the closed form for this censoring scheme. Using the property that the BS distribution can be written as an equal mixture of an IG distribution and its reciprocal [20] outlined an EM algorithm to obtained its MLEs. In this work, we use a computational tool introduced in [21] that is freely available in [22], which can be used to obtain MLEs of the BS parameters with all major censoring schemes.

Below, we outline the major steps of the Gibbs sampler, which employs progressively Type-II-censored BS data.

1. Calculate the MLE $\hat{\alpha}_{MLE}$ and $\hat{\beta}_{MLE}$ from the available right-censored data. Set $\hat{\alpha}_{MLE} = \alpha_1^{(0)}$ and $\hat{\beta}_{MLE} = \beta_1^{(0)}$.
2. Generate R_i random variates from a uniform distribution bounded by the BS CDF (F_T) value of the respective censored observation and one. Then, use the inverse CDF (F_T^{-1}) value of the newly sampled random variate to replace the censored value. For instance, for the jth censored observation in $(t_{(i)}, R_i)$,
   - Generate: $u_{(j:i)} \sim U\left[F_T\left(t_{(i)}\right), 1\right]$, where $F_T\left(t_{(i)}\right) = \Phi\left[\frac{1}{\alpha_1^{(0)}}\left(\sqrt{\frac{t_{(i)}}{\beta_1^{(0)}}} - \sqrt{\frac{\beta_1^{(0)}}{t_{(i)}}}\right)\right]$.
   - Then, set: $t_{(j:i)}^{(0)} = F_T^{-1}\left(u_{(j:i)}; \alpha_1^{(0)}, \beta_1^{(0)}\right)$.
3. Repeat Step 2 for all censored units in all r censored stages. The censored data will be replaced by the the newly simulated data $t_{(j:i)}^{(0)}\ (> t_{(i)})$, $\forall j = 1, 2, ..., R_i$ for each $i = 1, 2, ..., r$ and will be combined with the observed failure times $t_{(1)}, t_{(2)}, ..., t_{(r)}$ to form an updated and complete sample of size n.
4. Using the updated sample in Step 3, sample $\alpha_1^{(1)}$ and $\beta_1^{(1)}$ from their respective posterior distributions.
5. Repeat Steps 2–4 starting with the newly sampled parameters, $\alpha_1^{(1)}$ and $\beta_1^{(1)}$. This procedure will continue for k total iterations and conclude with the results for $\alpha_1^{(k)}$ and $\beta_1^{(k)}$. A new set of simulated BS observations should be picked in the same manner as in Step 3 using the $\alpha_1^{(k)}$ and $\beta_1^{(k)}$ as newly updated parameters.
6. At the conclusion of Step 5, the average remaining life of censored units defined in Equation (3) shall be calculated using the newly sampled data and is designated as $\bar{T}_1^{(k)}$.
7. Repeat the above process in Step 2–6 a large number of times, say m total replications. This will result:

$$(\alpha_1^{(k)}, \alpha_2^{(k)}, ..., \alpha_m^{(k)}), \quad (\beta_1^{(k)}, \beta_2^{(k)}, ..., \beta_m^{(k)}), \quad (\bar{T}_1^{(k)}, \bar{T}_2^{(k)}, ..., \bar{T}_m^{(k)}).$$

In the Gibbs sampler, we guarantee the convergence of the sampled data using both numerical and graphical summaries. This includes monitoring the scalar summary ψ and the scale reduction statistic $\hat{R}$ defined in [23]. As suggested in [24], we confirm that this scale reduction statistic is well below 1.1 and the trace plots behave appropriately to ensure the convergence of the Gibbs samples in all situations considered. After confirming the convergence, we report both point and interval estimates. This includes mean and its stand error estimates as well as the 95% equal-tailed credible intervals for all the parameters including $\tilde{T}$. Moreover, we use the Kernel density estimation procedure to make visual comparisons between estimation methods. A sample R code to exhibit this algorithm is included in the Supplementary Materials.

4. Monte–Carlo Simulation

We conduct a simulation study to compare the performance of the discussed Bayesian estimates. The data are generated from the $BS(\alpha, \beta)$ distribution with four different sample sizes $n = 10, 20, 30, 50$ and four different Type-II right-censoring percentages (CEP) at 10%(10%)40%. Without a loss of generality, we kept the scale parameter β fixed at 1.0 while varying the shape parameter $\alpha = 0.10, 0.30, 0.50, 1.00, 2.00$. In each experimental condition, we repeatedly generated 2000 BS data sets and applied the proposed Gibbs sampler.

We noticed that the Gibbs sampler converges in $k = 3000$ iterations for both Bayesian priors, and the scale reduction factor $\hat{R}$ for both parameters is less than 1.1. After assessing the convergence, we replicate the Gibbs sampler $m = 1000$ times to obtain the point and 95% equal-tailed credible intervals for α, β, and $\tilde{T}$ for each generated data set. Then for each parameter, the overall average of the posterior mean estimates (PE), its standard error (SE), and the coverage probability (CP) for 1000 randomly generated BS samples are acquired. To compare posterior point estimates, we refer to an observed bias as the difference between the true BS parameter and its PE. These results are shown in Tables 1–4.

Table 1. Mean and standard error of the point estimates and probability coverages of 95% credible intervals based on Monte–Carlo simulation ($n = 10$).

		$\hat{\alpha}$						$\hat{\beta}$						$\hat{\tilde{T}}$					
Param	**CEP%**	**Jeffrey's**			**Achcar's**			**Jeffrey's**			**Achcar's**			**Jeffrey's**			**Achcar's**		
α		**PE**	**SE**	**CP**	**PE**	**SE**	**CP**	**PE**	**SE**	**CP**	**PE**	**SE**	**CP**	**PE**	**SE**	**CP**	**PE**	**SE**	**CP**
0.1	10	0.100	0.025	0.939	0.108	0.027	0.957	1.003	0.034	0.927	1.001	0.031	0.952	0.063	0.019	0.940	0.071	0.021	0.942
	20	0.101	0.029	0.942	0.110	0.030	0.949	1.002	0.033	0.932	1.001	0.032	0.955	0.072	0.024	0.936	0.080	0.027	0.940
	30	0.101	0.031	0.934	0.113	0.035	0.956	1.002	0.033	0.916	1.006	0.034	0.951	0.078	0.028	0.925	0.091	0.033	0.954
	40	0.099	0.035	0.922	0.112	0.036	0.965	1.002	0.037	0.920	1.007	0.038	0.945	0.085	0.034	0.921	0.101	0.039	0.951
0.3	10	0.299	0.074	0.933	0.316	0.075	0.953	1.013	0.099	0.933	1.008	0.097	0.949	0.256	0.091	0.946	0.280	0.096	0.941
	20	0.293	0.079	0.932	0.319	0.082	0.960	1.008	0.099	0.931	1.014	0.100	0.947	0.265	0.102	0.928	0.301	0.108	0.943
	30	0.289	0.083	0.933	0.317	0.088	0.959	1.007	0.101	0.928	1.020	0.104	0.944	0.277	0.110	0.944	0.319	0.122	0.948
	40	0.289	0.091	0.918	0.320	0.094	0.952	1.013	0.110	0.922	1.026	0.117	0.938	0.297	0.125	0.923	0.346	0.137	0.944
0.5	10	0.489	0.115	0.938	0.517	0.123	0.945	1.032	0.159	0.941	1.026	0.166	0.936	0.543	0.218	0.940	0.592	0.244	0.951
	20	0.487	0.124	0.937	0.523	0.121	0.962	1.033	0.162	0.938	1.038	0.171	0.949	0.559	0.236	0.938	0.617	0.234	0.960
	30	0.475	0.125	0.949	0.515	0.128	0.960	1.025	0.172	0.927	1.046	0.168	0.950	0.552	0.235	0.942	0.629	0.247	0.945
	40	0.466	0.141	0.930	0.509	0.132	0.973	1.018	0.175	0.920	1.039	0.187	0.951	0.562	0.266	0.934	0.638	0.266	0.961
1	10	1.002	0.261	0.939	1.056	0.260	0.953	1.088	0.306	0.936	1.085	0.297	0.959	1.849	1.058	0.938	1.929	1.021	0.946
	20	1.002	0.289	0.924	1.073	0.291	0.947	1.085	0.307	0.943	1.104	0.304	0.961	1.899	1.188	0.948	2.072	1.180	0.940
	30	1.000	0.315	0.929	1.062	0.314	0.953	1.089	0.319	0.931	1.108	0.320	0.951	1.917	1.235	0.928	2.053	1.238	0.939
	40	0.983	0.337	0.930	1.079	0.344	0.957	1.067	0.318	0.922	1.116	0.328	0.956	1.873	1.246	0.929	2.141	1.339	0.961
2	10	1.961	0.465	0.946	2.013	0.473	0.948	1.111	0.416	0.954	1.109	0.420	0.965	6.634	4.577	0.918	6.923	4.658	0.917
	20	1.944	0.519	0.924	2.014	0.512	0.938	1.098	0.420	0.945	1.103	0.419	0.962	6.186	4.583	0.904	6.172	4.344	0.923
	30	1.868	0.545	0.927	1.943	0.541	0.938	1.065	0.425	0.949	1.103	0.433	0.957	5.193	3.955	0.921	5.529	4.439	0.922
	40	1.755	0.588	0.904	1.898	0.522	0.957	1.022	0.434	0.912	1.059	0.437	0.954	4.437	3.616	0.876	4.833	3.530	0.934

As shown in Table 1, for $n = 10$, Jeffrey's method slightly underestimates the true α value, and the size of the bias increases with the amount of the censoring percentage. The difference is more apparent for higher α values. Achcar's method slightly overestimates the true value of the α regardless of the censoring percentage, except for high censoring $\alpha = 2$ cases. The standard errors of the α estimates are somewhat similar for both methods. Interestingly, Achcar's prior maintains the coverage probability at the nominal 95% level while Jeffrey's prior becomes slightly liberal, as its coverage probability is around 93%. The

β estimates for both the methods are somewhat consistent for all α values. The coverage probability comparison for the β estimates is quite similar to that of the α.

For the average remaining time, Achcar's estimates provide somewhat higher estimates than Jeffrey's estimates. Again, the differences are greater for larger α values than for the smaller αs. As far as the standard error is concerned, both methods are equally good and proportional to the true α value. The coverage probability comparison is quite similar to that of the α and β comparisons.

Based on the estimates shown in Table 2, when $n = 20$, the comparisons we made earlier are still valid for all estimates, but the differences between estimates and the effects of high censoring are not as pronounced as in $n = 10$ cases, and their standard errors are also now lower. When the sample size increases to $n = 30$ and 50 (see Tables 3 and 4), both the methods provide better results with increasing precision. The differences between the point estimates for lower α values are further narrowing and the coverage probabilities of all estimates approach the nominal 95% level, showing greater precision in the interval estimations for large samples.

Table 2. Mean and standard error of the point estimates and probability coverages of 95% credible intervals based on Monte–Carlo simulation ($n = 20$).

		$\hat{\alpha}$						$\hat{\beta}$						$\hat{\tau}$					
Param	**CEP%**	**Jeffrey's**			**Achcar's**			**Jeffrey's**			**Achcar's**			**Jeffrey's**			**Achcar's**		
α		**PE**	**SE**	**CP**	**PE**	**SE**	**CP**	**PE**	**SE**	**CP**	**PE**	**SE**	**CP**	**PE**	**SE**	**CP**	**PE**	**SE**	**CP**
0.1	10	0.099	0.018	0.939	0.103	0.018	0.943	0.999	0.022	0.943	1.002	0.023	0.944	0.059	0.013	0.947	0.062	0.013	0.938
	20	0.100	0.019	0.936	0.104	0.020	0.951	1.000	0.023	0.940	1.002	0.024	0.944	0.066	0.015	0.937	0.071	0.016	0.951
	30	0.099	0.022	0.933	0.104	0.022	0.963	0.999	0.024	0.945	1.001	0.024	0.937	0.073	0.018	0.929	0.078	0.019	0.950
	40	0.100	0.024	0.936	0.105	0.025	0.957	1.000	0.025	0.934	1.003	0.026	0.945	0.081	0.022	0.929	0.087	0.023	0.946
0.3	10	0.302	0.054	0.944	0.310	0.054	0.950	1.004	0.066	0.939	1.007	0.068	0.949	0.245	0.066	0.954	0.257	0.068	0.954
	20	0.303	0.059	0.937	0.313	0.060	0.954	1.006	0.070	0.938	1.005	0.069	0.948	0.263	0.075	0.944	0.277	0.078	0.953
	30	0.299	0.062	0.946	0.308	0.064	0.948	1.006	0.071	0.938	1.010	0.076	0.934	0.274	0.081	0.944	0.288	0.086	0.949
	40	0.299	0.069	0.945	0.322	0.070	0.953	1.002	0.076	0.935	1.015	0.080	0.949	0.291	0.093	0.935	0.325	0.099	0.957
0.5	10	0.504	0.089	0.938	0.522	0.088	0.959	1.016	0.116	0.935	1.018	0.113	0.948	0.540	0.170	0.961	0.571	0.170	0.959
	20	0.499	0.096	0.937	0.513	0.093	0.953	1.019	0.114	0.954	1.020	0.115	0.939	0.548	0.179	0.945	0.573	0.179	0.959
	30	0.494	0.100	0.940	0.509	0.096	0.961	1.019	0.122	0.937	1.020	0.124	0.939	0.556	0.192	0.937	0.582	0.189	0.952
	40	0.501	0.110	0.941	0.519	0.111	0.951	1.017	0.125	0.952	1.029	0.136	0.945	0.586	0.212	0.945	0.625	0.222	0.962
1	10	0.998	0.177	0.947	1.029	0.182	0.947	1.049	0.218	0.942	1.050	0.220	0.951	1.841	0.745	0.948	1.956	0.798	0.954
	20	1.003	0.200	0.939	1.038	0.208	0.939	1.052	0.220	0.950	1.073	0.236	0.955	1.847	0.844	0.938	2.002	0.963	0.948
	30	1.004	0.218	0.942	1.051	0.234	0.943	1.051	0.230	0.945	1.070	0.255	0.951	1.843	0.917	0.945	2.054	1.129	0.957
	40	1.008	0.248	0.952	1.063	0.265	0.941	1.070	0.259	0.953	1.093	0.264	0.958	1.933	1.138	0.951	2.155	1.236	0.946
2	10	2.021	0.364	0.935	2.055	0.361	0.942	1.103	0.328	0.952	1.106	0.329	0.957	7.592	3.552	0.945	7.841	3.705	0.955
	20	1.988	0.395	0.928	2.025	0.374	0.951	1.103	0.360	0.934	1.118	0.365	0.943	7.070	3.777	0.944	7.367	3.807	0.951
	30	1.972	0.425	0.953	2.032	0.412	0.957	1.101	0.358	0.955	1.122	0.369	0.959	6.813	3.815	0.949	7.250	3.888	0.946
	40	1.997	0.458	0.950	2.046	0.443	0.966	1.106	0.381	0.953	1.136	0.376	0.963	6.844	4.108	0.957	7.219	3.982	0.963

Table 3. Mean and standard error of the point estimates and probability coverages of 95% credible intervals based on Monte–Carlo simulation ($n = 30$).

		$\hat{\alpha}$						$\hat{\beta}$						$\hat{\tau}$					
Param	**CEP%**	**Jeffrey's**			**Achcar's**			**Jeffrey's**			**Achcar's**			**Jeffrey's**			**Achcar's**		
α		**PE**	**SE**	**CP**	**PE**	**SE**	**CP**	**PE**	**SE**	**CP**	**PE**	**SE**	**CP**	**PE**	**SE**	**CP**	**PE**	**SE**	**CP**
0.1	10	0.099	0.014	0.943	0.101	0.014	0.956	1.000	0.018	0.946	0.999	0.019	0.938	0.058	0.010	0.949	0.060	0.010	0.954
	20	0.101	0.015	0.952	0.102	0.015	0.948	1.000	0.019	0.947	1.001	0.019	0.936	0.066	0.012	0.950	0.068	0.012	0.951
	30	0.100	0.017	0.937	0.103	0.018	0.939	1.001	0.020	0.938	1.000	0.020	0.955	0.073	0.015	0.953	0.076	0.015	0.949
	40	0.100	0.020	0.933	0.103	0.019	0.955	1.000	0.021	0.932	1.001	0.020	0.958	0.080	0.018	0.925	0.083	0.017	0.963
0.3	10	0.301	0.043	0.948	0.306	0.042	0.956	1.006	0.056	0.940	1.003	0.055	0.943	0.239	0.052	0.943	0.245	0.052	0.940
	20	0.298	0.046	0.941	0.308	0.047	0.957	1.001	0.056	0.940	1.005	0.057	0.957	0.251	0.057	0.940	0.265	0.059	0.956
	30	0.300	0.051	0.926	0.309	0.053	0.952	1.003	0.060	0.944	1.004	0.060	0.948	0.269	0.066	0.945	0.282	0.068	0.960
	40	0.295	0.057	0.933	0.311	0.058	0.949	1.002	0.061	0.938	1.006	0.062	0.959	0.281	0.075	0.934	0.302	0.081	0.947

Table 3. *Cont.*

		$\hat{\alpha}$						$\hat{\beta}$						$\hat{T}$					
Param	**CEP%**	**Jeffrey's**			**Achcar's**			**Jeffrey's**			**Achcar's**			**Jeffrey's**			**Achcar's**		
α		**PE**	**SE**	**CP**	**PE**	**SE**	**CP**	**PE**	**SE**	**CP**	**PE**	**SE**	**CP**	**PE**	**SE**	**CP**	**PE**	**SE**	**CP**
0.5	10	0.502	0.069	0.956	0.506	0.075	0.938	1.013	0.093	0.946	1.010	0.096	0.934	0.526	0.128	0.948	0.533	0.142	0.935
	20	0.502	0.075	0.952	0.513	0.084	0.932	1.010	0.093	0.951	1.013	0.095	0.948	0.537	0.140	0.952	0.560	0.159	0.932
	30	0.500	0.086	0.935	0.518	0.086	0.947	1.012	0.098	0.938	1.017	0.098	0.956	0.552	0.162	0.948	0.583	0.165	0.954
	40	0.502	0.094	0.946	0.517	0.092	0.962	1.015	0.106	0.937	1.015	0.104	0.955	0.574	0.177	0.925	0.599	0.179	0.962
1	10	0.994	0.145	0.945	1.024	0.149	0.956	1.038	0.175	0.952	1.042	0.180	0.937	1.785	0.593	0.942	1.895	0.660	0.936
	20	1.004	0.162	0.935	1.030	0.161	0.948	1.028	0.181	0.943	1.037	0.181	0.954	1.755	0.650	0.951	1.850	0.668	0.946
	30	1.002	0.179	0.946	1.024	0.186	0.938	1.040	0.205	0.937	1.053	0.200	0.945	1.755	0.763	0.945	1.840	0.781	0.953
	40	1.005	0.210	0.938	1.043	0.211	0.951	1.049	0.216	0.945	1.075	0.232	0.944	1.799	0.921	0.940	1.954	0.973	0.949
2	10	2.010	0.301	0.933	2.027	0.295	0.941	1.074	0.286	0.939	1.075	0.267	0.958	7.219	2.993	0.946	7.284	2.882	0.949
	20	2.008	0.324	0.945	2.024	0.336	0.929	1.078	0.299	0.937	1.066	0.295	0.943	6.914	3.202	0.948	6.970	3.344	0.937
	30	2.028	0.373	0.947	2.052	0.374	0.946	1.114	0.339	0.934	1.117	0.325	0.953	7.069	3.779	0.951	7.232	3.739	0.936
	40	1.996	0.411	0.943	2.053	0.409	0.953	1.101	0.347	0.959	1.148	0.355	0.962	6.656	3.848	0.941	7.221	4.098	0.955

Table 4. Mean and standard error of the point estimates and probability coverages of 95% credible intervals based on Monte–Carlo simulation ($n = 50$).

		$\hat{\alpha}$						$\hat{\beta}$						$\hat{T}$					
Param	**CEP%**	**Jeffrey's**			**Achcar's**			**Jeffrey's**			**Achcar's**			**Jeffrey's**			**Achcar's**		
α		**PE**	**SE**	**CP**	**PE**	**SE**	**CP**	**PE**	**SE**	**CP**	**PE**	**SE**	**CP**	**PE**	**SE**	**CP**	**PE**	**SE**	**CP**
0.1	10	0.100	0.011	0.950	0.101	0.011	0.949	1.000	0.014	0.945	0.999	0.014	0.958	0.057	0.007	0.950	0.058	0.008	0.944
	20	0.100	0.012	0.935	0.101	0.012	0.941	0.999	0.014	0.942	1.000	0.015	0.943	0.065	0.009	0.947	0.066	0.009	0.945
	30	0.100	0.013	0.934	0.102	0.013	0.953	1.000	0.015	0.940	1.000	0.016	0.936	0.072	0.011	0.935	0.073	0.011	0.932
	40	0.099	0.014	0.945	0.102	0.015	0.945	1.000	0.016	0.939	1.000	0.016	0.952	0.078	0.013	0.944	0.081	0.013	0.938
0.3	10	0.302	0.033	0.946	0.304	0.033	0.948	1.003	0.042	0.945	1.003	0.042	0.949	0.236	0.039	0.950	0.239	0.039	0.935
	20	0.299	0.035	0.952	0.306	0.034	0.954	1.003	0.045	0.928	1.000	0.042	0.949	0.249	0.043	0.945	0.256	0.042	0.952
	30	0.298	0.039	0.942	0.305	0.041	0.949	1.002	0.046	0.941	1.002	0.044	0.951	0.263	0.049	0.946	0.272	0.051	0.942
	40	0.301	0.045	0.930	0.306	0.045	0.945	1.004	0.049	0.944	1.002	0.049	0.947	0.282	0.059	0.946	0.289	0.060	0.939
0.5	10	0.500	0.056	0.943	0.506	0.055	0.946	1.004	0.071	0.937	1.007	0.069	0.959	0.511	0.103	0.954	0.522	0.103	0.933
	20	0.502	0.057	0.967	0.504	0.059	0.950	1.004	0.072	0.939	1.007	0.074	0.942	0.527	0.107	0.949	0.532	0.111	0.944
	30	0.500	0.067	0.944	0.507	0.067	0.942	1.007	0.076	0.945	1.014	0.075	0.946	0.540	0.125	0.963	0.554	0.126	0.947
	40	0.502	0.076	0.942	0.511	0.071	0.959	1.011	0.082	0.948	1.009	0.085	0.942	0.561	0.143	0.951	0.574	0.139	0.947
1	10	0.994	0.106	0.955	1.011	0.109	0.954	1.021	0.130	0.952	1.020	0.129	0.960	1.730	0.422	0.943	1.780	0.439	0.947
	20	1.006	0.118	0.963	1.016	0.120	0.953	1.013	0.137	0.946	1.022	0.144	0.939	1.699	0.460	0.934	1.744	0.484	0.934
	30	1.003	0.138	0.940	1.018	0.141	0.942	1.023	0.148	0.952	1.030	0.158	0.941	1.669	0.533	0.950	1.729	0.580	0.947
	40	1.008	0.169	0.919	1.017	0.159	0.944	1.035	0.169	0.941	1.043	0.171	0.942	1.694	0.684	0.941	1.724	0.644	0.957
2	10	1.992	0.227	0.936	2.017	0.231	0.945	1.033	0.207	0.948	1.050	0.218	0.949	6.746	2.200	0.943	7.021	2.326	0.947
	20	2.005	0.251	0.945	2.030	0.252	0.956	1.054	0.227	0.954	1.069	0.237	0.953	6.582	2.434	0.939	6.816	2.534	0.962
	30	2.008	0.299	0.939	2.031	0.301	0.937	1.070	0.262	0.953	1.074	0.286	0.938	6.447	3.002	0.953	6.594	3.095	0.938
	40	2.016	0.337	0.945	2.079	0.359	0.927	1.087	0.311	0.936	1.121	0.312	0.937	6.377	3.361	0.936	6.976	3.685	0.941

5. Illustrative Examples

In this section, we consider three examples to illustrate the Gibbs sampler procedure described in Section 3. These examples exhibit the parameter estimation in randomly right, Type-II, and progressively Type-II-censored data.

Example 01 (Cancer Patients Data): This data set was originally presented in [25] and consists of lifetimes (in months) of 20 cancer patients who received a new treatment. The complete lifetime of only 17 cancer patients was recorded and the rest of the three patients were right-censored and denoted by "+" in the following data set.

3	5	6	7	8	9	10	10^{+}	12	15
15^{+}	18	19	20	22	25	28	30	40	45^{+}

The Kolmogorov–Smirnov goodness-of-fit test indicates that these data adequately follow a BS distribution, and its MLEs are $\hat{\alpha}_{MLE} = 0.805$ and $\hat{\beta}_{MLE} = 14.899$. For these data, $\bar{T}$ represents the average remaining lifetime for each of three patients censored during the experiment until they die. With only three observations out of 20 being censored, the number of iteration $k = 2000$ was found to be sufficient to ensure the convergence, and m = 10,000 Gibbs sample chains were used for the parameter estimation. The resulting estimates are shown in Table 5.

In addition, in the lower portion of Table 5, we report both point and interval estimates obtained in [25] Bayesian work (A-M 2010) and also the [18]'s Bayesian and MLE results (S-N MLE and S-N Bayesian), where they applied a generalized Birnbaum–Saunders distribution for the same data.

Table 5. Parameter estimates on cancer data.

Parameter	α			β			$\bar{T}$	
	PE	95% CI	Width	PE	95% CI	Width	PE	95% CI
Jeffrey's	0.849	(0.603, 1.211)	0.608	15.335	(10.481, 22.127)	11.646	18.560	(3.113, 53.284)
Achcar's	0.874	(0.614, 1.284)	0.670	15.393	(10.376, 22.648)	12.272	19.393	(3.076, 59.307)
S-N MLE (2017)	0.974	(0.127, 1.821)	1.693	15.629	(9.614, 21.644)	12.030		
S-N Bayesian (2017)	0.962	(0.604, 1.510)	0.907	15.411	(10.489, 21.696)	11.207		
A-M (2010)	0.885	(0.610, 1.295)	0.685	16.030	(10.930, 24.360)	13.430		

We note that both the initial MLEs, $\hat{\alpha}_{MLE} = 0.805$ and $\hat{\beta}_{MLE} = 14.899$, fall well within all the corresponding 95% credible interval bounds (see Table 5). Both Jeffre's and Achcar's estimates compare favorably to one another. Lengths of the credible intervals are somewhat narrower for α when compared to the [18,25] results. The estimated average remaining lifetime for the censored patients ranges from 18 to 20 months after their observation period was completed.

Example 02 (Fatigue Life): This example consists of the fatigue life of 6061-T6 aluminum coupons cut parallel to the direction of rolling and oscillated at 18 cycles per second, with a maximum stress per cycle of 31,000 psi reported in [8]. We reconfirmed that these data can be adequately modeled using the BS distribution, and the MLEs for complete data are $\hat{\alpha} = 0.170$ and $\hat{\beta} = 131.819$.

70	90	96	97	99	100	103	104	104	105	107	108	108	108	109
109	112	112	113	114	114	114	116	119	120	120	120	121	121	123
124	124	124	124	124	128	128	129	129	130	130	130	131	131	131
131	131	132	132	132	133	134	134	134	134	134	136	136	137	138
138	138	139	139	141	141	142	142	142	142	142	142	144	144	145
146	148	148	149	151	151	152	155	156	157	157	157	157	158	159
162	163	163	164	166	166	168	170	174	196	212				

We applied the Type-II right-censoring scheme with censoring percentages (CEP) at 10%(10%)60% for these data, and the estimated MLEs at different censoring levels are shown in Table 6. Due to the relatively larger β and sample size, first, we transform these data using the scale transformation $t/\hat{\beta}$ suggested in Section 2.2 and adjust the MLEs accordingly to be used in the Gibbs sampler. We observed that the Gibbs sampler adequately converged with $k = 2000$ iterations and obtained m = 10,000 Gibbs sample chains to obtain estimates.

Also, Figure 1 shows the kernel density estimates of the parameters for Jeffrey's and Achcar's priors at 10%, 30%, and 60% censoring levels. The plots seem adequate and both methods seem to provide very similar estimates. However, as [26] indicated, the Gibbs output may not detect improper posteriors; the scale transformation we suggested should have scaled-down β to prevent such possible divergences.

The resulting point estimates along with the widths of the 95% credible intervals for both the priors are reported in Table 7. Interestingly, both $\hat{\alpha}$ and $\hat{\beta}$ estimates for both the methods for lower to mid-censoring percentages 10%, 20%, and 30% are very close to their uncensored MLEs for complete data ($\hat{\alpha} = 0.170$ and $\hat{\beta} = 131.819$). However, when censoring percentage increases, both $\hat{\alpha}$ and $\hat{\beta}$ overestimate the true values. As expected, the average remaining time $\bar{T}$ is also increased with respect to the censoring percentages. It is also noted that all six $\bar{T}$ estimates overestimated the true average remaining time; the increments are proportional to the true values for increasing the censoring percentages reported in Table 6.

Table 6. Initial Parameter estimates on Type-II-censored fatigue life data.

CEP	0.1	0.2	0.3	0.4	0.5	0.6
$\hat{\alpha}^{(0)}_{MLE}$	0.169	0.174	0.172	0.182	0.184	0.210
$\hat{\beta}^{(0)}_{MLE}$	131.489	131.900	131.804	132.940	133.225	137.270
True $\bar{T}$	10.20	11.55	15.00	14.85	17.28	16.25

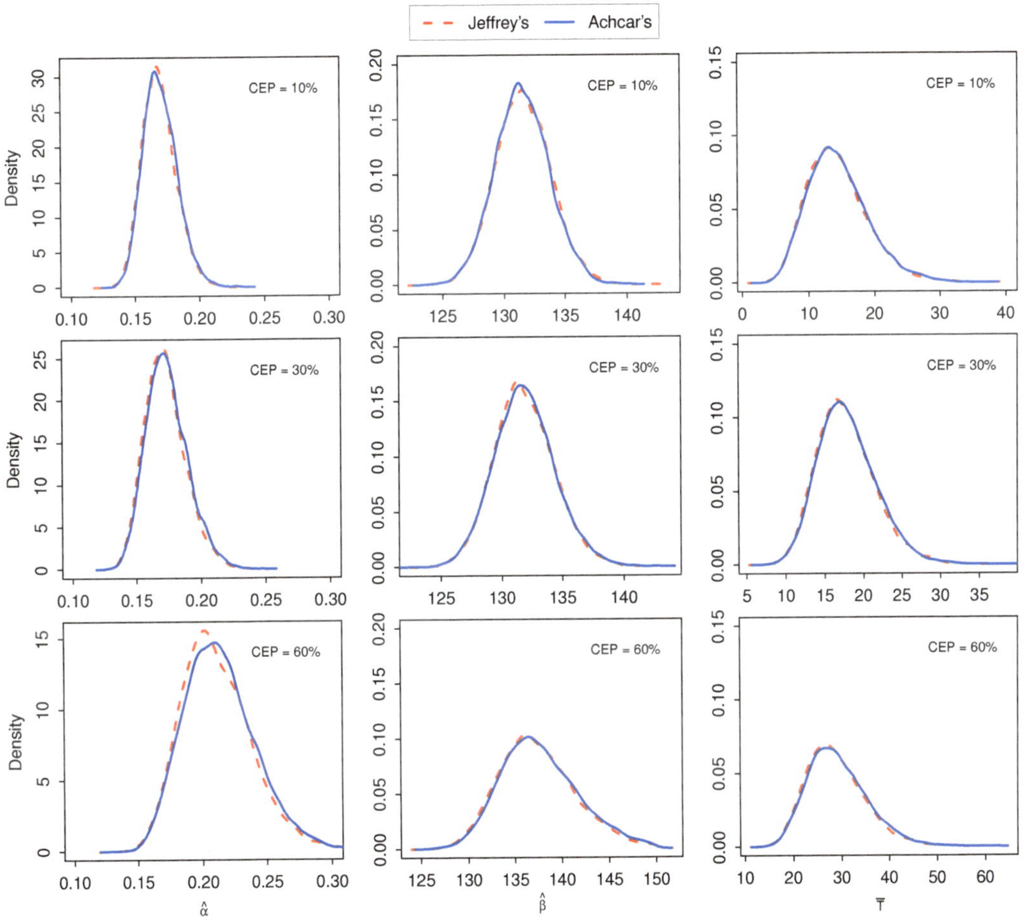

Figure 1. Kernel density estimates of Achcar's and Jeffrey's priors for censored fatigue life data. Top panel, middle, and bottom panels are for 10%, 30%, and 60% censoring schemes, respectively.

Table 7. Point estimates ($\hat{\alpha}$, $\hat{\beta}$, and $\bar{T}$) and widths of the corresponding credible intervals for different censoring percentages.

		Jeffrey's		Achcar's	
DOC%	**Param**	**PE**	**Width**	**PE**	**Width**
10	α	0.169	0.051	0.170	0.051
	β	131.582	8.926	131.501	8.796
	$\bar{T}$	14.348	17.628	14.519	18.105
20	α	0.174	0.058	0.175	0.058
	β	131.900	9.386	131.994	9.356
	$\bar{T}$	16.318	15.297	16.421	15.277
30	α	0.172	0.063	0.174	0.063
	β	131.830	9.601	131.883	9.876
	$\bar{T}$	17.759	14.654	17.951	14.705
40	α	0.182	0.072	0.184	0.074
	β	132.993	10.921	133.101	11.091
	$\bar{T}$	20.405	16.228	20.691	16.533
50	α	0.185	0.082	0.187	0.082
	β	133.276	12.267	133.469	12.271
	$\bar{T}$	22.541	17.959	22.881	18.037
60	α	0.211	0.106	0.214	0.108
	β	137.281	15.897	137.569	16.052
	$\bar{T}$	28.768	23.985	29.227	24.213

Example 03 (Ball Bearings' Data): This data set was originally presented in [27] and provides the fatigue life in hours of ten ball bearings of a certain type:

152.7	172.0	172.5	173.3	193.0	204.7	216.5	234.9	262.6	422.6

Ref. [9] used the full data set and fitted BS distribution and reported that unbiased MLEs of α and β are 0.314 and 211.528, respectively. Ref. [20] used these data to generate three different progressively Type-II-censored samples and estimated BS parameters. We use somewhat similar progressively Type-II-censored samples, as shown below.

- Scheme I: $n = 10, m = 6, R_1 = 4, R_2 = \cdots = R_6 = 0$;
- Scheme II: $n = 10, m = 6, R_1 = 0, R_2 = 2, R_3 = R_4 = R_5 = 0, R_6 = 2$.

The resulting parameter estimates, along with their 95% credible intervals, are reported in Table 8. Due to censoring in this small dataset, both Bayesian priors underestimate the unbiased MLEs. However, the credible intervals adequately capture these values. Achcar's estimates become slightly better, as they are closer to the unbiased MLEs obtained from the complete data. This example indicates that the suggested method can be used effectively even for small datasets, yielding decent results.

Table 8. Parameter estimates on Type-II progressively censored ball bearings' data.

Parameter	α		β		$\bar{T}$	
	PE	95% CI	PE	95% CI	PE	95% CI
			Scheme–I			
Jeffrey's	0.182	(0.107, 0.327)	201.939	(175.660, 236.367)	57.921	(21.599, 116.568)
Achcar's	0.199	(0.113, 0.368)	201.993	(174.342, 236.251)	60.627	(21.944, 126.152)
			Scheme–II			
Jeffrey's	0.173	(0.095, 0.337)	201.058	(178.361, 233.527)	36.467	(9.779, 94.211)
Achcar's	0.195	(0.102, 0.400)	201.686	(177.561, 235.060)	41.159	(10.182, 109.039)

6. Conclusions

This study reveals that the suggested Gibbs sampler performs reasonably well with both Bayesian priors. Achcar's priors appear to provide better coverage probability than Jeffrey's prior in the considered cases of this simulation study. Additionally, Achcar's priors tend to slightly overestimate the true parameter value, while Jeffrey's tends to underestimate it. The amount of censoring and sample size has an impact on the performance of both methods, and therefore, one should be aware of this limitation in practice. With an increase in sample size, all methods perform better, although the amount of censoring seems to slightly affect the estimates. Care must be taken regarding the size of the β parameter and the sample size when applying non-informative priors. The suggested scale transformation may need to be adopted to guarantee proper posteriors when using Achcar's reference prior. Also, because the marginal posterior distributions relied on the Laplace approximation, there may be limitations on estimating the average lifetime because the BS density $T \sim BS(\hat{\alpha}, \hat{\beta})$ is an approximation to its true underlying distribution. However, this study reveals that the Gibbs sampler is capable enough to provide accurate remaining average lifetime estimates.

The simulation results indicate that the method considered shows some improvements with regards to point estimates and coverage probabilities when compared to [15] Bayesian results. In particular, our algorithm shows no substantial effect on the coverage probability by the amount of censoring. Also, the posterior distributions discussed here have tractable closed forms that require no partial or hyper-prior information. Also, our results are consistent with regards to the bias and coverage probability for all parameter combinations we considered; this shows a clear improvement when compared to the simulation results shown in [18].

With the Gibbs sampler, there is less restriction on the type of prior distribution that can be chosen. However, caution must be exercised in programming to ensure the well-behaved nature of both prior and posterior distributions. If posterior distributions, whether conditional or otherwise, cannot be precisely determined, asymptotic distributions may be employed. The Gibbs sampler procedures offer a high degree of flexibility in implementation, allowing the adjustment of the number of iterations based on the trade-off between the speed and desired accuracy. Undoubtedly, the Gibbs sampler finds its place in developing complex models, particularly when dealing with censored data. Its computation involves a series of calculations that are easy to understand, and its implementation is relatively straightforward.

Supplementary Materials: The following supporting information can be downloaded at: https://www.mdpi.com/article/10.3390/math12060874/s1. Supplementary File: "R code for Fatigue Life data Analysis.R".

Funding: This research received no external funding.

Data Availability Statement: Data are contained within the article and supplementary materials.

Conflicts of Interest: The authors declare no conflicts of interest.

Appendix A

The Laplace's method for integrals provides an approximate to the integral of the form

$$I = \int f(\theta) \exp\{-nh(\theta)\} d\theta,$$

where $-h$ is a smooth function of θ, having its maximum at $\hat{\theta}$. Then, the Laplace's approximate for integral I becomes

$$\hat{I} \approx \sqrt{\frac{2\pi}{n}} \sigma f(\hat{\theta}) \exp\{-nh(\hat{\theta})\},$$

where $\sigma = 1/\sqrt{h''(\hat{\theta})}$.

Now, as outlined in [14], assuming Jeffrey's prior, the joint posterior distribution of α and β becomes

$$\pi(\alpha, \beta|\mathbf{T}) \propto \frac{\prod_{i=1}^{n}(\beta + t_i)\exp\{-Q(\beta)/\alpha^2\}}{\alpha^{n+1}\beta^{(n/2)+1}H(\alpha^2)}, \tag{A1}$$

where $Q(\beta) = \frac{ns}{2\beta} + \frac{n\beta}{2q} - n$ and $H(\alpha^2) = \left(\frac{1}{\alpha^2} + \frac{1}{4}\right)$.

For Achcar's prior $\pi(\alpha, \beta)$, $H(\alpha^2) = 1$ and the marginal posterior of α can be written as

$$\pi(\alpha|\mathbf{T}) \propto \frac{\exp\{n/\alpha^2\}}{\alpha^{n+1}} \int_0^\infty f(\beta)\exp\{-nh(\beta)\}d\beta, \tag{A2}$$

where $f(\beta) = \frac{\prod_{i=1}^{n}(\beta+t_i)}{\beta^{(n/2)+1}}$ and $h(\beta) = \frac{s}{2\beta\alpha^2} + \frac{\beta}{2q\alpha^2}$. The maximum of the $-h(\beta)$ occurs at $\hat{\beta} = \sqrt{sq}$ and therefore, $h(\hat{\beta}) = \frac{\sqrt{s/q}}{\alpha^2}$ and $h''(\hat{\beta}) = \frac{1}{\alpha^2 q\sqrt{sq}}$.

Then, using the Laplace approximation, the integral $I(\alpha) = \int_0^\infty f(\beta)\exp\{-nh(\beta)\}d\beta$ can be approximated by

$$\hat{I}(\alpha) \approx \sqrt{\frac{2\pi}{n}}\alpha\sqrt{q\sqrt{sq}}\left[\frac{\prod_{i=1}^{n}(\sqrt{sq} + t_i)}{(sq)^{n/4+1/2}}\right]\exp\left\{-\frac{n\sqrt{s/q}}{\alpha^2}\right\}$$

By neglecting all but α terms in $\hat{I}(\alpha)$, the approximate marginal posterior distribution of α becomes

$$\pi(\alpha|\mathbf{T}) \propto \alpha^{-n}\exp\left\{-\frac{n}{\alpha^2}(\sqrt{s/q} - 1)\right\}, \alpha > 0, \tag{A3}$$

To obtain the marginal posterior of the β, we integrate α in the joint posterior in Equation (A1).

$$\pi(\beta|\mathbf{T}) \propto \frac{\prod_{i=1}^{n}(\beta + t_i)}{\beta^{(n/2)+1}} \int_0^\infty \frac{\exp\{-Q(\beta)/\alpha^2\}}{\alpha^{n+1}} d\alpha, \tag{A4}$$

$$\propto \frac{\prod_{i=1}^{n}(\beta + t_i)}{\beta^{(n/2)+1}} \frac{\Gamma(n/2)}{2[(Q(\beta)]^{n/2}}, \tag{A5}$$

$$\propto \frac{\prod_{i=1}^{n}(\beta + t_i)}{\beta^{(n/2)+1}\{s/(2\beta) + \beta/(2q) - 1\}^{n/2}}, \beta > 0 \tag{A6}$$

Using similar arguments, Jeffrey's prior-based marginal posteriors given in Equations (8) and (9) can be obtained.

References

1. Birnbaum, Z.W.; Saunders, S.C. A new family of life distributions. *J. Appl. Probab.* **1969**, *6*, 319–327. [CrossRef]
2. Balakrishnan, N.; Kundu, D. Birnbaum-Saunders distribution: A review of models, analysis, and applications. *Appl. Stoch. Model. Bus. Ind.* **2019**, *35*, 4–49.
3. Desmond, A.F. On the relationship between two fatigue-life models. *IEEE Trans. Reliab.* **1986**, *35*, 167–169. [CrossRef]
4. Bhattacharyya, G.; Fries, A. Fatigue Failure Models—Birnbaum-Saunders vs. Inverse Gaussian. *IEEE Trans. Reliab.* **1982**, *31*, 439–441. [CrossRef]
5. Owen, W.J.; Ng, H.K.T. Revisit of relationships and models for the Birnbaum-Saunders and inverse-Gaussian distributions. *J. Stat. Distrib. Appl.* **2015**, *2*, 11.
6. Ng, H.K.T. Discussion of "Birnbaum-Saunders distribution: A review of models, analysis, and applications". *Appl. Stoch. Model. Bus. Ind.* **2019**, *35*, 64–71. [CrossRef]
7. Saunders, S.C. A family of random variables closed under reciprocation. *J. Am. Stat. Assoc.* **1974**, *69*, 533–539. [CrossRef]
8. Birnbaum, Z.W.; Saunders, S.C. Estimation for a family of life distributions with applications to fatigue. *J. Appl. Probab.* **1969**, *6*, 328–347. [CrossRef]
9. Ng, H.; Kundu, D.; Balakrishnan, N. Modified moment estimation for the two-parameter Birnbaum–Saunders distribution. *Comput. Stat. Data Anal.* **2003**, *43*, 283–298. [CrossRef]
10. Balakrishnan, N.; Zhu, X. An improved method of estimation for the parameters of the Birnbaum–Saunders distribution. *J. Stat. Comput. Simul.* **2014**, *84*, 2285–2294. [CrossRef]

11. Ng, H.; Kundu, D.; Balakrishnan, N. Point and interval estimation for the two-parameter Birnbaum–Saunders distribution based on Type-II censored samples. *Comput. Stat. Data Anal.* **2006**, *50*, 3222–3242. [CrossRef]
12. Wang, Z.; Desmond, A.F.; Lu, X. Modified censored moment estimation for the two-parameter Birnbaum–Saunders distribution. *Comput. Stat. Data Anal.* **2006**, *50*, 1033–1051. [CrossRef]
13. Jayalath, K.P. Fiducial Inference on the Right Censored Birnbaum–Saunders Data via Gibbs Sampler. *Stats* **2021**, *4*, 385–399. [CrossRef]
14. Achcar, J.A. Inferences for the Birnbaum—Saunders fatigue life model using Bayesian methods. *Comput. Stat. Data Anal.* **1993**, *15*, 367–380. [CrossRef]
15. Xu, A.; Tang, Y. Reference analysis for Birnbaum–Saunders distribution. *Comput. Stat. Data Anal.* **2010**, *54*, 185–192. [CrossRef]
16. Xu, A.; Tang, Y. Bayesian analysis of Birnbaum–Saunders distribution with partial information. *Comput. Stat. Data Anal.* **2011**, *55*, 2324–2333. [CrossRef]
17. Wang, M.; Sun, X.; Park, C. Bayesian analysis of Birnbaum–Saunders distribution via the generalized ratio-of-uniforms method. *Comput. Stat.* **2016**, *31*, 207–225. [CrossRef]
18. Sha, N.; Ng, T.L. Bayesian inference for Birnbaum–Saunders distribution and its generalization. *J. Stat. Comput. Simul.* **2017**, *87*, 2411–2429. [CrossRef]
19. Balakrishnan, N.; Cramer, E. The art of progressive censoring. In *Statistics for Industry and Technology*; Springer: Berlin/Heidelberg, Germany, 2014.
20. Pradhan, B.; Kundu, D. Inference and optimal censoring schemes for progressively censored Birnbaum–Saunders distribution. *J. Stat. Plan. Inference* **2013**, *143*, 1098–1108. [CrossRef]
21. Delignette-Muller, M.; Dutang, C. An R Package for Fitting Distributions.*J. Stat. Softw.* **2015**, *61*, 1–34.
22. R Core Team. *R: A Language and Environment for Statistical Computing;* R Foundation for Statistical Computing: Vienna, Austria, 2019.
23. Brooks, S.P.; Gelman, A. General methods for monitoring convergence of iterative simulations. *J. Comput. Graph. Stat.* **1998**, *7*, 434–455.
24. Gelman, A.; Carlin, J.B.; Stern, H.S.; Dunson, D.B.; Vehtari, A.; Rubin, D.B. *Bayesian Data Analysis*; Chapman and Hall/CRC: Boca Raton, FL, USA, 2013.
25. Achcar, J.A.; Moala, F.A. Use of MCMC methods to obtain Bayesian inferences for the Birnbaum-Saunders distribution in the presence of censored data and covariates. *Adv. Appl. Stat.* **2010**, *17*, 1–27.
26. Hobert, J.P.; Casella, G. The effect of improper priors on Gibbs sampling in hierarchical linear mixed models. *J. Am. Stat. Assoc.* **1996**, *91*, 1461–1473.
27. McCool, J. *Inferential Techniques for Weibull Populations. Aerospace Research Laboratories Report*; Technical Report, ARL TR 74-0180; Wright-Patterson AFB: Fairborn, OH, USA, 1974.

mathematics

MDPI

Article

General Mean-Field BDSDEs with Stochastic Linear Growth and Discontinuous Generator

Yufeng Shi and Jinghan Wang *

Institute for Financial Studies, Shandong University, Jinan 250100, China; yfshi@sdu.edu.cn
* Correspondence: wangjinghan@mail.sdu.edu.cn

Abstract: In this paper, we consider the general mean-field backward doubly stochastic differential equations (mean-field BDSDEs) whose generator f can be discontinuous in y. We prove the existence theorem of solutions under stochastic linear growth conditions and also obtain the related comparison theorem. Naturally, we present those results under the linear growth condition, which is a special case of the stochastic condition. Finally, a financial claim sale problem is discussed, which demonstrates the application of the general mean-field BDSDEs in finance.

Keywords: backward doubly stochastic differential equations; mean-field; Wasserstein metric; discontinuous; stochastic linear growth

MSC: 60H10

1. Introduction

It is well known that backward stochastic differential equations (BSDEs) can be regarded as a class of stochastic differential equations (SDEs) with a given terminal condition (not an initial condition). In 1990, Pardoux and Peng [1] published a famous article and studied nonlinear BSDEs for the first time,

$$Y_t = \xi + \int_t^T f(s, Y_s, Z_s)ds - \int_t^T Z_s dW_s. \tag{1}$$

In the past 30 years, research on nonlinear BSDEs has developed rapidly. Many scholars have discovered that this theory has important applications in many fields, such as mathematical finance, stochastic control, partial differential equations (PDEs), and so on. Afterward, Pardoux and Peng [2] proposed backward doubly stochastic differential equations (BDSDEs),

$$Y_t = \xi + \int_t^T f(s, Y_s, Z_s)ds + \int_t^T g(s, Y_s, Z_s)d\overleftarrow{B}_s - \int_t^T Z_s dW_s, \tag{2}$$

which contain two random integrals in opposite directions, leading to two opposite information flows, and thus have more complex measurability. Then. Shi, Gu, and Liu [3] proved the comparison theorem of BDSDEs. Recently, Owo [4–6] generalized these results under a series of stochastic conditions, including the existence and uniqueness theorem of solution for BDSDEs with stochastic Lipschitz generator, the existence theorem of solutions under stochastic linear growth and continuous or discontinuous conditions, and he also proved the associated comparison theorems. Inspired by this literature, in this paper, we study a new class of BDSDEs called general mean-field BDSDEs to obtain the corresponding results, and the equation's form is as follows:

$$Y_t = \xi + \int_t^T f(s, P_{Y_s}, Y_s, Z_s)ds + \int_t^T g(s, Y_s, Z_s)d\overleftarrow{B}_s - \int_t^T Z_s dW_s, \tag{3}$$

where the coefficients of BDSDEs depend not only on the solution processes but also on the law of the solution processes, which acts as the mean-field term.

Mean-field theory is also a hot research topic that has infiltrated various fields, such as statistical mechanics, physics, economics, finance, and so on. In 2007, Lasry and Lions [7] formally proposed the concept of mean-field games, which studied the problem of stochastic differential games with N particles and the limit behavior of random moving particles when N goes to infinity. Inspired by this idea, Buckdahn, Djehiche, Li, Peng [8] and Buckdahn, Li, Peng [9] used purely random methods to investigate a special class of mean-field problems, and proposed a new type of BSDEs, called mean-field BSDEs. Since then, more and more scholars have devoted their energies to the study of mean-field problems (see [10,11], etc.). Li, Liang and Zhang [12] studied mean-field BSDEs under continuous conditions and proposed a technical lemma by which the existence of solutions was obtained. Wang, Zhao and Shi [13] extended this result to discontinuous conditions. In recent years, Li and Xing [14] combined the results of BDSDEs and mean-field theory, and investigated the existence of a solution for general mean-field BDSDEs with continuous coefficients. Furthermore, Shi, Wang and Zhao [15] obtained the related results of the general mean-field BDSDEs under stochastic linear growth and continuous conditions.

It is worth emphasizing that the theory of mean-field is new, and there are still many conclusions to explore. On the one hand, the ordinary continuous condition or linear growth condition cannot be satisfied in many applications, which the example in Section 4 can reflect: Consider a financial claim with a contingent ξ and there is an investor who has additional information not detected in the financial market and wants to sell the claim. Moreover, suppose that the interest rate is applied only to portfolios whose value remains above a nominal value at any time. This problem is equivalent to solving the following mean-field BDSDE:

$$Y_t = \xi + \int_t^T (\theta(s)e^{-\frac{\beta A(s)}{2}} E[Y_s] + \mu(s)Y_s I_{\{Y_s>1\}} + \gamma(s)Z_s)ds + \int_t^T c(s)Z_s d\overleftarrow{B}_s - \int_t^T Z_s dW_s. \tag{4}$$

Since $f(t,p,y,z) = \theta(t)e^{-\frac{\beta A(t)}{2}} E[y] + r(t)yI_{\{y>1\}} + \gamma(t)z$ is not continuous in y, we cannot apply the existence result in [15]. Therefore, we relax the restriction on the generator $f(t,p,y,z)$ that f is discontinuous in y, continuous in p and z, and we solve the above problem, shown in Section 4. On the other hand, mean field theory is a useful tool when we study problems related to large numbers of particles. Because when the number of particles N tends to infinity, it is impractical to deal with the behavior of each particle, but through the mean-field term, we only need to pay attention to the limited behavior of randomly moving particles when N tends to infinity. In conclusion, it is meaningful to study the general mean-field BDSDE (3) with discontinuous and stochastic linear growth coefficients, which can solve some problems in physics, finance and so on.

Our paper is organized as follows: In Section 2, we give some preliminary results of general mean-field BDSDEs which are needed in what follows, and we also list some existing results related to our paper. Section 3 is devoted to giving the main results, including the existence theorem of solutions and the related comparison theorem under stochastic linear growth and discontinuous conditions. Then, we naturally introduce the existence theorem of solutions under linear growth conditions, which is a special case of stochastic conditions, and we also propose the associated comparison theorem. In Section 4, we study the application of the general mean-field BDSDEs to the financial claim sales problem. Finally, we conclude in Section 5.

2. Preliminaries

Now, we begin with introducing some necessary notations and concepts.

Let $(\Omega, \mathcal{F}, P)$ be a complete probability space, that is, all subsets of zero probability sets belong to $\mathcal{F}$, and let $T > 0$ be an arbitrarily fixed time horizon throughout this paper. Let $\{W_t; 0 \le t \le T\}$ and $\{B_t; 0 \le t \le T\}$ be two mutually independent standard Brownian Motions with values respectively in $\mathbb{R}^d$ and $\mathbb{R}^\ell$, defined on $(\Omega, \mathcal{F}, P)$. Let $\mathcal{N}$ denote the class of P-null sets of $\mathcal{F}$, and $\mathcal{P}_2(\mathbb{R}^k)$ denotes the set of the probability measures p over $(\mathbb{R}^k, \mathcal{B}(\mathbb{R}^k))$ with a finite second moment, that is, $\int_{\mathbb{R}^k} |x|^2 p(dx) < \infty$. Here, $\mathcal{B}(\mathbb{R}^k)$ denotes the Borel σ-field over $\mathbb{R}^k$, and the probability space $(\Omega, \mathcal{F}, P)$ needs to be rich, so we assume that there is a sub-σ-field $\mathcal{F}^0$, $\mathcal{N} \subset \mathcal{F}^0 \subset \mathcal{F}$, such that

(i) Brownian motion (B, W) is independent of $\mathcal{F}^0$;
(ii) $\mathcal{F}^0$ is 'rich enough', that is, for every $p \in \mathcal{P}_2(\mathbb{R}^k)$ there is a random variable $\xi \in L^2(\Omega, \mathcal{F}^0, P; \mathbb{R}^k)$ such that $P_\xi = p$.

Besides, $\{a(t)\}_{t\in[0,T]}$ is a jointly measurable process with positive values and square-integrable in $[0,T]$, and we define an increasing process $\{A(t)\}_{t\in[0,T]}$ by setting $A(t) = \int_0^t a^2(s)ds$. Every β that appears throughout this paper must satisfy $\beta > 0$ and be big enough. Here, are the following spaces:

- $L^{2,\beta}(\Omega, \mathcal{F}_t, P; \mathbb{R}^k) := \Big\{\mathbb{R}^k$-value $\mathcal{F}_t$-measurable random variables $\xi : \|\xi\|^2_{L^{2,\beta}} := E[e^{\beta A(t)}|\xi|^2] < +\infty\Big\}$;
- $\mathcal{H}^{2,\beta}(0,T;\mathbb{R}^k) := \Big\{\mathbb{R}^k$-value processes $\zeta :$ for any $t \in [0,T], \zeta(t)$ is $\mathcal{F}_t$-measurable with $\|\zeta\|^2_{\mathcal{H}^{2,\beta}} := E[\int_0^T e^{\beta A(t)}|\zeta(t)|^2 \mathrm{d}t] < +\infty\Big\}$;
- $\mathcal{H}^{2,\beta,a}(0,T;\mathbb{R}^k) := \Big\{\mathbb{R}^k$-value processes $\zeta :$ for any $t \in [0,T], \zeta(t)$ is $\mathcal{F}_t$-measurable with $\|a\zeta\|^2_{\mathcal{H}^{2,\beta}} := E[\int_0^T e^{\beta A(t)} a^2(t)|\zeta(t)|^2 \mathrm{d}t] < +\infty\Big\}$;
- $\mathcal{S}^{2,\beta}(0,T;\mathbb{R}^k) := \Big\{\mathbb{R}^k$-value continuous processes $\zeta :$ for any $t \in [0,T], \zeta(t)$ is $\mathcal{F}_t$-measurable with $\|\zeta\|^2_{\mathcal{S}^{2,\beta}} := E[\sup_{0\le t\le T} e^{\beta A(t)}|\zeta(t)|^2] < +\infty\Big\}$.

Note, that the space $\mathcal{H}^{2,\beta}(0,T;\mathbb{R}^k)$ with the norm $\|\cdot\|_{\mathcal{H}^{2,\beta}}$ is a Banach space, so is the space

$$\mathcal{M}^{2,\beta}(0,T) := \Big(\mathcal{H}^{2,\beta,a}(0,T;\mathbb{R}^k) \cap \mathcal{S}^{2,\beta}(0,T;\mathbb{R}^k)\Big) \times \mathcal{H}^{2,\beta}(0,T;\mathbb{R}^{k\times d}),$$

with the norm $\|(Y,Z)\|^2_{\mathcal{M}^{2,\beta}} = \|aY\|^2_{\mathcal{H}^{2,\beta}} + \|Y\|_{\mathcal{S}^{2,\beta}} + \|Z\|^2_{\mathcal{H}^{2,\beta}}$.

Now, let us consider the following general mean-field BDSDEs: for all $t \in [0,T]$, given $\xi \in L^{2,\beta}(\Omega, \mathcal{F}_T, P; \mathbb{R}^k)$,

$$Y_t = \xi + \int_t^T f(s, P_{Y_s}, Y_s, Z_s)\mathrm{d}s + \int_t^T g(s, Y_s, Z_s)\mathrm{d}\overleftarrow{B}_s - \int_t^T Z_s \mathrm{d}W_s. \tag{5}$$

Without loss of generality, in this paper, we consider the case of $k = 1$. Before discussing the main results of this paper, we will introduce some previous results of general mean-field BDSDEs under some stochastic conditions. Let, coefficients $f : [0,T] \times \Omega \times \mathcal{P}_2(\mathbb{R}) \times \mathbb{R} \times \mathbb{R}^d \to \mathbb{R}$, $g : [0,T] \times \Omega \times \mathbb{R} \times \mathbb{R}^d \to \mathbb{R}^\ell$ be jointly measurable and satisfy the following assumptions:

(A1) g is stochastic Lipschitz in $(y,z) \in \mathbb{R} \times \mathbb{R}^d$: There exists a non-negative $\mathcal{F}_t^W$-measurable process $\{v(t)\}_{t\in[0,T]}$ and a constant $\alpha, 0 < \alpha < 1$, such that for all $y_1, y_2 \in \mathbb{R}, z_1, z_2 \in \mathbb{R}^d$,

$$|g(t,y_1,z_1) - g(t,y_2,z_2)|^2 \le v(t)|y_1 - y_2|^2 + \alpha|z_1 - z_2|^2;$$

(A2) f is stochastic Lipschitz in $(p,y,z) \in \mathcal{P}_2(\mathbb{R}) \times \mathbb{R} \times \mathbb{R}^d$: There exist non-negative $\mathcal{F}_t^W$-measurable processes $\{\theta(t)\}_{t\in[0,T]}$, $\{\mu(t)\}_{t\in[0,T]}$ and $\{\gamma(t)\}_{t\in[0,T]}$ such that for all $p_1, p_2 \in \mathcal{P}_2(\mathbb{R}), y_1, y_2 \in \mathbb{R}, z_1, z_2 \in \mathbb{R}^d$,

$$|f(t,p_1,y_1,z_1) - f(t,p_2,y_2,z_2)| \le \theta(t)e^{-\frac{\beta A(t)}{2}} W_2(p_1,p_2) + \mu(t)|y_1 - y_2| + \gamma(t)|z_1 - z_2|;$$

(A3) For all $t \in [0,T]$, there exists a positive process $\{a(t)\}_{t\in[0,T]}$, which satisfies $a(t)^2 = \theta(t)^2 + \mu(t) + \gamma(t)^2 + \nu(t) \geq \iota > 0$ and the definitions of $\theta(t), \mu(t), \gamma(t)$ and $\nu(t)$ are same as those in assumptions (A1) and (A2). $A(t) = \int_0^t a(s)^2 ds < \infty$;

(A4) For any $(t,\mu,y,z) \in [0,T] \times \mathcal{P}_2(\mathbb{R}) \times \mathbb{R} \times \mathbb{R}^d$, there is

$$E[\int_0^T e^{\beta A(t)} \frac{|f(t,\delta_0,0,0)|^2}{a(t)^2} dt + \int_0^T e^{\beta A(t)} |g(t,0,0)|^2 dt] < +\infty,$$

where δ_0 denotes throughout the paper, the Dirac measure with mass at $0 \in \mathbb{R}$;

(A5) For any $\theta_1, \theta_2 \in L^2(\Omega, \mathcal{F}_t, P; \mathbb{R})$ and $(t,y,z) \in [0,T] \times \mathbb{R} \times \mathbb{R}^d$, there exists a non-negative $\mathcal{F}_t^W$ -measurable process $\{L(t)\}_{t\in[0,T]}$ such that

$$f(t,P_{\theta_1},y,z) - f(t,P_{\theta_2},y,z) \leq L(t) e^{-\frac{\beta A(t)}{2}} (E[|(\theta_1-\theta_2)^+|^2])^{\frac{1}{2}},$$

where $L(t)^2 \leq a(t)^2$, for all $t \in [0,T]$;

(A6) For almost every $(t,\omega) \in [0,T] \times \Omega$, $f(t,\omega,\cdot,\cdot,\cdot)$ is continuous, especially, with a continuity modulus $\rho : \mathbb{R}^+ \to \mathbb{R}^+$ with respect to p, for all $p_1, p_2 \in \mathcal{P}_2(\mathbb{R})$,$(y,z) \in \mathbb{R} \times \mathbb{R}^d$,

$$|f(t,\omega,p_1,y,z) - f(t,\omega,p_2,y,z)| \leq \rho(W_2(p_1,p_2));$$

(A7) There exist non-negative $\mathcal{F}_t^W$-measurable processes $\{\theta(t)\}_{t\in[0,T]}$, $\{\mu(t)\}_{t\in[0,T]}$, $\{\gamma(t)\}_{t\in[0,T]}$ and a non-negative $\mathcal{F}_t$-measurable process $\{\phi(t)\}_{t\in[0,T]}$ satisfying $E[\int_t^T e^{\beta A(s)} \phi(s)^2 ds] < \infty$, such that for all $p \in \mathcal{P}_2(\mathbb{R}), y \in \mathbb{R}, z \in \mathbb{R}^d$,

$$|f(t,p,y,z)| \leq \phi(t) + \theta(t) e^{-\frac{\beta A(t)}{2}} W_2(p,\delta_0) + \mu(t)|y| + \gamma(t)|z|;$$

(A8) Monotonicity in p : For all $\theta_1, \theta_2 \in L^2(\Omega, \mathcal{F}_t, P; \mathbb{R})$, and all $(y,z) \in \mathbb{R} \times \mathbb{R}^d$, when $\theta_1 \leq \theta_2$, P-a.s., we have

$$f(t,P_{\theta_1},y,z) \leq f(t,P_{\theta_2},y,z), \text{dtd}P\text{-a.e.}$$

Lemma 1 (Existence and Uniqueness). *Under the assumptions (A1)–(A4), the general mean-field BDSDE (5) has a unique solution* $(Y,Z) \in \mathcal{M}^{2,\beta}(0,T)$.

Lemma 2 (Comparison theorem). *Let* $g = g(t,\omega,y,z)$ *satisfy the assumptions (A1) and (A4), and* $f^{(i)} = f^{(i)}(t,\omega,p,y,z), i = 1,2$ *be two generators satisfying (A4). Moreover, we assume that*
(i) One of $f^{(i)}$ *satisfies the assumption (A2);*
(ii) One of $f^{(i)}$ *satisfies the assumption (A5).*

Denote by $(Y^{(1)},Z^{(1)})$ *and* $(Y^{(2)},Z^{(2)})$ *the solutions of the general mean-field BDSDE (5) with data* $(\xi^{(1)}, f^{(1)}, g)$ *and* $(\xi^{(2)}, f^{(2)}, g)$, *respectively. Then, if for all* $(p,y,z) \in \mathcal{P}_2(\mathbb{R}) \times \mathbb{R} \times \mathbb{R}^d$, $\xi^{(1)} \leq \xi^{(2)}$, *P-a.s.,* $f^{(1)}(t,p,y,z) \leq f^{(2)}(t,p,y,z)$, *dtdP-a.e., it holds that also* $Y_t^{(1)} \leq Y_t^{(2)}$, *for all* $t \in [0,T]$, *P-a.s.*

Lemma 3 (Existence). *Under the assumptions (A1), (A3), (A4) and (A6)–(A8), the general mean-field BDSDE (5) at least has one solution* $(Y,Z) \in \mathcal{M}^{2,\beta}(0,T)$. *Moreover, there is a minimal solution* $(\underline{Y},\underline{Z}) \in \mathcal{M}^{2,\beta}(0,T)$ *of the general mean-field BDSDE (5).*

Lemma 4 (Comparison theorem). *Let* $g = g(t,\omega,y,z)$ *satisfy the assumptions (A1) and (A4),* $f^{(1)} = f^{(1)}(t,\omega,p,y,z)$ *satisfy the assumptions (A3), (A4) and (A6)-(A8), and* $f^{(2)} = f^{(2)}(t,\omega,p,y,z)$ *satisfy the assumption (A4). Denote by* $(Y^{(1)},Z^{(1)})$ *and* $(Y^{(2)},Z^{(2)})$ *the solutions of general mean-field BDSDE (5) with data* $(\xi^{(1)}, f^{(1)}, g)$ *and* $(\xi^{(2)}, f^{(2)}, g)$, *respectively. Then, if for all* $(p,y,z) \in \mathcal{P}_2(\mathbb{R}) \times \mathbb{R} \times \mathbb{R}^d$, *there are* $\xi^{(1)} \leq \xi^{(2)}$ *P-a.s. and* $f^{(1)}(t,p,y,z) \leq f^{(2)}(t,p,y,z)$, *dtdP-a.e., it holds that also* $Y_t^{(1)} \leq Y_t^{(2)}$, *for all* $t \in [0,T]$, *P-a.s.*

For the detailed proofs of Lemmas 1–4, readers can refer to [15].

3. General Mean-Field BDSDEs with Stochastic Linear Growth and Discontinuous Generator

In this section, we focus on general mean-field BDSDEs (5) with stochastic linear growth and a discontinuous generator. We need to add some assumptions for the generator f as follows:

(B1) For a.e. $(t,\omega) \in [0,T]$, $f(t,p,y,z)$ is left-continuous in y, continuous in p and z, especially, with a continuity modulus $\rho : \mathbb{R}^+ \to \mathbb{R}^+$ for p: for all $p_1, p_2 \in \mathcal{P}_2(\mathbb{R}), (t,y,z) \in [0,T] \times \mathbb{R} \times \mathbb{R}^d$, there is

$$|f(t,p_1,y,z) - f(t,p_2,y,z)| \leq \rho(W_2(p_1,p_2)).$$

Here, ρ is supposed to be non-decreasing, such that $\rho(0_+) = 0$;

(B2) There exists a continuous function $K(t,p,y,z)$ defined on $[0,T] \times \mathcal{P}_2(\mathbb{R}) \times \mathbb{R} \times \mathbb{R}^d$, which is non-decreasing with respect to p, and there exist three non-negative $\mathcal{F}_t^W$-measurable processes $\{\theta(t)\}_{t\in[0,T]}$, $\{\mu(t)\}_{t\in[0,T]}$, $\{\gamma(t)\}_{t\in[0,T]}$ such that for all $t \in [0,T], p \in \mathcal{P}_2(\mathbb{R}), y \in \mathbb{R}, z \in \mathbb{R}^d$, there is

$$|K(t,p,y,z)| \leq \theta(t)e^{-\frac{\beta A(t)}{2}} W_2(p,\delta_0) + \mu(t)|y| + \gamma(t)|z|,$$

and for all $y_1 \geq y_2 \in \mathbb{R}, p_1, p_2 \in \mathcal{P}_2(\mathbb{R}), z_1, z_2 \in \mathbb{R}^d$, we have

$$f(t,p_1,y_1,z_1) - f(t,p_2,y_2,z_2) \geq K(t,\Delta(p_1,p_2),y_1-y_2,z_1-z_2),$$

where $\Delta(p_1,p_2) \in \mathcal{P}_2(\mathbb{R})$ and satisfies $W_2(\Delta(p_1,p_2),\delta_0) = W_2(p_1,p_2)$.

3.1. The Existence of Solutions

Next, we will give the first important conclusion of this paper, the existence of solutions for the general mean-field BDSDEs (5) under discontinuous and stochastic linear growth conditions. In order to facilitate readers to understand the logic of proof, we refer to the idea of proof in [16]. We first introduce the following technical lemma:

Lemma 5. *for $n \geq 1$, let us define*

$$K_n(t,p,y,z) = \inf_{(v,r,h)\in\mathcal{P}_2(\mathbb{R})\times\mathbb{R}\times\mathbb{R}^d} \Big\{ K(t,v,r,h) + n\big(\theta(t)e^{-\frac{\beta A(t)}{2}} W_{2,+}(\mu,v) + \mu(t)|y-r| + \gamma(t)|z-h|\big)\Big\}, \tag{6}$$

where $K(t,v,r,h)$ is similar to that in assumption (B2). From Lemma 3.1 in [12], we know these equations are well-defined and satisfy the following properties:

(i) Linear growth: for all $(t,p,y,z) \in [0,T] \times \mathcal{P}_2(\mathbb{R}) \times \mathbb{R} \times \mathbb{R}^d$, P-a.s., we have

$$|K_n(t,p,y,z)| \leq \theta(t)e^{-\frac{\beta A(t)}{2}} W_2(p,\delta_0) + \mu(t)|y| + \gamma(t)|z|;$$

(ii) Monotonicity in p: for all $\theta_1, \theta_2 \in L^{2,\beta}(\Omega, \mathcal{F}_T, P; \mathbb{R})$ with $\theta_1 \leq \theta_2$, P-a.s., we have

$$K_n(t,P_{\theta_1},y,z) \leq K_n(t,P_{\theta_2},y,z), dtdP\text{-a.s.};$$

(iii) Monotonicity in n: for all $(t,p,y,z) \in [0,T] \times \mathcal{P}_2(\mathbb{R}) \times \mathbb{R} \times \mathbb{R}^d$, P-a.s., $n < m$, we have

$$K_n(t,p,y,z) \leq K_m(t,p,y,z), dtdP\text{-a.s.};$$

(iv) Stochastic Lipschitz continuous: for all $(t, p_1, y_1, z_1), (t, p_2, y_2, z_2) \in [0, T] \times \mathcal{P}_2(\mathbb{R}) \times \mathbb{R} \times \mathbb{R}^d$, P-a.s., we have

$$\begin{aligned}&|K_n(t, p_1, y_1, z_1) - K_n(t, p_2, y_2, z_2)|\\ \leq& n\big(\theta(t)e^{-\frac{\beta A(t)}{2}} W_2(p_1, p_2) + \mu(t)|y_1 - y_2| + \gamma(t)|z_1 - z_2|\big);\end{aligned}$$

(v) Strong convergence: if $(p_n, y_n, z_n) \to (p, y, z)$ as $n \to \infty$ in $\mathcal{P}_2(\mathbb{R}) \times \mathbb{R} \times \mathbb{R}^d$, then

$$\lim_{n\to\infty} K_n(t, p_n, y_n, z_n) = K(t, p, y, z).$$

Proposition 1. *Let $\xi \in L^{2,\beta}(\Omega, \mathcal{F}_T, P; \mathbb{R})$, $\varphi_t \in \mathcal{H}^{2,\beta}(0, T; \mathbb{R})$, $K(t, p, u, v)$ and $G(t, u, v)$ satisfy the assumptions (A1), (A3), (A4) and (B2), and $G(t, 0, 0) = 0$. We consider the following general mean-field BDSDE: for all $t \in [0, T]$,*

$$U_t = \xi + \int_t^T (K(s, P_{U_s}, U_s, V_s) + \varphi_s)\, ds + \int_t^T G(s, U_s, V_s)\, d\overleftarrow{B}_s - \int_t^T V_s\, dW_s, \tag{7}$$

then, we have:
(i) The Equation (7) has at least one solution $(U, V) \in \mathcal{M}^{2,\beta}(0, T)$;
(ii) For any solution (U, V) of (7), if $\varphi_t \geq 0, \xi \geq 0$, we can obtain $U_t \geq 0$, P-a.s., $t \in [0, T]$.

Proof. Since K is continuous and $|K(t, p, y, z)| \leq \theta(t)e^{-\frac{\beta A(t)}{2}} W_2(p, \delta_0) + \mu(t)|y| + \gamma(t)|z|$, we note that (7) has at least one solution. For each n, because of Lemma 5, the following general mean-field BDSDEs are as follows: for all $t \in [0, T]$,

$$U_t^n = \xi + \int_t^T \big(K_n\big(s, P_{U_s^n}, U_s^n, V_s^n\big) + \varphi_s\big)\, ds + \int_t^T G(s, U_s^n, V_s^n)\, d\overleftarrow{B}_s - \int_t^T V_s^n\, dW_s, \quad n \geq 1 \tag{8}$$

has a unique adapted solution, and the solution $\{(U^n, V^n)\}_{n=1}^{\infty}$ of Equation (8) converge to the minimal solution $(\underline{U}, \underline{V})$ of Equation (7).

Next, we consider the following general mean-field BDSDEs: for all $t \in [0, T]$,

$$\tilde{U}_t^n = \int_t^T K_n\Big(s, P_{\tilde{U}_s^n}, \tilde{U}_s^n, \tilde{V}_s^n\Big)\, ds + \int_t^T G(s, \tilde{U}_s^n, \tilde{V}_s^n)\, d\overleftarrow{B}_s - \int_t^T \tilde{V}_s^n\, dW_s, \quad n \geq 1. \tag{9}$$

For each n, there exists a unique solution to Equation (9). Since $K_n(s, \delta_0, 0, 0) = 0$, $G(s, 0, 0) = 0$, then $(\tilde{U}^n, \tilde{V}^n) = (0, 0)$ is the unique solution to Equation (9). From the Lemma 2 and $\varphi_t \geq 0$, it follows that $U_t^n \geq \tilde{U}_t^n = 0$. Therefore, $\underline{U}_t \geq 0$. □

Before proving the existence of solutions of (5), we first construct a sequence of general mean-field BDSDEs as follows: given $\xi \in L^{2,\beta}(\Omega, \mathcal{F}_T, P; \mathbb{R})$, $t \in [0, T]$, $n \geq 1$,

$$\begin{aligned}\underline{Y}_t^0 =& \xi + \int_t^T \Big[-\theta(s)e^{-\frac{\beta A(s)}{2}} W_2(P_{\underline{Y}_s^0}, \delta_0) - \mu(s)|\underline{Y}_s^0| - \gamma(s)|\underline{Z}_s^0| - \phi(s)\Big] ds\\ &+ \int_t^T g(s, \underline{Y}_s^0, \underline{Z}_s^0) d\overleftarrow{B}_s - \int_t^T \underline{Z}_s^0 dW_s,\end{aligned} \tag{10}$$

$$\begin{aligned}\underline{Y}_t^n =& \xi + \int_t^T \Big[f\big(s, P_{\underline{Y}_s^{n-1}}, \underline{Y}_s^{n-1}, \underline{Z}_s^{n-1}\big) + K\big(s, \Delta(P_{\underline{Y}_s^n}, P_{\underline{Y}_s^{n-1}}), \underline{Y}_s^n - \underline{Y}_s^{n-1}, \underline{Z}_s^n - \underline{Z}_s^{n-1}\big)\Big] ds\\ &+ \int_t^T g(s, \underline{Y}_s^n, \underline{Z}_s^n) d\overleftarrow{B}_s - \int_t^T \underline{Z}_s^n dW_s,\end{aligned} \tag{11}$$

$$\begin{aligned}\overline{Y}_t^0 =& \xi + \int_t^T \Big[\theta(s)e^{-\frac{\beta A(s)}{2}} W_{2,+}(P_{\overline{Y}_s^0}, \delta_0) + \mu(s)|\overline{Y}_s^0| + \gamma(s)|\overline{Z}_s^0| + \phi(s)\Big]\, ds\\ &+ \int_t^T g(s, \overline{Y}_s^0, \overline{Z}_s^0)\, d\overleftarrow{B}_s - \int_t^T \overline{Z}_s^0\, dW_s.\end{aligned} \tag{12}$$

By Lemma 3, there exists at least one solution of (11). Here, we only consider the minimal solution, denoted as $(\underline{Y}^n, \underline{Z}^n)$. By Lemma 1 we know that (10) and (12) have unique solutions and are denoted as $(\underline{Y}^0, \underline{Z}^0)$ and $(\overline{Y}^0, \overline{Z}^0)$, respectively.

Proposition 2. *Under assumptions (A1), (A3), (A4), (A7), (B1) and (B2), then:*
(i) For any $n \geq 0$, $\underline{Y}_t^{n+1} \geq \underline{Y}_t^n$, $t \leq T$, P-a.s.
(ii) For any $n \geq 0$, $\overline{Y}_t^0 \geq \underline{Y}_t^n$, $t \leq T$, P-a.s.

Proof. Before the proof of this proposition, we first define

$$\begin{aligned} &G(s, Y_s^{n+1} - Y_s^n, Z_s^{n+1} - Z_s^n) \\ &:= g(s, Y_s^{n+1} - Y_s^n + Y_s^n, Z_s^{n+1} - Z_s^n + Z_s^n) - g(s, Y_s^n, Z_s^n) \\ &= g(s, Y_s^{n+1}, Z_s^{n+1}) - g(s, Y_s^n, Z_s^n), \end{aligned} \tag{13}$$

thus, we know $G(s, 0, 0) = 0$.

(i) The conclusion can be proved by the induction method. First, prove that $\underline{Y}_t^1 \geq \underline{Y}_t^0$. From the Equations (10), (11) and (13) we have

$$\begin{aligned} \underline{Y}_t^1 - \underline{Y}_t^0 = &\int_t^T \left[K\left(s, \Delta(P_{\underline{Y}_s^1}, P_{\underline{Y}_s^0}), \underline{Y}_s^1 - \underline{Y}_s^0, \underline{Z}_s^1 - \underline{Z}_s^0\right) + \psi_s^0\right] ds \\ &+ \int_t^T G(s, \underline{Y}_s^1 - \underline{Y}_s^0, \underline{Z}_s^1 - \underline{Z}_s^0)\, d\overleftarrow{B}_s \int_t^T \left(\underline{Z}_s^1 - \underline{Z}_s^0\right) dW_s, \end{aligned}$$

where $\psi_s^0 = f(s, P_{\underline{Y}_s^0}, \underline{Y}_s^0, \underline{Z}_s^0) + \theta(s) e^{-\frac{\beta A(s)}{2}} W_2(P_{\underline{Y}_s^0}, \delta_0) + \mu(s)|\underline{Y}_s^0| + \gamma(s)|\underline{Z}_s^0| + \phi(s)$. From (A7), we know $\psi_s^0 \geq 0$. Because $\left(\underline{Y}_t^0, \underline{Z}_t^0\right)$ is the solution of Equation (10), so $\psi_s^0 \in \mathcal{H}^{2,\beta}(0, T, \mathbb{R})$. Therefore, from Proposition 1, we can obtain $\underline{Y}_t^1 - \underline{Y}_t^0 \geq 0$, i.e., $\underline{Y}_t^1 \geq \underline{Y}_t^0$, for all $t \in [0, T]$, P-a.s.

Next, suppose $\underline{Y}_t^n \geq \underline{Y}_t^{n-1}$, then we prove $\underline{Y}_t^{n+1} \geq \underline{Y}_t^n$.

From Equations (11) and (13), we can obtain

$$\begin{aligned} \underline{Y}_t^{n+1} - \underline{Y}_t^n = &\int_t^T \left[K\left(s, \Delta(P_{\underline{Y}_s^{n+1}}, P_{\underline{Y}_s^n}), \underline{Y}_s^{n+1} - \underline{Y}_s^n, \underline{Z}_s^{n+1} - \underline{Z}_s^n\right) + \psi_s^n\right] ds \\ &+ \int_t^T G(s, \underline{Y}_s^{n+1} - \underline{Y}_s^n, \underline{Z}_s^{n+1} - \underline{Z}_s^n)\, d\overleftarrow{B}_s - \int_t^T \left(\underline{Z}_s^{n+1} - \underline{Z}_s^n\right) dW_s, \end{aligned}$$

where $\psi_s^n = f(s, P_{\underline{Y}_s^n}, \underline{Y}_s^n, \underline{Z}_s^n) - f(s, P_{\underline{Y}_s^{n-1}}, \underline{Y}_s^{n-1}, \underline{Z}_s^{n-1}) - K(\Delta(P_{\underline{Y}_s^n}, P_{\underline{Y}_s^{n-1}}), \underline{Y}_s^n - \underline{Y}_s^{n-1}, \underline{Z}_s^n - \underline{Z}_s^{n-1})$. From (B2), we know $\psi_s^n \geq 0$. Similarly, we can also obtain that $\underline{Y}_t^{n+1} \geq \underline{Y}_t^n$, for all $t \in [0, T]$, P-a.s.

(ii) We still use the induction method to prove $\overline{Y}_t^0 \geq \underline{Y}_t^n, n \geq 0$.

Before proving $\overline{Y}_t^0 \geq \underline{Y}_t^0$, we first consider the following general mean-field BDSDEs:

$$\begin{aligned} I_t' &= \int_t^T \theta(s) e^{-\frac{\beta A(s)}{2}} W_2\left(P_{I_s'}, \delta_0\right) ds + \int_t^T G(s, I_s', J_s')\, d\overleftarrow{B}_s - \int_t^T J_s' dW_s, \\ I_t &= \int_t^T \left(-\theta(s) e^{-\frac{\beta A(s)}{2}} W_2(P_{I_s}, \delta_0) - \mu(s) I_s - \gamma(s) J(s)\right) ds \\ &\quad + \int_t^T G(s, I_s, J_s) d\overleftarrow{B}_s - \int_t^T J_s dW_s, \end{aligned}$$

where $G(s, 0, 0) = 0$. Under assumptions (A1), (A3) and (A4), each of these two equations has a unique solution $(I', J') = (0, 0)$ and $(I, J) = (0, 0)$.

From (10) and (12), we can obtain

$$\overline{Y}_t^0 - \underline{Y}_t^0 = \int_t^T \left(\theta(s)e^{-\frac{\beta A(s)}{2}} W_2\left(P_{\overline{Y}_s^0}, P_{\underline{Y}_t^0}\right) + \Phi_s^0\right) ds$$
$$+ \int_t^T G(s, \overline{Y}_s^0 - \underline{Y}_s^0, \overline{Z}_s^0 - \underline{Z}_s^0)\, d\overleftarrow{B}_s - \int_t^T \left(\overline{Z}_s^0 - \underline{Z}_s^0\right) dW_s,$$

where

$$\Phi_s^0 = \theta(s)e^{-\frac{\beta A(s)}{2}} (W_{2,+}(P_{\overline{Y}_s^0}, \delta_0) + W_2(P_{\underline{Y}_s^0}, \delta_0) - W_2(P_{\overline{Y}_s^0}, P_{\underline{Y}_s^0})) + \mu(s)(|\overline{Y}_s^0| + |\underline{Y}_s^0|)$$
$$+ \gamma(s)(|\overline{Z}_s^0| + |\underline{Z}_s^0|) + 2\phi(s) \geq 0.$$

From Lemma 2, it follows

$$\overline{Y}_t^0 - \underline{Y}_t^0 \geq I_t' = 0.$$

Therefore, $\overline{Y}_t^0 \geq \underline{Y}_t^0$, for all $t \in [0, T]$, P-a.s.

Next, for $n = 1$, we have

$$\overline{Y}_t^0 - \underline{Y}_t^1 = \int_t^T \left(-\theta(s)e^{-\frac{\beta A(s)}{2}} W_2(P_{\overline{Y}_s^0}, P_{\underline{Y}_s^1}) - \mu(s)|\overline{Y}_s^0 - \underline{Y}_s^1| - \gamma(s)|\overline{Z}_s^0 - \underline{Z}_s^1| + \Phi_s^1\right) ds$$
$$+ \int_t^T G(s, \overline{Y}_s^0 - \underline{Y}_s^1, \overline{Z}_s^0 - \underline{Z}_s^1)\, d\overleftarrow{B}_s - \int_t^T (\overline{Z}_s^0 - \underline{Z}_s^1) dW_s,$$

where

$$\Phi_s^1 = \theta(s)e^{-\frac{\beta A(s)}{2}} W_2(P_{\overline{Y}_s^0}, P_{\underline{Y}_s^1}) + \mu(s)|\overline{Y}_s^0 - \underline{Y}_s^1| + \gamma(s)|\overline{Z}_s^0 - \underline{Z}_s^1| + \theta(s)e^{-\frac{\beta A(s)}{2}} W_{2,+}(P_{\overline{Y}_s^0}, \delta_0)$$
$$+ \mu(s)|\overline{Y}_s^0| + \gamma(s)|\overline{Z}_s^0| + \phi(s) - f\left(s, P_{\underline{Y}_s^0}, \underline{Y}_s^0, \underline{Z}_s^0\right) - K\left(s, \Delta(P_{\underline{Y}_s^1}, P_{\underline{Y}_s^0}), \underline{Y}_s^1 - \underline{Y}_s^0, \underline{Z}_s^1 - \underline{Z}_s^0\right)$$
$$\geq f\left(s, P_{\underline{Y}_s^1}, \underline{Y}_s^1, \underline{Z}_s^1\right) - f\left(s, P_{\underline{Y}_s^0}, \underline{Y}_s^0, \underline{Z}_s^0\right) - K\left(s, \Delta(P_{\underline{Y}_s^1}, P_{\underline{Y}_s^0}), \underline{Y}_s^1 - \underline{Y}_s^0, \underline{Z}_s^1 - \underline{Z}_s^0\right)$$
$$\geq 0.$$

From Lemma 2, it follows

$$\overline{Y}_t^0 - \underline{Y}_t^1 \geq I_t = 0.$$

Therefore, $\overline{Y}_t^0 \geq \underline{Y}_t^1$, for all $t \in [0, T]$, P-a.s.

Next, suppose $\overline{Y}_t^0 \geq \underline{Y}_t^{n-1}$, then we prove $\overline{Y}_t^0 \geq \underline{Y}_t^n$.

$$\overline{Y}_t^0 - \underline{Y}_t^n = \int_t^T \left(-\theta(s)e^{-\frac{\beta A(s)}{2}} W_2(P_{\overline{Y}_s^0}, P_{\underline{Y}_s^n}) - \mu(s)|\overline{Y}_s^0 - \underline{Y}_s^n| - \gamma(s)|\overline{Z}_s^0 - \underline{Z}_s^n| + \Phi_s^n\right) ds$$
$$+ \int_t^T G(s, \overline{Y}_s^0 - \underline{Y}_s^n, \overline{Z}_s^0 - \underline{Z}_s^n)\, d\overleftarrow{B}_s - \int_t^T \left(\overline{Z}_s^0 - \underline{Z}_s^n\right) dW_s,$$

where

$$\Phi_s^n = \theta(s)e^{-\frac{\beta A(s)}{2}} (W_2(P_{\overline{Y}_s^0}, P_{\underline{Y}_s^n}) + W_{2,+}(P_{\overline{Y}_s^0}, \delta_0)) + \mu(s)(|\overline{Y}_s^0 - \underline{Y}_s^n| + |\overline{Y}_s^0|) + \gamma(s)(|\overline{Z}_s^0 - \underline{Z}_s^n|$$
$$+ |\overline{Z}_s^0|) + \phi(s) - f\left(s, P_{\underline{Y}_s^{n-1}}, \underline{Y}_s^{n-1}, \underline{Z}_s^{n-1}\right) - K\left(s, \Delta(P_{\underline{Y}_s^n}, P_{\underline{Y}_s^{n-1}}), \underline{Y}_s^n - \underline{Y}_s^{n-1}, \underline{Z}_s^n - \underline{Z}_s^{n-1}\right)$$
$$\geq f\left(s, P_{\underline{Y}_s^n}, \underline{Y}_s^n, \underline{Z}_s^n\right) - f\left(s, P_{\underline{Y}_s^n}, \underline{Y}_s^n, \underline{Z}_s^n\right) - K\left(s, \Delta(P_{\underline{Y}_s^n}, P_{\underline{Y}_s^{n-1}}), \underline{Y}_s^n - \underline{Y}_s^{n-1}, \underline{Z}_s^n - \underline{Z}_s^{n-1}\right)$$
$$\geq 0.$$

Similarly, $\overline{Y}_t^0 \geq \underline{Y}_t^n$, for all $t \in [0, T]$, P-a.s. □

Remark 1. *Proposition 2 implies that the minimal solution sequence of general mean-field BDSDEs (11) is increasing and has an upper bound, i.e.,*

$$\overline{Y}_t^0 \geq \underline{Y}_t^{n+1} \geq \underline{Y}_t^n \geq \underline{Y}_t^0,\ t \leq T,\ P\text{-a.s.},\ n \geq 1. \tag{14}$$

Furthermore, we obtain our main theorem:

Theorem 1. *Under the assumptions (A1), (A3), (A4), (A7), (B1) and (B2), the sequence of solutions of the family of Equation (11) $\{(Y^n, Z^n)\}_{n=1}^{\infty} \in \mathcal{M}^{2,\beta}(0,T)$ converges to $(\underline{Y}, \underline{Z})$, which is the minimal solution of Equation (5).*

Proof. From Equation (14), we know that $(\underline{Y}^n)_{n=1}^{\infty}$ is increasing and bounded in $\mathcal{H}^{2,\beta}(0,T;\mathbb{R})$. By the monotone convergence theorem, we can deduce that $(\underline{Y}^n)_{n=1}^{\infty}$ converges in $\mathcal{H}^{2,\beta}(0,T;\mathbb{R})$, and denote $\underline{Y}$ as the limit of $\{\underline{Y}^n\}_{n=1}^{\infty}$. Notice that

$$\sup_n E[\sup_{0\leq t\leq T} e^{\beta A(t)}|\underline{Y}_t^n|^2] \leq E[\sup_{0\leq t\leq T} e^{\beta A(t)}|\underline{Y}_t^0|^2] + E[\sup_{0\leq t\leq T} e^{\beta A(t)}|\overline{Y}_t^0|^2] < \infty.$$

Using the Itô formula to $e^{\beta A(t)}\left|\underline{Y}_t^{n+1}\right|^2$, then we have

$$\begin{aligned}
&\left|\underline{Y}_0^{n+1}\right|^2 + \beta\int_0^T e^{\beta A(t)} a^2(t)\left|\underline{Y}_t^{n+1}\right|^2 dt + \int_0^T e^{\beta A(t)}\left|\underline{Z}_t^{n+1}\right|^2 dt \\
=& e^{\beta A(T)}|\xi|^2 + 2\int_0^T e^{\beta A(t)}\underline{Y}_t^{n+1}\Big(f\Big(t, P_{\underline{Y}_t^n}, \underline{Y}_t^n, \underline{Z}_t^n\Big) + K(t, \Delta(P_{\underline{Y}_t^{n+1}}, P_{\underline{Y}_t^n}), \underline{Y}_t^{n+1} - \underline{Y}_t^n, \\
&\underline{Z}_t^{n+1} - \underline{Z}_t^n)\Big)dt + \int_0^T e^{\beta A(t)}|g(t, \underline{Y}_t^{n+1}, \underline{Z}_t^{n+1})|^2 dt + 2\int_0^T e^{\beta A(t)}\underline{Y}_t^{n+1} g(t, \underline{Y}_t^{n+1}, \underline{Z}_t^{n+1}) d\overleftarrow{B}_t \\
&- 2\int_0^T e^{\beta A(t)}\underline{Y}_t^{n+1}\underline{Z}_t^{n+1} dW_t.
\end{aligned}$$

Noticing that $\int_0^T e^{\beta A(t)}\underline{Y}_t^{n+1}\underline{Z}_t^{n+1}dW_t$ and $\int_0^T e^{\beta A(t)}\underline{Y}_t^{n+1}g(t,\underline{Y}_t^{n+1}, \underline{Z}_t^{n+1})d\overleftarrow{B}_t$ are martingales. Next, we take the expectation of the above equation. From $2ab \leq \frac{1}{\delta}a^2 + \delta b^2$, $\delta > 0$, we know that there exist constants $\delta_1, \delta_2 > 0$ such that

$$\begin{aligned}
&E[|\underline{Y}_0^{n+1}|^2] + \beta E[\int_0^T e^{\beta A(t)} a^2(t)|\underline{Y}_t^{n+1}|^2 dt] + E[\int_0^T e^{\beta A(t)}|\underline{Z}_t^{n+1}|^2 dt] \\
=& E[e^{\beta A(T)}|\xi|^2] + 2E[\int_0^T e^{\beta A(t)}\underline{Y}_t^{n+1}(f(t, P_{\underline{Y}_t^n}, \underline{Y}_t^n, \underline{Z}_t^n) + K(t, \Delta(P_{\underline{Y}_t^{n+1}}, P_{\underline{Y}_t^n}), \underline{Y}_t^{n+1} - \underline{Y}_t^n, \\
&\underline{Z}_t^{n+1} - \underline{Z}_t^n))dt] + E[\int_0^T e^{\beta A(t)}|g(t, \underline{Y}_t^{n+1}, \underline{Z}_t^{n+1})|^2 dt] \\
\leq& E[e^{\beta A(T)}|\xi|^2] + 2E[\int_0^T e^{\beta A(t)}\underline{Y}_t^{n+1} f(t, P_{\underline{Y}_t^{n+1}}, \underline{Y}_t^{n+1}, \underline{Z}_t^{n+1})dt] + E[\int_0^T e^{\beta A(t)}|g(t, \underline{Y}_t^{n+1}, \underline{Z}_t^{n+1})|^2 dt] \\
\leq& E[e^{\beta A(T)}|\xi|^2] + 2E[\int_0^T e^{\beta A(t)}|\underline{Y}_t^{n+1}|(\phi(t) + \theta(t)e^{-\frac{\beta A(t)}{2}} W_2(P_{\underline{Y}_t^{n+1}}, \delta_0) + \mu(t)|\underline{Y}_t^{n+1}| + \gamma(t) \\
&|\underline{Z}_t^{n+1}|)dt] + E[\int_0^T e^{\beta A(t)}((1+\delta_1)|g(t, \underline{Y}_t^{n+1}, \underline{Z}_t^{n+1}) - g(t,0,0)|^2 + (1 + \frac{1}{\delta_1})|g(t,0,0)|^2)dt] \\
\leq& E[e^{\beta A(T)}|\xi|^2] + E[\int_0^T e^{\beta A(t)}|\underline{Y}_t^{n+1}|^2 dt] + E[\int_0^T e^{\beta A(t)}\phi(t)^2 dt] + E[\int_0^T e^{\beta A(t)}\theta(t)^2|\underline{Y}_t^{n+1}|^2 dt] \\
&+ E[\int_0^T E[|\underline{Y}_t^{n+1}|^2]dt] + 2E[\int_0^T e^{\beta A(t)}\mu(t)|\underline{Y}_t^{n+1}|^2 dt] + \delta_2 E[\int_0^T e^{\beta A(t)}\gamma(t)^2|\underline{Y}_t^{n+1}|^2 dt]
\end{aligned}$$

$$+\frac{1}{\delta_2}E[\int_0^T e^{\beta A(t)}|\underline{Z}_t^{n+1}|^2 dt] + (1+\delta_1)E[\int_t^T e^{\beta A(t)}v(t)|\underline{Y}^{n+1}(t)|^2 dt]$$
$$+ (1+\delta_1)\alpha E[\int_0^T e^{\beta A(t)}|\underline{Z}_s^{n+1}|^2 dt] + (1+\frac{1}{\delta_1})E[\int_0^T e^{\beta A(t)}|g(t,0,0)|^2 dt]$$
$$\leq E[e^{\beta A(T)}|\xi|^2] + 2E[\int_0^T e^{\beta A(t)}|\underline{Y}_t^{n+1}|^2 dt] + E[\int_0^T e^{\beta A(t)}\left(\theta(t)^2 + 2\mu(t) + \delta_2\gamma(t)^2 + (1+\delta_1)v(t)\right)$$
$$|\underline{Y}_t^{n+1}|^2 dt] + (\frac{1}{\delta_2} + (1+\delta_1)\alpha)E[\int_0^T e^{\beta A(t)}|\underline{Z}_t^{n+1}|^2 dt] + E[\int_0^T e^{\beta A(t)}\left(\phi(t)^2 + (1+\frac{1}{\delta_1})|g(t,0,0)|^2\right)dt].$$

As we mentioned earlier, β is big enough, so let $\beta > 4 + \delta_1 + \delta_2$. Taking $\delta_1 = \frac{1-\alpha}{4\alpha}$ and $\delta_2 = \frac{4}{1-\alpha}$, then the above inequality can be simplified as follows

$$E[|\underline{Y}_0^{n+1}|^2] + (\beta - 4 - \frac{1-\alpha}{4\alpha} - \frac{4}{1-\alpha})E[\int_0^T e^{\beta A(t)}a^2(t)|\underline{Y}_t^{n+1}|^2 dt] + \frac{1-\alpha}{2}E[\int_0^T e^{\beta A(t)}|\underline{Z}_t^{n+1}|^2 dt]$$
$$\leq E[e^{\beta A(T)}|\xi|^2] + 2TE[\sup_{0\leq t\leq T} e^{\beta A(t)}|\underline{Y}_t^{n+1}|^2] + E[\int_0^T e^{\beta A(t)}(\phi(t)^2 + \frac{1+3\alpha}{1-\alpha}|g(t,0,0)|^2)dt] < \infty,$$

which implies that $\sup_n E[\int_0^T e^{\beta A(t)}\left|\underline{Z}_t^{n+1}\right|^2 dt] < \infty$, and $\eta_t^{n+1} = f(t, P_{\underline{Y}_t^n}, \underline{Y}_t^n, \underline{Z}_t^n) + K(t, \Delta(P_{\underline{Y}_t^{n+1}}, P_{\underline{Y}_t^n}), \underline{Y}_t^{n+1} - \underline{Y}_t^n, \underline{Z}_t^{n+1} - \underline{Z}_t^n)$ is uniformly bounded in $\mathcal{H}^{2,\beta}(0,T;\mathbb{R})$. Let $C_0 = \sup_n E[\int_0^T e^{\beta A(t)}|\eta_t^n|^2 dt]$. For any $m,n > 0$, using Itô formula to $e^{\beta A(t)}|\underline{Y}_t^m - \underline{Y}_t^n|^2$, we can obtain

$$E[\int_0^T e^{\beta A(t)}|\underline{Z}_t^m - \underline{Z}_t^n|^2 dt]$$
$$\leq 2E[\int_0^T e^{\beta A(t)}(\underline{Y}_t^m - \underline{Y}_t^n)(\eta_t^m - \eta_t^n)dt] + E[\int_0^T e^{\beta A(t)}|g(t,\underline{Y}_t^m,\underline{Z}_t^m) - g(t,\underline{Y}_t^n,\underline{Z}_t^n)|^2 dt]$$
$$\leq 2\left(E[\int_0^T e^{\beta A(t)}|\underline{Y}_t^m - \underline{Y}_t^n|^2 dt]\right)^{\frac{1}{2}}\left(E[\int_t^T e^{\beta A(t)}(|\eta_t^m| + |\eta_t^n|)^2 dt]\right)^{\frac{1}{2}}$$
$$+ E[\int_0^T e^{\beta A(t)}v(t)|\underline{Y}_t^m - \underline{Y}_t^n|^2 dt] + E[\int_0^T e^{\beta A(t)}\alpha|\underline{Z}_t^m - \underline{Z}_t^n|^2 dt]$$
$$\leq \frac{4\sqrt{C_0}}{1-\alpha}\left(E[\int_0^T e^{\beta A(t)}|\underline{Y}_t^m - \underline{Y}_t^n|^2 dt]\right)^{\frac{1}{2}} + \frac{1}{1-\alpha}E[\int_0^T e^{\beta A(t)}v(t)|\underline{Y}_t^m - \underline{Y}_t^n|^2 dt].$$

Because $\{\underline{Y}^n\}_{n=1}^\infty$ is a Cauchy sequence in $\mathcal{H}^{2,\beta}(0,T;\mathbb{R})$, $\{\underline{Z}^n\}_{n=1}^\infty$ is also a Cauchy sequence in $\mathcal{H}^{2,\beta}(0,T;\mathbb{R})$. Therefore, $\{\underline{Z}^n\}_{n=1}^\infty$ converges in $\mathcal{H}^{2,\beta}(0,T;\mathbb{R})$, we denote it by $\underline{Z}$. Now, we pass to the limit, as $n \to \infty$ on both sides of (11), it follows that

$$\underline{Y}_t = \xi + \int_t^T f(s, P_{\underline{Y}_s}, \underline{Y}_s, \underline{Z}_s)ds + \int_t^T g(s, \underline{Y}_s, \underline{Z}_s)d\overleftarrow{B}_s - \int_t^T \underline{Z}_s dW_s.$$

Obviously, $(\underline{Y}, \underline{Z})$ solves the general mean-field BDSDEs (5).

Let, $(Y,Z) \in \mathcal{M}^{2,\beta}(0,T)$ be any solution of (5) and consider (11) with its minimal solution $(\underline{Y}^n, \underline{Z}^n) \in \mathcal{M}^{2,\beta}(0,T)$ for every $n \geq 0$.

For $n = 0$, we first denote $\underline{f}_0(s, P_{Y_s}, Y_s, Z_s) := -\theta(s)e^{-\frac{\beta A(s)}{2}}W_2(P_{Y_s}, \delta_0) - \mu(s)|Y_s| - \gamma(s)|Z_s| - \phi(s)$. From assumption (A7), there is

$$f(s, P_{Y_s}, Y_s, Z_s) \geq \underline{f}_0(s, P_{Y_s}, Y_s, Z_s), \text{ for all } s \in [0,T].$$

Since $\underline{f}_0$ satisfies assumptions (A2), (A4) and (A5), we obtain from Lemma 2 that $\underline{Y}_s^0 \leq Y_s$, P-a.s., for all $s \in [0,T]$.

Now, suppose that there exists $n > 1$ such that $\underline{Y}_s^n \le Y_s$ and prove that $\underline{Y}_s^{n+1} \le Y_s$, P-a.s., for all $s \in [0,T]$. Denote $\underline{f}_{n+1}(s, P_{Y_s}, Y_s, Z_s) := f(s, P_{\underline{Y}_s^n}, \underline{Y}_s^n, \underline{Z}_s^n) + K(s, \Delta(P_{Y_s}, P_{\underline{Y}_s^n}), Y_s - \underline{Y}_s^n, Z_s - \underline{Z}_s^n)$, from assumption (B2) and $Y_s \ge \underline{Y}_s^n$, it follows that

$$f(s, P_{Y_s}, Y_s, Z_s) \ge \underline{f}_{n+1}(s, P_{Y_s}, Y_s, Z_s), \text{ for all } s \in [0,T].$$

Since, $\underline{f}_{n+1}$ satisfies assumptions (A2), (A4) and (A5), we obtain from Lemma 2 that, $\underline{Y}_s^{n+1} \le Y_s$, a.s., for all $s \in [0,T]$. Consequently, for all $n \ge 0$, we have $\underline{Y}_s^n \le Y_s$, P-a.s., for all $s \in [0,T]$.

Since $(\underline{Y}^n, \underline{Z}^n)$ converges to $(\underline{Y}, \underline{Z})$, we can obtain $\underline{Y}_s \le Y_s$, P-a.s., for all $s \in [0,T]$, which proves that $(\underline{Y}, \underline{Z})$ is the minimal solution of (5). □

Remark 2. *Similar to the proof of Theorem 1, we can obtain another existence result that Equation (5) has a maximal solution. Replace (B1) with (B1)′:*

(B1)′: For a.e. $(s,\omega) \in [0,T]$, $f(s,p,y,z)$ *is right-continuous in* y, *and continuous in* p *and* z, *especially with a continuity modulus* $\rho : \mathbb{R}^+ \to \mathbb{R}^+$ *for* p: *for all* $p_1, p_2 \in \mathcal{P}_2(\mathbb{R})$, $(s,y,z) \in [0,T] \times \mathbb{R} \times \mathbb{R}^d$, *there is* $|f(s,p_1,y,z) - f(s,p_2,y,z)| \le \rho(W_2(p_1,p_2))$. *Here* ρ *is supposed to be non-decreasing and such that* $\rho(0_+) = 0$.

Consider the Equation (12) and the following equation: Given $\xi \in L^{2,\beta}(\Omega, \mathcal{F}_T, P; \mathbb{R}), t \in [0,T]$,

$$\begin{aligned} \overline{Y}_t^n =& \xi + \int_t^T \left[f(s, P_{\overline{Y}_s^{n-1}}, \overline{Y}_s^{n-1}, \overline{Z}_s^{n-1}) + K(s, \Delta(P_{\overline{Y}_s^{n-1}}, P_{\overline{Y}_s^n}), \overline{Y}_s^{n-1} - \overline{Y}_s^n, \overline{Z}_s^{n-1} - \overline{Z}_s^n) \right] ds \\ &+ \int_t^T g(s, \overline{Y}_s^n, \overline{Z}_s^n) d\overleftarrow{B}_s - \int_t^T \overline{Z}_s^n dW_s, \ n \ge 1. \end{aligned} \tag{15}$$

For all $n \ge 1$, *there exists at least one solution to the general mean-field BDSDEs (15), and here we give the sequence of maximal solutions denoted by* $\{(\overline{Y}^n, \overline{Z}^n)\}_{n=1}^{\infty}$, *which will limit to the maximal solution of Equation (5).*

Working similarly to Lemma 5 and Theorem 1, we conclude the following:

Corollary 1. *Under the assumptions (A1), (A3), (A4), (A7), (B1)′ and (B2), if* $\{(\overline{Y}^n, \overline{Z}^n)\}_{n=1}^{\infty}$ *is the maximal solution of the Equation (15), then*

(i) For $n \ge 0$, $\overline{Y}_t^0 \ge \overline{Y}_t^n \ge \overline{Y}_t^{n+1} \ge \underline{Y}_t^0$, $t \in [0,T]$, *P-a.s.;*

(ii) $\{(\overline{Y}^n, \overline{Z}^n)\}_{n=1}^{\infty} \in \mathcal{M}^{2,\beta}(0,T)$ *converges to* $(\overline{Y}, \overline{Z})$, *which is the maximal solution of Equation (5).*

3.2. Comparison Theorem

The comparison theorem is also an important result in the theory of general mean-field BDSDEs; therefore, we will prove the comparison theorem to the case where the generator f is discontinuous.

Theorem 2. *Assume that* $\xi^{(1)}, \xi^{(2)} \in L^{2,\beta}(\Omega, \mathcal{F}_T, P; \mathbb{R})$, g *and* $f^{(i)}$, $i = 1,2$ *satisfy the assumptions (A1), (A3), (A4), (A7), (B1) and (B2). Let* $(\underline{Y}^{(1)}, \underline{Z}^{(1)})$ *be the minimal solution of the general mean-field BDSDEs (5) with the data* $\left(\xi^{(1)}, f^{(1)}, g\right)$; $(Y^{(2)}, Z^{(2)})$ *be a solution of the general mean-field BDSDEs (5) with the data* $\left(\xi^{(2)}, f^{(2)}, g\right)$. *Then, if* $\xi^{(1)} \le \xi^{(2)}$, *P-a.s. and* $f^{(1)}(t,p,y,z) \le f^{(2)}(t,p,y,z)$, *dtdP-a.e., it holds that* $\underline{Y}_t^{(1)} \le Y_t^{(2)}$, *for all* $t \in [0,T]$, *P-a.s..*

Proof. Let $(\underline{Y}_t^n, \underline{Z}_t^n)_{t\in[0,T]} (n = 0, 1, \cdots)$ be the minimal solutions of the following general mean-field BDSDEs:

$$\underline{Y}_t^0 = \xi^{(1)} + \int_t^T \Big[-\theta(s)e^{-\frac{\beta A(s)}{2}} W_2(P_{\underline{Y}_s^0}, \delta_0) - \mu(s)|\underline{Y}_s^0| - \gamma(s)|\underline{Z}_s^0| - \phi(s) \Big] ds$$
$$+ \int_t^T g(s, \underline{Y}_s^0, \underline{Z}_s^0) d\overleftarrow{B}_s - \int_t^T \underline{Z}_s^0 dW_s, \tag{16}$$
$$\underline{Y}_t^n = \xi^{(1)} + \int_t^T \Big[f^{(1)}(s, P_{\underline{Y}_s^{n-1}}, \underline{Y}_s^{n-1}, \underline{Z}_s^{n-1}) + K(s, \Delta(P_{\underline{Y}_s^n}, P_{\underline{Y}_s^{n-1}}), \underline{Y}_s^n - \underline{Y}_s^{n-1}, \underline{Z}_s^n - \underline{Z}_s^{n-1}) \Big] ds$$
$$+ \int_t^T g(s, \underline{Y}_s^n, \underline{Z}_s^n) d\overleftarrow{B}_s - \int_t^T \underline{Z}_s^n dW_s. \tag{17}$$

For any $(s, p, y, z) \in [0, T] \times \mathcal{P}(\mathbb{R}) \times \mathbb{R} \times \mathbb{R}^d$, we denote

$$F_0^{(1)}(s, p, y, z) = -\theta(s)e^{-\frac{\beta A(s)}{2}} W_2(p, \delta_0) - \mu(s)|y| - \gamma(s)|z| - \phi(s),$$
$$F_n^{(1)}(s, p, y, z) = f^{(1)}(s, P_{\underline{Y}_s^{n-1}}, \underline{Y}_s^{n-1}, \underline{Z}_s^{n-1}) + K(s, \Delta(p, P_{\underline{Y}_s^{n-1}}), y - \underline{Y}_s^{n-1}, z - \underline{Z}_t^{n-1}), \quad n \geq 1.$$

First, we prove $Y_s^{(2)} \geq \underline{Y}_s^0$. From the assumption (A7), we have

$$\begin{aligned} &f^{(2)}(s, P_{Y_s^{(2)}}, Y_s^{(2)}, Z_s^{(2)}) \\ &\geq -\theta(s)e^{-\frac{\beta A(s)}{2}} W_2(P_{Y_s^{(2)}}, \delta_0) - \mu(s)|Y_s^{(2)}| - \gamma(s)|Z_s^{(2)}| - \phi(s) \\ &= F_0^{(1)}(s, P_{Y_s^{(2)}}, Y_s^{(2)}, Z_s^{(2)}). \end{aligned}$$

Since $F_0^{(1)}$ satisfies the assumptions (A6)–(A8), we obtain from Lemma 4 that $Y_s^{(2)} \geq \underline{Y}_s^0$, for all $s \in [0, T]$, P-a.s.

Next, we prove $Y_s^{(2)} \geq \underline{Y}_s^1$. From the assumption (B2), it follows that

$$\begin{aligned} &f^{(2)}(s, P_{Y_s^{(2)}}, Y_s^{(2)}, Z_s^{(2)}) \\ &\geq f^{(2)}(s, P_{\underline{Y}_s^0}, \underline{Y}_s^0, \underline{Z}_s^0) + K(s, \Delta(Y_s^{(2)}, \underline{Y}_s^0), Y_s^{(2)} - \underline{Y}_s^0, Z_s^{(2)} - \underline{Z}_s^0) \\ &\geq f^{(1)}(s, P_{\underline{Y}_s^0}, \underline{Y}_s^0, \underline{Z}_s^0) + K(s, \Delta(Y_s^{(2)}, \underline{Y}_s^0), Y_s^{(2)} - \underline{Y}_s^0, Z_s^{(2)} - \underline{Z}_s^0) \\ &= F_1^{(1)}(s, P_{Y_s^2}, Y_s^2, Z_s^2). \end{aligned} \tag{18}$$

Since $F_1^{(1)}$ satisfies the assumptions (A6)–(A8), we obtain from Lemma 4 that $Y_s^{(2)} \geq \underline{Y}_s^1$, for all $s \in [0, T]$, P-a.s.

Then, we assume that there exists $n \geq 1$ such that $Y_s^{(2)} \geq \underline{Y}_s^n$, P-a.s., following the same procedure as (18), we can prove that $Y_s^{(2)} \geq \underline{Y}_s^{n+1}$, for all $s \in [0, T]$, P-a.s.

Finally, from Theorem 1 we know $\{(\underline{Y}^n, \underline{Z}^n)\}_{n \geq 0}$ converges in $\mathcal{M}^{2,\beta}(0, T)$ to the minimal solution $(\underline{Y}^{(1)}, \underline{Z}^{(1)})$ of general mean-field BDSDEs $(\xi^{(1)}, f^{(1)}, g)$, so there is $\underline{Y}_s^{(1)} \leq Y_s^{(2)}$, for all $s \in [0, T]$, P-a.s. □

3.3. A Special Case: General Mean-Field BDSDEs with Linear Growth and Discontinuous Generator

Next, we will discuss the general mean-field BDSDEs under non-stochastic conditions, which is a special case of that under the above stochastic conditions. Let $\beta = 0$, and for all $t \in [0, T]$, let processes $\theta(t), \mu(t), \gamma(t), \phi(t), \nu(t)$ equal to the constant A, then the results under stochastic conditions will degenerate into some classical results, which are shown in Theorems 3 and 4.

At first, when $\beta = 0, \theta(t), \mu(t), \gamma(t), \phi(t), \nu(t) \equiv A$, for all $t \in [0, T]$, the corresponding assumptions will be modified as follows:

(C1) $g(t,\omega,0,0) \in \mathcal{H}^{2,0}(0,T,\mathbb{R}^{\ell})$;

(C2) g is Lipschitz in (y,z) : There are constants $\alpha_1 > 0$ and $0 < \alpha_2 < 1$, such that for all $y_1, y_2 \in \mathbb{R}, z_1, z_2 \in \mathbb{R}^d$,

$$|g(t,y_1,z_1) - g(t,y_2,z_2)|^2 \leq \alpha_1 |y_1 - y_2|^2 + \alpha_2 |z_1 - z_2|^2;$$

(C3) Linear growth: There exists $A \geq 0$, such that for all $(p,y,z) \in \mathcal{P}(\mathbb{R}) \times \mathbb{R} \times \mathbb{R}^d$, there is

$$|f(t,p,y,z)| \leq A(1 + W_2(p,\delta_0) + |y| + |z|), \text{ dtd}P\text{-a.e.};$$

(C4) Monotonicity in p : For all $\theta_1, \theta_2 \in L^2(\Omega,\mathcal{F},P;\mathbb{R})$, and all $(y,z) \in \mathbb{R} \times \mathbb{R}^d$, when $\theta_1 \leq \theta_2$, P-a.s., we have

$$f(t,P_{\theta_1},y,z) \leq f(t,P_{\theta_2},y,z), \text{dsd}P\text{-a.e.};$$

(C5) There exists a continuous function $K(t,p,y,z)$ defined on $[0,T] \times \mathcal{P}_2(\mathbb{R}) \times \mathbb{R} \times \mathbb{R}^d$, which is non-decreasing with respect to p and for all $A \geq 0$ satisfying

$$|K(t,p,y,z)| \leq A(W_2(p,\delta_0) + |y| + |z|),$$

such that for all $y_1 \geq y_2 \in \mathbb{R}, p_1, p_2 \in \mathcal{P}_2(\mathbb{R}), z_1, z_2 \in \mathbb{R}^d$, we have

$$f(t,p_1,y_1,z_1) - f(t,p_2,y_2,z_2) \geq K(t,\Delta(p_1,p_2),y_1 - y_2, z_1 - z_2),$$

where $\Delta(p_1,p_2) \in \mathcal{P}_2(\mathbb{R})$ and satisfies $W_2(\Delta(p_1,p_2),\delta_0) = W_2(p_1,p_2)$.

Theorem 3. *Under the assumptions (C1)-(C5) and (B1), the general mean-field BDSDE (5) at least has one solution $(Y,Z) \in \mathcal{M}^{2,0}(0,T)$. Moreover, there is a minimal solution $(\underline{Y}, \underline{Z}) \in \mathcal{M}^{2,0}(0,T)$ of the general mean-field BDSDE (5).*

Here, we give an example to show the rationality of those mentioned assumptions.

Example 1. *Let $\xi \in L^{2,0}(\Omega,\mathcal{F}_T,P;\mathbb{R})$, consider the following mean-field BDSDE: for $t \in [0,T]$,*

$$Y_t = \xi + \int_t^T \left(1 + E[Y_s] + Y_s I_{\{Y_s > 1\}} + Z_s\right) ds + \int_t^T \left(\frac{1}{2}Y_s + \frac{1}{2}Z_s\right) d\overleftarrow{B}_s - \int_t^T Z_s dW_s. \quad (19)$$

Taking $A = 1$, $\alpha_1 = \frac{1}{2}$ and $\alpha_2 = \frac{1}{2}$, the above equation satisfies assumptions (C1)–(C4) and (B1). Given the continuous function $K(t,p,y,z) = z$, the assumptions (C5) will also be satisfied. Therefore, from Theorem 3 we know that the Equation (19) at least has one solution $(Y,Z) \in \mathcal{M}^{2,0}(0,T)$.

Theorem 4 (Comparison theorem). *Assume that $\xi^{(1)}, \xi^{(2)} \in L^{2,0}(\Omega,\mathcal{F}_T,P;\mathbb{R})$, g and $f^{(i)}$, $i = 1,2$ satisfy the assumptions (C1)–(C5) and (B1). Let $(\underline{Y}^{(1)}, \underline{Z}^{(1)})$ be the minimal solution of the general mean-field BDSDEs (5) with the data $(\xi^{(1)}, f^{(1)}, g)$; $(Y^{(2)}, Z^{(2)}) \in \mathcal{M}^{2,0}(0,T)$ be a solution of the general mean-field BDSDEs (5) with the data $(\xi^{(2)}, f^{(2)}, g)$. If $\xi^{(1)} \leq \xi^{(2)}$, P-a.s. and $f^{(1)}(t,p,y,z) \leq f^{(2)}(t,p,y,z)$, dtdP-a.e., it holds that $\underline{Y}_t^{(1)} \leq Y_t^{(2)}$, for all $t \in [0,T]$, P-a.s.*

Proof. The proof of Theorems 3 and 4 is similar to that of Theorems 1 and 2, so it is omitted here. □

4. Application in Finance: Selling a Financial Claim

Considering a financial claim with a contingent ξ and there an investor who wants to sell the claim and hedge it. Suppose that the investor has additional information not detected in the financial market, and his decision is also affected by the distribution of all investors' decisions in the market. Moreover, suppose that the interest rate is applied only to portfolios whose value remains above a nominal value at any time. This problem is equivalent to solving the following mean-field BDSDE: $\xi \in L^{2,\beta}(\Omega, \mathcal{F}_T, P; \mathbb{R})$, for $t \in [0, T]$,

$$Y_t = \xi + \int_t^T \left(\theta(s)e^{-\frac{\beta A(s)}{2}} E[Y_s] + \mu(s)Y_s I_{\{Y_s>1\}} + \gamma(s)Z_s\right)\mathrm{d}s + \int_t^T c(s)Z_s\mathrm{d}\overleftarrow{B}_s - \int_t^T Z_s\mathrm{d}W_s, \tag{20}$$

where the mean-field term $E[y]$ reflects that the investor relies on the distribution of all investors' decisions in the market to make a decision, $\mu(t)$ is the interest rate, $\gamma(t)$ is the risk premium vector and $c(t)$ is the volatility caused by the systemic risks.

We have $f(t,p,y,z) = \theta(t)e^{-\frac{\beta A(t)}{2}} E[y] + \mu(t)yI_{\{y>1\}} + \gamma(t)z$ and $g(t,y,z) = c(t)z$. Obviously, it follows that the assumptions (A7), (B1) and (B2) are satisfied with $\phi(t) \equiv 0$ and $K(t,p,y,z) = \gamma(t)z$. If we let $c(t) = \alpha 1_{\{B_T - B_t > 0\}}$ and $\nu(t) \equiv 0, 0 < \alpha < 1$, then assumption (A1) is also satisfied. For any $t \in [0, T]$, let $X_t = \sqrt{2t}\,(X \wedge 1)$, where $X \sim \mathcal{N}(0, 1)$. Now, for any $\varepsilon > 0$, we put

$$\theta(t) = \sqrt{\frac{1}{2}X_t^2 1_{\{W_t \geq 0\}}}, \quad \mu(t) = \frac{1}{2}X_t^2 1_{\{W_t \geq 0\}}, \quad \text{and} \quad \gamma(t) = \sqrt{X_t^2 1_{\{W_t<0\}} + \varepsilon}.$$

Then, $\theta(t), \mu(t), \gamma(t)$ and $\nu(t)$ are positive $\mathcal{F}_t^W$-adapted processes. Indeed, for any $t \in [0, T]$, we have

$$\begin{aligned} a^2(t) &= \theta(t)^2 + \mu(t) + \gamma^2(t) + \nu(t) = X_t^2 + \varepsilon > 0, \quad \text{and} \\ A(t) &= \int_0^t \left(X_s^2 + \varepsilon\right)ds \leq (X \wedge 1)^2 T^2 + \varepsilon T < +\infty, \end{aligned}$$

thus, the assumptions (A3) and (A4) are satisfied. Therefore, from Theorem 1 we know, the Equation (20) at least has one solution $(Y, Z) \in \mathcal{M}^{2,\beta}(0, T)$, that is, the investor can sell the financial claim at a certain price Y.

5. Conclusions

This paper studies a class of general mean-field BDSDEs whose generator f depends not only on the solution processes but also on their distribution.

We present the main result in Section 3, that is, the existence of the solutions for the general mean-field BDSDEs and the comparison theorem under discontinuous and stochastic linear growth conditions.

It is worth emphasizing that the general mean-field BDSDEs with discontinuous generators can help to deal with some financial problems, for example, we discuss a financial claim sale problem in Section 4, which can be solved by a class of general mean-field BDSDE.

Author Contributions: Formal analysis, J.W.; resources, J.W. and Y.S.; writing—original draft preparation, J.W.; writing—review and editing, J.W. and Y.S.; funding acquisition, Y.S. All authors have read and agreed to the published version of the manuscript.

Funding: This research article was supported by the Major Fundamental Research Project of Shandong Province of China under Grant No. ZR2023ZD33, National Key R&D Program of China under Grant Nos. 2023YFA1008903 and 2018YFA0703900, National Natural Science Foundation of China under Grant Nos. 11871309 and 11371226.

Data Availability Statement: Data availability is not applicable to this article as no new data were created or analyzed in this study.

Conflicts of Interest: The authors declare no conflicts of interests.

References

1. Pardoux, E.; Peng, S. Adapted solution of a backward stochastic differential equation. *Syst. Control Lett.* **1990**, 14, 55–61. [CrossRef]
2. Pardoux, E.; Peng, S. Backward doubly stochastic differential equations and systems of quasilinear SPDEs. *Probab. Theory Relat. Fields* **1994**, *98*, 209–227. [CrossRef]

3. Shi, Y.; Gu, Y.; Liu, K. Comparison theorems of backward doubly stochastic differential equations and applications. *Stoch. Anal. Appl.* **2005**, *23*, 97–110. [CrossRef]
4. Owo, J.M. Backward doubly stochastic differential equations with stochastic Lipschitz condition. *Stat. Probab. Lett.* **2015**, *96*, 75–84. [CrossRef]
5. Owo, J.M. Backward doubly SDEs with continuous and stochastic linear growth coefficients. *Random Oper. Stoch. Equ.* **2018**, *26*, 175–184. [CrossRef]
6. Owo, J.M. Backward doubly stochastic differential equations with discontinuous and stochastic linear growth generator. *Stoch. Anal. Appl.* **2022**, *41*, 958–973. [CrossRef]
7. Lasry, J.; Lions, P. Mean field games. *Jpn. J. Math.* **2007**, *2*, 229–260. [CrossRef]
8. Buckdahn, R.; Djehiche, B.; Li, J.; Peng, S. Mean-field backward stochastic differential equation: A limit approach. *Ann. Probab.* **2009**, *37*, 1524–1565. [CrossRef]
9. Buckdahn, R.; Li, J.; Peng, S. Mean-field backward stochastic differential equations and related partial differential equations. *Stoch. Process. Their Appl.* **2009**, *119*, 3133–3154. [CrossRef]
10. Moon, J.; Kim, W. Explicit characterization of feedback nash equilibria for indefinite, linear-quadratic, mean-field-type stochastic zero-sum differential games with jump-diffusion Models. *Mathematics* **2020**, *8*, 1669. [CrossRef]
11. Zhang, P.; Mohamed, N.A.; Ibrahim, A.I.N. Mean-field and anticipated BSDEs with time-felayed generator. *Mathematics* **2023**, *11*, 888. [CrossRef]
12. Li, J.; Liang, H.; Zhang, X. General mean-field BSDEs with continuous coefficients. *J. Math. Anal. Appl.* **2018**, *466*, 264–280. [CrossRef]
13. Wang, J.; Zhao, N.; Shi, Y. General mean-field backward stochastic differential equations with discontinuous coefficients. In Proceedings of the 41th Chinese Control Conference, Hefei, China, 25–27 July 2022; pp. 1287–1292.
14. Li, J.; Xing, C. General mean-field BDSDEs with continuous coefficients. *J. Math. Anal. Appl.* **2022**, *506*, 125699. [CrossRef]
15. Shi, Y.; Wang, J.; Zhao, N. General mean-field BDSDEs with continuous and stochastic linear growth coefficients. *J. Syst. Sci. Complex.* **2024**. *in press*
16. Bibi Ruhomally, Y.; Zaid Dauhoo, M.; Dumas, L. Stochastic modelling of marijuana use in Washington: Pre-and post-Initiative-502 (I-502). *IMA J. Appl. Math.* **2022**, *87*, 1121–1150. [CrossRef]

mathematics

MDPI

Article

The Maximal and Minimal Distributions of Wealth Processes in Black–Scholes Markets

Shuhui Liu

Department of Applied Mathematics, The Hong Kong Polytechnic University, Hung Hom, Kowloon, Hong Kong, China; shuhui.liu@polyu.edu.hk

Abstract: The Black–Scholes formula is an important formula for pricing a contingent claim in complete financial markets. This formula can be obtained under the assumption that the investor's strategy is carried out according to a self-financing criterion; hence, there arise a set of self-financing portfolios corresponding to different contingent claims. The natural questions are: If an investor invests according to self-financing portfolios in the financial market, what are the maximal and minimal distributions of the investor's wealth on some specific interval at the terminal time? Furthermore, if such distributions exist, how can the corresponding optimal portfolios be constructed? The present study applies the theory of backward stochastic differential equations in order to obtain an affirmative answer to the above questions. That is, the explicit formulations for the maximal and minimal distributions of wealth when adopting self-financing strategies would be derived, and the corresponding optimal (self-financing) portfolios would be constructed. Furthermore, this would verify the benefits of diversified portfolios in financial markets: that is, do not put all your eggs in the same basket.

Keywords: self-financing portfolio; optimal investment; maximal distribution; backward stochastic differential equation; diversified portfolio

MSC: 60G05; 60H05; 60H30; 91-10

1. Introduction

In the realm of financial markets, the continuous trading of securities such as stocks forms the backbone of economic dynamics. This paper delves into a market comprising N securities operating within a fixed time horizon. The price trajectories of these securities are modeled by geometric Brownian motion: each is characterized by distinct drifts and volatilities. We explore the scenario of an investor investing his/her initial endowment into these N securities. The investor's portfolio, $\Pi(t) := (\pi_1(t), \cdots, \pi_N(t))$, represents the proportion of wealth invested in each stock. The notation V_t^{Π} represents the investor's wealth trajectory under the self-financing portfolio strategy $\Pi(t)$. In the context of modern portfolio theory, investors aim to balance risk and reward, with risk-averse individuals prioritizing predictability and lower risk over potentially higher but uncertain returns; see, for example, [1–4]. This preference underscores the importance of understanding the risk associated with a portfolio, particularly through the probability of the wealth process V_T^{π} falling within a specific interval.

Therefore, a natural question is: Can we obtain the maximal and minimal distributions of the wealth process V_T^{Π} on any specific interval over the portfolio set Θ. If this is possible, how can these two optimal portfolios, Π^* and Π_*, be constructed to achieve the maximal and minimal distributions, respectively? This is, for any given positive numbers $a < b$ and $0 \leq T < \infty$,

$$\mathbb{P}(V_T^{\Pi^*} \in [a,b]) = \sup_{\Pi \in \Theta} \mathbb{P}(V_T^{\Pi} \in [a,b]), \tag{1}$$

and

$$\mathbb{P}(V_T^{\Pi_*} \in [a,b]) = \inf_{\Pi \in \Theta} \mathbb{P}(V_T^{\Pi} \in [a,b]). \tag{2}$$

In the above proposed financial market model, the drift terms of the securities' price processes are not precisely known, introducing ambiguity into the market dynamics. This ambiguity reflects the real-world uncertainty that investors face when the true probabilities of future events are unclear or indeterminate. Unlike risk, which can be quantified and managed through probabilistic models, ambiguity challenges traditional decision-making frameworks and necessitates novel approaches to portfolio optimization.

The current study addresses this ambiguity by considering the range of possible drift values within known bounds $[\underline{\mu}, \overline{\mu}]$. By doing so, we aim to characterize the maximal and minimal distributions of the wealth process V_T^{Π}, which represent the best- and worst-case scenarios for an investor's wealth at time T given the uncertain drift terms. These distributions provide valuable insights for investors, particularly those who are risk-averse, as they offer a way to gauge the potential outcomes of their investment strategies in the face of ambiguous market conditions.

The study on ambiguity models dates back to Frank [5], who explains how uncertainty can create imperfect market structures. The portfolio optimization problem is studied by Hansen and Sargent [6], who model the volatility of stocks as a stochastic process such that the volatility of stocks is uncertain. Chen and Epstein [2] conceptualize the theoretical framework of ambiguity, risk and asset return with respect to a set of 'objective' probability measures. Cvitanic, Ma and Zhang [7] study the problem of computing hedging portfolios for options that may have discontinuous payoffs. Schied [8] uses risk assessment operators to solve the portfolio maximization problem. A robust mean-variance maximization problem is studied by Maccheroni, Marinacci and Ruffino [9]. Bielecki, Jin, Pliska and Zhou [10] study continuous-time mean-variance portfolio selection with bankruptcy prohibition. Jin and Zhou [11] study continuous-time portfolio selection under ambiguity, in which the appreciation rates are only known to be in a certain convex closed set, and the portfolios are allowed to be only based on historical stock prices. Bai, Ma and Xing [12] study a class of optimal dividend and investment problems with the assumption that the underlying reserve process follows the Sparre Andersen model. Hu, Jin and Zhou [13] study portfolio selection in a complete, continuous time market, in which the preference is dictated by the rank-dependent utility. Chen, Feng and Zhang [14] study sampling-strategy-driven limit theorems that generate the maximum or minimum average reward in the two-armed bandit problem.

To date, the above model has been widely studied. However, the explicit formulations of the maximal and minimal distributions remain unknown. The present study introduces a new method to investigate the above model. Specifically, based on the theory of backward stochastic differential equations (BSDEs), a confirmed answer can be obtained for the above question. That is, the explicit expression of Π^* and Π_* would be established, and the closed form of $\mathbb{P}(V_T^{\Pi^*} \in [a,b])$ and $\mathbb{P}(V_T^{\Pi_*} \in [a,b])$ would be obtained. Actually, we shall show that the maximal and minimal distributions are closely related to a BSDE that is nonlinear in z_t. Nonlinear BSDEs were initially studied by Pardoux and Peng [15]. It has been widely recognized that BSDEs provide a useful framework for formulating problems in various fields, such as financial mathematics, stochastic optimal control, and partial differential equations (PDEs). For example, El Karoui, Peng and Quenez [16] study different properties of BSDEs and their applications in finance, especially contingent claim valuation and recursive utility (independently introduced by Duffie and Epstein [17]). Pardoux and Peng [18] establish some estimates and regularity results for the solution of BSDEs and provide a Feynman–Kac representation for solutions to some nonlinear parabolic PDEs. Peng [19] obtain the general stochastic maximum principle through the theory of BSDEs. Yong [20] discusses the solvability of BSDEs with possibly unbounded coefficients and their applications in a Black–Scholes type security market with unbounded risk premium processes and/or interest rates. Chen and Epstein [21] study a central limit theorem for a sequence of random variables with a mean uncertainty, and it was revealed that the limit is defined by a BSDE, which can be interpreted as modeling an ambiguous continuous-time random walk.

Although BSDEs have been used in various problems, this method still has some limitations since the properties of z_t and the explicit solution of general nonlinear BSDEs cannot be easily established. For the z_t part, Chen, Kupperger and Wei [22] obtain an interesting comonotonic theorem of z_t for a nonlinear but special generator. Although it is difficult to obtain the explicit formulations for the solution of a general nonlinear BSDE, Chen, Liu, Qian and Xu [23] obtain explicit solutions to an interesting class of nonlinear BSDEs, which is the k-ignorance model that arose from modeling the ambiguity of asset pricing (e.g., Chen and Epstein [2]).

Motivated by these above results, the present paper uses BSDEs to study the optimal investment problem. The main ideas are as follows: First, the correlation between the maximal distribution $\sup_{\Pi\in\Theta} \mathbb{P}(V_T^{\Pi} \in [a,b])$ and the solution for a special kind of nonlinear BSDE (Theorem 1) is established. Second, through the formulation of the BSDE, the corresponding optimal portfolio is constructed (Theorem 2). Third, after obtaining the explicit solution for the derived BSDE, the maximal distribution is explicitly computed (Theorem 4). Similarly, the minimal distribution $\inf_{\Pi\in\Theta} \mathbb{P}(V_T^{\Pi} \in [a,b])$ and the corresponding optimal portfolio are similarly studied. For wider applications, a general utility function φ including the indicator function $\mathbf{1}_{[a,b]}$ is considered (Theorem 3). From the explicit formulations of the optimal strategy and the optimal distribution, it can easily be observed that diversified portfolios with two stocks would be better than portfolios with only one stock.

The present study is organized as follows. Section 2 presents the definition of maximal and minimal distributions and some basic results for the BSDEs used for the study. Section 3 presents the explicit representations of optimal portfolios Π^* and Π_*, which correspond to the maximal and minimal distributions, respectively. The explicit expressions for the maximal and minimal distributions and a general utility function case are presented in Section 4. The maximal distribution is applied to explain the benefits of diversified portfolios in Section 5.

2. Preliminaries

In this section, some notations and lemmas are provided. Let $(\Omega, \mathcal{F}, \mathbb{P})$ refer to the probability space, $(B_t)_{t\geq 0}$ refer to the standard Brownian motion on this probability space, and $(\mathcal{F}_t)_{t\geq 0}$ refer to the σ-filtration generated by the Brownian motion, which is augmented by all $\mathbb{P}$-null sets $\mathcal{N}(\mathbb{P})$. That is, $\mathcal{F}_t = \sigma\{B_s; 0 \leq s \leq t\} \vee \mathcal{N}(\mathbb{P})$. Let $L^2(\Omega, \mathcal{F}_T, \mathbb{P})$ refer to the set of all $\mathcal{F}_T$-measurable and square-integrable random variables, $\mathcal{S}(0,T;\mathbb{R})$ refer to the set of all real-valued $\mathcal{F}_t$-adapted processes with $\mathbb{E}\left[\sup_{t\in[0,T]} |y_t|^2\right] < +\infty$, and $\mathcal{M}(0,T;\mathbb{R})$ refer to the set of all $\mathcal{F}_t$-progressively measurable real-valued processes with $\mathbb{E}\left[\int_0^T |z_t|^2 dt\right] < \infty$. Throughout the study, $\mathbf{1}_A$ represents the indicator function on set A, $\mathbb{E}_{\mathbb{P}}[\cdot]$ denotes the expectation under probability measure $\mathbb{P}$, and the sign function $\text{sgn}(x)$ is given by

$$\text{sgn}(x) = \begin{cases} 1, & x > 0, \\ -1, & x \leq 0. \end{cases}$$

The definition of a maximal distribution is initially given. The minimal distribution is similarly defined.

Definition 1 (Maximal distribution). *Let X^θ refer to the family of random variables over a given index set Θ. The maximal distribution of X^θ over the set Θ is denoted by the following:*

$$\sup_{\theta\in\Theta} \mathbb{P}\left(X^\theta \in [a,b]\right), \quad \textit{for all } a,b \in R_+.$$

We now introduce the model of our study, which is set within a finite time horizon $0 \leq T < \infty$. The price dynamics of the securities are governed by the following system of stochastic differential equations (SDEs):

$$\begin{cases} dS_i(t) = \mu_i\, S_i(t)dt + \sigma_i\, S_i(t)dB_t, \\ S_i(0) = x_i, \quad i = 1, 2, \cdots, N, \end{cases} \tag{3}$$

where μ_i represents the drift, $\sigma_i > 0$ is the volatility, x_i is the initial price, and B_t is a Brownian motion within the probability space $(\Omega, \mathcal{F}, \mathbb{P})$. A feature of our model is the ambiguity of the exact values of μ_i, with only their maximum and minimum known. For simplicity, we only consider the case $N = 2$ and $x_i = 1$ for $i = 1, 2$. This simplification does not detract from the generality of our results, which can be extended to scenarios with $N > 2$.

We explore the scenario of an investor investing his/her initial endowment into two stocks. The investor's portfolio, $\Pi(t) := (\pi(t), 1 - \pi(t))$, represents the proportion of wealth invested in each stock. The evolution of the investor's wealth, V_t^{π}, is governed by the stochastic differential equation:

$$\begin{cases} dV_t^{\Pi} = V_t^{\Pi}[\pi(t)\mu_1 + (1 - \pi(t))\mu_2]dt + V_t^{\Pi}[\pi(t)\sigma_1 + (1 - \pi(t))\sigma_2]dB_t, \quad t \in [0, T], \\ V_0^{\Pi} = 1. \end{cases} \tag{4}$$

The set of all possible self-financing portfolios, Θ, is defined as:

$$\Theta := \left\{ \Pi(t) = (\pi(t), 1 - \pi(t)) : \pi(t) \in [\underline{\rho}, \overline{\rho}] \text{ is a predictable process} \right\},$$

where $\underline{\rho}, \overline{\rho} \in [0, 1]$ refer to two fixed numbers that represent the constraints on the investment proportion of these two stocks.

At the end of this section, nonlinear BSDEs are briefly introduced, which were initially investigated in [15]:

$$y_t = \xi + \int_t^T g(y_s, z_s)ds - \int_t^T z_s dB_s. \tag{5}$$

Lemma 1 ([15])**.** *Assume that $g : \mathbb{R}^2 \to \mathbb{R}$ is uniformly Lipschitz continuous. Hence, for any $\xi \in L^2(\Omega, \mathcal{F}_T, \mathbb{P})$ and $T > 0$, the BSDE (5) has a unique pair of solution $(y, z) \in \mathcal{S}(0, T; \mathbb{R}) \times \mathcal{M}(0, T; \mathbb{R})$.*

Usually, it is difficult to obtain the closed form for the solution of the BSDE (5) when g is nonlinear. Interestingly, as shown in the following lemma, for cases $g(z) = k|z|$ and $\xi = \varphi(B_T)$, the following BSDE has a pair of explicit solutions:

$$Y_t = \varphi(B_T) + \int_t^T k|Z_s|ds - \int_t^T Z_s dB_s, \tag{6}$$

where φ satisfies the following assumption:

Hypothesis 1. *There exists some $c \in \mathbb{R}$ such that φ is symmetric on c. That is, $\varphi(c - x) = \varphi(c + x)$ for all $x \in \mathbb{R}$.*

Lemma 2 ([23])**.** *Assume that $\varphi \in C^3(\mathbb{R})$ satisfies (H.1) for some $c \in \mathbb{R}$, and $\varphi^{(i)}$ (where $i = 0, 1, 2, 3$) have, at most, polynomial growth. Then BSDE (6) has a pair of explicit solutions*

$$Y_t = H(B_t),\ Z_t = \partial_h H(B_t),$$

with H defined as follows:

(i) If $\varphi' \geq 0$ and $\varphi' \not\equiv 0$ on (c, ∞), then

$$H(h) = e^{-\frac{1}{2}k^2(T-t)} \int_{\mathbb{R}} \int_{y \geq 0} \varphi(x+h) e^{k|x-c+h|-k|c-h|-ky} P(B_{T-t} \in dx, L_{T-t}^{c-h} \in dy);$$

(ii) If $\varphi' \leq 0$ and $\varphi' \not\equiv 0$ on (c, ∞), then

$$H(h) = e^{-\frac{1}{2}k^2(T-t)} \int_{\mathbb{R}} \int_{y \geq 0} \varphi(x+h) e^{-k|x-c+h|+k|c-h|+ky} P(B_{T-t} \in dx, L_{T-t}^{c-h} \in dy),$$

where $\mathbb{P}(B_t \in dx, L_t^{\ell} \in dy)$ is the joint distribution of B_t and its local time L_t^{ℓ} with respect to ℓ and is given by

$$\begin{aligned} &\mathbb{P}(B_t \in dx, L_t^{\ell} \in dy) \\ &= \frac{1}{\sqrt{2\pi t^3}}(y + |x-\ell| + |\ell|) \exp\left\{ \frac{-(y+|x-\ell|+|\ell|)^2}{2t} \right\} \cdot \mathbf{1}_{\{y>0\}} dxdy \\ &+ \frac{1}{\sqrt{2\pi t}} \left[\exp\left\{ -\frac{x^2}{2t} \right\} - \exp\left\{ -\frac{(|x-\ell|+|\ell|)^2}{2t} \right\} \right] \cdot \mathbf{1}_{\{y=0\}} dxdy. \end{aligned} \tag{7}$$

3. Explicit Representation of Optimal Portfolios

For simplicity, in the following, we will suppress the time variable t in $\pi(t)$ when there is no confusion. This section provides the optimal portfolios $\Pi^* = (\pi^*, 1-\pi^*)$ and $\Pi_* = (\pi_*, 1-\pi_*)$ such that

$$\mathbb{P}(V_T^{\Pi^*} \in [a,b]) = \sup_{\Pi \in \Theta} \mathbb{P}(V_T^{\Pi} \in [a,b]) = \sup_{\Pi \in \Theta} \mathbb{P}(\log V_T^{\Pi} \in [\log a, \log b]),$$

and

$$\mathbb{P}(V_T^{\Pi_*} \in [a,b]) = \inf_{\Pi \in \Theta} \mathbb{P}(V_T^{\Pi} \in [a,b]) = \inf_{\Pi \in \Theta} \mathbb{P}(\log V_T^{\Pi} \in [\log a, \log b]).$$

Moreover, in the following it is assumed that $\sigma_1 = \sigma_2 = \sigma$ and $x = 1$. Then, the wealth process takes the following form:

$$\begin{cases} dV_t^{\Pi} = V_t^{\Pi}[\Pi(t)\mu_1 + (1-\Pi(t))\mu_2]dt + \sigma V_t^{\Pi} dB_t, \\ V_0^{\Pi} = 1, \quad t \in (0,T]. \end{cases} \tag{8}$$

Denote

$$\mu(t) := \pi(t)\left(\mu_1 - \frac{1}{2}\sigma^2\right) + (1-\pi(t))\left(\mu_2 - \frac{1}{2}\sigma^2\right).$$

Similarly, $\mu^*(t)$ and $\mu_*(t)$ are denoted corresponding to Π^* and Π_*, respectively. In order to study the optimal portfolios, the following result needs to be initially obtained.

Theorem 1. *Suppose that V_t^{Π} is the wealth process defined in (8) with $\sigma_1 = \sigma_2 = \sigma$, and $\Pi(t) = (\pi(t), 1-\pi(t))$ is the related portfolio. Assume that $\varphi(\sigma B_T) \in L^2(\Omega, \mathcal{F}_T, \mathbb{P})$. Then*

(1) $\sup_{\Pi \in \Theta} \mathbb{E}[\varphi(\log V_T^{\Pi})]$ is the value of the solution Y_t of the following BSDE at $t = 0$:

$$Y_t = \varphi(\sigma B_T) + \int_t^T \left(\frac{\overline{\mu}}{\sigma} Z_s^+ - \frac{\underline{\mu}}{\sigma} Z_s^- \right) ds - \int_t^T Z_s dB_s, \tag{9}$$

(2) $\inf_{\Pi \in \Theta} \mathbb{E}[\varphi(\log V_T^{\Pi})]$ is the value of the solution y_t of the following BSDE at $t = 0$:

$$y_t = \varphi(\sigma B_T) + \int_t^T \left(\frac{\underline{\mu}}{\sigma} z_s^+ - \frac{\overline{\mu}}{\sigma} z_s^- \right) ds - \int_t^T z_s dB_s, \tag{10}$$

where

$$\overline{\mu} = \Big[\frac{\overline{\rho}-\underline{\rho}}{2} sgn(\mu_1-\mu_2) + \frac{\overline{\rho}+\underline{\rho}}{2}\Big](\mu_1-\mu_2) + \mu_2 - \frac{1}{2}\sigma^2,$$
$$\underline{\mu} = \Big[\frac{\underline{\rho}-\overline{\rho}}{2} sgn(\mu_1-\mu_2) + \frac{\overline{\rho}+\underline{\rho}}{2}\Big](\mu_1-\mu_2) + \mu_2 - \frac{1}{2}\sigma^2,$$

and $\bar{\rho}, \underline{\rho} \in [0,1]$ *are the upper bound and lower bound, respectively, of* $\pi(t)$.

Proof. Note that
$$d\log V_t^{\Pi} = \mu(t)dt + \sigma dB_t,\ \log V_0^{\Pi} = 0.$$
Let $\mathcal{H}$ be the set of $\{\mathcal{F}_t\}$-progressively measurable processes $\theta_s, 0 \le s \le T$ taking values in $[\underline{\mu}, \overline{\mu}]$. Then, from

$$\mu(t) = \pi(t)\Big(\mu_1 - \frac{1}{2}\sigma^2\Big) + (1-\pi(t))\Big(\mu_2 - \frac{1}{2}\sigma^2\Big),$$

we have
$$\Pi(t) \in \Theta \Longleftrightarrow \mu(t) \in \mathcal{H}.$$
Therefore,

$$\begin{aligned}\sup_{\Pi\in\Theta} \mathbb{E}\Big[\varphi\Big(\log V_T^{\Pi}\Big)\Big] &= \sup_{\Pi\in\Theta} \mathbb{E}\Big[\varphi\Big(\sigma B_T + \int_0^T \pi(s)\Big(\mu_1 - \frac{1}{2}\sigma^2\Big) + (1-\pi(s))\Big(\mu_2 - \frac{1}{2}\sigma^2\Big)ds\Big)\Big] \\ &= \sup_{\mu\in\mathcal{H}} \mathbb{E}\Big[\varphi\Big(\sigma B_T + \int_0^T \mu(s)ds\Big)\Big].\end{aligned} \tag{11}$$

Let (Y_t, Z_t) be the solution of BSDE (9). Define

$$a_s = \frac{\overline{\mu}}{\sigma}\mathbf{1}_{Z_s>0} + \frac{\underline{\mu}}{\sigma}\mathbf{1}_{Z_s\le 0}, \quad \text{and} \quad \widetilde{B}_s = B_s - \int_0^s a_r dr. \tag{12}$$

By Girsanov's theorem (see for example [24]), we know $\widetilde{B}_s$ is a Brownian motion under $\mathbb{Q}$, where

$$\frac{d\mathbb{Q}}{d\mathbb{P}}\Big|_{\mathcal{F}_t} = \exp\Big(\int_0^t a_r dB_r - \frac{1}{2}\int_0^t a_r^2 dr\Big). \tag{13}$$

Therefore,

$$\begin{aligned}Y_t =& \varphi(\sigma B_T) + \int_t^T \Big(\frac{\overline{\mu}}{\sigma}Z_s^+ - \frac{\underline{\mu}}{\sigma}Z_s^-\Big)ds - \int_t^T Z_s dB_s \\ =& \varphi(\sigma B_T) - \int_t^T Z_s d\widetilde{B}_s \\ =& \varphi\Big(\sigma\widetilde{B}_T + \sigma\int_0^T a_r dr\Big) - \int_t^T Z_s d\widetilde{B}_s.\end{aligned}$$

Hence,

$$Y_0 = \mathbb{E}_{\mathbb{Q}}\Big[\varphi\Big(\sigma\widetilde{B}_T + \sigma\int_0^T a_r dr\Big)\Big] \le \sup_{\mu\in\mathcal{H}} \mathbb{E}_{\mathbb{Q}}\Big[\varphi\Big(\sigma\widetilde{B}_T + \int_0^T \mu(r)dr\Big)\Big]. \tag{14}$$

For any $\sigma\theta_s \in \mathcal{H}$, consider the following BSDE:

$$Y_t^{\theta} = \varphi(\sigma B_T) + \int_t^T \theta_s Z_s^{\theta} ds - \int_t^T Z_s^{\theta} dB_s. \tag{15}$$

Define $B_s^\theta = B_s - \int_0^s \theta_r dr$. Then B_s^θ is a Brownian motion under $\mathbb{P}^\theta$, where

$$\frac{d\mathbb{P}^\theta}{d\mathbb{P}}\Big|_{\mathcal{F}_t} = \exp\Big(\int_0^t \theta_r dB_r - \frac{1}{2}\int_0^t \theta_r^2 dr\Big).$$

Thus,

$$Y_t^\theta = \varphi(\sigma B_T) + \int_t^T \theta_s Z_s^\theta ds - \int_t^T Z_s^\theta dB_s = \varphi\Big(\sigma B_T^\theta + \sigma\int_0^T \theta_r dr\Big) - \int_t^T Z_s^\theta dB_s^\theta.$$

Hence,

$$Y_0^\theta = \mathbb{E}_{\mathbb{P}^\theta}\Big[\varphi\Big(\sigma B_T^\theta + \sigma\int_0^T \theta_r dr\Big)\Big].$$

It follows from the comparison theorem of BSDE (e.g., [16]) that

$$Y_0^\theta \leq Y_0.$$

Consequently,

$$\sup_{\theta\in\mathcal{H}} \mathbb{E}_{\mathbb{P}^\theta}\Big[\varphi\Big(\sigma B_T^\theta + \int_0^T \theta_r dr\Big)\Big] \leq Y_0. \tag{16}$$

Note

$$\sup_{\theta\in\mathcal{H}} \mathbb{E}_{\mathbb{P}^\theta}\Big[\varphi\Big(\sigma B_T^\theta + \int_0^T \theta_r dr\Big)\Big] = \sup_{\theta\in\mathcal{H}} \mathbb{E}_{\mathbb{P}}\Big[\varphi\Big(\sigma B_T + \int_0^T \theta_r dr\Big)\Big] = \sup_{\mu\in\mathcal{H}} \mathbb{E}_{\mathbb{Q}}\Big[\varphi\Big(\sigma \widetilde{B}_T + \int_0^T \mu(r) dr\Big)\Big].$$

Combining (11), (14) and (16), we have

$$Y_0 = \sup_{\Pi\in\Theta} \mathbb{E}[\varphi(\log V_T^\pi)].$$

Similarly, part (2) of Theorem 1 can be proved. □

Now, we can give the main result of this section, which is about the optimal portfolios.

Theorem 2. *The optimal portfolios $\Pi^* = (\pi^*, 1-\pi^*)$ and $\Pi_* = (\pi_*, 1-\pi_*)$ defined by* (1) *and* (2) *are given as follows: For $t \in [0,T]$,*

$$\begin{aligned}
\pi^*(t) =& \frac{\overline{\rho}+\underline{\rho}}{2} + \frac{(\overline{\rho}-\underline{\rho})sgn(\mu_1-\mu_2)}{2} sgn\Big(-\overline{R}_t + \frac{\log(ab)}{2\sigma} - \frac{\overline{\mu}+\underline{\mu}}{2\sigma}(T-t)\Big) \\
=& \begin{cases} \frac{\overline{\rho}+\underline{\rho}}{2} + \frac{\overline{\rho}-\underline{\rho}}{2} sgn\Big(-\overline{R}_t + \frac{\log(ab)}{2\sigma} - \frac{\overline{\mu}+\underline{\mu}}{2\sigma}(T-t)\Big), & \mu_1 > \mu_2, \\ \frac{\overline{\rho}+\underline{\rho}}{2} - \frac{\overline{\rho}-\underline{\rho}}{2} sgn\Big(-\overline{R}_t + \frac{\log(ab)}{2\sigma} - \frac{\overline{\mu}+\underline{\mu}}{2\sigma}(T-t)\Big), & \mu_1 \leq \mu_2. \end{cases}
\end{aligned} \tag{17}$$

and

$$\begin{aligned}
\pi_*(t) =& \frac{\overline{\rho}+\underline{\rho}}{2} + \frac{(\underline{\rho}-\overline{\rho})sgn(\mu_1-\mu_2)}{2} sgn\Big(-\underline{R}_t + \frac{\log(ab)}{2\sigma} - \frac{\overline{\mu}+\underline{\mu}}{2\sigma}(T-t)\Big) \\
=& \begin{cases} \frac{\overline{\rho}+\underline{\rho}}{2} + \frac{\underline{\rho}-\overline{\rho}}{2} sgn\Big(-\underline{R}_t + \frac{\log(ab)}{2\sigma} - \frac{\overline{\mu}+\underline{\mu}}{2\sigma}(T-t)\Big), & \mu_1 > \mu_2, \\ \frac{\overline{\rho}+\underline{\rho}}{2} - \frac{\underline{\rho}-\overline{\rho}}{2} sgn\Big(-\underline{R}_t + \frac{\log(ab)}{2\sigma} - \frac{\overline{\mu}+\underline{\mu}}{2\sigma}(T-t)\Big), & \mu_1 \leq \mu_2. \end{cases}
\end{aligned} \tag{18}$$

where

$$d\overline{R}_t = \Big[\frac{\overline{\mu}-\underline{\mu}}{2\sigma}sgn\Big(-\overline{R}_t + \frac{\log(ab)}{2\sigma} - \frac{\overline{\mu}+\underline{\mu}}{2\sigma}(T-t)\Big) + \frac{\overline{\mu}+\underline{\mu}}{2\sigma}\Big]dt + dB_t,\ \overline{R}_0 = 0,$$

and

$$d\underline{R}_t = \Big[\frac{\underline{\mu}-\overline{\mu}}{2\sigma}sgn\Big(-\underline{R}_t + \frac{\log(ab)}{2\sigma} - \frac{\overline{\mu}+\underline{\mu}}{2\sigma}(T-t)\Big) + \frac{\overline{\mu}+\underline{\mu}}{2\sigma}\Big]dt + dB_t,\ \underline{R}_0 = 0.$$

In this case,

$$\begin{cases} d\Big(\frac{\log V_t^{\Pi^*}}{\sigma}\Big) = \Big[\pi^*(t)\Big(\mu_1 - \frac{1}{2}\sigma^2\Big) + (1-\pi^*(t))\Big(\mu_2 - \frac{1}{2}\sigma^2\Big)\Big]dt + dB_t \\ \qquad = \Big[\frac{\overline{\mu}-\underline{\mu}}{2\sigma}sgn\Big(-\overline{R}_t + \frac{\log ab}{2\sigma} - \frac{\overline{\mu}+\underline{\mu}}{2\sigma}(T-t)\Big) + \frac{\overline{\mu}+\underline{\mu}}{2\sigma}\Big]dt + dB_t, \\ \log V_0^{\Pi^*} = 0, \end{cases}$$

and

$$\begin{cases} d\Big(\frac{\log V_t^{\Pi_*}}{\sigma}\Big) = \Big[\pi_*(t)\Big(\mu_1 - \frac{1}{2}\sigma^2\Big) + (1-\pi_*(t))\Big(\mu_2 - \frac{1}{2}\sigma^2\Big)\Big]dt + dB_t \\ \qquad = \Big[\frac{\underline{\mu}-\overline{\mu}}{2\sigma}sgn\Big(-\underline{R}_t + \frac{\log ab}{2\sigma} - \frac{\overline{\mu}+\underline{\mu}}{2\sigma}(T-t)\Big) + \frac{\overline{\mu}+\underline{\mu}}{2\sigma}\Big]dt + dB_t, \\ \log V_0^{\Pi_*} = 0. \end{cases}$$

That is, $e^{\sigma\overline{R}_t}$ is the wealth at time t with respect to $\Pi^* = (\pi^*, 1-\pi^*)$, and $e^{\sigma\underline{R}_t}$ is the wealth at time t with respect to $\Pi_* = (\pi_*, 1-\pi_*)$

Proof. By Theorem 1, we have

$$\sup_{\Pi\in\Theta}\mathbb{P}(V_T^{\Pi} \in [a,b]) = \sup_{\Pi\in\Theta}\mathbb{P}(\log V_T^{\Pi} \in [\log a, \log b]) = Y_0,$$

where

$$Y_t = \mathbf{1}_{[\log a, \log b]}(\sigma B_T) + \int_t^T \Big(\frac{\overline{\mu}}{\sigma}Z_s^+ - \frac{\underline{\mu}}{\sigma}Z_s^-\Big)ds - \int_t^T Z_s dB_s,$$

and $\mathbf{1}_{[\log a, \log b]}(\cdot)$ is the indicator function on $[\log a, \log b]$. Moreover,

$$Y_0 = \mathbb{E}_{\mathbb{Q}}\Big[\mathbf{1}_{[\log a, \log b]}\Big(\sigma\widetilde{B}_T + \sigma\int_0^T a_s ds\Big)\Big],$$

where a_s and $\mathbb{Q}$ are given by (12) and (13), respectively. Define $\widehat{B}_t = B_t - \frac{\overline{\mu}+\underline{\mu}}{2\sigma}t$. We know from Girsanov's theorem that $\widehat{B}_t$ is a Brownian motion under $\widehat{\mathbb{P}}$ with

$$\frac{d\widehat{\mathbb{P}}}{d\mathbb{P}}\Big|_{\mathcal{F}_t} = \exp\Big\{\frac{\overline{\mu}+\underline{\mu}}{2\sigma}B_t - \frac{1}{2}\Big|\frac{\overline{\mu}+\underline{\mu}}{2\sigma}\Big|^2 t\Big\},$$

and

$$\begin{aligned} Y_t =& \mathbf{1}_{[\log a, \log b]}(\sigma B_T) + \int_t^T \Big(\frac{\overline{\mu}}{\sigma}Z_s^+ - \frac{\underline{\mu}}{\sigma}Z_s^-\Big)ds - \int_t^T Z_s dB_s \\ =& \mathbf{1}_{[\frac{\log a}{\sigma} - \frac{\overline{\mu}+\underline{\mu}}{2\sigma}T, \frac{\log b}{\sigma} - \frac{\overline{\mu}+\underline{\mu}}{2\sigma}T]}(\widehat{B}_T) + \int_t^T \frac{\overline{\mu}-\underline{\mu}}{2\sigma}|Z_s|ds - \int_t^T Z_s d\widehat{B}_s. \end{aligned}$$

It follows from ([23] Corollary 6) that

$$\text{sgn}(-Z_s) = sgn\Big(\widehat{B}_s - \frac{\log(ab)}{2\sigma} + \frac{\overline{\mu}+\underline{\mu}}{2\sigma}T\Big) = \text{sgn}\Big(B_s - \frac{\log(ab)}{2\sigma} + \frac{\overline{\mu}+\underline{\mu}}{2\sigma}(T-s)\Big).$$

Therefore,

$$Y_0 = \mathbb{E}_{\widetilde{\mathbb{P}}}\Big[\mathbf{1}_{[\log a,\log b]}\Big(\sigma\widetilde{B}_T + \int_0^T\Big[\frac{\overline{\mu}-\underline{\mu}}{2}\text{sgn}\Big(-B_s + \frac{\log(ab)}{2\sigma} - \frac{\overline{\mu}+\underline{\mu}}{2\sigma}(T-s)\Big) + \frac{\overline{\mu}+\underline{\mu}}{2}\Big]ds\Big)\Big].$$

Define

$$d\overline{R}_t = \Big[\frac{\overline{\mu}-\underline{\mu}}{2\sigma}\text{sgn}\Big(-\overline{R}_t + \frac{\log(ab)}{2\sigma} - \frac{\overline{\mu}+\underline{\mu}}{2\sigma}(T-t)\Big) + \frac{\overline{\mu}+\underline{\mu}}{2\sigma}\Big]dt + dB_t,\ \overline{R}_0 = 0.$$

We have

$$Y_0 = \mathbb{E}_{\mathbb{P}}\Big[\mathbf{1}_{[\log a,\log b]}\Big(\sigma B_T + \int_0^T\Big[\frac{\overline{\mu}-\underline{\mu}}{2}\text{sgn}\Big(-\overline{R}_s + \frac{\log(ab)}{2\sigma} - \frac{\overline{\mu}+\underline{\mu}}{2\sigma}(T-s)\Big) + \frac{\overline{\mu}+\underline{\mu}}{2}\Big]ds\Big)\Big].$$

Since

$$\begin{aligned}
&\sup_{\Pi\in\Theta}\mathbb{E}_{\mathbb{P}}[\mathbf{1}_{[\log a,\log b]}(\log V_T^{\pi})] \\
&= \sup_{\mu\in\mathcal{H}}\mathbb{E}_{\mathbb{P}}\Big[\mathbf{1}_{[\log a,\log b]}\Big(\sigma B_T + \int_0^T\mu(t)dt\Big)\Big] \\
&= \mathbb{E}_{\mathbb{P}}\Big[\mathbf{1}_{[\log a,\log b]}\Big(\sigma B_T + \int_0^T\Big[\frac{\overline{\mu}-\underline{\mu}}{2}\text{sgn}\Big(-\overline{R}_t + \frac{\log(ab)}{2\sigma} - \frac{\overline{\mu}+\underline{\mu}}{2\sigma}(T-t)\Big) + \frac{\overline{\mu}+\underline{\mu}}{2}\Big]dt\Big)\Big],
\end{aligned}$$

and $\sup_{\Pi\in\Theta}\mathbb{E}[\varphi(\log V_T^{\Pi})] = \sup_{\mu\in\mathcal{H}}\mathbb{E}\Big[\varphi\Big(\sigma B_T + \int_0^T\mu(s)ds\Big)\Big]$, from (11), we obtain that

$$\mu^*(t) = \frac{\overline{\mu}-\underline{\mu}}{2}\text{sgn}\Big(-\overline{R}_t + \frac{\log(ab)}{2\sigma} - \frac{\overline{\mu}+\underline{\mu}}{2\sigma}(T-t)\Big) + \frac{\overline{\mu}+\underline{\mu}}{2}.$$

Moreover, we know

$$\mu^*(t) = \pi^*(t)(\mu_1 - \frac{1}{2}\sigma^2) + (1-\pi^*(t))(\mu_2 - \frac{1}{2}\sigma^2).$$

Thus,

$$\begin{aligned}
\pi^*(t) &= \frac{\overline{\rho}+\underline{\rho}}{2} + \frac{\overline{\mu}-\underline{\mu}}{2(\mu_1-\mu_2)}\text{sgn}\Big(-\overline{R}_t + \frac{\log(ab)}{2\sigma} - \frac{\overline{\mu}+\underline{\mu}}{2\sigma}(T-t)\Big) \\
&= \frac{\overline{\rho}+\underline{\rho}}{2} + \frac{(\overline{\rho}-\underline{\rho})\text{sgn}(\mu_1-\mu_2)}{2}\text{sgn}\Big(-\overline{R}_t + \frac{\log(ab)}{2\sigma} - \frac{\overline{\mu}+\underline{\mu}}{2\sigma}(T-t)\Big) \\
&= \begin{cases} \frac{\overline{\rho}+\underline{\rho}}{2} + \frac{\overline{\rho}-\underline{\rho}}{2}\text{sgn}\Big(-\overline{R}_t + \frac{\log(ab)}{2\sigma} - \frac{\overline{\mu}+\underline{\mu}}{2\sigma}(T-t)\Big),\ \mu_1 > \mu_2, \\ \frac{\overline{\rho}+\underline{\rho}}{2} - \frac{\overline{\rho}-\underline{\rho}}{2}\text{sgn}\Big(-\overline{R}_t + \frac{\log(ab)}{2\sigma} - \frac{\overline{\mu}+\underline{\mu}}{2\sigma}(T-t)\Big),\ \mu_1 \le \mu_2. \end{cases}
\end{aligned} \tag{19}$$

Similarly, by Theorem 1, we have

$$\inf_{\Pi\in\Theta}\mathbb{P}(V_T^{\Pi}\in[a,b]) = \inf_{\Pi\in\Theta}\mathbb{P}(\log V_T^{\Pi}\in[\log a,\log b]) = y_0,$$

where

$$y_t = \mathbf{1}_{[\log a,\log b]}(\sigma B_T) + \int_t^T\Big(\frac{\underline{\mu}}{\sigma}z_s^+ - \frac{\overline{\mu}}{\sigma}z_s^-\Big)ds - \int_t^T z_s dB_s,$$

and

$$y_0 = \mathbb{E}_{\check{\mathbb{P}}}\Big[\mathbf{1}_{[\log a, \log b]}\Big(\sigma \check{B}_T + \sigma \int_0^T \beta_s ds\Big)\Big],$$

$\check{B}_t = B_t - \int_0^t \beta_s ds$ is a Brownian motion under $\check{\mathbb{P}}$ with

$$\frac{d\check{\mathbb{P}}}{d\mathbb{P}}\Big|_{\mathcal{F}_t} = \exp\Big(\int_0^t \beta_s dB_s - \frac{1}{2}\int_0^t \beta_s^2 ds\Big),$$

and

$$\beta_s = \frac{\underline{\mu}}{\sigma}\mathbf{1}_{z_s>0} + \frac{\overline{\mu}}{\sigma}\mathbf{1}_{z_s\le 0} = \frac{\underline{\mu} - \overline{\mu}}{2\sigma}\mathrm{sgn}(z_s) + \frac{\underline{\mu} + \overline{\mu}}{2\sigma}.$$

It follows from ([23] Corollary 6) that

$$\mathrm{sgn}(-z_s) = \mathrm{sgn}\Big(B_s - \frac{\log(ab)}{2\sigma} + \frac{\overline{\mu} + \underline{\mu}}{2\sigma}(T-s)\Big).$$

Therefore,

$$\begin{aligned} y_0 =& \mathbb{E}_{\check{\mathbb{P}}}\Big[\mathbf{1}_{[\log a, \log b]}\Big(\sigma \check{B}_T + \int_0^T \Big[\frac{\underline{\mu} - \overline{\mu}}{2}\mathrm{sgn}\Big(-B_s + \frac{\log(ab)}{2\sigma} - \frac{\overline{\mu} + \underline{\mu}}{2\sigma}(T-s)\Big) + \frac{\underline{\mu} + \overline{\mu}}{2}\Big]ds\Big)\Big] \\ =& \mathbb{E}_{\mathbb{P}}\Big[\mathbf{1}_{[\log a, \log b]}\Big(\sigma B_T + \int_0^T \Big[\frac{\underline{\mu} - \overline{\mu}}{2}\mathrm{sgn}\Big(-\underline{R}_s + \frac{\log(ab)}{2\sigma} - \frac{\overline{\mu} + \underline{\mu}}{2\sigma}(T-s)\Big) + \frac{\overline{\mu} + \underline{\mu}}{2}\Big]ds\Big)\Big]. \end{aligned}$$

Then we have

$$\mu_*(t) = \frac{\underline{\mu} - \overline{\mu}}{2}\mathrm{sgn}\Big(-\underline{R}_t + \frac{\log(ab)}{2\sigma} - \frac{\overline{\mu} + \underline{\mu}}{2\sigma}(T-t)\Big) + \frac{\underline{\mu} + \overline{\mu}}{2}.$$

From

$$\mu_*(t) = \pi_*(t)(\mu_1 - \frac{1}{2}\sigma^2) + (1 - \pi_*(t))(\mu_2 - \frac{1}{2}\sigma^2),$$

we have

$$\begin{aligned} \pi_*(t) =& \frac{\overline{\rho} + \underline{\rho}}{2} + \frac{\underline{\mu} - \overline{\mu}}{2(\mu_1 - \mu_2)}\mathrm{sgn}\Big(-\underline{R}_t + \frac{\log(ab)}{2\sigma} - \frac{\overline{\mu} + \underline{\mu}}{2\sigma}(T-t)\Big) \\ =& \frac{\overline{\rho} + \underline{\rho}}{2} + \frac{(\underline{\rho} - \overline{\rho})\mathrm{sgn}(\mu_1 - \mu_2)}{2}\mathrm{sgn}\Big(-\underline{R}_t + \frac{\log(ab)}{2\sigma} - \frac{\overline{\mu} + \underline{\mu}}{2\sigma}(T-t)\Big) \\ =& \begin{cases} \frac{\overline{\rho} + \underline{\rho}}{2} + \frac{\underline{\rho} - \overline{\rho}}{2}\mathrm{sgn}\Big(-\underline{R}_t + \frac{\log(ab)}{2\sigma} - \frac{\overline{\mu} + \underline{\mu}}{2\sigma}(T-t)\Big), & \mu_1 > \mu_2, \\ \frac{\overline{\rho} + \underline{\rho}}{2} - \frac{\underline{\rho} - \overline{\rho}}{2}\mathrm{sgn}\Big(-\underline{R}_t + \frac{\log(ab)}{2\sigma} - \frac{\overline{\mu} + \underline{\mu}}{2\sigma}(T-t)\Big), & \mu_1 \le \mu_2. \end{cases} \end{aligned}$$

This completes the proof. □

Remark 1. *If the drifts μ_1 and μ_2 of the prices are known, based on* (17) *and* (18)*, the optimal portfolios can be obtained with reference to the processes/wealth $\overline{R}_t$ and $\underline{R}_t$, respectively. For the case that μ_1 and μ_2 are unknown, the optimal portfolios cannot be applied directly. However, if $\mu_1 \vee \mu_2$ and $\mu_1 \wedge \mu_2$ are known while μ_1 and μ_2 are unknown, under the criterion of exploration and exploitation, the reinforcement learning technique (e.g., the ε-greedy method, ([25] Chapter 2) and [26]) and the above optimal portfolios can be combined together to construct the desired portfolios. With the estimated drifts (based on the historic data), a portfolio can be constructed to achieve the largest coverage probability on any interval $[a, b]$, for which the stock deduced by the optimal portfolios* (17) *and* (18) *with the estimated drifts is selected most of the time. However, every once in a while, such as with a small probability ε, the two stocks are chosen randomly (i.e., chosen with equal probabilities) independent of the estimated drifts for portfolios* (17) *and* (18)*. Specifically, when the sign function in* (17) *is positive, the stock with the larger estimated drift is chosen with probability $1 - \varepsilon$, and the two stocks are chosen randomly with the probability ε. Otherwise, the stock with the smaller estimated drift* *is chosen with probability $1-\varepsilon$, and the two stocks are chosen randomly with the probability ε. Similarly, when the sign function in* (18) *is positive, the stock with smaller estimated drift is chosen with probability $1-\varepsilon$, and the two stocks are chosen randomly with the probability ε. Otherwise, the stock with the larger estimated drift is chosen with probability $1-\varepsilon$, and the two stocks are chosen randomly with the probability ε. The algorithm with $\varepsilon = 0.1$ is presented in Appendix A.*

4. Maximal and Minimal Distributions

Next, the explicit distributions of the ambiguity portfolio model will be provided: that is, the explicit expressions of $\sup\limits_{\Pi\in\Theta}\mathbb{P}(V_T^{\Pi}\in[a,b])$ and $\inf\limits_{\Pi\in\Theta}\mathbb{P}(V_T^{\Pi}\in[a,b])$. In particular, the representations of $\sup\limits_{\Pi\in\Theta}\mathbb{E}[\varphi(\log V_T^{\Pi})]$ and $\inf\limits_{\Pi\in\Theta}\mathbb{E}[\varphi(\log V_T^{\Pi})]$ for general utility function φ are initially given. Then, the maximal and minimal distributions are obtained.

Theorem 3. *Assume that $\varphi\in C^3(\mathbb{R})$ satisfies (H.1) for some $c\in\mathbb{R}$, and $\varphi^{(i)}$ $(i=0,1,2,3)$ have, at most, polynomial growth. Set $k=\frac{\overline{\mu}-\underline{\mu}}{2\sigma}$. Then the representations of $\sup\limits_{\Pi\in\Theta}\mathbb{E}[\varphi(\log V_T^{\Pi})]$ and $\inf\limits_{\Pi\in\Theta}\mathbb{E}[\varphi(\log V_T^{\Pi})]$ are given as follows:*

(1) *If $\varphi'\geq 0$ and $\varphi'\not\equiv 0$ on (c,∞), then*

$$\sup_{\Pi\in\Theta}\mathbb{E}[\varphi(\log V_T^{\Pi})]=e^{-\frac{1}{2}k^2T}\times\Big\{\int_{\mathbb{R}}\int_{y\geq 0}\varphi\Big(\sigma x+\frac{\overline{\mu}+\underline{\mu}}{2}T\Big)\cdot\exp\{k|x-c|-k|c|-ky\}\mathbb{P}(B_T\in dx, L_T^c\in dy)\Big\},$$

$$\inf_{\pi\in\Theta}\mathbb{E}[\varphi(\log V_T^{\pi})]=e^{-\frac{1}{2}k^2T}\times\Big\{\int_{\mathbb{R}}\int_{y\geq 0}\varphi\Big(\sigma x+\frac{\overline{\mu}+\underline{\mu}}{2}T\Big)\cdot\exp\{-k|x-c|+k|c|+ky\}\mathbb{P}(B_T\in dx, L_T^c\in dy)\Big\},$$

where $\mathbb{P}(B_T\in dx, L_T^c\in dy)$ is given by (7).

(2) *If $\varphi'\leq 0$ and $\varphi'\not\equiv 0$ on (c,∞), then*

$$\sup_{\Pi\in\Theta}\mathbb{E}[\varphi(\log V_T^{\Pi})]=e^{-\frac{1}{2}k^2T}\times\Big\{\int_{\mathbb{R}}\int_{y\geq 0}\varphi\Big(\sigma x+\frac{\overline{\mu}+\underline{\mu}}{2}T\Big)\cdot\exp\{-k|x-c|+k|c|+ky\}\mathbb{P}(B_T\in dx, L_T^c\in dy)\Big\},$$

$$\inf_{\Pi\in\Theta}\mathbb{E}[\varphi(\log V_T^{\Pi})]=e^{-\frac{1}{2}k^2T}\times\Big\{\int_{\mathbb{R}}\int_{y\geq 0}\varphi\Big(\sigma x+\frac{\overline{\mu}+\underline{\mu}}{2}T\Big)\cdot\exp\{k|x-c|-k|c|-ky\}\mathbb{P}(B_T\in dx, L_T^c\in dy)\Big\}.$$

Proof. Let $\widetilde{\varphi}(x)=\varphi(\sigma x)$. Then $\mathbb{E}[\varphi(\log V_T^{\pi})]=\mathbb{E}\Big[\widetilde{\varphi}\Big(\frac{\log V_T^{\pi}}{\sigma}\Big)\Big]$. We will only give the proof of $\sup\limits_{\Pi\in\Theta}\mathbb{E}[\varphi(\log V_T^{\Pi})]$ when $\varphi'\geq 0$ and $\varphi'\not\equiv 0$ on (c,∞) since the other case can be treated similarly. Using Theorem 1, we have

$$\sup_{\Pi\in\Theta}\mathbb{E}\Big[\widetilde{\varphi}\Big(\frac{\log V_T^{\Pi}}{\sigma}\Big)\Big]=Y_0,$$

where Y_0 is the solution Y_t of the following BSDE at $t = 0$:

$$Y_t = \widetilde{\varphi}(B_T) + \int_t^T \Big(\frac{\overline{\mu}}{\sigma} Z_s^+ - \frac{\underline{\mu}}{\sigma} Z_s^-\Big) ds - \int_t^T Z_s dB_s. \tag{20}$$

Set $\widehat{B}_s = B_s - \frac{\underline{\mu}+\overline{\mu}}{2\sigma} s$ and $\widehat{\varphi}(x) = \widetilde{\varphi}(x + \frac{\underline{\mu}+\overline{\mu}}{2\sigma} T)$. Then BSDE (20) is equivalent to the following equation:

$$Y_t = \widehat{\varphi}(\widehat{B}_T) + \int_t^T \frac{\overline{\mu}-\underline{\mu}}{2\sigma} |Z_s| ds - \int_t^T Z_s d\widehat{B}_s, \tag{21}$$

where $\widehat{B}_t$ is a Brownian motion under measure $\widehat{\mathbb{Q}}$ defined by

$$\frac{d\widehat{\mathbb{Q}}}{d\mathbb{P}}\Big|_{\mathcal{F}_t} = \exp\left\{ \int_0^t \frac{\underline{\mu}+\overline{\mu}}{2\sigma} dB_s - \frac{1}{2}\int_0^t \Big(\frac{\underline{\mu}+\overline{\mu}}{2\sigma}\Big)^2 ds \right\}.$$

Thus, it suffices to solve BSDE (21) on $(\Omega, \mathcal{F}, \widehat{\mathbb{Q}})$. By Lemma 2, we have

$$\sup_{\Pi\in\Theta} \mathbb{E}[\varphi(\log V_T^\Pi)] = Y_0 = e^{-\frac{1}{2}k^2 T} \times \left\{ \int_{\mathbb{R}} \int_{y\geq 0} \widehat{\varphi}(x) e^{k|x-c|-k|c|-ky} \widehat{\mathbb{Q}}(\widehat{B}_T \in dx, \widehat{L}_T^c \in dy) \right\},$$

where

$$\begin{aligned} &\widehat{\mathbb{Q}}(\widehat{B}_T \in dx, \widehat{L}_T^c \in dy) = \mathbb{P}(B_T \in dx, L_T^c \in dy) \\ &= \frac{1}{\sqrt{2\pi T^3}} (y + |x-c| + |c|) \exp\left\{ \frac{-(y+|x-c|+|c|)^2}{2T} \right\} \cdot I_{\{y>0\}} dxdy \\ &+ \frac{1}{\sqrt{2\pi T}} \left[\exp\left\{ -\frac{x^2}{2T} \right\} - \exp\left\{ -\frac{(|x-c|+|c|)^2}{2T} \right\} \right] \cdot I_{\{y=0\}} dxdy. \end{aligned}$$

So we obtain the expression of $\sup\limits_{\Pi\in\Theta} \mathbb{E}[\varphi(\log V_T^\Pi)]$.

Similarly, applying Theorem 1, we have

$$\inf_{\Pi\in\Theta} \mathbb{E}\Big[\varphi(\log V_T^\Pi)\Big] = y_0,$$

where y_0 is the solution y_t of the following BSDE when $t = 0$:

$$y_t = \widetilde{\varphi}(B_T) + \int_t^T \Big(\frac{\underline{\mu}}{\sigma} z_s^+ - \frac{\overline{\mu}}{\sigma} z_s^-\Big) ds - \int_t^T z_s dB_s = \widehat{\varphi}(\widehat{B}_T) - \int_t^T \frac{\overline{\mu}-\underline{\mu}}{2\sigma} |z_s| ds - \int_t^T z_s d\widehat{B}_s.$$

It then follows from Lemma 2 that

$$\inf_{\Pi\in\Theta} \mathbb{E}\Big[\varphi(\log V_T^\Pi)\Big] = y_0 = e^{-\frac{1}{2}k^2 T} \times \left\{ \int_{\mathbb{R}} \int_{y\geq 0} \widehat{\varphi}(x) e^{-k|x-c|+k|c|+ky} \widehat{\mathbb{Q}}(\widehat{B}_T \in dx, \widehat{L}_T^c \in dy) \right\};$$

thus, the expression of $\inf\limits_{\Pi\in\Theta} \mathbb{E}[\varphi(\log V_T^\Pi)]$ is obtained. □

Applying Theorem 3, the explicit formulations of the maximal and minimal distributions when $\varphi(x) = \mathbf{1}_{[a,b]}(x)$ with $0 < a < b < +\infty$ can be obtained.

Theorem 4. *Let $k = \frac{\overline{\mu}-\underline{\mu}}{2\sigma}$ and $c = \frac{\log(ab)}{2\sigma} - \frac{\underline{\mu}+\overline{\mu}}{2\sigma} T$ with $0 < a < b < +\infty$; then the maximal and minimal distributions are given by*

$$\sup_{\Pi\in\Theta} \mathbb{P}(V_T^\Pi \in [a,b]) = \Phi\left(-\frac{|c| - kT - \frac{\log(b/a)}{2\sigma}}{\sqrt{T}} \right) - e^{-\frac{k}{\sigma}\log(b/a)} \Phi\left(-\frac{|c| - kT + \frac{\log(b/a)}{2\sigma}}{\sqrt{T}} \right),$$

and

$$\inf_{\Pi\in\Theta}\mathbb{P}(V_T^{\Pi}\in[a,b])=\Phi\left(-\frac{|c|+kT-\frac{\log(b/a)}{2\sigma}}{\sqrt{T}}\right)-e^{\frac{k}{\sigma}\log(b/a)}\Phi\left(-\frac{|c|+kT+\frac{\log(b/a)}{2\sigma}}{\sqrt{T}}\right), \tag{22}$$

where $\Phi(\cdot)$ is the distribution function of the standard normal distribution.

Proof. First, recall that $\sup_{\Pi\in\Theta}\mathbb{E}\left[\varphi(\log V_T^{\Pi})\right]$ is the value of the solution Y_t of the following BSDE at $t=0$:

$$\begin{aligned}Y_t=&\mathbf{1}_{[a,b]}(\sigma B_T)+\int_t^T\left(\frac{\overline{\mu}}{\sigma}Z_s^+-\frac{\underline{\mu}}{\sigma}Z_s^-\right)ds-\int_t^T Z_s dB_s\\=&\mathbf{1}_{[\frac{\log a}{\sigma}-\frac{\overline{\mu}+\underline{\mu}}{2\sigma}T,\frac{\log b}{\sigma}-\frac{\overline{\mu}+\underline{\mu}}{2\sigma}T]}(\widehat{B}_T)+\int_t^T\frac{\overline{\mu}-\underline{\mu}}{2\sigma}|Z_s|ds-\int_t^T Z_s d\widehat{B}_s,\end{aligned} \tag{23}$$

where $\widehat{B}_t=B_t-\frac{\overline{\mu}+\underline{\mu}}{2\sigma}t$ is a Brownian motion under $\widehat{\mathbb{P}}$ with

$$\frac{d\widehat{\mathbb{P}}}{d\mathbb{P}}\Big|_{\mathcal{F}_t}=\exp\left\{\frac{\overline{\mu}+\underline{\mu}}{2\sigma}B_t-\frac{1}{2}\left|\frac{\overline{\mu}+\underline{\mu}}{2\sigma}\right|^2 t\right\}.$$

For simplicity, let

$$\hat{a}=\frac{\log a}{\sigma}-\frac{\overline{\mu}+\underline{\mu}}{2\sigma}T,\ \ \hat{b}=\frac{\log b}{\sigma}-\frac{\overline{\mu}+\underline{\mu}}{2\sigma}T.$$

For any $\varepsilon>0$, define

$$\varphi_\varepsilon(x):=\mathbb{E}_{\widehat{\mathbb{P}}}\left[\mathbf{1}_{[\hat{a},\hat{b}]}(x+\sqrt{\varepsilon}\xi)\right]=\int_{-\infty}^{\infty}\mathbf{1}_{[\hat{a},\hat{b}]}(v)\frac{1}{\sqrt{2\pi\varepsilon}}\exp\left[-\frac{(v-x)^2}{2\varepsilon}\right]dv,$$

where ξ is a standard normal distribution under probability measure $\widehat{\mathbb{P}}$. Then $\varphi_\varepsilon\in C^\infty(\mathbb{R})$ and $\varphi_\varepsilon(x)\to I_{[\hat{a},\hat{b}]}(x)$ as $\varepsilon\to0$. Consider the following BSDE:

$$Y_t^\varepsilon=\varphi_\varepsilon(\widehat{B}_T)+\int_t^T k|Z_s^\varepsilon|ds-\int_t^T Z_s^\varepsilon d\widehat{B}_s.$$

By Theorem 3, we have

$$Y_t^\varepsilon=H^\varepsilon(\widehat{B}_t),$$

where

$$\begin{aligned}H^\varepsilon(h)=&e^{-\frac{1}{2}k^2(T-t)}\left\{\int_{\mathbb{R}}\int_{y\geq0}\varphi_\varepsilon(x+h)e^{-k|x-c+h|+k|c-h|+ky}\widehat{\mathbb{P}}\left(\widehat{B}_{T-t}\in dx,\widehat{L}_{T-t}^{c-h}\in dy\right)\right\}\\=&e^{-\frac{1}{2}k^2(T-t)}\int_{\mathbb{R}}\int_{y>0}\frac{\varphi_\varepsilon(x+h)}{\sqrt{2\pi(T-t)^3}}e^{-k|x-c+h|+k|c-h|+ky}(y+|x-(c-h)|+|c-h|)\\&\exp\left\{\frac{-(y+|x-(c-h)|+|c-h|)^2}{2(T-t)}\right\}dxdy\\&+e^{-\frac{1}{2}k^2(T-t)}\int_{\mathbb{R}}\frac{\varphi_\varepsilon(x+h)}{\sqrt{2\pi(T-t)}}e^{-k|x-c+h|+k|c-h|}\\&\left[\exp\left\{-\frac{x^2}{2(T-t)}\right\}-\exp\left\{-\frac{(|x-(c-h)|+|c-h|)^2}{2(T-t)}\right\}\right]dxdy.\end{aligned}$$

Define

$$H(h) := e^{-\frac{1}{2}k^2(T-t)}\Big\{\int_{\mathbb{R}}\int_{y\geq 0}\mathbf{1}_{[\hat{a},\hat{b}]}(x+h)e^{k|x-c+h|-k|c-h|-ky}\widehat{\mathbb{P}}\Big(\widehat{B}_{T-t}\in dx,\widehat{L}^{c-h}_{T-t}\in dy\Big)\Big\}$$

$$= e^{-\frac{1}{2}k^2(T-t)}\int_{\mathbb{R}}\int_{y>0}\frac{\mathbf{1}_{[\hat{a},\hat{b}]}(x+h)}{\sqrt{2\pi(T-t)^3}}e^{-k|x-c+h|+k|c-h|+ky}(y+|x-(c-h)|+|c-h|)$$

$$\exp\Big\{\frac{-(y+|x-(c-h)|+|c-h|)^2}{2(T-t)}\Big\}dxdy$$

$$+e^{-\frac{1}{2}k^2(T-t)}\int_{\mathbb{R}}\frac{\mathbf{1}_{[\hat{a},\hat{b}]}(x+h)}{\sqrt{2\pi(T-t)}}e^{-k|x-c+h|+k|c-h|}$$

$$\Big[\exp\Big\{-\frac{x^2}{2(T-t)}\Big\}-\exp\Big\{-\frac{(|x-(c-h)|+|c-h|)^2}{2(T-t)}\Big\}\Big]dxdy.$$

After some computations, we have

$$H(h)=\Phi\Big(-\frac{|h-c|-k(T-t)-\frac{\hat{b}-\hat{a}}{2}}{\sqrt{T-t}}\Big)-e^{-k(\hat{b}-\hat{a})}\Phi\Big(-\frac{|h-c|-k(T-t)+\frac{\hat{b}-\hat{a}}{2}}{\sqrt{T-t}}\Big).$$

By Lebesgue's dominated convergence theorem, we have that $H^{\varepsilon}(h)$ converges to $H(h)$ as $\varepsilon\to 0$, which means $H^{\varepsilon}(\widehat{B}_t)$ converges to $H(\widehat{B}_t)$ almost surely. Therefore, Y_t of (23) is given by

$$Y_t=H(\widehat{B}_t)=\Phi\Big(-\frac{|\widehat{B}_t-c|-k(T-t)-\frac{\hat{b}-\hat{a}}{2}}{\sqrt{T-t}}\Big)-e^{-k(\hat{b}-\hat{a})}\Phi\Big(-\frac{|\widehat{B}_t-c|-k(T-t)+\frac{\hat{b}-\hat{a}}{2}}{\sqrt{T-t}}\Big).$$

Finally,

$$\sup_{\Pi\in\Theta}\mathbb{E}[\mathbf{1}_{[a,b]}(V_t^{\Pi})]=\sup_{\Pi\in\Theta}\mathbb{E}[\mathbf{1}_{[\log a,\log b]}(\log V_t^{\Pi})]=Y_0$$

$$=\Phi\Big(-\frac{|c|-kT-\frac{\hat{b}-\hat{a}}{2}}{\sqrt{T}}\Big)-e^{-k(\hat{b}-\hat{a})}\Phi\Big(-\frac{|c|-kT+\frac{\hat{b}-\hat{a}}{2}}{\sqrt{T}}\Big).$$

Similarly, we have (22). □

Remark 2. *It can be observed from Theorem 4 that the maximal and minimal distributions of wealth V_T^{π} are no longer* log-normal *when $\underline{\mu}\neq\overline{\mu}$. That is, if a random disturbance $\mu(t)$ is given to the Brownian motion (or the price process of the stocks), then its distribution will no longer be normal. That is, it would be a mixture of normal distributions. This is explained in the following example: If the process $(\log V_t)_{t\in[0,T]}$ follows the following SDE with some random disturbance $\mu(t)$,*

$$d\log V_t=\mu(t)dt+dB_t,\ \log V_0=0,$$

where $|\mu(t)|\leq\varepsilon$. Take $T=1,\varepsilon=1/2,a=-b$ and set

$$\mathbb{F}_{B_1}(b):=\mathbb{P}(B_1\in[e^{-b},e^{b}]),\bar{\mathbb{F}}_{\log V_1}(b):=\sup_{|\mu(t)|\leq\varepsilon}\mathbb{P}(\log V_1\in[-b,b]),\underline{\mathbb{F}}_{\log V_1}(b):=\inf_{|\mu(t)|\leq\varepsilon}\mathbb{P}(\log V_1\in[-b,b]).$$

Let $f_1(z)$ refer to the density function of B_1, and let $\bar{f}(z)$ and $\underline{f}(z)$ refer to the density functions of $\bar{\mathbb{F}}_{\log V_1}(\cdot)$ and $\underline{\mathbb{F}}_{\log V_1}(\cdot)$, respectively. Based on Theorem 4, it is not difficult to obtain

$$\begin{cases}\bar{\mathbb{F}}_{\log V_1}(b)=\Phi(1/2+b)-e^{-b}\cdot\Phi(1/2-b),\\ \underline{\mathbb{F}}_{\log V_1}(b)=\Phi(-1/2+b)-e^{b}\cdot\Phi(-1/2-b),\end{cases}$$

and consequently,

$$\begin{cases} \bar{f}(z) = \frac{1}{\sqrt{2\pi}} e^{-\frac{z^2+|z|+1/4}{2}} + 1/2 \cdot e^{-|z|} \cdot \Phi(-|z|+1/2), \\ \underline{f}(z) = \frac{1}{\sqrt{2\pi}} e^{-\frac{z^2-|z|+1/4}{2}} - 1/2 \cdot e^{|z|} \cdot \Phi(-|z|-1/2). \end{cases}$$

The differences in $\mathbb{F}_{B_1}$, $\bar{\mathbb{F}}_{\log V_1}$ *and* $\underline{\mathbb{F}}_{\log V_1}$ *and the differences in* f_1, $\bar{f}$ *and* $\underline{f}$ *can be intuitively observed from Figure 1. This shows that the maximal and minimal distributions of* V_1 *are no longer* log-*normal.*

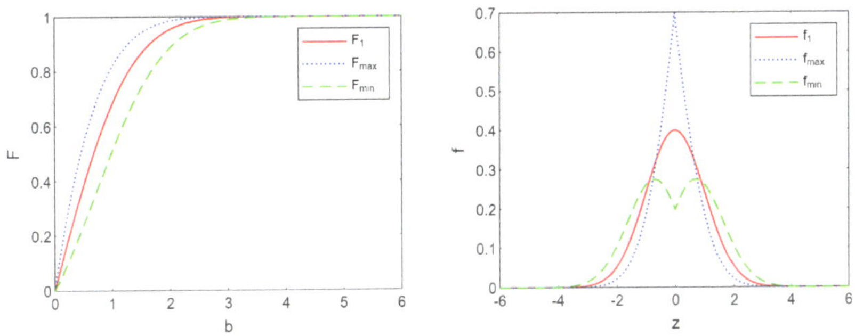

Figure 1. Differences among $\mathbb{F}_{B_1}$, $\bar{\mathbb{F}}_{\log V_1}$ and $\bar{\mathbb{F}}_{\log V_1}$ and differences in f, $\bar{f}$ and $\underline{f}$ when $a = -b$, $\varepsilon = 0.5$, $T = 1$.

5. Do Not Put All the Eggs in One Basket

'Do not put all your eggs in the same basket' is a widespread proverb that means that diversified investment is necessary in order to avoid great losses due to a single investment. On the one hand, this advice can be partly formalized by considering the volatility of the portfolio. For example, by constructing portfolios with assets that are imperfectly correlated with one another, the risk inherent in the portfolio would decline as more assets are added to the portfolio until, eventually, the volatility of the portfolio would converge to the average covariance of assets that comprise the portfolio. Therefore, diversified risks can be reduced when compared to undiversified risks. On the other hand, after obtaining the explicit formulation for the maximal distribution and the corresponding portfolio, the benefits of the diversified portfolios can be explained and the proverb from the probability framework can be formalized, as shown in the following results.

Let $\bar{\rho} = 1$ and $\underline{\rho} = 0$. Then, $\Pi_1(\cdot) \equiv (1,0)$ and $\Pi_2(\cdot) \equiv (0,1)$ refer to two self-financing portfolios. By applying Theorem 4, the following result can be obtained.

Proposition 1. *For* $0 < a < b < +\infty$,

$$\mathbb{P}(V_T^{\Pi^*} \in [a,b]) = \sup_{\Pi \in \Theta} \mathbb{P}(V_T^{\pi} \in [a,b]) \geq \mathbb{P}(V_T^1 \in [a,b]) \vee \mathbb{P}(V_T^2 \in [a,b]), \tag{24}$$

where $\Pi^* = (\pi^*, 1-\pi^*)$, $\pi^*(\cdot)$ *is defined in* (19), $V_\cdot^1$ *and* $V_\cdot^2$ *are the wealth processes corresponding to portfolios* $\Pi_1(\cdot)$ *and* $\Pi_2(\cdot)$, *respectively: that is, investing only in the first stock and only in the second stock respectively. Furthermore, let* $\sigma = T = 1$, $\log b = \bar{\mu} + \delta$ *and* $\log a = \bar{\mu} - \delta$ *for some* $\delta > 0$*; we have*

$$\mathbb{P}(V_1^{\Pi^*} \in [a,b]) - \mathbb{P}(V_1^1 \in [a,b]) \vee \mathbb{P}(V_1^2 \in [a,b]) = (1 - e^{-(\bar{\mu}+\underline{\mu})\delta})\Phi(-\delta) > 0. \tag{25}$$

The two portfolios, $\Pi_1(\cdot) \equiv (1,0)$ and $\Pi_2(\cdot) \equiv (0,1)$, correspond to the cases for which all wealth is invested solely in the first and second stock, respectively. From (25), it can be observed that neither of the above portfolios is optimal in the probability framework. Instead, investing in both stocks according to $\pi^*(\cdot)$ would deduce a larger probability on any interval around the larger drift/return, thereby achieving a greater coverage probability to win a larger drift/return and reducing the risk. Therefore, a diversified portfolio with two stocks is better than a portfolio with only one stock (even when the stock has a larger drift/return). That is, the existence of a stock with a smaller drift/return does not always cause bad influences on the market. Interestingly, the combination of these two stocks would induce a larger coverage probability of wealth on any specific interval, consequently reducing the risk of the investment. Therefore, this verifies the benefits of diversified portfolios and implies the mathematical explanations for the proverb.

Remark 3. *The results for the maximal and minimal distributions can be extended to a case with more than two stocks. For example, consider that there are N $(N > 2)$ stocks in the financial market; the wealth process would follow the following SDE:*

$$\begin{cases} dV_t^{\Pi} = V_t^{\Pi}[\sum_{i=1}^{N} \mu_i \pi_i(t)]dt + \sigma V_t^{\pi} dB_t, \\ V_0^{\Pi} = 1, \quad t \in (0, T], \end{cases} \tag{26}$$

in which $\sum_{i=1}^{N} \pi_i(t) = 1$, and the set of self-financing portfolios is

$$\Theta^N := \{\Pi(t) = (\pi_1(t), \cdots, \pi_N(t)) : \pi_i(t) \in [0,1] \text{ is a predictable processes}\}.$$

Let

$$\overline{\mu} := \sup\{\mu_1 - \frac{1}{2}\sigma^2, \cdots, \mu_N - \frac{1}{2}\sigma^2\} \text{ and } \underline{\mu} := \inf\{\mu_1 - \frac{1}{2}\sigma^2, \cdots, \mu_N - \frac{1}{2}\sigma^2\}. \tag{27}$$

Then, similar to Theorem 1, it can be proved that $\sup_{\Pi \in \Theta} \mathbb{E}[\varphi(\log V_T^{\Pi})]$ is equal to Y_0 of BSDE (9), with $\overline{\mu}$ and $\underline{\mu}$ given by (27). Thus, through solving BSDE (9), the maximal distributions of this case can be obtained based on Theorem 4. Furthermore, the minimal distribution can be similarly obtained.

Funding: This research was funded by Research Grants of The Hong Kong Polytechnic University under grant numbers S-ZG9U and 1-W32B.

Data Availability Statement: No new data were created or analyzed in this study. Data sharing is not applicable to this article.

Conflicts of Interest: The author declares no conflict of interest.

Appendix A

The algorithm is as follows:

Algorithm A1: ϵ-greedy algorithm

```
Input: time partition K; returns μ1, μ2; reward interval [a, b];
Output: Wealth log V_1^{π*}.
terminal time T = 1, t_k = k/K, k = 0, 1, ..., K, initial condition log V_0^{π*} = 0,
 maximal drift coefficient μ̄ = μ1 ∨ μ2, minimal drift coefficient μ_ = μ1 ∧ μ2.
for i = 1, 2 do
  sample means μ̄_i(0) = 0;
  the number of times each state has been observed T_i = 1;
end for
for each k ∈ [0, K] do
  if  k  mod 10 == 0, then
     j = randperm(2, 1);
```

Algorithm A1: *Cont.*

$\Delta = \frac{1}{K}\mu_j + \sigma B(\frac{1}{K})$;
$\overline{\mu}_j(t_{k+1}) = \frac{T_j-1}{T_j}\overline{\mu}_j(t_k) + \frac{\Delta}{T_j}$;
$\overline{\mu}_i(t_{k+1}) = \overline{\mu}_i(t_k), i \neq j$;
$\log V^{\pi^*}_{t_{k+1}} = \log V^{\pi^*}_{t_k} + \Delta$;
$T_j = T_j + 1$;
else
  if $\log V^{\pi^*}_{t_k} \leq \frac{\log(ab)}{2\sigma} - \frac{\overline{\mu}+\underline{\mu}}{2\sigma}(1-t_k)$, **then**
    find j such that $\overline{\mu}_j(t_k) = \overline{\mu}_1(t_k) \vee \overline{\mu}_2(t_k)$;
    $\Delta = \frac{1}{K}\mu_j + \sigma B(\frac{1}{K})$;
    $\overline{\mu}_j(t_{k+1}) = \frac{T_j-1}{T_j}\overline{\mu}_j(t_k) + \frac{\Delta}{T_j}$;
    $\overline{\mu}_i(t_{k+1}) = \overline{\mu}_i(t_k), i \neq j$;
    $\log V^{\pi^*}_{t_{k+1}} = \log V^{\pi^*}_{t_k} + \Delta$;
    $T_j = T_j + 1$;
  else
    find j such that $\overline{\mu}_j(t_k) = \overline{\mu}_1(t_k) \wedge \overline{\mu}_2(t_k)$;
    $\Delta = \frac{1}{K}\mu_j + \sigma B(\frac{1}{K})$;
    $\overline{\mu}_j(t_{k+1}) = \frac{T_j-1}{T_j}\overline{\mu}_j(t_k) + \frac{\Delta}{T_j}$;
    $\overline{\mu}_i(t_{k+1}) = \overline{\mu}_i(t_k), i \neq j$;
    $\log V^{\pi^*}_{t_{k+1}} = \log V^{\pi^*}_{t_k} + \Delta$;
    $T_j = T_j + 1$;
  end if
end if
end for

References

1. Barberis, N. Investing for the Long Run when Returns Are Predictable. *J. Financ.* **2000**, *55*, 225–264. [CrossRef]
2. Chen, Z.; Epstein, L. Ambiguity, risk, and asset returns in continuous time. *Econometrica* **2002**, *70*, 1403–1443. [CrossRef]
3. Markowitz, H.M. Portfolio Selection. *J. Financ.* **1952**, *7*, 77–91.
4. Pedersen, L.H. *Efficiently Inefficient: How Smart Money Invests and Market Prices Are Determined*; Princeton University Press: Princeton, NJ, USA, 2019.
5. Frank, H.K. *Risk, Uncertainty and Profit*; BN Publishing: Hawthorne, CA, USA, 1921.
6. Hansen, L.P.; Sargent, T.J. Robust control and model uncertainty. *Am. Econ. Rev.* **2001**, *91*, 60–66. [CrossRef]
7. Cvitanic, J.; Ma, J.; Zhang, J. Efficient Computation of Hedging Portfolios for Options with Discontinuous Payoffs. *Math. Financ.* **2003**, *13*, 131–151. [CrossRef]
8. Schied, A. Risk measures and robust optimization problems. *Stoch. Model.* **2006**, *22*, 753–831. [CrossRef]
9. Maccheroni, F.; Marinacci, M.; Ruffino, D. Alpha as ambiguity: Robust mean-variance portfolio analysis. *Econometrica* **2013**, *81*, 1075–1113. [CrossRef]
10. Bielecki, T.; Jin, H.; Pliska, S.; Zhou, X. Continuous-time mean-variance portfolio selection with bankruptcy prohibition. *Math. Financ.* **2005**, *15*, 213–244. [CrossRef]
11. Jin, H.; Zhou, X. Continuous-time portfolio selection under ambiguity. *Math. Control. Relat. Fields* **2015**, *5*, 475–488. [CrossRef]
12. Bai, L.; Ma, J.; Xing, X. Optimal Dividend and Investment Problems under Sparrer-Andersen Model. *Ann. Appl. Probab.* **2017**, *27*, 3588–3632. [CrossRef]
13. Hu, Y.; Jin, H.; Zhou, X. Consistent investment of sophisticated rank-dependent utility agents in continuous time. *Math. Financ.* **2021**, *31*, 1056–1095. [CrossRef]
14. Chen, Z.; Feng, S.; Zhang, G. Strategy-Driven Limit Theorems Associated with Bandit Problems. *arXiv* **2022**, arXiv:2204.04442.
15. Pardoux, E.; Peng, S. Adapted solution of a backward stochastic differential equation. *Syst. Control. Lett.* **1990**, *14*, 55–61. [CrossRef]
16. Karoui, N.E.; Peng, S.; Quenez, M.C. Backward stochastic differential equations in finance. *Math. Financ.* **1997**, *7*, 1–71. [CrossRef]
17. Duffie, D.; Epstein, L.G. Stochastic differential utility. *Econometrica* **1992**, *60*, 353–394. [CrossRef]
18. Pardoux, E.; Peng, S. Backward stochastic differential equations and quasilinear parabolic partial differential equations. In *Stochastic Partial Differential Equations and Their Applications*; Springer: Berlin/Heidelberg, Germany, 1992; Volume 176, pp. 200–217.

19. Peng, S. Backward stochastic differential equations and applications to optimal control. *Appl. Math. Optim.* **1993**, *27*, 125–144. [CrossRef]
20. Yong, J. Completeness of security markets and solvability of linear backward stochastic differential equations. *J. Math. Anal. Appl.* **2006**, *319*, 333–356. [CrossRef]
21. Chen, Z.; Epstein, L. A Central Limit Theorem for sets of probability measures. *Stoch. Process. Their Appl.* **2022**, *152*, 424–451. [CrossRef]
22. Chen, Z.; Kulperger, R.; Wei, G. A comonotonic theorem of BSDEs. *Stoch. Process. Their Appl.* **2005**, *115*, 41–54. [CrossRef]
23. Chen, Z.; Liu, S.; Qian, Z.; Xu, X. Explicit solutions for a class of nonlinear BSDEs and their nodal sets. *Probab. Uncertain. Quant. Risk* **2022**, *7*, 283–300. [CrossRef]
24. Karatzas, I.; Shreve, S. *Brownian Motion and Stochastic Calculus*; Springer: New York, NY, USA, 1988.
25. Sutton, R.S.; Barto, A.G. *Reinforcement Learning: An Introduction*; MIT Press: Cambridge, MA, USA, 1998.
26. Agrrawal, P. An automation algorithm for harvesting capital market information from the web. *Manag. Financ.* **2009**, *35*, 427–438.

mathematics

Article

Demystifying the Two-Armed Futurity Bandit's Unfairness and Apparent Fairness

Huaijin Liang [1,†], Jin Ma [2,†], Wei Wang [3,†,*] and Xiaodong Yan [1,†]

1 Zhongtai Securities Institute for Financial Studies, Shandong University, Jinan 250100, China; 201711877@mail.sdu.edu.cn (H.L.); yanxiaodong@sdu.edu.cn (X.Y.)
2 School of Mathematics, Shandong University, Jinan 250100, China; janemj0311@163.com
3 School of Statistics and Mathematics, Shandong University of Finance and Economics, Jinan 250014, China
* Correspondence: wangwei_0115@outlook.com
† These authors contributed equally to this work.

Abstract: While a gambler may occasionally win, continuous gambling inevitably results in a net loss to the casino. This study experimentally demonstrates the profitability of a particularly deceptive casino game: a two-armed antique Mills Futurity slot machine. The main findings clearly show that both non-random and random two-arm strategies, predetermined by the player and repeated without interruption, are always profitable for the casino, despite two coins being refunded for every two consecutive losses by the gambler. We theoretically explore the cyclical nature of slot machine strategies and speculate on the impact of the frequency of switching strategies on casino returns. Our results not only assist casino owners in developing and improving casino designs, but also guide gamblers to participate more cautiously in gambling.

Keywords: fairness; multi-armed bandit; futurity slot machine

MSC: 60J10; 60F05

1. Introduction

The origin of human gambling is estimated to coincide with the emergence of human civilization. Evidence suggests that people engaged in "taking chances" as early as the late Paleolithic Age. For example, divination was widely practiced to discern good and bad outcomes in prehistoric China. More recently, the establishment of casinos has significantly boosted the longstanding prosperity of the gambling industry. Over the centuries, various forms of gambling have been developed, including horse racing, lotteries, dice, baccarat, slot machines, roulette, and blackjack.

Today, some governments support and encourage the development of the gambling industry because it stimulates domestic economic growth, even during global economic downturns. This highlights not only the profitability of the gambling industry but also an implicit truth: casino games reliably generate revenue, at least partly due to their inherent design.

Gambling attracts players through the illusion of fairness, including the misconception that casinos are unprofitable. When gambler enthusiasm is heightened by ostensibly honest advertisements of fairness, gamblers indulge in fantasies of winning vast sums of money. Casinos are particularly captivating to individuals with gambling-related pathologies [1] who become deeply immersed in gambling, subsequently experiencing depressive symptoms, heightened gambling expectancy, and increased dark flow ratings [2].

Such ostensibly honest advertisements of fairness are often promoted through casino loyalty programs, which offer equal rewards to gamblers who wager equal amounts [3]. The aim of these loyalty programs is to enhance both attitudinal and behavioral loyalty. Attitudinal loyalty refers to the extent to which individuals trust and are satisfied with the casino, including a sense of identification with the casino brand. Behavioral loyalty, on the other hand, refers to the actual behaviors that demonstrate loyalty, such as repeatedly visiting the casino to gamble. However, despite the appearance of fairness, all casino games are inherently unfair. Indeed, casinos have consistently reported profits from players, with the notable exception of the Kelly formula [4], which determines the optimal proportion to wager in each period in a series of blackjack ("21") hands or repeated investments, ensuring a win rate greater than 50%. Nonetheless, attitudinal loyalty remains high among casino players.

This article uses a multi-armed Futurity bandit to mathematically explore the profound mystery of attitudinal and behavioral loyalty in the face of casino profitability. The multi-armed bandit (MAB) [5], a popular entertainment tool, is selected because it has been meticulously designed by casinos to appear fair and attract gamblers [6]. The MAB has also been extensively studied theoretically to analyze various complex decision problems [7–9] in fields such as science, society, economy, and management. It also plays a central role in research on reinforcement learning [10–12]. Specifically, this study introduces a two-armed Futurity bandit to elucidate the pervasive absorption of gamblers at casinos. The two-armed slot machine contrasts with the seemingly fair one-armed slot machine, which can be unprofitable for the casino depending on the Futurity award design. For example, a Futurity slot machine may offer a truly fair reward: when the current number of consecutive gambler losses reaches a value of J, all coins invested by the gambler in these losses are refunded. However, two-armed slot machines disrupt this fairness and exhibit the phenomenon of Parrondo's paradox [13,14]: the game becomes profitable for the casino when a player alternates between arms in any random or non-random manner, despite the true advertisement that each of the two arms is fair individually.

In the rest of this paper, Section 2 reviews the related researches. Section 3 describes the model and results. Section 4 conduct experiments to show the result. Section 5 offers the method of this paper and the related lemma. Section 6 concludes this paper.

2. Recent Work

Parrondo's Paradox is a counterintuitive phenomenon where the combination of two losing strategies can lead to a winning outcome. This paradox was first proposed in 1996 by physicist Juan Parrondo of the Complutense University of Madrid. Several studies [15] have examined this paradox from perspectives including game theory, quantum game theory, and information theory. Pyke [16] introduced a fairness assumption applicable to our model suggesting that the two fair arms of the slot machine may lead to long-term profits for the casino through random or non-random strategy combinations.

Many people learn from their experiences in casinos, but the underlying inevitability of their outcomes is dictated by the "law of large numbers" in probability theory. Consequently, the mystery behind casino profitability and inherent unfairness remains elusive to those without a background in probability theory. This article employs probabilistic tools to examine the law of large numbers as it applies to a two-armed antique Mills Futurity slot machine designed by the Chicago Mills Novelty Company in 1936 [6,17,18]. The Futurity slot machine offers a reward whereby when the current number of consecutive gambler losses reaches a of value J, all coins invested by the gambler in these losses are refunded. The long-term profitability of such a machine exposes the deception of the apparent fairness of this game—the "fairness illusion". According to the game's compensation rule, two coins are returned to the gambler each time their consecutive losses reach two. In this context, the deception can be articulated as follows: casinos honestly but shrewdly advertise that the one-armed Futurity bandit is unprofitable due to its fairness, implying long-term unprofitability. This portrayal of fairness for the one-armed Futurity bandit enhances the casino's reputation among gamblers. However, statistical artifacts emerge with the two-armed Futurity bandit when its left and right arms are alternately played, resulting in consistent profitability for the casino under the rule of returning two coins after two consecutive losses by the same gambler. This outcome aligns with the conjecture proposed by Ethier and Lee [6], who suggested that such a two-armed Futurity bandit adheres to Parrondo's paradox when executing any non-random mixed strategy after proving this rule for any random mixed strategy. The present article employs experiments to validate these theoretical results.

Therefore, our results, along with the conclusions of Ethier and Lee [6], demonstrate that a non-random or random two-arm strategy decided by the player before playing and then repeated without interruption is always profitable for the casino, even though two coins are refunded for every two consecutive gambler losses. This phenomenon is theoretically exemplified. This model was ingeniously proven by Chen and Liang [19], who provided an expression for the casino's asymptotic profit expectation.

The main contributions of this article include the following:

- This study experimentally demonstrates the profitability of a deceptively unfair game for gamblers under a mixed strategy. The Kelly formula not only aids blackjack owners in better developing and improving the design of the game, but also helps gamblers participate cautiously in gambling. Furthermore, the formula is widely used in financial risk management as a component of modern financial technology.
- This paper provides a preliminary theoretical proof of the traditional two-arm Futurity slot machine ($J = 10$) model. It also presents our conjecture on the underlying mechanisms of slot machine profitability and offers inspiring ideas for the further exploration of Parrondo's paradox.

In Section 3, this paper provides a detailed introduction to the model of the Futurity two-armed slot machine and presents the theoretical results of both random and non-random strategies under the condition of $J = 2$. Section 4 employs the Monte Carlo method to simulate four different strategic scenarios to verify the theoretical results from Section 3, and then compares the theoretical gains with the benefits obtained from the simulation results. In the latter part of Section 4, we conduct experimental simulations of the traditional $J = 10$ Futurity two-armed slot machine model and compare the casino's empirical average profits for each of the four strategies. This comparison aims to demonstrate, from an experimental perspective, that the casino can achieve long-term profits. In Section 5, we prospectively prove the periodic impact of non-random strategies on casino returns and speculate that the frequency of player strategy exchanges is positively related to the casino's asymptotic return expectations. This provides a theoretical direction for further research on the Futurity two-armed slot machine and Parrondo's paradox.

3. Model and Results

The antique Futurity slot machine, designed by the Chicago Mills Novelty Company [6,17,18], was in production from 1936 to 1941. After 7 December 1941, Mills Novelty ceased slot machine production and became a defense contractor for the duration of the war. When slot machine production resumed in 1945, it did so with new designs. In this article, we use the antique Futurity slot machine designed by the Chicago Mills Novelty in 1936 as an example to explore the scientific mystery of why "long bets will lose".

In the antique Futurity slot machine, a player spends one coin per play. There are two screens on the machine: one screen's pointer records the current number of consecutive gambler losses. When this number reaches 10 (which can be set to another value by the casino), all 10 coins are refunded to the gambler. This refund is called the futurity award. The other screen displays the current mode. The machine's internal structure features a periodic cam with several fixed modes, each having different winning conditions and rewards. With each play, the cam rotates to the next mode. Each arm has its own mode cam, different from the others, resulting in independent payoff distributions for each arm. The gambler pulls one arm to play. For the futurity award, the number of consecutive losses is recorded regardless of the order in which the player plays the arms. When the pointer reaches value J (where $J \geq 2$) set by the casino, J coins are refunded to the gambler. The casino advertises that each arm on its multiple-armed machine is "fair," meaning each arm has a 50% chance of profit for the gambler. The gambler can play either arm in a deterministic order or at random.

For simplicity, we consider a simple two-armed Futurity bandit, with two arms denoted as A and B, each arm with a different i.i.d payoff sequence. For the convenience of analysis, we can regard each arm's distribution of wins as a Bernoulli distribution, that is, the probability of winning a game is p_A (resp. p_B), with $0 < p_A < 1$ and $0 < p_B < 1$. The gambler must pay one coin to the casino for each coup and alternates between arms according to a pre-determined repeating sequence called a strategy. The casino also offers a futurity award each time a gambler suffers consecutive losses in gambling, as described above. Casinos usually advertise the design of $J = 2$, which is the considered case in this work and the most attractive to gamblers. We consider the case in which the gambler chooses a pre-formulated non-random mixed strategy D before the game starts, where D contains at least 1 A and 1 B. For instance, for strategy $D = ABB$, the gambler pulls arm A, then arm B, then arm B, repeating that sequence indefinitely. This work considers a "fairness" design for the one-armed Futurity bandit by adjusting the payoff distribution of each arm, where the reward is assumed to be $(3-2p)/(2-p)$ under win probabilities $p = p_A$ and p_B for arms A and B, respectively. If the game is played according to the above rules, it seems that the gambler is playing a fair game with no long-term loss, but in fact, the casino definitely makes a profit in the long run, as demystified in Theorem 1 [19] below.

Subtle mathematical induction shows that any non-random repeating mixed strategy D can be arranged in the following asymptotic form $D(a(h,r,s))$:

$$D(a(h,r,s)) = \underbrace{A\cdots A}_{r_1}\underbrace{B\cdots B}_{s_1}\cdots\underbrace{A\cdots A}_{r_k}\underbrace{B\cdots B}_{s_k}\cdots\underbrace{A\cdots A}_{r_h}\underbrace{B\cdots B}_{s_h} := A^{r_1}B^{s_1}\cdots A^{r_h}B^{s_h}.$$

Here, $r_k > 0$, $s_k > 0$, $\sum_{k=1}^{h} r_k = r$, $\sum_{k=1}^{h} s_k = s$ and vector $a(h,r,s) = (a_1, a_2, \cdots, a_{2h}) = (r_1, s_1, \cdots, r_k, s_k, \cdots, r_h, s_h)$. In order to make our results more concise, we define function b_i of vector a for $-2h+1 \le i \le 4h$ as follows:

- $b_{2j-1} = (-1)^{a_{2j-1}}(1-p_A)^{a_{2j-1}}$, $b_{2j} = (-1)^{a_{2j}}(1-p_B)^{a_{2j}}$ for $1 \le j \le h$,
- $b_i = b_{i-2h}$ for $2h+1 \le i \le 4h$, $b_i = b_{i+2h}$ for $-2h+1 \le i \le 0$.

Theorem 1 (Chen and Liang [19] (2023)). *The casino's asymptotic profit expectation R is $2QS$, where*

$$Q := Q(D(a(h,r,s))) = h + \sum_{m=1}^{2h}\sum_{j=1}^{2h-1}(-1)^j \prod_{i=m}^{m+j-1} b_i + h\prod_{i=1}^{2h} b_i,$$

$$S := S(r,s,p_A,p_B) = \frac{(p_A-p_B)^2(1+(-1)^{r+s}(1-p_A)^r(1-p_B)^s)}{(r+s)(2-p_A)^2(2-p_B)^2(1-(1-p_A)^{2r}(1-p_B)^{2s})}.$$

This theoretical result demonstrates that the game is always profitable for the casino in the long term for all $p_A \neq p_B$. The asymptotic profit expectation $R = 0$ applies if and only if $p_A = p_B$. These results make clear that the win probability discrepancy between the two arms favors the casino. In detail, the expression of the casino's asymptotic profit expectation R consists of three parts. The first part is the number two, representing settlement rule $J = 2$ of the futurity bandit award. The second part, function Q, denotes the gambler's playing rule across the two arms as laid out in the internal structure of strategy D. The last part, function S, characterizes the changes in profitability to the casino accompanying changes in the values of the considered parameters p_A, p_B and the considered playing number r, s. Figure 1 show the casino's payoff of a single arm across different probabilities.

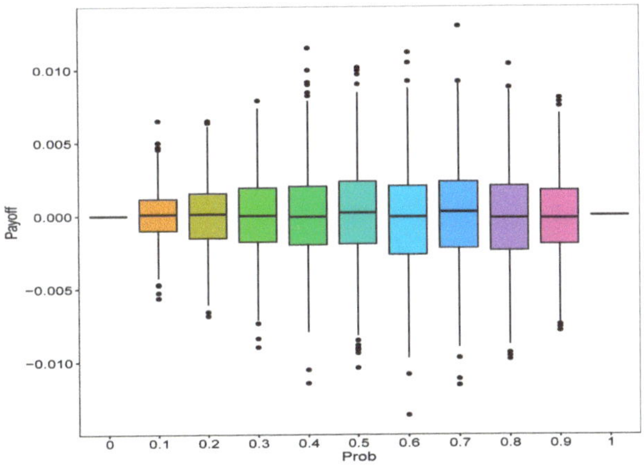

Figure 1. Payoff of a single arm across the full range of win probabilities.

Figure 2 shows three-dimensional surfaces for the casino's payoff as functions of win probabilities p_A and p_B for arms A and B, respectively, under four different but representative non-random strategies. The four panels, each with a different vertical scale, show that each non-random strategy generates distinct profit modes, but each is dominated by a region of casino profitability. Figure 2a implies that playing the two arms in direct alternation generates the greatest profits for the casino. Playing the two arms in equal numbers of pulls guarantees the symmetric form of the payoffs (see Figure 2a,b).

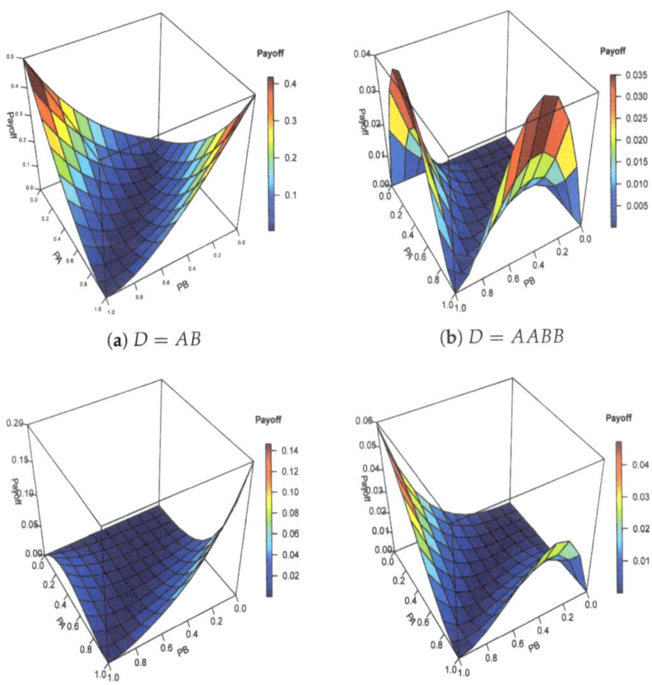

(**a**) $D = AB$ (**b**) $D = AABB$

(**c**) $D = AAABB$ (**d**) $D = A^4B^4A^6B^3$

Figure 2. Casino payoffs (theoretical values) for the full range of win probabilities for arms A and B under four different non-random strategies D. Note that the vertical scale differs among panels.

Now, suppose a gambler plays the two-armed Futurity bandit according to a strategy of randomness C with probability p_γ of pulling arm A and correspondingly probability $1 - p_\gamma$ of pulling arm B. Previous research has shown that the asymptotic profit expectation R_C of the casino [6] is

$$R_C = f(p_\gamma(1 - p_A) + (1 - p_\gamma)(1 - p_B)) - p_\gamma f(1 - p_A) - (1 - p_\gamma)f(1 - p_B),$$

where $f(z) = \frac{2z^2}{1+z}$. Since $f(z)$ is a convex function, the casino is profitable in the long run for all $p_A \neq p_B$. $R_C = 0$ if and only if $p_A = p_B$. Figure 3 shows the payoff performance under a strategy of randomness with probabilities p_γ of 0.1, 0.3, 0.5, 0.7, and 0.9 of selecting arm A. Each panel displays non-negative payoffs under all combinations of p_A and p_B. For $p_\gamma = 0.5$, meaning equal numbers of pulls of the two arms, the payoff surface is symmetric, in line with the symmetry of the results shown in Figure 2a,b.

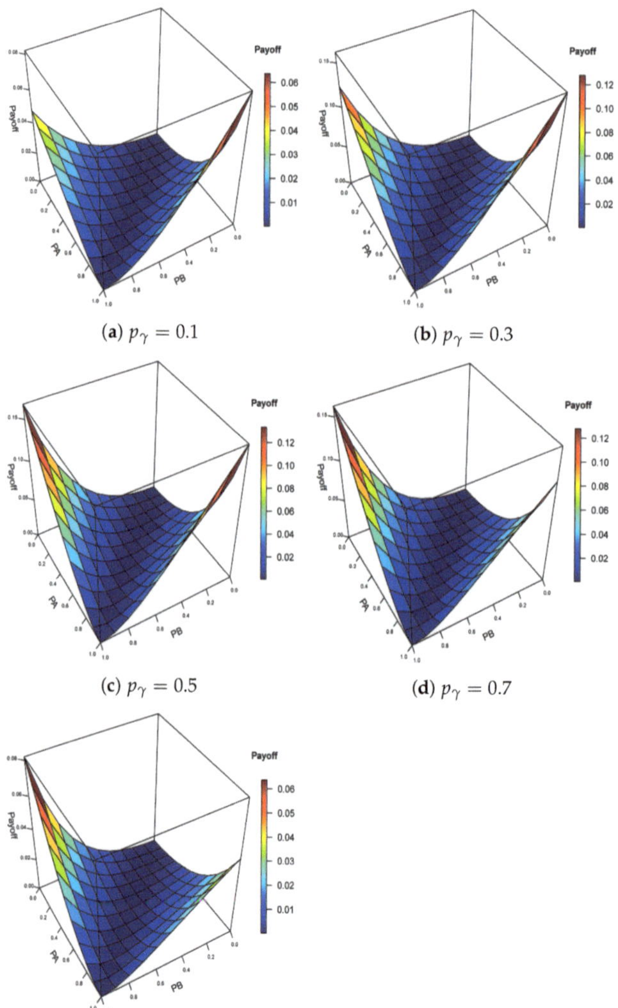

(a) $p_\gamma = 0.1$ **(b)** $p_\gamma = 0.3$

(c) $p_\gamma = 0.5$ **(d)** $p_\gamma = 0.7$

(e) $p_\gamma = 0.9$

Figure 3. True mean casino payoff under a strategy of randomness with probability p_γ of selecting arm A.

4. Experiments

4.1. Simulation Verifying Theoretical Results

This section implements Monte Carlo simulations to verify the theoretical results above for four cases corresponding to the non-random mixed strategies $D = AB$, $D = AABB := A^2B^2$, $D = A^3B^2$, and $D = A^4B^4A^6B^3$. The number of coups is $M = 100,000$, and the true mean profit for the casino equals $(M - W - J * C)/M$, where W represents the total number of wins for the gambler and C denotes the count of futurity awards for J consecutive gambler losses, where $J = 2$. Ten thousand replicates are conducted in each simulation.

As stated above, the casino can adjust the win probability distribution of each of the two arms so as to adjust its own profit while ensuring the fairness of each arm. In an initial simulation of a single arm, Figure 1 shows that the long-term payoff to the gambler or the casino always lies close to zero for any given win probability on interval [0, 1] for the single arm. This result represents the fairness of each individual arm. In particular, the long-term payoff to the gambler is zero without uncertainty when the win probability is zero, while the long-term payoff to the casino is zero without uncertainty when the win probability is one.

Since the value of Q in Theorem 1 is also related to the win probability distributions of the two arms, the impact of Q on profits should also be considered by the casino when adjusting the win probability distributions of the arms. Figure 2 shows three-dimensional surfaces of the payoff to the casino for all combinations of win probabilities of the two arms. These graphs vividly illustrate that the casino can select the win probabilities for A and B that maximize its profit.

Next, we aim to compare the theoretical payoff with that obtained from the simulation results by examining four vertical cross-sections of the three-dimensional surfaces in Figure 2. Without loss of generality, we fix the win probability of arm B at $p_B = 0.5$. Figure 4 shows the theoretical and simulated curves for those four non-random strategies. This agreement demonstrates that the theoretical conclusions are highly consistent with the simulated results, thus verifying Theorem 1 for these four cases.

Last, we simulate the results of mixed random and non-random strategy, some non-random strategy followed by random strategy. Figure 5a examines vertical cross-sections of the three-dimensional surfaces, showing the sample mean casino payoffs for the full range of win probabilities for arms A and B under mixed strategy. Without loss of generality, we fix the win probability of arm B at $p_B = 0.5$ in Figure 5b under the mixed strategy. It obviously shows that the casino loss could inspire gamblers to choose mixed strategy to win if they could choose their own strategy for the gambling machines.

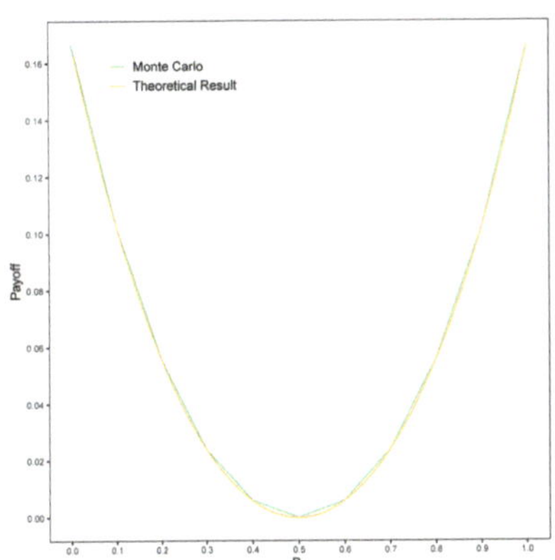

(**a**) $D = AB$

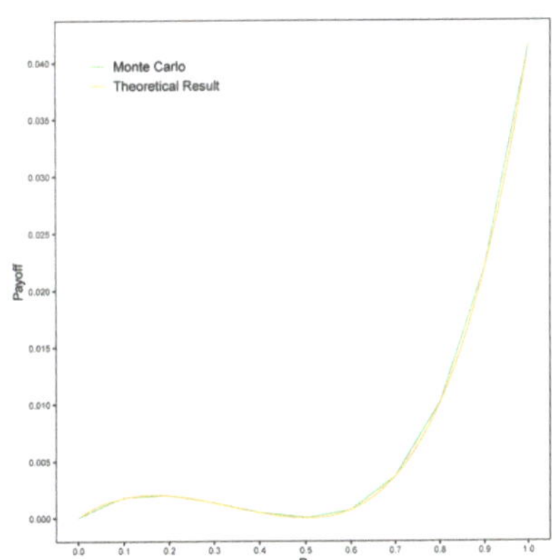

(**b**) $D = AABB$

Figure 4. *Cont.*

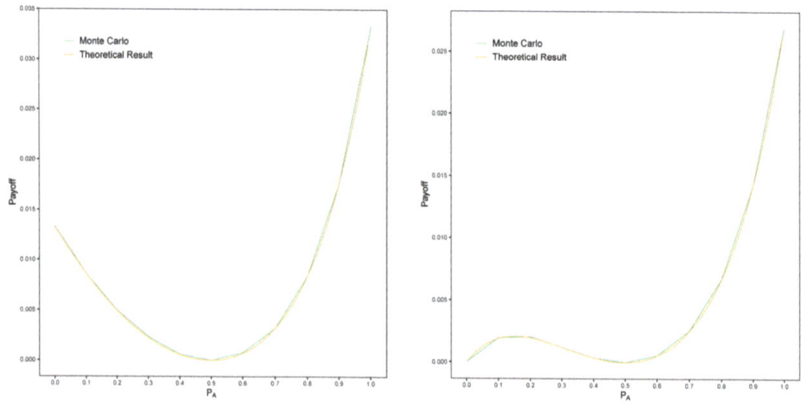

(c) $D = AAABB$ (d) $D = A^4B^4A^6B^3$

Figure 4. Sample mean casino payoff for the full range of win probabilities for an arm A pull under the fixed probability $p_B = 0.5$ of an arm B pull, for various non-random strategies D.

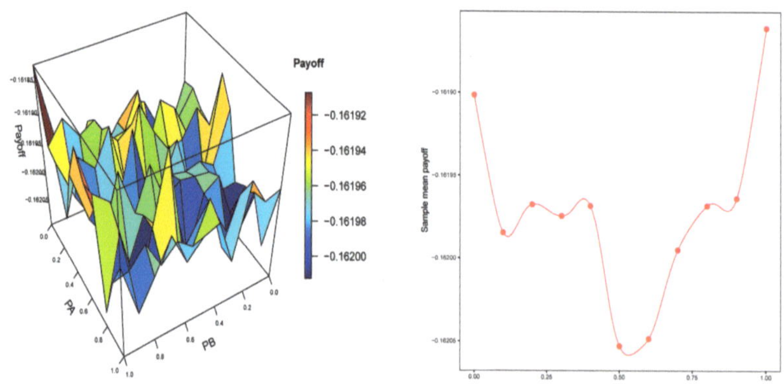

(**a**) Mixed Strategy (**b**) Mixed Strategy

Figure 5. (**a**): Sample mean casino payoffs for the full range of win probabilities for arms A and B under mixed strategy. (**b**): Sample mean casino payoff for the full range of win probabilities for an arm A pull under fixed probability $p_B = 0.5$ of an arm B pull, for mixed strategy. Note that the vertical scale differs among panels.

4.2. Empirical Study with a Real Two-Armed Futurity Slot Machine

This section considers a real antique Mills Futurity slot machine designed in 1936 by the Chicago Mills Novelty Company. There are two screens on the slot machine, one screen recording the current number of consecutive gambler losses and the other displaying the current mode. In detail, a player consumes 1 coin per coup, and when the number of consecutive gambler losses reaches $J = 10$, all 10 coins are refunded. The machine's J value of 10 in this machine is replaced by the case of $J = 2$ because the latter is even more attractive to gamblers. The machine's internal structure includes a periodic cam switching between Modes E and O, corresponding to arm A and arm B. Both closely follow the multi-point distribution shown in Table 1. The win probabilities and rewards are distinct for the two modes, and the two-armed machines are "fair" in the sense that each arm has a 50% chance of profiting the gambler, as honestly advertised by the casino. However, the casino does not allow for a gambler to play solely on one arm, since such an experiment would reveal that it is the alternation between the two "fair" arms that makes money for the casino.

Table 1. Multi-point distribution of reward values in Modes E and O for the actual two-armed antique Mills Futurity slot machine.

Reward\Probability	0	3	5	10	14	18	150
Mode E	0.968	0.003	0.007	0.018	0.004	0	0
Mode O	0.357	0.576	0.064	0	0	0.002	0.001

In this application, we transform the multi-point distribution of each mode into a two-point distribution. For each mode, we split the distribution into gain and loss, allowing the obtention of reward of each model, thereby revealing that each individual mode is indeed fair. In particular, we show the casino's empirical mean profit for each of the four strategies in Figure 6, revealing that the sample mean casino profit converges long-term to a positive value in each case. This finding again confirms the conclusion that the casino can earn money, in the long run, using a two-armed Futurity bandit under a compensation rule equivalent to that for $J = 10$ certified by Ethier and Lee [6].

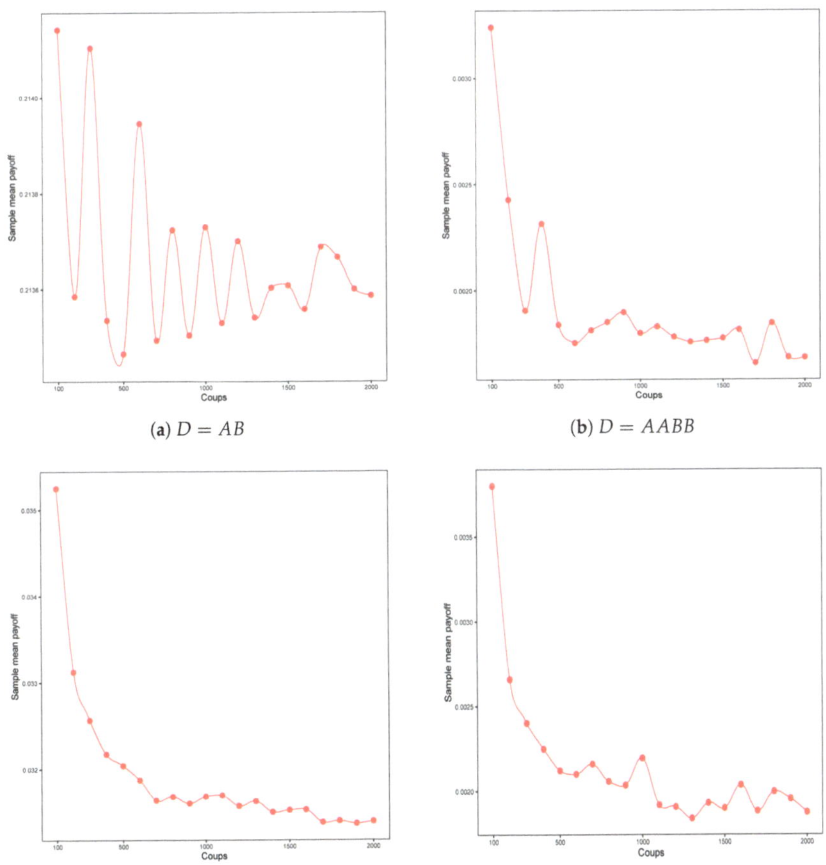

(**a**) $D = AB$ (**b**) $D = AABB$

(**c**) $D = AAABB$ (**d**) $D = A^4B^4A^6B^3$

Figure 6. Casino's cumulative payoff vs. the number of coups for four strategies D applied to an actual two-armed antique Mills Futurity slot machine [6].

5. Method

Chen and Liang [19] demonstrated the long-term profitability of this slot machine, and their theoretical proof provides enlightening ideas for proving the profitability of the classic two-arm slot machine ($J = 10$). The gambler's motivation to gamble is presumably tied to the casino's claim that each arm is fair. Although a given strategy D implemented by the player may yield a range of results, gamblers often believe they can formulate profitable strategies in advance. Therefore, we must examine the relationship among the various strategies. When a casino is confronted with strategy D, it must determine how this strategy is expected to affect its profitability. This slot machine can also be regarded as a confrontation game between the casino and the player. In this context, how is the asymptotic profit expectation difference between the casino and the player calculated? Based on the casino's calculation of the asymptotic profit expectation, we can ingeniously determine that the value of this profit is strictly positive, thus explaining why the casino is profitable in the long run.

Below, we conduct a preliminary theoretical analysis of the characteristics of the model based on the assumptions of the classic two-arm bandit machine. We explain why a casino can claim that slot machines are fair and how certain player strategies can have a cyclical impact on the casino's asymptotic returns. Finally, we elaborate on future work on this model and propose our conjectures.

5.1. Why Can Casinos Claim Each Arm of the Slot Machine Is Fair?

The source of the casino's profit is every single coin paid by the gambler before each coup. The player's profit from the slot machine is divided into two parts: one part is payoff u obtained by winning a single coup, and the other part is the refund obtained by losing two consecutive coups. We can choose either arm for initial analysis. If the gambler plays only the A arm, then p_A° represents the asymptotic probability, per coup, of the player obtaining the futurity award. The player's expected asymptotic revenue per coup is then $\mu_A^* = p_A u_A + 10 p_A^\circ$, where u_A is the payoff obtained by the gambler by winning a single coup. The casino can set $\mu_A^* = 1$ by tuning parameters p_A and u_A. In such a case, the player's asymptotic payoff expectation per coup is equal to the 1-coin payoff received by the casino before each coup. Ethier and Lee [6] calculated the value of p_A° as $p_A^\circ = \frac{p_A q_A^{10}}{1-q_A^{10}}$, where $q_A = 1 - p_A$. Then, to maintain fairness, the casino must ensure that $u_A = \frac{10p_A(1-p_A)^{10}+(1-p_A)^{10}-1}{p_A((1-p_A)^{10}-1)}$ while modifying the arm's payoff distribution to maintain or maximize profitability. In the same way, the casino can also make the B arm fair, but the set parameters need to be $p_A \neq p_B, 0 < p_A < 1, 0 < p_B < 1$.

5.2. What Is the Relationship among Various Non-Random Mixing Strategies?

By implementing a general fixing of values $r, s > 0$, the casino can ignore everything about a gambler's strategy D other than how the strategy affects the casino's asymptotic profit expectation. We let p_D° denote the asymptotic probability, per coup, of the gambler obtaining the futurity award under strategy D, and we let p_i^D denote the win probability of the ith game under strategy D. Ethier and Lee [6] preliminarily provided the form of p_D°. On this basis, we preliminarily calculated the casino's asymptotic profit expectation and the value of p_D°.

Lemma 1. *The casino's asymptotic profit expectation R is*

$$R = 10\left(p_D^\circ - \frac{r}{r+s}p_A^\circ - \frac{s}{r+s}p_B^\circ\right),$$

where

$$p_D^\circ = \frac{1}{r+s}\sum_{k=1}^{r+s}\left(\sum_{j=1}^{r+s} p_j^D \prod_{i=j+1}^{j+10k} q_i^D\right)\frac{1}{1-(q_A^r q_B^s)^{10}},$$

where $q_i^D = 1 - p_i^D$.

Proof. Based on the casino's claim that each arm is fair and the discussion above, we have

$$R = 1 - \mu_D^* = 1 - \mu_D - 10p_D^\circ,$$

where μ_D is the asymptotic payoff expectation for the player per coup, disregarding the Futurity award. From the law of large numbers, we know that

$$\mu_D = \frac{r}{r+s} p_A u_A + \frac{s}{r+s} p_B u_B.$$

Ethier and Lee [6] showed that p_D° has the following form:

$$p_D^\circ = \frac{1}{r+s} \sum_{k=1}^{r+s} \left(\sum_{j=1}^{r+s} p_j \prod_{i=j+1}^{j+10k-(r+s)\lceil 10k/(r+s) \rceil} q_i \right) \frac{(q_A^r q_B^s)^{\lceil 10k/(r+s) \rceil}}{1-(q_A^r q_B^s)^{10}}. \tag{1}$$

For any nonrandom-pattern strategy D, we have

$$q_A^r q_B^s = \prod_{i=1}^{r+s} q_i = \prod_{i=1}^{m} q_i \prod_{i=m+1}^{r+s} q_i = \prod_{i=1}^{m} q_{i+r+s} \prod_{i=m+1}^{r+s} q_i = \prod_{i=m+1}^{m+r+s} q_i$$

for any $m = 1, 2, \cdots, r+s$, and similarly for $m = r+s+1, r+s+2, \cdots, 10r+10s$, we also have $q_A^r q_B^s = \prod_{i=1}^{r+s} q_{i+r+s} = \prod_{i=m+1}^{m+r+s} q_i$. Then, by Equation (1), we note that $1 \le j \le j + 10k - (r+s)\lceil 10k/(r+s) \rceil < j + r + s \le 10r + 10s$. We let $m = j + 10k - (r+s)\lceil 10k/(r+s) \rceil$, and then we have $(q_A^r q_B^s)^{\lceil 10k/(r+s) \rceil} = \prod_{i=m+1}^{j+10k} q_i$. Then, Equation (1) can be rewritten as follows:

$$p_D^\circ = \frac{1}{r+s} \sum_{k=1}^{r+s} \left(\sum_{j=1}^{r+s} p_j^D \prod_{i=j+1}^{j+10k} q_i^D \right) \frac{1}{1-(q_A^r q_B^s)^{10}},$$

and

$$R = \frac{r}{r+s} \mu_A^* + \frac{s}{r+s} \mu_B^* - \mu_D - 10p_D^\circ = 10\left(p_D^\circ - \frac{r}{r+s} p_A^\circ - \frac{s}{r+s} p_B^\circ \right).$$

□

From the above lemma, we can observe that (1) the value of p_D° summarizes all relevant effects of a given strategy D and that (2) the value of p_D° affects the casino's asymptotic profit expectation R. From the expression for p_D°, we observe that the value of p_D° is relatively insensitive to the choice of strategy.

Lemma 2. *For any set of fixed values of r, s, and l, where* $l = 1, 2, \cdots, r+s$, *and non-random-pattern strategies* D_1 *and* D_2, $p_i^{D_1} = p_{i+l}^{D_2}$ *for all* $i = 1, 2, \cdots, r+s$. *Then, the casino asymptotic profit expectations of the two strategies are equal, that is,* $R_{D_1} = R_{D_2}$.

Proof. We consider strategies D_1 and D_2 where $p_i^{D_1} = p_{i+l}^{D_2}$ for any $i = 1, 2, \cdots, r+s$. Then, it also holds for $i = r+s+1, r+s+2, \cdots, 11r+11s$ by the periodic, and by Lemma 1, we have

$$
\begin{aligned}
&\sum_{j=1}^{r+s} p_j^{D_1} \prod_{i=j+1}^{j+10k} q_i^{D_1} = \sum_{j=1}^{r+s} p_{j+l}^{D_2} \prod_{i=j+1}^{j+10k} q_{i+l}^{D_2} \\
&= \sum_{j=1}^{r+s-l} p_{j+l}^{D_2} \prod_{i=j+1}^{j+10k} q_{i+l}^{D_2} + \sum_{j=r+s-l+1}^{r+s} p_{j+l}^{D_2} \prod_{i=j+1}^{j+10k} q_{i+l}^{D_2} \\
&= \sum_{j=l+1}^{r+s} p_j^{D_2} \prod_{i=j+1-l}^{j+10k-l} q_{i+l}^{D_2} + \sum_{j=1}^{l} p_{j+r+s}^{D_2} \prod_{i=j+1-l}^{j+10k-l} q_{i+r+s+l}^{D_2} \\
&= \sum_{j=l+1}^{r+s} p_j^{D_2} \prod_{i=j+1}^{j+10k} q_i^{D_2} + \sum_{j=1}^{l} p_j^{D_2} \prod_{i=j+1}^{j+10k} q_i^{D_2} = \sum_{j=1}^{r+s} p_j^{D_2} \prod_{i=j+1}^{j+10k} q_i^{D_2}.
\end{aligned}
$$

That is, $p^{\circ}_{D_1} = p^{\circ}_{D_2}$, and by Lemma 1,

$$
R_{D_1} = 10(p^{\circ}_{D_1} - \frac{r}{r+s} p^{\circ}_A - \frac{s}{r+s} p^{\circ}_B) = 10(p^{\circ}_{D_2} - \frac{r}{r+s} p^{\circ}_A - \frac{s}{r+s} p^{\circ}_B) = R_{D_2}.
$$

Then, we complete the proof. □

To understand the above lemma more intuitively, we can consider Steps A and B in the strategy as number r of "A" balls and number s of "B" balls. If these balls are placed in a cycle, then the values of p°_D for different starting points in the same arrangement are equal. For example, for $r = 4$, $s = 2$, the following two arrangements yield the same p° value, that is, $p^{\circ}_{AABABA} = p^{\circ}_{ABABAA}$. Hence, $R_{AABABA} = R_{ABABAA}$.

$$
\begin{array}{ccccc}
 & A & \longrightarrow & A & \\
\nearrow & & & & \searrow \\
A & & & & B \\
\nwarrow & & & & \swarrow \\
 & B & \longleftarrow & A &
\end{array}
\qquad\qquad
\begin{array}{ccccc}
 & A & \longrightarrow & B & \\
\nearrow & & & & \searrow \\
A & & & & A \\
\nwarrow & & & & \swarrow \\
 & A & \longleftarrow & B &
\end{array}
$$

In this way, any non-random pattern strategy provided by the player can be regarded by the casino as a strategy starting from arm A in the process of calculating profitability. Vector $a(h, r, s)$ can be used to represent the structure of this strategy, that is, Equation (1), where $2h$ is the number of times the arm is switched during a single cycle of the strategy. We conjecture that in any non-random pattern strategy provided by the player for fixed values of r and s, the more frequent the switching of arms, the higher the casino's profitability; that is, R and h are positively correlated.

Conjecture 1. *We consider non-random pattern strategy $D_1 = a(h, r, s)$, where $h < \min\{r, s\}$; then, there is strategy $D_2 = a(h+1, r, s)$ such that $R_{D_1} > R_{D_2}$. In particular, player strategy $D = AB$ is most beneficial to the casino, and strategy $D = A^r B^s$ is most beneficial to the player.*

Ethier and Lee [6] showed that if no restrictions are provided to the player strategy, the casino may not be profitable in the long term. They pointed out that the player strategy must include A or B only once, or the casino sets the winning rate of the arm $p_A + p_B > 1/3$, or the player strategy $r + s \le J$ can ensure the long-term profitability of the casino, and these are still a open question. We relate simple and easy-to-calculate strategies to complex strategies provided by players based on the heuristic conjectures we provide, exploiting the periodicity of the impact of player strategies on casino returns, and calculating the difference in expected house asymptotic returns between different similar strategies. Then, we may obtain theoretical proofs of other conjectures of Ethier and Lee, which also reveals the principle of the Parrondo's paradox and provides a theoretical explanation for casino profits.

6. Conclusions

This article suggests that the root cause of gamblers' losses lies in the intricate mathematical logic of gambling equipment and the sophisticated program design based on probability modelling and random calculation. This work rigorously demystifies the so-called casino loyalty programs that advertise fair returns with one-armed Futurity bandits to attract gamblers but then continuously profit from them using two-armed Futurity bandits. We thus expose the fraud of the seemingly fair two-armed Futurity bandit. The explicit mathematical expression of expected casino profits, as found in the Results and illustrated in the corresponding figures, vividly elucidates how expected profit changes accompany variations in the considered parameters, again implying that the game can always be profitable for the casino in the long run. The experiments conducted were designed to validate the theoretical results through simulation, and a real two-armed Futurity slot machine with a more complex output was also tested to verify this conclusion.

We anticipate that this study will benefit gamblers by helping them recognize the fundamental unfairness within the gambling industry, particularly regarding so-called loyalty programs that are typically advertised with claims of fairness. On the other hand, we do not intend for our theoretical findings to be used in the further design of slot machines, nor by other businesses such as those engaging in discount marketing, bundled sales, or other induced consumption tactics. This article may serve as a starting point for further study of the mathematically inherent profitability of casino games, including more sophisticated multi-armed Futurity bandits, based on the probabilistic tools presented herein. We also hope this study will assist casino owners in better designing their casinos and helping gamblers participate in gambling more cautiously.

Author Contributions: Methodology, H.L.; Software, J.M.; Writing—review & editing, X.Y.; Project administration, W.W. All authors have read and agreed to the published version of the manuscript.

Funding: This work was funded by the National Key R&D Program of China (No. 2023YFA1008701), the National Natural Science Foundation of China (No. 12371292), the National Statistical Science Research Project (No. 2022LY080), the Shandong Provincial Natural Science Foundation (No. ZR2022QA109), and the Jinan Science and Technology Bureau (No. 2021GXRC056).

Data Availability Statement: The data is freely available for academic use from Github at https://github.com/yanxiaodong128/datareconstruction (accessed on 1 April 2024).

Conflicts of Interest: The funders had no role in the design of the study; in the collection, analyses, or interpretation of data; in the writing of the manuscript; or in the decision to publish the results.

References

1. Dixon, M.J.; Graydon, C.; Harrigan, K.A.; Wojtowicz, L.; Siu, V.; Fugelsang, J.A. The allure of multi-ine games in modern slot machines. *Addiction* **2014**, *109*, 1920–1928. [CrossRef] [PubMed]
2. Dixon, M.J.; Stange, M.; Larche, C.J.; Graydon, C.; Fugelsang, J.A.; Harrigan, K.A. Dark flow, depression and multiline slot machine play. *J. Gambl. Stud.* **2018**, *34*, 73–84. [CrossRef] [PubMed]
3. Hollingshead, S.J.; Davis, C.G.; Wohl, M.J. The customer-brand relationship in the gambling industry: Positive play predicts attitudinal and behavioral loyalty. *Int. Gambl. Stud.* **2023**, *23*, 118–138. [CrossRef]
4. Kelly, J.L. A new interpretation of information rate. *Bell Syst. Tech. J.* **1956**, *35*, 917–926. [CrossRef]
5. Sutton, R.S.; Barto, A.G. *Reinforcement Learning: An Introcution*, 2nd ed.; MIT press: Cambridge, MA, USA, 2018.
6. Ethier, S.N.; Lee, J. A Markovian slot machine and Parrondo's paradox. *Ann. Appl. Probab.* **2010**, *20*, 1098–1125. [CrossRef]
7. Auer, P.; Cesa-Bianchi, N.; Fischer, P. Finite-time analysis of the multi-armed bandit problem. *Mach. Learn.* **2002**, *47*, 235–256. [CrossRef]
8. Chen, Z.; Epstein, L.G. A central limit theorem for sets of probability measures. *Stoch. Process. Their Appl.* **2022**, *152*, 424–451. [CrossRef]
9. Chen, Z.; Feng, S.; Zhang, G. Strategic limit theorems associated bandit problems. *arXiv* **2022**, arXiv:2204.04442.
10. Agrawal, R. Sample mean based index policies by $O(logn)$ regret for the multi-armed bandit problem. *Adv. Appl. Probab.* **1995**, *27*, 1054–1078. [CrossRef]
11. Collins, A.G.; Cockburn, J. Beyond dichotomies in reinforcement learning. *Nat. Rev. Neurosci.* **2020**, *21*, 576–586. [CrossRef] [PubMed]

12. Narisawa, N.; Chauvet, N.; Hasegawa, M.; Naruse, M. Arm order recognition in multi-armed bandit problem with laser chaos time series. *Sci. Rep.* **2021**, *11*, 4459. [CrossRef] [PubMed]
13. Harmer, G.P.; Abbott, D. A review of Parrondo's paradox. *Fluct. Nois Lett.* **2002**, *2*, 71–107. [CrossRef]
14. Parrondo, J.M.; Harmer, G.P.; Abbott, D. New paradoxical games based on Brownian ratchets. *Phys. Rev. Lett.* **2000**, *85*, 5226–5229. [CrossRef] [PubMed]
15. Abbott, D. Asymmetry and disorder: A decade of Parrondo's paradox. *Fluct. Noise Lett.* **2010**, *9*, 129–156. [CrossRef]
16. Pyke, R. On random walks and diffusions related to Parrondo's games. *Lect.-Notes-Monogr. Ser.* **2003**, *42*, 185–216.
17. Geddes, R.N. The Mills Futurity. *Loose Chang.* **1980**, *3*, 10–14.
18. Geddes, R.N.; Saul, D.L. The mathematics of the Mills Futurity slot machine. *Loose Chang.* **1980**, *3*, 22–27.
19. Chen, Z.; Liang, H. Proof of a conjecture about Parrondo's paradox for two-armed slot machines. *arXiv* **2023**, arXiv:2310.08935v2.

mathematics

MDPI

Review

From Classical to Modern Nonlinear Central Limit Theorems

Vladimir V. Ulyanov [1,2]

[1] Faculty of Computer Science, HSE University, 109028 Moscow, Russia; vulyanov@hse.ru
[2] Faculty of Computational Mathematics and Cybernetics, Lomonosov Moscow State University, 119991 Moscow, Russia

Abstract: In 1733, de Moivre, investigating the limit distribution of the binomial distribution, was the first to discover the existence of the normal distribution and the central limit theorem (CLT). In this review article, we briefly recall the history of classical CLT and martingale CLT, and introduce new directions of CLT, namely Peng's nonlinear CLT and Chen–Epstein's nonlinear CLT, as well as Chen–Epstein's nonlinear normal distribution function.

Keywords: central limit theorem; martingale CLT; nonlinear Peng's CLT; nonlinear Chen—Epstein CLT

MSC: 60F05; 60-03

1. Introduction

The central limit theorem (CLT) is one of the gems of probability theory. Its importance can hardly be overestimated both from the theoretical point of view and from the point of view of its applications in various fields. The CLT is usually associated with the normal distribution, or Gaussian distribution, which acts as the limiting distribution in the theorem. In this review article, we recall the history of the CLT, briefly focusing on classical and martingale CLTs and discussing the newer directions of CLT, namely Peng's nonlinear CLT and Chen–Epstein's nonlinear CLT, in more detail, as well as the Chen–Epstein nonlinear normal distribution.

Speaking of the classical and martingale CLTs, we only touch upon the basic results involving the de Moivre–Laplace theorem, the Lindeberg–Feller theorem, the Lévy theorem and Hall's theorem. We point out that the classical CLT is related to sums of independent random variables. In the martingale CLT, the summands are already dependent. But, in both cases, we consider a linear expectation and a probability space with one probability measure. This part of the review is rather short, since there are numerous publications on classical and martingale CLTs. A detailed and extensive review of the classical and martingale CLTs can be found in Rootzén [1], Hall and Heyde [2], Adams [3], and Fischer [4]. Further research was carried out in several directions, including the rates of convergance, see, e.g., Petrov [5], Götze et al. [6], Shevtsova [7], Fujikoshi and Ulyanov [8], and Dedecker et al. [9]; generalization of CLT to the multivariate case, see, e.g., Bhattacharya and Ranga Rao [10] and Sazonov [11], and to infinite dimensional case, see, e.g., Bentkus and Götze [12], Götze and Zaitsev [13], and Prokhorov and Ulyanov [14].

The main part of the paper is devoted to the nonlinear CLT. The motivation for its emergence comes from real life, where we often face decision-making problems under uncertainty. In most cases, classical CLT and normal distribution are not suitable. For example, we cannot directly construct a confidence interval using the martingale CLT. Nonlinear probability and expectation theory has developed rapidly over the last thirty years and has become an important tool for investigating model uncertainty or ambiguity. Nonlinear CLT is an important research area that describes the asymptotic behavior of a sequence of random variables with distribution uncertainty. Its limiting distribution is no longer represented by the classical normal distribution, but by a number of "new nonlinear normal distributions", such as the g-expectation distribution and the G-normal distribution. Nonlinear CLT can fill the huge gaps between martingale CLT and real life.

Nonlinear CLT can be applied in many areas. For example, two-sample tests analyze whether the difference between two population parameters is more significant than a given positive equivalence margin. Chen et al. [15] developed a strategy-specific test statistic using nonlinear CLT and the law of large numbers. Furthermore, inspired by the nonlinear CLT and sublinear expectation theory, Peng et al. [16] introduced G-VaR, which is a new methodology for financial risk management. The inherent volatility of financial returns is not restricted to a single distribution; instead, it is reflected by an infinite set of distributions. By carefully assessing the most unfavorable scenario in this spectrum of possibilities, the G-VaR predictor can be accurately determined; see also Hölzermann [?] on pricing interest rate derivatives under volatility uncertainty and Ji et al. [18] on imbalanced binary classification under distribution uncertainty.

This paper is organised as follows: in Section 2, we consider the classical CLT. Section 3 presents the CLT for martingales. Section 4 introduces the theory of nonlinear expectations and nonlinear CLT. In Section 5, we discuss the differences between classical CLT and nonlinear CLT. Section 6 presents some future research problems of nonlinear CLT.

2. The Classical Central Limit Theorems

The first version of the CLT appeared as the de Moivre–Laplace theorem. De Moivre's investigation was motivated by a need to compute the probabilities of winning in various games of chance. In the proof, de Moivre [19] used Stirling's formula to obtain the following theorem.

Theorem 1 (de Moivre (1733) [19]). *Let $\{X_n\}_{n\geq 1}$ be a sequence of independent Bernoulli random variables, each with a success probability $p \in (0,1)$; that is, for each i,*

$$\mathsf{P}(X_i = 1) = p = 1 - \mathsf{P}(X_i = 0).$$

Let $S_n = \sum_{i=1}^n X_i$ denote the total number of successes in the first n Bernoulli trials. Then, for any $a < b \in \mathbb{R}$,

$$\mathsf{P}\left(a < \frac{S_n - np}{\sqrt{np(1-p)}} \leq b\right) \to \Phi(b) - \Phi(a),$$

where

$$\Phi(x) = \frac{1}{\sqrt{2\pi}} \int_{-\infty}^{x} e^{-y^2/2} dy$$

is the standard normal distribution function.

Thus, de Moivre discovered the probability distribution, which, in the late 19th century, came to be called the normal distribution. Another name—Gaussian distribution—is used in honor of Gauss, who arrived at this distribution as "the law of error" in his famous work, Gauss [20], on the problems of measurement in astronomy and the least squares method.

Laplace [21] proved the Moivre–Laplace theorem anew using the Euler– McLaurin summation formula.

Theorem 2 (Laplace (1781) [21]). *In the notation of Theorem 1, for any $a \in \mathbb{R}$, we have*

$$\mathsf{P}(|S_n - np - z| \leq a) = 2\left(\Phi\left(\frac{a\sqrt{n}}{\sqrt{x\,x'}}\right) - \Phi(0)\right) + \frac{\sqrt{n}}{\sqrt{2\pi x' x}} \exp\left(-\frac{a^2 n}{2x' x}\right),$$

where $z \in \mathbb{R}$, $|z| < 1$, and $x = np + z$, $x' = n(1-p) - z$.

This theorem, besides convergence to the normal law, also provides a good estimate of the accuracy of the normal approximation.

After the first CLT appeared, many famous mathematicians studied the CLT, such as Possion, Dirichlet, and Cauchy. The first significant generalization of the Moivre–Laplace theorem was the Lyapunov theorem [22,23]:

Theorem 3 (Lyapunov(1900, 1901) [22,23]). *Let $\{X_n\}_{n\geq 1}$ be a sequence of independent random variables with mean $\mathsf{E}[X_n] = \mu_n$, variance $\mathsf{Var}[X_n] = \sigma_n^2$ and finite moment $\mathsf{E}[|X_n - \mathsf{E}X_n|^{2+\delta}]$, $\delta > 0$. Let $S_n = \sum_{i=1}^n X_i$, $B_n = \sum_{i=1}^n \sigma_i^2$. If, for some $\delta > 0$,*

$$\lim_{n\to\infty} \frac{1}{B_n^{1+\delta/2}} \sum_{i=1}^n \mathsf{E}[|X_i - \mathsf{E}[X_i]|^{2+\delta}] = 0,$$

then, for any $a < b \in \mathbb{R}$,

$$\mathsf{P}\left(a < \frac{S_n - \mathsf{E}[S_n]}{\sqrt{B_n}} \leq b\right) \to \Phi(b) - \Phi(a),$$

uniformly with respect to a and b.

This theorem was proved by a new method: the method of characteristic functions. The formulation of the problem and a possible solution were proposed in 1887 by Chebyshev, who suggested using the method of moments by comparing the moments of sums of independent random variables with the moments of the Gaussian distribution. The method of moments is still helpful in some cases.

In the 1920s, the study of CLT introduced modern probability theory. The most crucial CLT in the early years of the century belongs to Lévy. In 1922, Lévy's fundamental theorems on characteristic functions were proved; see [24].

At the same time, Lindeberg also used characteristic functions to study CLT, and a fundamental CLT, called the Lindeberg–Feller CLT, was formulated:

Theorem 4. *In the notation of Theorem 3, for*

$$\lim_{n\to\infty} \frac{\max_{1\leq i\leq n} \sigma_i^2}{B_n} = 0$$

and for any b, the limit

$$\mathsf{P}\left(\frac{S_n - \mathsf{E}[S_n]}{\sqrt{B_n}} \leq b\right) \to \Phi(b), \quad n \to \infty,$$

holds; it is necessary and sufficient that the condition (the Lindeberg condition) for any $\varepsilon > 0$:

$$\lim_{n\to\infty} \frac{1}{B_n} \sum_{i=1}^n \mathsf{E}[(X_i - \mathsf{E}[X_i])^2 1_{\{|X_i - \mathsf{E}[X_i]| > \varepsilon\sqrt{B_n}\}}] = 0$$

is met.

Sufficiency was proved by Lindeberg [25] and necessity by Feller [26].

3. The Martingale Central Limit Theorems

The classical result is that independent and identically distributed variables lead to a normal distribution under the proper moment condition. Counterexamples show that violation of the independence or identity of the distributions may lead to a non-normal limit distribution. However, numerous examples also show that the violation of independence or identity of distribution can still lead to a normal distribution. Bernstein [27] and Lévy [28] independently put forward a new direction of study: how to prove the CLT for sums of dependent random variables. In 1935, Lévy [28] established a CLT under some conditions, which can be regarded as the first version of the martingale CLT.

In the classical CLT, $S_n = \sum_{i=1}^n X_i$, where $\{X_n\}_{n\geq 1}$ is a sequence of independent random variables. In the contents of the martingale CLT, $S_n = \sum_{i=1}^n X_i$ is a martingale and $\{X_n\}_{n\geq 1}$ is assumed to be a martingale difference sequence, i.e., $\mathsf{E}[X_n|\mathcal{F}_{n-1}] = 0$, where $\{\mathcal{F}_n\}_{n\geq 0}$ is a sequence of a given σ-algebras filtration.

Theorem 5 (Lévy (1935) [28]). *Let $\{X_n\}_{n\geq 1}$ be a sequence of random variables defined on $(\Omega, \mathcal{F}, \{\mathcal{F}_n\}_{n\geq 0}, \mathsf{P})$, with $\mathsf{E}[X_n|\mathcal{F}_{n-1}] = 0$. Denote $S_n = \sum_{i=1}^n X_i$, $\sigma_n^2 = \mathsf{E}[X_n^2|\mathcal{F}_{n-1}]$ and $b_n^2 = \sum_{i=1}^n \sigma_i^2$. Let*

$$\sum_{n=1}^{\infty} \sigma_n^2 = \infty, \quad \mathsf{P}\text{-a.s.},$$

and for any $\varepsilon > 0$, the relations

$$\begin{aligned}
&\lim_{n\to\infty} \sum_{i=1}^n \mathsf{P}(|X_i| > \varepsilon b_n|\mathcal{F}_{i-1}) = 0, && \mathsf{P}\text{-a.s.},\\
&\lim_{n\to\infty} \frac{1}{b_n} \sum_{i=1}^n \mathsf{E}\left[X_i 1_{\{|X_i|>\varepsilon b_n\}}|\mathcal{F}_{i-1}\right] = 0, && \mathsf{P}\text{-a.s.},\\
&\lim_{n\to\infty} \frac{1}{b_n^2} \sum_{i=1}^n \mathsf{E}\left[X_i^2 1_{\{|X_i|>\varepsilon b_n\}}|\mathcal{F}_{i-1}\right] = 0, && \mathsf{P}\text{-a.s.},\\
&\lim_{n\to\infty} \frac{1}{b_n^2} \sum_{i=1}^n \left(\mathsf{E}\left[X_i 1_{\{|X_i|>\varepsilon b_n\}}|\mathcal{F}_{i-1}\right]\right)^2 = 0, && \mathsf{P}\text{-a.s.}
\end{aligned}$$

hold. Then,

$$\frac{S_n}{\sqrt{n}} \xrightarrow{d} N(0, c^2),$$

where c is a constant.

Lévy's result depends on the conditions for σ_n^2, which are random variables. The assumptions of Lévy's theorem are too strict. Many authors tried to relax the assumptions, including Doob [29], Billingsley [30], Ibragimov [31], and Csörgö [?]. Their works led to the CLT being used under some other conditions, including the following:

$$\frac{b_n^2}{\mathsf{E}[S_n^2]} \xrightarrow{\mathsf{P}} C,$$

where C is a constant.

Brown [33] improved the previous martingale CLT:

Theorem 6 (Brown (1971) [33]). *Let $\{X_n\}_{n\geq 1}$ be a sequence of random variables defined on $(\Omega, \mathcal{F}, \{\mathcal{F}_n\}_{n\geq 0}, \mathsf{P})$, with $\mathsf{E}[X_n|\mathcal{F}_{n-1}] = 0$. Denote $S_n = \sum_{i=1}^n X_i$, $\sigma_n^2 = \mathsf{E}[X_n^2|\mathcal{F}_{n-1}]$, $\varphi_n(t) = \mathsf{E}[e^{itX_n}|\mathcal{F}_{n-1}]$, $b_n^2 = \sum_{i=1}^n \sigma_i^2$, and $s_n^2 = \mathsf{E}[S_n^2]$. If*

$$\frac{b_n^2}{s_n^2} \xrightarrow{\mathsf{P}} 1,$$

$$\prod_{j=1}^n \varphi_j\left(\frac{t}{\sqrt{s_n^2}}\right) \xrightarrow{\mathsf{P}} e^{-\frac{t^2}{2}}, \tag{1}$$

and

$$\frac{\max_{1\leq i\leq n} \sigma_i^2}{s_n^2} \xrightarrow{\mathsf{P}} 0,$$

then

$$\frac{S_n}{\sqrt{s_n^2}} \xrightarrow{d} N(0,1).$$

The condition (1) is a critical condition. In 1974, McLeish [34] introduced an elegant method and proved a new martingale CLT.

Theorem 7 (McLeish (1974) [34]). *Let $\{X_{n,i}, n \geq 1, 1 \leq i \leq k_n\}$ be an array of random variables defined on $(\Omega, \mathcal{F}, \mathsf{P})$, with $\mathsf{E}[X_{n,i}|\mathcal{F}_{n,i-1}] = 0$, where $\mathcal{F}_{n,i} = \sigma(X_{n,j}, 1 \leq j \leq i)$. Denote $S_n = \sum_{i=1}^{k_n} X_{n,i}$, $T_n = \prod_{i=1}^{k_n}(1 + itX_{n,i})$. If for all real t, $\{T_n\}$ is uniformly integrable, and*

$$\lim_{n\to\infty} \mathsf{E}[T_n] = 1, \quad \sum_{i=1}^{k_n} X_{n,i}^2 \xrightarrow{\mathsf{P}} 1,$$

$$\max_{1\leq i\leq k_n} |X_{n,i}| \xrightarrow{\mathsf{P}} 0,$$

then

$$S_n \xrightarrow{d} N(0,1).$$

The elegant MacLeish's method proves that condition (1) holds. It follows from condition (1) that the limiting distribution of martingales S_n is Gaussian. However, condition (1) means that the conditional characteristic function converges to a non-random function of t. This is an unnatural condition. The limiting distribution will be different if the conditional characteristic function or conditional variance converges to a random variable. Hall [35] obtained the following result, which is an essential step in the development of martingale CLT.

Theorem 8 (Hall (1977) [35]). *Let $\{X_{n,i}, n \geq 1, 1 \leq i \leq k_n\}$ be an array of random variables defined on $(\Omega, \mathcal{F}, \mathsf{P})$, with $\mathsf{E}[X_{n,i}|\mathcal{F}_{n,i-1}] = 0$, where $\mathcal{F}_{n,i} = \sigma(X_{j,k_n}, 1 \leq j \leq i)$ and for $n \geq 1$, $1 \leq i \leq k_n$, $\mathcal{F}_{n,i} \subset \mathcal{F}_{n+1,i}$. Denote $S_n = \sum_{i=1}^{k_n} X_{n,i}$. If*

$$\lim_{n\to\infty} \mathsf{E}[\max_{1\leq i\leq k_n} X_{n,i}^2] = 0,$$

$$\sum_{i=1}^{k_n} X_{n,i}^2 \xrightarrow{\mathsf{P}} T, \tag{2}$$

then

$$S_n \xrightarrow{d} T' N(0,1),$$

where T' is an independent copy of T.

It follows from Hall's result that the limiting distribution of the martingale may not be Gaussian. It may be a conditional Gaussian. In the study of economics and finance, the condition (2) usually corresponds to the real-life situation. More often than not, final decisions can only be made in an ambiguous context.

4. Nonlinear Central Limit Theorems

There are two main frameworks for studying nonlinear CLT. The nonlinear expectation framework $(\Omega, \mathcal{H}, \mathbb{E})$ proposed by Peng is one approach to characterizing distributional uncertainty. Another approach involves using a set of probability measures $\mathcal{P}$ on $(\Omega, \mathcal{F})$ to study nonlinear CLT, as was achieved by Chen, Epstein and their co-authors.

4.1. Nonlinear CLT under Nonlinear Expectations

Peng [36] constructed a large class of dynamically consistent nonlinear expectations through backward stochastic differential equations, known as the g-expectation, with the corresponding dynamic risk measure referred to as the g-risk measure. The g-expectation can handle uncertain probability sets $\{P_\theta, \theta \in \Theta\}$ controlled by a given probability measure P. However, for singular cases (i.e., $P(A) = 0$ while $P_\theta(A) > 0$), the g-expectation is no longer applicable. Peng, breaking free from the framework of the original probability space, created the theory of nonlinear expectation spaces and introduced a more general nonlinear expectation G-expectation; see Peng [37].

Definition 1. *Given a set Ω, let $\mathcal{H}$ be a linear space of real-valued functions defined on Ω. Let the functional $\mathbb{E}$: $\mathcal{H} \to \mathbb{R}$ satisfy the following four conditions:*

(1) *Monotonicity: If $X \geqslant Y$, then $\mathbb{E}[X] \geqslant \mathbb{E}[Y]$;*
(2) *Preserving constants: $\mathbb{E}[c] = c$, for all $c \in \mathbb{R}$;*
(3) *Subadditivity: $\mathbb{E}[X+Y] \leqslant \mathbb{E}[X] + \mathbb{E}[Y]$, for all $X, Y \in \mathcal{H}$;*
(4) *Positive homogeneity: $\mathbb{E}[\lambda X] = \lambda \mathbb{E}[X]$, for all $\lambda \geqslant 0$.*

Then, the functional $\mathbb{E}$ is called a sublinear expectation. The triple $(\Omega, \mathcal{H}, \mathbb{E})$ is referred to as a sublinear expectation space. If only conditions (1) and (2) are satisfied, $\mathbb{E}$ is termed a nonlinear expectation, and $(\Omega, \mathcal{H}, \mathbb{E})$ is called a nonlinear expectation space.

Within the framework of nonlinear expectations, based on fundamental assumptions, one can also derive such concepts as the distribution of random variables, independence, correlation, stationarity, Markov processes, etc. At the same time, nonlinear Brownian motion and the corresponding stochastic analysis represent a significant extension of the classical stochastic analysis. Moreover, the limit theorems are still valid under nonlinear expectations. Peng [38] developed an elegant partial differential equation method and obtained the first nonlinear CLT under sublinear expectations.

Theorem 9 (Peng (2008) [38])**.** *Let $\{X_i\}_{i\geq 1}$ be a sequence of independent and identically distributed random variables in a sublinear expectation space $(\Omega, \mathcal{H}, \mathbb{E})$. Assume that*

$$\mathbb{E}[X_1] = \mathbb{E}[-X_1] = 0, \quad \lim_{c\to\infty} \mathbb{E}\left[\left(|X_1|^2 - c\right)^+\right] = 0.$$

Let $S_n := \sum_{i=1}^n X_i$. Then, for any $\varphi \in C(\mathbb{R})$ with linear growth, one has

$$\lim_{n\to\infty} \mathbb{E}\left[\varphi\left(\frac{S_n}{\sqrt{n}}\right)\right] = \mathbb{E}[\varphi(\xi)], \tag{3}$$

where $\xi \sim \mathcal{N}(0, [\underline{\sigma}^2, \overline{\sigma}^2])$ is a G-normally distributed random variable and the corresponding sublinear function $G : \mathbb{R} \mapsto \mathbb{R}$ is defined by

$$G(a) := \mathbb{E}\left[\frac{a}{2} X_1^2\right], a \in \mathbb{R}.$$

4.2. Nonlinear CLT under a Set of Probability Measures

Peng's nonlinear CLT opens a new way to replace martingale CLT in the study of economics and finance. In economic markets, random variables objectively exist, but the uncertain probability measure P may not be deterministic. The well-known Ellsberg paradox illustrates that random variables exist, but finding a probabilistic measure P to quantify a given random variable is not always possible. This example shows that, in practical applications of probability theory, there can be ambiguity in people's understanding of probability measures, and it is necessary to clarify which measure should be used to better quantify uncertainty. The economic community often refers to this as ambiguity, pointing to the uncertainty arising from the market and people's limited cognitive abilities. In terms of the development of economic markets, economists have concluded that the probability axioms established by Kolmogorov can quantify the internal laws of development of economic markets. However, they cannot accurately characterize the external effects of human behavior on the laws of market development. Thus, classical and martingale CLTs do not work. Therefore, a new discipline called behavioral economics has emerged, which studies the laws of economic markets using different perspectives (probability measures). One of the fundamental problems of the new discipline is the presence of non-IID data. Establishing universal asymptotic results for non-IID random variables is an important and challenging issue in this situation.

Inspired by this, Chen, Epstein, and their co-authors, in contrast to Peng, who started with nonlinear expectations, investigated nonlinear CLT for a set of probability measures (i.e., in the context of ambiguity). They use a set of probability measures $\mathcal{P}$, which is assumed to be "rectangular" (or closed with respect to the pasting of alien marginals and conditionals), to describe the distribution uncertainty of the random variables $\{X_n\}$ defined on $(\Omega, \mathcal{F})$. Given the history information $\{\mathcal{G}_{n-1}\}$, the conditional mean and variance of $\{X_n\}$ will vary under different probability measures $Q \in \mathcal{P}$, which leads to the concepts of upper and lower conditional means and variances; see (4) and (17). Thus, they focused on two characteristics, mean uncertainty and variance uncertainty, respectively, to obtain the nonlinear CLT. The restriction of the uniqueness of the probability measure in Kolmogorov's axiom is overcome.

Chen, Epstein and their co-authors established two types of nonlinear normal distributions, which have explicit probability densities, given by (15) and (24), to characterize the limit distribution in the nonlinear CLT. These explicit expressions are the first explicit formulae for nonlinear CLT since de Moivre (1733), Laplace (1781) and Gauss (1809) [19–21] discovered and proved the classical (linear) CLT and the normal distribution for a single probability measure more than two hundred years ago. It is worth noting that these two types of nonlinear normal distributions also play a crucial role in the study of multi-armed bandits and quantum computing, as well as nonlinear statistics (see, e.g., Chen et al. [39]).

Case I: CLT with mean uncertainty

Chen and Epstein [40] established a family of CLT with mean uncertainty under a set of probability measures. Under the assumptions of the constant conditional variance of the random variable sequence and conditional mean constrained to a fixed interval $[\underline{\mu}, \overline{\mu}]$, they proved that the limiting distribution can be described by the g-expectation or a solution of a backward stochastic differential equation (BSDE). Moreover, for a class of symmetric test functions, they showed that the limiting distribution has an explicit density function, given by (15), see, e.g., [41].

Theorem 10 (Chen and Epstein (2022) [40])**.** *Let $(\Omega, \mathcal{F})$ be a measurable space, $\mathcal{P}$ be a family of probability measures on $(\Omega, \mathcal{F})$, and $\{X_i\}$ be a sequence of real-valued random variables defined on this space. The history information is represented by the filtration $\{\mathcal{G}_i\}_{i\geq 1}$, ($\mathcal{G}_0 = \{\emptyset, \Omega\}$), such that $\{X_i\}$ is adapted to $\{\mathcal{G}_i\}$.*

Assume that the upper and lower conditional means of $\{X_i\}$ satisfy the following:

$$\text{ess sup}_{Q\in\mathcal{P}} E_Q[X_i|\mathcal{G}_{i-1}] = \overline{\mu} \text{ and ess inf}_{Q\in\mathcal{P}} E_Q[X_i|\mathcal{G}_{i-1}] = \underline{\mu}, \text{for all } i \geq 1. \tag{4}$$

Assume that $\{X_i\}$ has an unambiguous conditional variance σ^2; that is,

$$E_Q\left[(X_i - E_Q[X_i|\mathcal{G}_{i-1}])^2|\mathcal{G}_{i-1}\right] = \sigma^2 > 0 \text{ for all } Q \in \mathcal{P} \text{ and all } i. \tag{5}$$

Furthermore, assume that $\mathcal{P}$ is rectangular and $\{X_i\}$ satisfies the Lindeberg condition:

$$\lim_{n\to\infty} \frac{1}{n} \sum_{i=1}^{n} \sup_{Q\in\mathcal{P}} E_Q\left[|X_i|^2 I_{\{|X_i|>\sqrt{n\varepsilon}\}}\right] = 0, \forall \varepsilon > 0. \tag{6}$$

Then, for all $\varphi \in C([-\infty, \infty])$,

$$\lim_{n\to\infty} \sup_{Q\in\mathcal{P}} E_Q\left[\varphi\left(\frac{1}{n}\sum_{i=1}^{n} X_i + \frac{1}{\sqrt{n}}\sum_{i=1}^{n}\frac{1}{\sigma}(X_i - E_Q[X_i|\mathcal{G}_{i-1}])\right)\right] = \mathbb{E}_{[\underline{\mu},\overline{\mu}]}[\varphi(B_1)], \tag{7}$$

or equivalently,

$$\lim_{n\to\infty} \inf_{Q\in\mathcal{P}} E_Q\left[\varphi\left(\frac{1}{n}\sum_{i=1}^{n} X_i + \frac{1}{\sqrt{n}}\sum_{i=1}^{n}\frac{1}{\sigma}(X_i - E_Q[X_i|\mathcal{G}_{i-1}])\right)\right] = \mathcal{E}_{[\underline{\mu},\overline{\mu}]}[\varphi(B_1)], \tag{8}$$

where $\mathbb{E}_{[\underline{\mu},\overline{\mu}]}[\varphi(B_1)] \equiv Y_0$ *is called g-expectation by Peng (1997) [36], given that* (Y_t, Z_t) *is the solution of the BSDE*

$$Y_t = \varphi(B_1) + \int_t^1 \max_{\underline{\mu}\le\mu\le\overline{\mu}}(\mu Z_s)ds - \int_t^1 Z_s dB_s,\ 0 \le t \le 1, \tag{9}$$

and $\mathcal{E}_{[\underline{\mu},\overline{\mu}]}[\varphi(B_1)] \equiv y_0$, *given that* (y_t, z_t) *is the solution of the BSDE*

$$y_t = \varphi(B_1) + \int_t^1 \min_{\underline{\mu}\le\mu\le\overline{\mu}}(\mu z_s)ds - \int_t^1 z_s dB_s,\ 0 \le t \le 1. \tag{10}$$

Here, (B_t) *is a standard Brownian motion*

Particularly, when φ *is symmetric with the center* $c \in \mathbb{R}$, *that is,* $\varphi(c + x) = \varphi(c - x)$, *and is monotonic on* (c, ∞), *the limits in (7) and (8) can be expressed explicitly.*

(1) *If* φ *is increasing on* (c, ∞), *then*

$$\lim_{n\to\infty} \sup_{Q\in\mathcal{P}} E_Q\left[\varphi\left(\frac{1}{n}\sum_{i=1}^{n} X_i + \frac{1}{\sqrt{n}}\sum_{i=1}^{n}\frac{1}{\sigma}(X_i - E_Q[X_i|\mathcal{G}_{i-1}])\right)\right] = \int_{\mathbb{R}} \varphi(y) f^{\frac{\overline{\mu}-\underline{\mu}}{2},\frac{\overline{\mu}+\underline{\mu}}{2},c}(y)dy \tag{11}$$

$$\lim_{n\to\infty} \inf_{Q\in\mathcal{P}} E_Q\left[\varphi\left(\frac{1}{n}\sum_{i=1}^{n} X_i + \frac{1}{\sqrt{n}}\sum_{i=1}^{n}\frac{1}{\sigma}(X_i - E_Q[X_i|\mathcal{G}_{i-1}])\right)\right] = \int_{\mathbb{R}} \varphi(y) f^{\frac{\underline{\mu}-\overline{\mu}}{2},\frac{\overline{\mu}+\underline{\mu}}{2},c}(y)dy \tag{12}$$

(2) *If* φ *is decreasing on* (c, ∞), *then*

$$\lim_{n\to\infty} \sup_{Q\in\mathcal{P}} E_Q\left[\varphi\left(\frac{1}{n}\sum_{i=1}^{n} X_i + \frac{1}{\sqrt{n}}\sum_{i=1}^{n}\frac{1}{\sigma}(X_i - E_Q[X_i|\mathcal{G}_{i-1}])\right)\right] = \int_{\mathbb{R}} \varphi(y) f^{\frac{\underline{\mu}-\overline{\mu}}{2},\frac{\overline{\mu}+\underline{\mu}}{2},c}(y)dy \tag{13}$$

$$\lim_{n\to\infty} \inf_{Q\in\mathcal{P}} E_Q\left[\varphi\left(\frac{1}{n}\sum_{i=1}^{n} X_i + \frac{1}{\sqrt{n}}\sum_{i=1}^{n}\frac{1}{\sigma}(X_i - E_Q[X_i|\mathcal{G}_{i-1}])\right)\right] = \int_{\mathbb{R}} \varphi(y) f^{\frac{\overline{\mu}-\underline{\mu}}{2},\frac{\overline{\mu}+\underline{\mu}}{2},c}(y)dy \tag{14}$$

where the density function $f^{\alpha,\beta,c}$ *is given as follows:*

$$f^{\alpha,\beta,c}(y) = \frac{1}{\sqrt{2\pi}} e^{-\frac{(y-\beta)^2 - 2\alpha(|y-c|-|c-\beta|)+\alpha^2}{2}} - \alpha e^{2\alpha|y-c|}\Phi(-|c-\beta| - |y-c| - \alpha), \tag{15}$$

The above density function of the Chen–Epstein distribution degenerates into the density function of the classical normal (Gaussian) distribution only when $\alpha = 0$.

Remark 1. *Let* $\beta = 0$ *and* $c = 0$. *Then, the density function* $f^{\alpha,\beta,c}$ *has the following properties:*

- *If* $\alpha < 0$, *the curve of* $f^{\alpha,\beta,c}$ *has more spike than the normal distribution, referred to as the spike distribution. When we use* $f^{\alpha,\beta,c}$ *to denote maximum probability density in (13) and the minimum probability density in (12), the corresponding* $\alpha < 0$.
- *If* $\alpha > 0$, *the curve of* $f^{\alpha,\beta,c}$ *is similar to two linked normal distributions, referred to as the binormal distribution. When we use* $f^{\alpha,\beta,c}$ *to denote maximum probability density in (11) and the minimum probability density in (14), the corresponding* $\alpha > 0$.

- *If $\alpha = 0$, the curve of $f^{\alpha,\beta,c}$ is degenerated to a standard normal distribution. It follows from (11)–(14) that when $\overline{\mu} = \underline{\mu}$, the corresponding $\alpha = 0$.*

  The density function of the Chen–Epstein distribution is shown in the figures below.

The curves of the density function $f^{\alpha,\beta,c}$, for the cases where $\beta = 0, c = 0$ and α take different values, are shown in the following Figures 1 and 2.

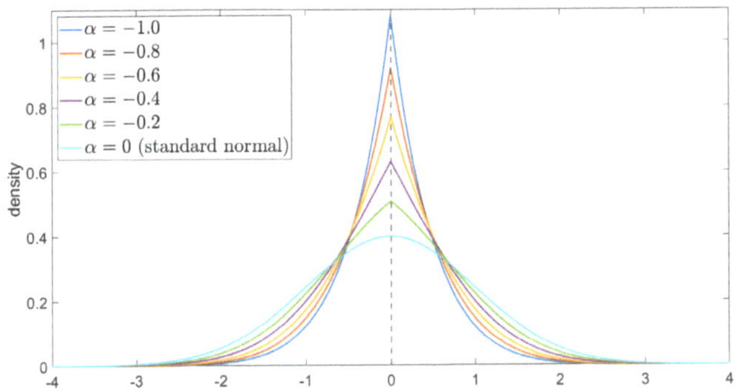

Figure 1. Plots of $f^{\alpha,\beta,c}$ for $\beta = 0, c = 0$ and $\alpha \leq 0$. and $\alpha \leq 0$.

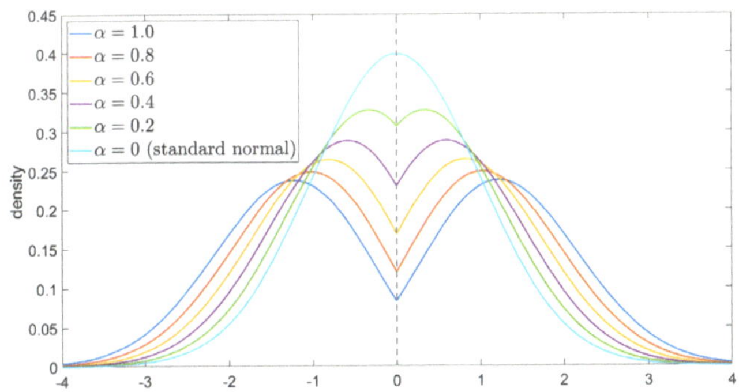

Figure 2. Plots of $f^{\alpha,\beta,c}$ for $\beta = 0, c = 0$ and $\alpha \geq 0$. and $\alpha \geq 0$.

Case II: CLT with variance uncertainty

Chen et al. [39] investigated the CLT with variance uncertainty under a set of probability measures. The considered random variables sequence has an unambiguous conditional mean and its conditional variance is constrained to vary within the interval $[\underline{\sigma}^2, \bar{\sigma}^2]$. First of all, the limiting distribution can still be described by the G-normal distribution. More significantly, for a class of "S-Shaped" test functions, which are important indexes for characterizing loss aversion in behavioral economics, they demonstrated that the limiting distribution also has an explicit probability density function, given by (24).

Theorem 11 (Chen, Epstein and Zhang (2023) [39])**.** *Let $(\Omega, \mathcal{F})$ be a measurable space, $\mathcal{P}$ be a family of probability measures on $(\Omega, \mathcal{F})$, and $\{X_i\}$ be a sequence of real-valued random variables defined on this space. The history information is represented by the filtration $\{\mathcal{G}_i\}_{i \geq 1}$, $(\mathcal{G}_0 = \{\emptyset, \Omega\})$, such that $\{X_i\}$ is adapted to $\{\mathcal{G}_i\}$.*

Assume that $\{X_i\}$ has an unambiguous conditional mean 0, that is,

$$E_Q[X_i|\mathcal{G}_{i-1}] = \mu = 0 \text{ for all } Q \in \mathcal{P} \text{ and all } i, \tag{16}$$

Assume that the upper and lower conditional variances of $\{X_i\}$ satisfy the following:

$$ess\ sup_{Q\in\mathcal{P}} E_Q[X_i^2|\mathcal{G}_{i-1}] = \overline{\sigma}^2 \text{ and } ess \inf_{Q\in\mathcal{P}} E_Q[X_i^2|\mathcal{G}_{i-1}] = \underline{\sigma}^2, \text{for all } i \geq 1. \tag{17}$$

Assume also that the Lindeberg condition (6) is met and that $\mathcal{P}$ is rectangular. Put $S_n = \sum_{i=1}^n X_i$. For any $\varphi \in C([-\infty,\infty])$, we have

$$\lim_{n\to\infty} \sup_{Q\in\mathcal{P}} E_Q\left[\varphi\left(\frac{S_n}{\sqrt{n}}\right)\right] = \mathbb{E}[\varphi(\xi)]$$

where $\xi \sim \mathcal{N}(0,[\underline{\sigma}^2,\overline{\sigma}^2])$ is a G-Normal distribution under the sublinear expectation space $(\Omega,\mathcal{H},\mathbb{E})$.

Particularly, for any $c \in \mathbb{R}$ and $\varphi_1 \in C_b^3(\mathbb{R})$, set $\theta = \underline{\sigma}/\overline{\sigma}$ and define functions

$$\phi(x) = \begin{cases} \varphi_1(x) & x \geq c, \\ \varphi_2(x) = -\theta\varphi_1\left(-\frac{1}{\theta}(x-c)+c\right) + (1+\theta)\varphi_1(c) & x < c, \end{cases} \tag{18}$$

$$\overline{\phi}(x) = \begin{cases} \varphi_1(x) & x \geq c, \\ \overline{\varphi}_2(x) = -\frac{1}{\theta}\varphi_1(-\theta(x-c)+c) + \left(1+\frac{1}{\theta}\right)\varphi_1(c) & x < c. \end{cases} \tag{19}$$

(1) *If $\varphi_1''(x) \leq 0$ for $x \geq c$, then*

$$\lim_{n\to\infty} \sup_{Q\in\mathcal{P}} E_Q\left[\overline{\phi}\left(\frac{S_n}{\sqrt{n}}\right)\right] = \int_{\mathbb{R}} \overline{\phi}(y) q^{\underline{\sigma},\overline{\sigma},c}(y)dy, \tag{20}$$

$$\lim_{n\to\infty} \inf_{Q\in\mathcal{P}} E_Q\left[\phi\left(\frac{S_n}{\sqrt{n}}\right)\right] = \int_{\mathbb{R}} \phi(y) q^{\overline{\sigma},\underline{\sigma},c}(y)dy. \tag{21}$$

(2) *If $\varphi_1''(x) > 0$ for $x \geq c$, then*

$$\lim_{n\to\infty} \sup_{Q\in\mathcal{P}} E_Q\left[\phi\left(\frac{S_n}{\sqrt{n}}\right)\right] = \int_{\mathbb{R}} \phi(y) q^{\overline{\sigma},\underline{\sigma},c}(y)dy, \tag{22}$$

$$\lim_{n\to\infty} \inf_{Q\in\mathcal{P}} E_Q\left[\overline{\phi}\left(\frac{S_n}{\sqrt{n}}\right)\right] = \int_{\mathbb{R}} \overline{\phi}(y) q^{\underline{\sigma},\overline{\sigma},c}(y)dy. \tag{23}$$

The density function of $q^{\alpha,\beta,c}$ is given as follows:

$$q^{\alpha,\beta,c}(y) = \frac{1}{\sqrt{2\pi}\sigma(y)} e^{-\frac{\left(\frac{c}{\sigma(0)}+\frac{y-c}{\sigma(y)}\right)^2}{2}} + \frac{\beta-\alpha}{\beta+\alpha} \frac{sgn(y-c)}{\sqrt{2\pi}\sigma(y)} e^{-\frac{\left(\left|\frac{c}{\sigma(0)}\right|+\left|\frac{y-c}{\sigma(y)}\right|\right)^2}{2}}, \tag{24}$$

and $\sigma(y) = \alpha I_{[c,\infty)}(y) + \beta I_{(-\infty,c)}(y)$, $\forall y \in \mathbb{R}$.

The above density function of the Chen–Epstein–Zhang distribution degenerates into the density function of the normal distribution $N(0,\sigma^2)$ only when $\alpha = \beta = \sigma$.

Remark 2. *The assumptions and results of Theorem 11 are slightly different from those in the publication of Chen, Epstein and Zhang (2023). The frameworks and assumptions in the publication are slightly more complicated due to the consideration of the bandit problem and the construction of the optimal strategies in the Bayesian framework.*

The following figure shows the curves of the density function $q^{\alpha,\beta,c}$ of the Chen–Epstein–Zhang distribution.

The curve of the density function $q^{\alpha,\beta,c}$ for $\alpha = 1, \beta = 2, c = 0$ is shown as follows (Figure 3).

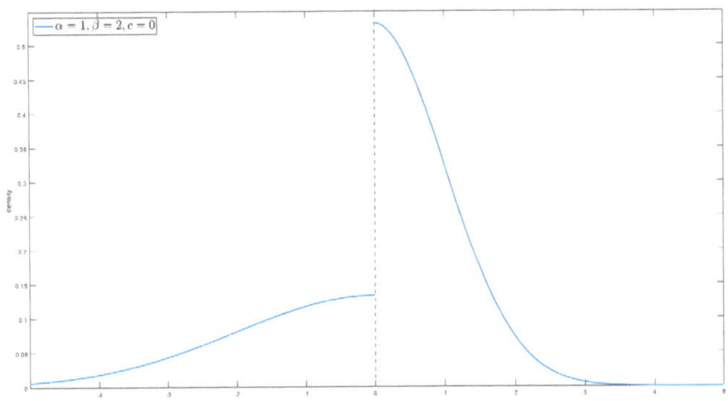

Figure 3. Plot of $q^{\alpha,\beta,c}$ for $\alpha = 1, \beta = 2, c = 0$.

The curve of the density function $q^{\alpha,\beta,c}$ for $\alpha = 2, \beta = 1, c = 0$ is shown as follows (Figure 4).

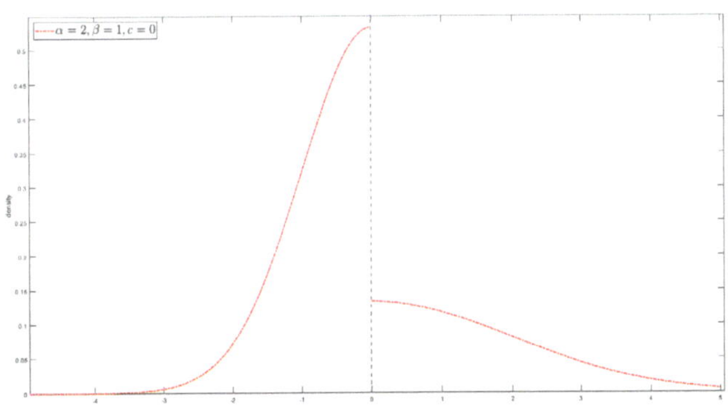

Figure 4. Plot of $q^{\alpha,\beta,c}$ for $\alpha = 2, \beta = 1, c = 0$.

When comparing the curves of classical normal distribution with the minimum–maximum probability density functions, one can clearly see that the minimum–maximum probability density functions are no longer continuous.

5. Differences between Classical CLT and Nonlinear CLT

For convenience, we used C-CLT to denote the classical CLT , NE-CLT to denote the nonlinear Peng's CLT on the nonlinear expectations given by Peng, and NP-CLT to denote the nonlinear Chen–Epstein CLT under a set of probability measures given by Chen and Epstein as well as Zhang.

5.1. Frameworks

- C-CLT: The classical CLT is mainly considered on a probability space $(\Omega, \mathcal{F}, \mathsf{P})$ with a single probability measure P. And $\{X_i\}$ is a sequence of random variables defined on $(\Omega, \mathcal{F}, \mathsf{P})$. The distribution of each X_i is fixed under the probability measure P.
- NE-CLT: The NE-CLT is considered on the sublinear expectation space $(\Omega, \mathcal{H}, \mathbb{E})$, and the random variables sequence $\{X_i\}$ is defined on $(\Omega, \mathcal{H}, \mathbb{E})$. One can use the sublinear expectation $\mathbb{E}$ to describe the distribution uncertainty of $\{X_i\}$. When $\mathbb{E}$ becomes a linear expectation, the nonlinear CLT degenerates into a classical one.
- NP-CLT: The NP-CLT is considered under a set of probability measures $\mathcal{P}$ on $(\Omega, \mathcal{F})$, and the random variables sequence $\{X_i\}$ is defined on $(\Omega, \mathcal{F})$. One can use $\mathcal{P}$ to describe the distribution uncertainty of $\{X_i\}$. When $\mathcal{P}$ equals the singlton $\{\mathsf{P}\}$, the nonlinear CLT degenerates into a classical one.

5.2. Assumptions

5.2.1. Independence

- C-CLT: Usually, $\{X_i\}$ are independent or $\{X_i\}$ is a sequence of martingale differences.
- NE-CLT: Peng provided the concept of independence on sublinear expectation space. That is, $\{X_i\}$ are independent on $(\Omega, \mathcal{H}, \mathbb{E})$, if

$$\mathbb{E}[f(X_1, \cdots, X_n)] = \mathbb{E}\Big[\mathbb{E}[f(x, X_n)]_{x=(X_1,\cdots,X_{n-1})}\Big].$$

- NP-CLT: When the CLT is considered on $(\Omega, \mathcal{F}, \mathcal{P})$, there is no concept of independence. However, one should assume that $\mathcal{P}$ and $\{X_i\}$ satisfy a property similar to independence, which can be described as follows

$$\sup_{Q\in\mathcal{P}} E_Q[f(X_1, \cdots, X_n)] = \sup_{Q\in\mathcal{P}} E_Q\Big[\text{ess sup}_{Q\in\mathcal{P}} E_Q[f(X_1, \cdots, X_n)|\mathcal{G}_{n-1}]\Big]$$

In fact, this holds naturally when $\mathcal{P}$ is rectangular; see Lemma 2.2 from [40].

5.2.2. Mean and Variance

- C-CLT: Usually $\{X_i\}$ are identically distributed; notably, $\{X_i\}$ have the same mean and variance.
- NE-CLT: Peng defined the upper and lower means as follows

$$\overline{\mu} = \mathbb{E}[X_1] \text{ and } \underline{\mu} = -\mathbb{E}[-X_1]$$

when $\mathbb{E}[X_1] = \mathbb{E}[-X_1] = 0$, he stated that $\{X_i\}$ has no mean uncertainty, and defined the upper and lower variances as follows:

$$\overline{\sigma}^2 = \mathbb{E}[X_1^2] \text{ and } \underline{\sigma}^2 = -\mathbb{E}[-X_1^2]$$

- NP-CLT: There are two main assumptions for the conditional means and variances of $\{X_i\}$. Since there is no independence here, and the conditional means and variances of $\{X_i\}$, given the information $\mathcal{G}_{i-1}$, will vary for different measures in $\mathcal{P}$, Chen and co-authors focused on the conditional means and variances of $\{X_i\}$.
When investigating CLT with an uncertain mean, it is assumed that $\{X_i\}$ have uncertain conditional means but common conditional variance, i.e., we have (4) and (5).
When investigating CLT with variance uncertainty, it is assumed that $\{X_i\}$ have uncertain conditional variances but a common conditional mean, i.e., we have (17) and (16).

5.3. Results

5.3.1. Expression Form

- C-CLT: One usually investigates the limit behavior of

$$\frac{\sum_{i=1}^n (X_i - \mu)}{\sqrt{n}\sigma} \text{ with } \mu = \mathsf{E}[X_1], \sigma^2 = \mathsf{Var}(X_1),$$

which is the standardization of $S_n = \sum_{i=1}^n X_i$.
One has

$$\frac{\sum_{i=1}^n (X_i - \mu)}{\sqrt{n}\sigma} \xrightarrow{d} N(0,1),$$

which has many equivalent expressions:

$$\mathsf{P}\left(\frac{\sum_{i=1}^{n}(X_i-\mu)}{\sqrt{n}\sigma}\leq x\right)\to \mathsf{P}(Z\leq x), Z\sim N(0,1),$$
$$\mathsf{E}\left[f\left(\frac{\sum_{i=1}^{n}(X_i-\mu)}{\sqrt{n}\sigma}\right)\right]\to \mathsf{E}[f(Z)].$$

- NE-CLT: Usually, $\{X_i\}$ has no mean uncertainty, and the limit behavior of $S_n/\sqrt{n}$ is investigated. Peng also introduced the corresponding notion of convergence in distribution in sublinear expectation space: we say that $S_n/\sqrt{n}$ converges in distribution to G-normal distribution ξ, if

$$\mathbb{E}\left[\varphi\left(\frac{S_n}{\sqrt{n}}\right)\right]\to \mathbb{E}[\varphi(\xi)],\ \forall\varphi\in C_{b,Lip}(\mathbb{R}).$$

- NP-CLT: Considering CLT with variance uncertainty, Chen and co-authors similarly investigated the limiting behavior of $S_n/\sqrt{n}$, assuming that $\{X_i\}$ has a common conditional mean of 0.
  Considering CLT with mean uncertainty, they investigated the limiting behavior of

$$T_n^Q := \frac{1}{n}\sum_{i=1}^{n}X_i+\frac{1}{\sqrt{n}}\sum_{i=1}^{n}\frac{1}{\sigma}(X_i-E_Q[X_i|\mathcal{G}_{i-1}])$$

  The second part is the S_n standardization, which is similar in form to the classical CLT. Since they wanted to consider the mean uncertainty, and the standardization in the second part does not actually reflect the mean uncertainty, they added a sample mean to reflect the mean uncertainty.
  On the other hand, they investigated the limit behavior of the upper (or lower) expectation of the statistics for given test function, that is:

$$\lim_{n\to\infty}\sup_{Q\in\mathcal{P}}E_Q\left[\varphi\left(\frac{S_n}{\sqrt{n}}\right)\right]=?\quad\text{and}\quad\lim_{n\to\infty}\sup_{Q\in\mathcal{P}}E_Q\left[\varphi\left(T_n^Q\right)\right]=?$$

  Since, for a set of measures $\mathcal{P}$, the upper expectation or probability, that is $\sup_{Q\in\mathcal{P}}E_Q[\cdot]$ or $\sup_{Q\in\mathcal{P}}Q(\cdot)$ resp., do not have the additivity property, the above limit behavior is not equivalent to the problems (but contains them)

$$\lim_{n\to\infty}\sup_{Q\in\mathcal{P}}Q\left(\frac{S_n}{\sqrt{n}}\leq x\right)=?\quad\text{and}\quad\lim_{n\to\infty}\sup_{Q\in\mathcal{P}}Q\left(T_n^Q\leq x\right)=?$$

5.3.2. Limit Distribution

- C-CLT: The normal distribution is mostly used to describe the limit distribution.
- NE-CLT: Peng introduced the notion of G-normal distribution $\mathcal{N}(0,[\underline{\sigma}^2,\overline{\sigma}^2])$ to characterize the limit distribution. When $\underline{\sigma}^2=\overline{\sigma}^2$, it degenerated to the classical normal distribution.
- NP-CLT:
  (1) For the CLT with mean uncertainty, Chen and Epstein use the g-expectation $\mathbb{E}_{[\underline{\mu},\overline{\mu}]}[\varphi(B_1)]$ or $\mathcal{E}_{[\underline{\mu},\overline{\mu}]}[\varphi(B_1)]$, which corresponds to the solution of BSDE (9) or (10), to describe the limit distribution. We know that the BSDE usually does not have an explicit solution, i.e., it does not have an explicit expression like the density of normal distribution. However, for some classes of symmetric test functions φ, Chen and coauthors found the explicit density $f^{\alpha,\beta,c}$ to describe the limit distribution.

(2) For the CLT with variance uncertainty, similar to the NE-CLT, one can still use the G-normal distribution to describe the limit distribution. It is also known that the G-normal distribution usually does not have an explicit expression like the density of the normal distribution. Therefore, similar to CLT with mean uncertainty, Chen and coauthors tried to find some class of functions that provides an explicit expression for the limit distribution. Then, they considered two classes of functions, ϕ and $\overline{\phi}$, given by (18) and (19), which are two kinds of "S-Shaped" function. For these test functions, they found the explicit expression for the density function $q^{\alpha,\beta,c}$ of the limit distribution.

5.4. Proofs

5.4.1. Methods to Prove C-CLT

There are four common methods of proving the CLT:

- Method of characteristic functions;
- Method of moments;
- Stein's method;
- The Lindeberg exchange method.

5.4.2. Methods to Prove NE-CLT

Peng first established the connection between G-normal distribution and the following nonlinear parabolic PDE, which he called G-heat equation:

$$\begin{cases} \partial_t u(t,x) + \frac{\overline{\sigma}^2}{2}(\partial^2_{xx}u(t,x))^+ - \frac{\underline{\sigma}^2}{2}(\partial^2_{xx}u(t,x))^- = 0, \ (t,x) \in [0,1) \times \mathbb{R}, \\ u(1,x) = \varphi(x). \end{cases}$$

He found that $v(0,0) = \mathbb{E}[\varphi(\xi)]$, where $\xi \sim \mathcal{N}(0,[\underline{\sigma}^2,\overline{\sigma}^2])$ is the G-normal distribution.

Then, he represented the difference between $\mathbb{E}[\varphi(S_n/\sqrt{n})]$ and $\mathbb{E}[\varphi(\xi)]$ in terms of $u(t,x)$, and split it into n terms:

$$\begin{aligned} \mathbb{E}\left[\varphi\left(\frac{S_n}{\sqrt{n}}\right)\right] - \mathbb{E}[\varphi(\xi)] &= u\left(1,\frac{S_n}{\sqrt{n}}\right) - u(0,0) \\ &= \sum_{m=1}^{n}\left\{u\left(\frac{m}{n},\frac{S_m}{\sqrt{n}}\right) - u\left(\frac{m-1}{n},\frac{S_{m-1}}{\sqrt{n}}\right)\right\}. \end{aligned}$$

Finally, he applied the Taylor expansion and the G-heat equation to prove that the above sums converge to 0.

5.4.3. Methods to Prove NP-CLT

The idea of the proof is similar to the idea of the Lindeberg exchange method, as well as Peng's method. It can be described in the following steps:

- Step 1: Guess the form of the limiting distribution, for example, the solution of BSDE or the G-Normal distribution. Use it to construct a family of basic functions $\{H_t(x)\}$, such that

  $$H_t(x) = \mathbb{E}_{[\underline{\mu},\overline{\mu}]}[\varphi(x + B_1 - B_t)] \quad (25)$$

  $$H_t(x) = \mathbb{E}[\varphi(x + \sqrt{1-t}\xi)] \quad (26)$$

  where $\mathbb{E}_{[\underline{\mu},\overline{\mu}]}$ is the g-expectation corresponding to the BSDE (9).

  The key to constructing the function $H_t(x)$ is to ensure that $H_1(x) = \varphi(x)$ and $H_0(0)$ equals the limit distribution.

  Note: In fact, the above definition is not rigorous; this is just to make it easier to understand. In the formal proof, the actual definition of H_t differs slightly from the above definition to facilitate the proof of properties such as the smoothness and boundedness of H_t. For example, the terminal time should not be 1 but $1+h$ for a sufficiently small h, and the generators of the g-expectation should be modified. See (6.3) in [40] and (A.3) in [39].

- Step 2: Prove that $\{H_t\}$ has some nice properties, such as smoothness, boundedness, and the dynamic consistency (something like the Dynamic Programming Principles). This step is in preparation for the Taylor's expansion, which will be used later; see [40] (Lemma 6.1) and [39] (Lemma A.1).
- Step 3: We use the function H_t to connect the left- and right-hand sides of the equation in the limit theorem. Therefore, to prove the CLT, it suffices to prove that

$$\sup_{Q\in\mathcal{P}} E_Q[H_1(T_n^Q)] - H_0(0) \to 0,\ H_t \text{ is defined by } (25)$$

$$\sup_{Q\in\mathcal{P}} E_Q\left[H_1\left(\frac{S_n}{\sqrt{n}}\right)\right] - H_0(0) \to 0,\ H_t \text{ is defined by } (26).$$

Similar to Lindeberg's exchange method, as well as Peng's method, we can divide the above differences into n parts, e.g., for CLT with variance uncertainty, we have the following:

$$\begin{aligned}
&\sup_{Q\in\mathcal{P}} E_Q\left[H_1\left(\frac{S_n}{\sqrt{n}}\right)\right] - H_0(0)\\
=&\sum_{m=1}^{n}\left\{\sup_{Q\in\mathcal{P}} E_Q\left[H_{\frac{m}{n}}\left(\frac{S_m}{\sqrt{n}}\right)\right] - \sup_{Q\in\mathcal{P}} E_Q\left[H_{\frac{m-1}{n}}\left(\frac{S_{m-1}}{\sqrt{n}}\right)\right]\right\}\\
=&\sum_{m=1}^{n}\left\{\sup_{Q\in\mathcal{P}} E_Q\left[H_{\frac{m}{n}}\left(\frac{S_m}{\sqrt{n}}\right)\right] - \sup_{Q\in\mathcal{P}} E_Q\left[L_{m,n}\left(\frac{S_{m-1}}{\sqrt{n}}\right)\right]\right\}\\
&+\sum_{m=1}^{n}\left\{\sup_{Q\in\mathcal{P}} E_Q\left[L_{m,n}\left(\frac{S_{m-1}}{\sqrt{n}}\right)\right] - \sup_{Q\in\mathcal{P}} E_Q\left[H_{\frac{m-1}{n}}\left(\frac{S_{m-1}}{\sqrt{n}}\right)\right]\right\}\\
=:&\Delta_n^1+\Delta_n^2,
\end{aligned}$$

where $L_{m,n}(x) = H_{\frac{m}{n}}(x) + \frac{\overline{\sigma}^2}{2n}\left(H''_{\frac{m}{n}}(x)\right)^+ - \frac{\underline{\sigma}^2}{2n}\left(H''_{\frac{m}{n}}(x)\right)^-$.

For the CLT with mean uncertianty, the corresponding $L_{m,n}$ is defined as follows

$$L_{m,n}(x) = H_{\frac{m}{n}}(x) + \frac{\overline{\mu}}{n}\left(H'_{\frac{m}{n}}(x)\right)^+ - \frac{\underline{\mu}}{n}\left(H'_{\frac{m}{n}}(x)\right)^- + \frac{1}{2n}H''_{\frac{m}{n}}(x).$$

- Step 4: Using Taylor's expansion for $H_{\frac{m}{n}}\left(\frac{S_m}{\sqrt{n}}\right)$ at $\frac{S_{m-1}}{\sqrt{n}}$, prove that the sum of the residuals converges to 0; that is,

$$\sum_{m=1}^{n}\left|\sup_{Q\in\mathcal{P}} E_Q\left[H_{\frac{m}{n}}\left(\frac{S_m}{\sqrt{n}}\right)\right] - \sup_{Q\in\mathcal{P}} E_Q\left[H_{\frac{m}{n}}\left(\frac{S_{m-1}}{\sqrt{n}}\right) + H'_{\frac{m}{n}}\left(\frac{S_{m-1}}{\sqrt{n}}\right)\frac{X_m}{\sqrt{n}} + H''_{\frac{m}{n}}\left(\frac{S_{m-1}}{\sqrt{n}}\right)\frac{X_m^2}{2n}\right]\right| \to 0$$

Further, using the dynamic consistency of $\{X_i\}$ under $\mathcal{P}$, one can prove that

$$\begin{aligned}
&\sup_{Q\in\mathcal{P}} E_Q\left[H_{\frac{m}{n}}\left(\frac{S_{m-1}}{\sqrt{n}}\right) + H'_{\frac{m}{n}}\left(\frac{S_{m-1}}{\sqrt{n}}\right)\frac{X_m}{\sqrt{n}} + H''_{\frac{m}{n}}\left(\frac{S_{m-1}}{\sqrt{n}}\right)\frac{X_m^2}{2n}\right]\\
=&\sup_{Q\in\mathcal{P}} E_Q\left[L_{m,n}\left(\frac{S_{m-1}}{\sqrt{n}}\right)\right].
\end{aligned}$$

This leads to relation $\Delta_n^1 \to 0$.

On the other hand, using the dynamic consistency of H_t, one has, for example

$$H_{\frac{m-1}{n}}(x) = \mathbb{E}\left[H_{\frac{m}{n}}\left(x + \sqrt{\frac{1}{n}}\xi\right)\right].$$

Then, combining this with Taylor's expansion, one can prove that $\Delta_n^2 \to 0$.
See [40] (Lemma 6.4) and [39] (Lemma A.2).

6. Conclusions

Based on the axiomatic definition of probability theory, modern probability theory has made a number of achievements. After Kolmogorov, such scientists as the French mathematician Lévy, the Soviet mathematicians Khinchin and Prokhorov, the American mathematician Doob, the Japanese mathematician Itô, and many others made great contributions to the development of probability theory. The CLTs for random variables laid the foundation for the creation and development of stochastic analysis. This paper first provides a brief overview of the classical CLT and CLT for martingales, and then presents recent advances in CLT in the framework of nonlinear expectations. In particular, recent significant results on nonlinear CLT from the Chinese school of nonlinear expectations, including Peng, Chen, and Zhang, as well as their co-authors, are highlighted.

Among the future directions of research on nonlinear CPT, two important questions should be emphasized:

- How should the nonlinear CLT be interpreted in the case of multidimensional or high-dimensional situations?
- The convergence rate in the classical CLT has been studied quite well and has been successfully used in many applications. However, the rate of convergence in the nonlinear central limit theorem is much less investigated. How should it be treated?

The above directions are also relevant due to the active work on the mathematical justification of models and methods used in machine learning, where we often have to deal with data analysis under uncertainty.

Funding: This research received no external funding.

Acknowledgments: The research was conducted within the framework of the HSE University Basic Research Programs and within the program of the Moscow Center for Fundamental and Applied Mathematics, Lomonosov Moscow State University. The author thanks the Editor for his support and the Reviewers for their appropriate comments which have improved the quality of this paper.

Conflicts of Interest: The author declares no conflicts of interest.

References

1. Rootzén, H. On the Functional Central Limit Theorem for Martingales. *Z. Wahrscheinlichkeitstheorie Verw. Geb.* **1977**, *38*, 199–210. [CrossRef]
2. Hall, P.; Heyde, C.C. *Martingale Limit Theory and Its Application*; Academic Press: New York, NY, USA, 1980.
3. Adams, W.J. The Life and Times of the Central Limit Theorem, 2nd ed. In *History of Mathematics, Volume 35*; American Mathematical Society: Providence, RI, USA, 2009.
4. Fischer, H. *A History of the Central Limit Theorem, From Classical to Modern Probability Theory*; Springer: Berlin, Germany, 2011.
5. Petrov, V.V. *Limit Theorems of Probability Theory*; Oxford Science Publications: Oxford, UK, 1995.
6. Götze, F.; Naumov, A.A.; Ulyanov, V.V. Asymptotic analysis of symmetric functions. *J. Theor. Probab.* **2017**, *30*, 876–897. [CrossRef]
7. Shevtsova, I.G. On absolute constants in inequalities of Berry-Esseen type. *Dokl. Math.* **2014**, *89*, 378–381. [CrossRef]
8. Fujikoshi, F.; Ulyanov, V.V. *Non-Asymptotic Analysis of Approximations for Multivariate Statistics*; SpringerBriefs in Statistics; Springer: Singapore, 2020.
9. Dedecker, J.; Merlevède, F.; Rio, E. Rates of convergence in the central limit theorem for martingales in the non-stationary setting. *Ann. Inst. H. Poincaré Probab. Statist.* **2022**, *58*, 945–966. [CrossRef]
10. Bhattacharya, R.N.; Ranga Rao, R. *Normal Approximation and Asymptotic Expansions*; Wiley: New York, NY, USA, 1976.
11. Sazonov, V.V. *Normal Approximation—Some Recent Advances*; Springer: Berlin, Germany, 1981.
12. Bentkus, V.; Götze, F. Optimal rates of convergence in the CLT for quadratic forms. *Ann. Probab.* **1996**, *24*, 466–490. [CrossRef]
13. Götze F.; Zaitsev, A.Y. Explicit rates of approximation in the CLT for quadratic forms. *Ann. Probab.* **2014**, *42*, 354–397. [CrossRef]

14. Prokhorov, Y.V.; Ulyanov, V.V. Some Approximation Problems in Statistics and Probability. In *Limit Theorems in Probability, Statistics and Number Theory. Springer Proceedings in Mathematics and Statistics*; Eichelsbacher, P., Elsner, G., Kösters, H., Löwe, M., Merkl, F., Rolles, S. Eds.; Springer: Berlin, Germany, 2013; Volume 42, pp. 235–249.
15. Chen, Z.; Yan, X.; Zhang, G. Strategic two-sample test via the two-armed bandit process. *J. R. Stat. Soc. Ser. B Stat. Methodol.* **2023**, *85*, 1271–1298. [CrossRef]
16. Peng, S.; Yao, J.; Yang, S. Improving Value-at-Risk prediction under model uncertainty. *J. Financ. Econom.* **2023**, *21*, 228–259. [CrossRef]
17. Hölzermann, J. Pricing interest rate derivatives under volatility uncertainty. *Ann. Oper. Res.* bf 2024, *336*, 153–182. [CrossRef]
18. Ji, X.; Peng, S.; Jang, S. Imbalanced binary classification under distribution uncertainty. *Inf. Sci.* **2023**, *621*, 156–171. [CrossRef]
19. de Moivre, A. *The Doctrine of Chances*, 2nd ed.; Woodfall: London, UK, 1738.
20. Gauss, C.F. *Theoria Motus Corporum Coelestium*; Perthes & Besser: Hamburg, Germany, 1809.
21. Laplace, P.S.. Mémoire sur la probabilités. *Mémoires de l'Académie Royale des Sciences de Paris Année* **1781**, *1778*, 227–332.
22. Lyapunov, A.M. Sur une proposition de la théorie des probabilités. *Bulletin de l'Académie Impériale des Sciences de St.-Pétersbourg* **1900**, *13*, 359–386.
23. Lyapunov, A.M. *Nouvelle Forme du Théorème sur la Limite de Probabilité*; Mémoires de l'Académie Impériale des Sciences de St.-Pétersbourg VIIIe Série, Classe Physico-Mathématique; Imperial Academy Nauk: Russia, 1901; Volume 12, pp. 1–24. Available online: https://books.google.com/books/about/Nouvelle_forme_du_th%C3%A9or%C3%A8me_sur_la_limi.html?id=XDZinQEACAAJ (accessed on 17 July 2024).
24. Lévy, P. Sur la rôle de la loi de Gauss dans la théorie des erreurs. *Comptes Rendus Hebdomadaires de l'Académie des Sciences de Paris* **1922**, *174*, 855–857.
25. Lindeberg, J.W. Eine neue Herleitung des Exponentialgesetzes in der Wahrscheinlichkeitsrechnung. *Math. Z.* **1922**, *15*, 211–225. [CrossRef]
26. Feller, W. Über den zentralen Grenzwertsatz der Wahrscheinlichkeitsrechnung. *Math. Z.* **1935**, *40*, 521–559. [CrossRef]
27. Bernstein, S. Sur l'extension du théorème limite du calcul des probabilités aux sommes de quantités dépendantes. *Math. Ann.* **1926**, *97*, 1–59. [CrossRef]
28. Lévy, P. Propriétés asymptotiques des sommes de variables aléatoires indépendantes ou enchaînées. *J. Math. Appl.* **1935**, *14*, 347–402.
29. Doob, J.L. *Stochastic Processes*; Wiley: New York, NY, USA, 1953.
30. Billingsley, P. The Lindeberg-Lévy theorem for martingales. *Proc. Am. Math. Soc.* **1961**, *12*, 788–792.
31. Ibragimov, I.A. A central limit theorem for a class of dependent random variables. *Theory Probab. Its Appl.* **1963**, *8*, 83–89. [CrossRef]
32. Csörgő, M. On the strong law of large numbers and the central limit theorem for martingales. *Trans. Am. Math. Soc.* **1968**, *131*, 259–275. [CrossRef]
33. Brown, B.M. Martingale central limit theorems. *Ann. Math. Stat.* **1971**, *42*, 59–66. [CrossRef]
34. McLeish, D.L. Dependent central limit theorems and invariance principles. *Ann. Probab.* **1974**, *2*, 620–628. [CrossRef]
35. Hall, P. Martingale invariance principles. *Ann. Probab.* **1977**, *5*, 875–887. [CrossRef]
36. Peng, S. Backward SDE and related g-expectation. In *Backward Stochastic Differential Equations. Pitman Research Notes in Math. Series*; El Karoui, N., Mazliak, L., Eds.; Longman: London, UK, 1997; pp. 141–159.
37. Peng, S. *Nonlinear Expectations and Stochastic Calculus under Uncertainty: With Robust CLT and G-Brownian Motion*; Springer: Berlin, Germany, 2019, Volume 95.
38. Peng, S. A new central limit theorem under sublinear expectations. *arXiv* **2008**, arXiv:0803.2656.
39. Chen, Z.; Epstein, L.G.; Zhang, G. A central limit theorem, loss aversion and multi-armed bandits. *J. Econ. Theory* **2023**, *209*, 105645. [CrossRef]
40. Chen, Z.; Epstein, L.G. A central limit theorem for sets of probability measures. *Stoch. Process. Their Appl.* **2022**, *152*, 424–451. [CrossRef]
41. Chen, Z.; Liu, S.; Qian, Z.; Xu, X. Explicit solutions for a class of nonlinear BSDEs and their nodal sets. *Probab. Uncertain. Quant. Risk* **2022**, *7*, 283–300. [CrossRef]

mathematics

MDPI

Article

Pointwise Sharp Moderate Deviations for a Kernel Density Estimator

Siyu Liu [1], Xiequan Fan [1,*], Haijuan Hu [1] and Paul Doukhan [2]

[1] School of Mathematics and Statistics, Northeastern University at Qinhuangdao, Qinhuangdao 066004, China
[2] CY University, AGM UMR 8088, Saint-Martin, 95000 Cergy-Pontoise, France
* Correspondence: fanxiequan@neuq.edu.cn

Abstract: Let f_n be the non-parametric kernel density estimator based on a kernel function K and a sequence of independent and identically distributed random vectors taking values in $\mathbb{R}^d$. With some mild conditions, we establish sharp moderate deviations for the kernel density estimator. This means that we provide an equivalent for the tail probabilities of this estimator.

Keywords: Cramér moderate deviations; kernel density estimator; kernel function

MSC: 60F10; 62G07; 60E05; 62E20

1. Introduction

Let $\{X_i; i \geqslant 1\}$ be a sequence of independent and identically distributed (i.i.d.) random vectors taking values in $\mathbb{R}^d$ on probability space $(\Omega, \mathcal{F}, \mathbf{P})$ with density function f. Let $K : \mathbb{R}^d \mapsto \mathbb{R}$ be a kernel function. The kernel density estimator of f is defined by

$$f_n(x) = \frac{1}{na_n^d} \sum_{i=1}^{n} K\Big(\frac{x - X_i}{a_n}\Big), \qquad x = (x_1, x_2, ..., x_d)^T \in \mathbb{R}^d,$$

where $\{a_n, n \geqslant 1\}$ is a bandwidth sequence, that is, a sequence of positive numbers satisfying

$$a_n \to 0, \qquad na_n^d \to +\infty \qquad as \quad n \to +\infty.$$

A great and synthetic reference for such estimates is [1]. Among the huge number of applications of kernel density estimation, let us cite the elegant paper in [2] which makes use of this estimator for an important problem related with green algae: using our results may be used to derive a decision rule for this important ecological question.

In this paper, we are interested in the pointwise sharp moderate deviations for $\{f_n, n \geqslant 1\}$ by the empirical process approach; the volume in [3] is a perfect overview for such questions. In order to present our main result, let us first introduce some notations and assumptions. Let $g : \mathbb{R}^d \mapsto \mathbb{R}$ be a real function. As usual, denote by

$$\|g\|_p = \Big(\int_{x\in\mathbb{R}^d} |g(x)|^p dx \Big)^{\frac{1}{p}}, \ 1 \le p < \infty \quad \text{and} \quad \|g\|_\infty = \sup_{x\in\mathbb{R}^d} |g(x)|$$

the L_p-norm of g and the supermum norm, respectively.

The consistency for the kernel density estimator has been studied widely. Let f be continuously differentiable on $\mathbb{R}$ such that $\|f\|_\infty < \infty$ and $\|f'\|_\infty < \infty$ (f' is the derivative of f). In addition, suppose that $\lim_{N\to\infty} na_n = \infty$ and $\lim_{N\to\infty} na_n^2 = c \ge 0$, where c is a constant. With some mild conditions, Joutard [4] proved the following pointwise sharp large deviation: for any $\alpha > 0$ and $n \to \infty$,

$$\mathbf{P}\Big(f_n(x) - f(x) > \alpha\Big) = \frac{\exp\{-na_n\Lambda^*(\alpha) + cH(\tau)\}}{\tau(2\pi na_n f(x)I''(\tau))^{\frac{1}{2}}}\Big(1 + O(1)\Big),$$

where $\Lambda^*(\alpha) = \tau(\alpha + f(x)) - f(x)I(\tau), \tau \in [0, \alpha]$, is such that $\alpha + f(x) = f(x)I'(\tau)$ and $H(\tau) = -(f^2(x)I^2(\tau)/2 + f'(x)J(\tau))$, with $J(t) = \int_{\mathbb{R}} z\exp\{tK(z)\}dz$. For uniform consistency, with some mild conditions, Gao [5] proved the following moderate deviation principle (MDP) result. Let $\{b_n, n \geq 1\}$ be a sequence of positive real numbers satisfying

$$\frac{na_n^d}{b_n} \to +\infty, \qquad \frac{na_n^d \log a_n^{-1}}{b_n^2} \to +\infty \quad as \quad n \to +\infty.$$

Gao [5] proved that for any $\lambda > 0$,

$$\lim_{n\to\infty} \frac{na_n^d}{b_n} \ln \mathbf{P}\Big(\frac{na_n^d}{b_n}\|f_n - \mathbf{E}f_n\|_\infty > \lambda\Big) = -I(\lambda),$$

where

$$I(\lambda) = \frac{\lambda^2}{2\|f\|_\infty\|K\|_2^2}.$$

A pointwise MDP is also established in Gao [5]. A class of refinements of pointwise MDP is called sharp moderate deviations. Sharp moderate deviations are also known as Cramér moderate deviations, and have attracted a lot of interest. We refer to Cramér [6], Petrov [7], Beknazaryan et al. [8] and Fan et al. [9] for such type results. In this paper, we are interested in establishing sharp moderate deviations for the kernel density estimator.

The paper is organized as follows. Our main result is stated and discussed in Section 2. The proof of our theorem is given in Section 3.

2. Main Results

The following assumptions will be used in this paper.

(A) Assume that the kernel function K satisfies

$$\int_{x\in\mathbb{R}^d} K(x)\,dx = 1 \quad \text{and} \quad \|K\|_\infty < +\infty.$$

(B) There exist a constant $\beta \in (0, 1]$ and a non-negative integer s such that for any $x, y, z \in \mathbb{R}^d$,

$$|(z\cdot\nabla)^s f(x) - (z\cdot\nabla)^s f(y)| \leqslant A\,\|x - y\|_2^\beta \|z\|_2^s,$$

where A is a positive constant, $\|\cdot\|_2$ is the Euclidean distance and

$$z\cdot\nabla = z_1\frac{\partial}{\partial x_1} + z_2\frac{\partial}{\partial x_2} + \cdots + z_d\frac{\partial}{\partial x_d}.$$

(C) Assume

$$\int_{x\in\mathbb{R}^d} K^2(x)\|x\|_2^{s+\beta}\,dx < +\infty \quad \text{and} \quad \int_{x\in\mathbb{R}^d} K(x)\prod_{i=1}^d x_i^{j_i}\,dx = 0, \quad 0 < \sum_{i=1}^d j_i \leq s.$$

Remark 1. *After [1], we recall that the previous assumptions are pretty standard and we restate them in the current multivariate setting:*

1. *The first condition in Assumption (A) is necessary to ensure that the estimate remains a function with integral 1;*

the second one is not necessary but no striking or useful unbounded kernel was used in the frame of density estimation. Moreover, this condition makes it useless to assume that $\int_{x\in\mathbb{R}^d} K^2(x)\,dx < \infty$*, for example.*

2. *Assumption (B) is a regularity condition on* f *with order* $s+\beta$*, with* $\beta > 0$ *and* $s \in \mathbb{N}$ *as considered before.*
3. *The first condition in Assumption (C) is useful to prove that the involved expressions are square-integrable. The second part of this condition is more tricky and ensures that the Taylor expansion up to order* s *provides the relation*

$$\int_{z\in\mathbb{R}^d} K(z)f(x+z)\,dz = f(x) + \mathcal{O}(\|x\|^{s+\beta}), \tag{1}$$

since all the intermediate terms simply vanish. It is important to also quote that such kernels K *exist. A very simple and usual case is* $s = \beta = 1$ *(second-order regularity), which holds in case* K *is symmetric with respect to each of its coordinates; it this case, it is possible to obtain* $K(z) \geq 0$ *and then the estimator* f_n *is still a density (since it is non-negative). For the general case* $s \in \mathbb{N}$*, a standard procedure to prove the existence of such kernels is to define* $K(z) = P(z)\delta(z)$ *for a fixed bounded density function and* $d^\circ P = s$*, where* $d^\circ P$ *is the degree of the polynomial* P*. Then, it is easy to prove that the system of equations in (C) together with the first part of (A) is invertible and linear because the matrix with coefficients*

$$a_{j,k} = \int_{z\in\mathbb{R}^d} K(x)\prod_{i=1}^{d} x_i^{j_i+k_i}\,dx, \qquad 0 < \sum_{i=1}^{d} j_i \leq s,\ 0 < \sum_{i=1}^{d} k_i \leq s,$$

is symmetric non-negative definite; this point is a straightforward extension of Lemma 3.3.1 in [10] to our multidimensional setting.

Assume that $f(x) > 0$ for some $x \in \mathbb{R}^d$. Denote

$$D_n(x) = \frac{\sqrt{na_n^d}\,(f_n(x) - \mathbf{E}f_n(x))}{\sqrt{f(x)\|K\|_2^2 + \sum_{t=1}^{s} a_n^t \frac{1}{t!}\int_{z\in\mathbb{R}^d}(z\cdot\nabla)^t f(x)K^2(z)\,dz}}.$$

We have the following pointwise sharp moderate deviations for the kernel density estimator.

Theorem 1. *Assume that Conditions (A)–(C) are satisfied. Assume* $f(x) > 0$ *for some* $x \in \mathbb{R}^d$*. Then, it holds that*

$$\ln\frac{\mathbf{P}(D_n(x) \geq t)}{1-\Phi(t)} = O\Big(\frac{1+t^3}{\sqrt{na_n^d}} + t^2 a_n^{(s+\beta)\wedge d}\Big) \tag{2}$$

uniformly for $0 \leq t = o(\sqrt{na_n^d}\,)$ *as* $n \to \infty$*. Moreover, the same equality remains valid when* $\ln\frac{\mathbf{P}(D_n(x)\geq t)}{1-\Phi(t)}$ *is replaced by* $\ln\frac{\mathbf{P}(D_n(x)\leq -t)}{1-\Phi(t)}$.

For the non-centered case, we have the following pointwise sharp moderate deviations for the kernel density estimator. Denote

$$\widehat{D}_n(x) = \frac{\sqrt{na_n^d}}{\|K\|_2\sqrt{f(x)}}\Big(f_n(x) - f(x) - \sum_{t=1}^{s}\frac{1}{t!}\int_{x\in\mathbb{R}^d} K(z)(z\cdot\nabla)^t f(x)\,dz\,a_n^t\Big).$$

Theorem 2. *Assume that conditions (A)–(C) are satisfied. Assume* $f(x) > 0$ *for some* $x \in \mathbb{R}^d$*. Then, it holds that*

$$\ln\frac{\mathbf{P}(\widehat{D}_n(x) \geq t)}{1-\Phi(t)} = O\Big(\frac{1+t^3}{\sqrt{na_n^d}} + t^2 a_n^{(s+\beta)\wedge d} + (1+t)\sqrt{n}a_n^{s+\beta+d/2}\Big) \tag{3}$$

uniformly for $0 \le t = o(\sqrt{na_n^d})$ *as* $n \to \infty$. *Moreover, the same equality remains valid when* $\ln \frac{\mathbf{P}(\widehat{D}_n(x) \ge t)}{1-\Phi(t)}$ *is replaced by* $\ln \frac{\mathbf{P}(\widehat{D}_n(x) \le -t)}{1-\Phi(t)}$.

Remark 2. *Let us comment on Theorem 2.*

1. *In the expression of* D_n, *recall that* (1) *in Remark 1 entails that* $\mathbf{E}f_n(x) - f(x) = O(a_n^{s+\beta})$.
2. *This result makes it possible to provide a practitioner with precise confidence intervals that are easy to compute in the case of hypothesis testing. Explicit asymptotic p-values can thus be straightforwardly obtained. For instance, consider the following hypothesis testing:*

$$H_0 : f(x_0) = t_0 \quad \textit{versus} \quad H_1 : f(x_0) \neq t_0,$$

with $t_0 > 0$. *Denote*

$$z_0 = \frac{\sqrt{na_n^d}}{\|K\|_2 \sqrt{f(x_0)}} \Big(f_n(x_0) - t_0 \Big).$$

Then, by Theorem 2, the p-value is asymptotically equal to $2(1 - \Phi(z_0))$, *provided that* z_0 *satisfies*

$$\frac{1+z_0^3}{\sqrt{na_n^d}} + z_0^2 a_n^{(s+\beta)\wedge d} + (1+z_0)\sqrt{n} a_n^{s+\beta+d/2} \to 0.$$

as $n \to \infty$.

3. *Cases of other non parametric estimators, such as the Nadaraya–Watson kernel regression estimator (cf. El Machkouri et al. [11] for instance), non-linear regression estimates or conditional expectations, for predictions issues or estimates of derivatives or even quantile regression estimators, see Rosenblatt [1], will be derived in further subsequent papers.*
4. *Even if a non-independent version of this result is accessible, we prefer to give a simple result in the current i.i.d. case.*

By Theorem 2, we have the following Berry–Esseen bound for $\widehat{D}_n(x)$, that is,

$$\sup_{t \in \mathbb{R}} \Big| \mathbf{P}(\widehat{D}_n(x) \le t) - \Phi(t) \Big| = O\bigg(\frac{1}{\sqrt{na_n^d}} + a_n^{(s+\beta)\wedge d} + \sqrt{n} a_n^{s+\beta+d/2} \bigg). \tag{4}$$

In particular, by taking $a_n = n^{-1/(s+\beta+d)}$, we obtain

$$\sup_{t \in \mathbb{R}} \Big| \mathbf{P}(\widehat{D}_n(x) \le t) - \Phi(t) \Big| = O\Big(n^{-(s+\beta)/(2s+2\beta+d)} \Big).$$

Moreover, if $s = 0$ and $\beta = d = 1$, i.e., f is 1-Hölder-continuous, then it holds that

$$\sup_{t \in \mathbb{R}} \bigg| \mathbf{P}\bigg(\frac{n^{\frac{1}{4}}}{\|K\|_2 \sqrt{f(x)}} (f_n(x) - f(x)) \le t \bigg) - \Phi(t) \bigg| = O\Big(n^{-1/3} \Big).$$

Conclusions. When $f \in C^1(\mathbb{R}^d)$ and $K(z)$ is symmetric with respect to 0, which implies that $\int_{z \in \mathbb{R}^d} z_i K^2(z)\, dz = 0$ for all $1 \le i \le d$, by taking $s = 1$ in Assumptions (C), then we have

$$\int_{x \in \mathbb{R}^d} K(z) z \cdot \nabla f(x)\, dz = 0,$$

which implies

$$D_n(x) = \frac{\sqrt{na_n^d}}{\|K\|_2 \sqrt{f(x)}} (f_n(x) - \mathbf{E}f_n(x)) \quad \text{and} \quad \widehat{D}_n(x) = \frac{\sqrt{na_n^d}}{\|K\|_2 \sqrt{f(x)}} (f_n(x) - f(x)).$$

Then, Theorems 1 and 2 hold with $s = 1$. Theorems 1 and 2 provide moderate deviations for the expressions D_n and $\widehat{D}_n$, which are related through the expression of f_n's bias; see Remark 2. Remarks 1 and 2 provide a detailed description of the calculation of the bias essential here.

3. Proof of Theorem 1

For $n \geq 1$, let $\{Y_i, 1 \leq i \leq n\}$ be i.i.d. and centered random variables. Denote $\sigma^2 = \mathbf{E}Y_1^2$ and $T_n = \sum_{i=1}^n Y_i$. Assume that $\sigma > 0$. Fan et al. [12] (see also Cramér [6]) established the following asymptotic expansion on the tail probabilities of moderate deviations for T_n.

Lemma 1. *Assume that there exists a constant α_n such that for all $1 \leq i \leq n$,*

$$\mathbf{E}|Y_i|^k \leq \frac{1}{2}k!\left(\frac{1}{\alpha_n}\right)^{k-2}\mathbf{E}Y_i^2, \quad k \geq 2. \tag{5}$$

Then,

$$\ln \frac{\mathbf{P}(T_n \geq t\sigma\sqrt{n})}{1-\Phi(t)} = O\left(\frac{1+t^3}{\sqrt{n}\alpha_n}\right) \quad as \ n \to \infty \tag{6}$$

holds uniformly for $0 \leq t = o(\sqrt{n}\alpha_n)$.

Proof. Lemma 1 is a simple consequence of Fan et al. [12]. □

With the preliminary lemma above, we are in the position to begin the proof of Theorem 1. It is easy to see that

$$\sqrt{na_n^d}\Big(f_n(x) - \mathbf{E}f_n(x)\Big) = \frac{1}{\sqrt{na_n^d}}\sum_{k=1}^n\left[K\left(\frac{x-X_i}{a_n}\right) - \mathbf{E}K\left(\frac{x-X_i}{a_n}\right)\right]. \tag{7}$$

In the sequel, we give an estimate for the right-hand side of the last equality. Notice that

$$\begin{aligned}\frac{1}{\sqrt{na_n^d}}&\sum_{k=1}^n\left[K\left(\frac{x-X_i}{a_n}\right) - \mathbf{E}K\left(\frac{x-X_i}{a_n}\right)\right]\\ &= \frac{1}{\sqrt{n}}\sum_{k=1}^n\frac{1}{\sqrt{a_n^d}}\left[K\left(\frac{x-X_i}{a_n}\right) - \mathbf{E}K\left(\frac{x-X_i}{a_n}\right)\right].\end{aligned} \tag{8}$$

Denote

$$Y_i = \frac{1}{\sqrt{a_n^d}}\left[K\left(\frac{x-X_i}{a_n}\right) - \mathbf{E}K\left(\frac{x-X_i}{a_n}\right)\right], \ 1 \leq i \leq n.$$

We can prove that Y_i satisfies the Bernstein condition Equation (5). Indeed, we can deduce that for all $k \geq 2$,

$$\begin{aligned}\mathbf{E}|Y_i|^k &\leqslant \left(\frac{1}{\sqrt{a_n^d}}\right)^k\mathbf{E}\left|K\left(\frac{x-X_i}{a_n}\right) - \mathbf{E}K\left(\frac{x-X_i}{a_n}\right)\right|^k\\ &\leqslant \left(\frac{1}{\sqrt{a_n^d}}\right)^k\|K\|_\infty^{k-2}\mathbf{E}\left|K\left(\frac{x-X_i}{a_n}\right) - \mathbf{E}K\left(\frac{x-X_i}{a_n}\right)\right|^2\\ &\leqslant \left(\frac{\|K\|_\infty}{\sqrt{a_n^d}}\right)^{k-2}\mathbf{E}|Y_i|^2\\ &\leqslant \frac{1}{2}k!\left(\frac{\|K\|_\infty}{\sqrt{a_n^d}}\right)^{k-2}\mathbf{E}|Y_i|^2.\end{aligned}$$

For the variance of Y_i, we have the following estimation:

$$\begin{aligned}\mathrm{Var}(Y_i) &= \frac{1}{a_n^d}\mathrm{Var}\left(K\left(\frac{x-X_i}{a_n}\right)\right)\\ &= \frac{1}{a_n^d}\left(\mathbf{E}K^2\left(\frac{x-X_i}{a_n}\right)-\left[\mathbf{E}K\left(\frac{x-X_i}{a_n}\right)\right]^2\right).\end{aligned}$$

It is easy to see that

$$\begin{aligned}\mathbf{E}K^2\left(\frac{x-X_i}{a_n}\right) &= a_n^d\left[\int_{z\in\mathbb{R}^d}K^2(z)f(x-za_n)\,dz\right]\\ &= a_n^d\left[\int_{z\in\mathbb{R}^d}K^2(z)f(x)\,dz+\int_{z\in\mathbb{R}^d}K^2(z)(f(x-za_n)-f(x))\,dz\right].\end{aligned}$$

By Assumption (B), it is easy to see that

$$\begin{aligned}&\left|f(x-za_n)-f(x)-\sum_{t=1}^{s}\frac{1}{t!}(z\cdot\nabla)^t f(x)a_n^t\right|\\ &\quad=\left|\frac{1}{s!}\Big((z\cdot\nabla)^s f(x+\theta za_n)-(z\cdot\nabla)^s f(x)\Big)a_n^s\right|\\ &\quad\le C_dAa_n^{s+\beta}\|z\|_2^{s+\beta},\end{aligned}\tag{9}$$

where $|\theta|\le 1$ and A is given by Assumption (B). Again by Condition (C), we can deduce that

$$\begin{aligned}\mathbf{E}K^2\left(\frac{x-X_i}{a_n}\right) &= a_n^d\left[\int_{z\in\mathbb{R}^d}K^2(z)f(x)\,dz+\int_{z\in\mathbb{R}^d}K^2(z)(f(x-za_n)-f(x))\,dz\right]\\ &= a_n^d f(x)\int_{z\in\mathbb{R}^d}K^2(z)\,dz+\sum_{t=1}^{s}\frac{1}{t!}\int_{z\in\mathbb{R}^d}(z\cdot\nabla)^t f(x)K^2(z)\,dz\,a_n^{d+t}\\ &\quad+O(1)a_n^{d+s+\beta}\int_{z\in\mathbb{R}^d}K^2(z)\|z\|_2^{s+\beta}\,dz\\ &= a_n^d f(x)\int_{z\in\mathbb{R}^d}K^2(z)\,dz+\sum_{t=1}^{s}a_n^{d+t}\frac{1}{t!}\int_{z\in\mathbb{R}^d}(z\cdot\nabla)^t f(x)K^2(z)\,dz\\ &\quad+O(a_n^{d+s+\beta}).\end{aligned}\tag{10}$$

By Condition (B), it is easy to see that

$$\begin{aligned}\mathbf{E}K\left(\frac{x-X_i}{a_n}\right) &= a_n^d\left[\int_{z\in\mathbb{R}^d}K(z)f(x)\,dz+\int_{z\in\mathbb{R}^d}K(z)[f(x-za_n)-f(x)]\,dz\right]\\ &= a_n^d f(x)\int_{z\in\mathbb{R}^d}K(z)\,dz+o(a_n^d)\\ &= a_n^d f(x)+o(a_n^d).\end{aligned}\tag{11}$$

From Equations (10) and (11), we have

$$\begin{aligned}\mathrm{Var}(Y_i) &= \frac{1}{a_n^d}\left(a_n^d f(x)\int_{z\in\mathbb{R}^d}K^2(z)\,dz+\sum_{t=1}^{s}a_n^{d+t}\frac{1}{t!}\int_{z\in\mathbb{R}^d}(z\cdot\nabla)^t f(x)K^2(z)\,dz\right.\\ &\quad\left.+O(a_n^{d+s+\beta})-\left(a_n^d f(x)+o(a_n^d)\right)^2\right)\\ &= f(x)\int_{z\in\mathbb{R}^d}K^2(z)\,dz+\sum_{t=1}^{s}a_n^t\frac{1}{t!}\int_{z\in\mathbb{R}^d}(z\cdot\nabla)^t f(x)K^2(z)\,dz+O(a_n^{(s+\beta)\wedge d}).\end{aligned}$$

When $f(x) > 0$, we obtain

$$\gamma_n := \frac{\|K\|_\infty / \sqrt{a_n^d}}{\sqrt{n\mathrm{Var}(Y_1)}} = O\Big(\frac{1}{\sqrt{na_n^d}}\Big)$$

and

$$\frac{\mathrm{Var}(Y_i)}{f(x)\|K\|_2^2 + \sum_{t=1}^{s} a_n^t \frac{1}{t!} \int_{z\in\mathbb{R}^d} (z\cdot\nabla)^t f(x) K^2(z)\, dz} = 1 + O(a_n^{(s+\beta)\wedge d}). \tag{12}$$

Therefore, by Lemma 1, we can deduce that for all $0 \le t = o(\sqrt{na_n^d}\,)$

$$\begin{aligned}\mathbf{P}\Big(\sqrt{na_n^d}\Big(f_n(x) - \mathbf{E}f_n(x)\Big) \geqslant t\sqrt{\mathrm{Var}(Y_1)}\Big) &= \mathbf{P}\Big(\frac{1}{\sqrt{n\mathrm{Var}(Y_1)}} \sum_{k=1}^{n} Y_i \geqslant t\Big) \\ &= \Big(1 - \Phi(t)\Big) \exp\Big\{O(1)\frac{1+t^3}{\sqrt{na_n^d}}\Big\}.\end{aligned}$$

Applying inequality Equation (12) to the last inequality, we deduce that for all $0 \le t = o(\sqrt{na_n^d}\,)$

$$\begin{aligned}&\mathbf{P}(D_n(x) \ge t) \\ &= \mathbf{P}\Bigg(\sqrt{na_n^d}\Big(f_n(x) - \mathbf{E}f_n(x)\Big) \geqslant t\sqrt{f(x)\|K\|_2^2 + \sum_{t=1}^{s} a_n^t \frac{1}{t!} \int_{z\in\mathbb{R}^d} (z\cdot\nabla)^t f(x) K^2(z)\, dz}\Bigg) \\ &= \mathbf{P}\Bigg(\sqrt{na_n^d}\Big(f_n(x) - \mathbf{E}f_n(x)\Big) \geqslant t\sqrt{\mathrm{Var}(Y_1)}\sqrt{1 + O(a_n^{(s+\beta)\wedge d})}\Bigg) \\ &= \Big(1 - \Phi(t(1 + O(a_n^{(s+\beta)\wedge d})))\Big) \exp\Big\{O(1)\frac{1+t^3}{\sqrt{na_n^d}}\Big\}.\end{aligned}$$

Because of

$$\frac{1}{1+\lambda} e^{-\lambda^2/2} \le \sqrt{2\pi}(1 - \Phi(\lambda)), \quad \lambda \ge 0,$$

it is easy to see that for all $0 \le \lambda \le x$,

$$\begin{aligned}1 \le \frac{\int_\lambda^\infty \exp\{-t^2/2\}dt}{\int_x^\infty \exp\{-t^2/2\}dt} &\le 1 + \frac{\int_\lambda^x \exp\{-t^2/2\}dt}{\int_x^\infty \exp\{-t^2/2\}dt} \\ &\le 1 + c_1 x(x-\lambda) \exp\Big\{(x^2 - \lambda^2)/2\Big\} \\ &\le \exp\Big\{c_2\, x|x-\lambda|\Big\}.\end{aligned}$$

Hence, we obtain for any $\lambda, x \ge 0$,

$$1 - \Phi(\lambda) = (1 - \Phi(x)) \exp\Big\{O(1)(x+\lambda)|x-\lambda|\Big\}.$$

By the last equality, it follows that

$$1 - \Phi(x(1 + O(a_n^{(s+\beta)\wedge d}))) \;=\; (1 - \Phi(x)) \exp\Big\{O(1) x^2 a_n^{(s+\beta)\wedge d}\Big\}.$$

Therefore, we have, for all $0 \leq t = o(\sqrt{na_n^d})$,

$$\mathbf{P}\big(D_n(x) \geq t\big) = \Big(1 - \Phi(t)\Big) \exp\Big\{O(1)\Big(\frac{1+t^3}{\sqrt{na_n^d}} + t^2 a_n^{(s+\beta)\wedge d}\Big)\Big\}. \tag{13}$$

This completes the proof of Theorem 1.

4. Proof of Theorem 2

It is easy to see that

$$\begin{aligned} \mathbf{E}f_n(x) - f(x) &= \frac{1}{na_n^d} \sum_{k=1}^{n} \int_{x\in\mathbb{R}^d} K\Big(\frac{x-t}{a_n}\Big) f(t)\, dt - f(x) \\ &= \int_{x\in\mathbb{R}^d} K(z) f(x - a_n z)\, dz - f(x) \\ &= \int_{x\in\mathbb{R}^d} K(z)[f(x - a_n z) - f(x)]\, dz. \end{aligned}$$

By inequality Equation (9), we deduce that

$$\begin{aligned} \mathbf{E}f_n(x) - f(x) &= \sum_{t=1}^{s} \frac{1}{t!} \int_{x\in\mathbb{R}^d} K(z)(z\cdot\nabla)^t f(x)\, dz\, a_n^t \\ &\quad + C_d A \int_{x\in\mathbb{R}^d} K(z)\|z\|_2^{s+\beta} dz\, a_n^{s+\beta} \\ &= \sum_{t=1}^{s} \frac{1}{t!} \int_{x\in\mathbb{R}^d} K(z)(z\cdot\nabla)^t f(x)\, dz\, a_n^t + O(a_n^{s+\beta}). \end{aligned}$$

Applying the last line to Equation (13), we obtain, for all $0 \leq t = o(\sqrt{na_n^d})$,

$$\begin{aligned} \mathbf{P}\Big(\widehat{D}_n(x) \geq t\Big) &= \mathbf{P}\left(D_n(x) \geq t - \frac{\sqrt{na_n^d}\, O(a_n^{s+\beta})}{\|K\|_2 \sqrt{f(x)}} \right) \\ &= \Big(1 - \Phi(t)\Big) \exp\Big\{O(1)\Big(\frac{1+t^3}{\sqrt{na_n^d}} + t^2 a_n^{(s+\beta)\wedge d} + (1+t)\sqrt{n} a_n^{s+\beta+d/2}\Big)\Big\}. \end{aligned}$$

This completes the proof of Theorem 2.

Author Contributions: Writing—original draft preparation, X.F., P.D., S.L. and H.H.; supervision, X.F.; funding acquisition, S.L. All authors have read and agreed to the published version of the manuscript.

Funding: This work was also funded in the frame of the chair FIME: https://fime-lab.org/ and CY-AS ("Investissements d'Avenir" ANR-16-IDEX-0008), "EcoDep" PSI-AAP2020-0000000013.

Data Availability Statement: Data sharing is not applicable to this article as no new data were created or analyzed in this study.

Acknowledgments: The authors would like to thank the anonymous referees for their valuable comments and remarks.

Conflicts of Interest: The authors declare no conflicts of interest.

References

1. Rosenblatt, R. *Stochastic Curve Estimation*; NSF-CBMS Regional Conference Series in Probability and Statistics; Institute of Mathematical Statistics: Waite Hill, OH, USA, 1991; Volume 3.
2. Ciret, T.; Damien, P.; Ciutat, A.; Durrieu, G.; Massabuau, J.-C. Estimation of potential and limits of bivalve closure response to detect contaminants: Application to cadmium. *Environ. Toxicol. Chem.* **2003**, *22*, 914–920.
3. de la Peña, V.H.; Lai, T.L.; Shao Q.M. *Self-Normalized Processes: Limit Theory and Statistical Applications (Probability and Its Applications)*; Springer: Berlin/Heidelberg, Germany, 2009.

4. Joutard, C. Sharp large deviations in nonparametric estimation. *J. Nonparam. Stat.* **2006**, *18*, 293–306. [CrossRef]
5. Gao, F. Moderate deviations and large deviations for kernel density estimators. *J. Theoret. Probab.* **2003**, *16*, 401–418. [CrossRef]
6. Cramér, H. Sur un nouveau théorème-limite de la théorie des probabilités. *Actual. Sci. Indust.* **1938**, *736*, 5–23.
7. Petrov, V.V. *Sums of Independent Random Variables*; Springer: Berlin/Heidelberg, Germany, 1975.
8. Beknazaryan, A.; Sang, H.; Xiao, Y. Cramér type moderate deviations for random fields. *J. Appl. Probab.* **2019**, *56*, 223–245. [CrossRef]
9. Fan, X.; Hu, H.; Xu, L. Cramér-type moderate deviations for Euler-Maruyama scheme for SDE. *Sci. China Math.* **2024**, *67*, 1865–1880. [CrossRef]
10. Doukhan, P. *Stochastic Models for Time Series*; Series Mathématiques et Applications; Springer: Berlin/Heidelberg, Germany, 2018; Volume 80.
11. El Machkouri, M.; Fan, X.; Reding, L. On the Nadaraya-Watson kernel regression estimator for irregularly spaced spatial data. *J. Statist. Plann. Infer.* **2020**, *205*, 92–114. [CrossRef]
12. Fan, X.; Grama, I.; Liu, Q. Cramér large deviation expansions for martingales under Bernstein's condition. *Stoch. Process. Appl.* **2013**, *123*, 3919–3942. [CrossRef]

mathematics

MDPI

Article

Borel–Cantelli Lemma for Capacities

Chunyu Kao [1,*] **and Gaofeng Zong** [2]

[1] Zhongtai Securities Institute for Financial Studies, Shandong University, Jinan 250100, China
[2] School of Mathematics and Quantitative Economics, Shandong University of Finance and Economics, Jinan 250014, China; zonggf@sdufe.edu.cn
* Correspondence: kcy@mail.sdu.edu.cn

Abstract: In this paper, we investigate the second Borel–Cantelli lemma for capacity without the assumption of independence for events. We obtain a sufficient condition under which the second Borel–Cantelli lemma for capacity holds. Our results are natural extensions of the classical Borel–Cantelli lemma. However, the proof is different from the existing literature.

Keywords: capacity; Choquet expectation; exponential independence; law of large numbers; sub-linear expectation

MSC: 60A10; 60H05

1. Introduction

In probability theory, the Borel–Cantelli lemma, which was first obtained by Borel (1909, 1912) [1,2] and Cantelli (1917) [3], is an important theorem about sequences of events, such a lemma consists of two parts, which are called the first and second Borel–Cantelli lemma. The lemma states that, under certain conditions, an event will occur with either probability zero or probability one. The second Borel–Cantelli lemma is a partial converse of the first Borel–Cantelli lemma since the second Borel–Cantelli lemma needs the additional assumption of independence.

Since then, there has been a large amount of literature to extend the Borel–Cantelli lemma (see, for example, Chandra (2012) [4] in detail). For the first Borel–Cantelli lemma, we refer the reader to Barndorff-Nielsen (1961) [5], Martikainen and Petrov (1990) [6], and Balakrishnan and Stepanov (2010) [7]. For the second Borel–Cantelli lemma, we refer the reader to Erdös and Rényi (1959) [8], Kochen and Stone (1964) [9], Petrov (2002, 2004) [10,11], Yan (2006) [12], (which provides a new and simple proof about Kochen and Stone (1964) [9]), and Xie (2009) [13] and Zong et al. (2016) [14], in which many attempts can be founded to weaken the independence condition.

Recently, motivated by mathematical finance and robust statistics, non-additive measures or non-linear expectations have already caught many scholars' attention; see Huber (1973) [15], Denneberg (1994) [16], Wang and Klir (2009) [17], Peng (2006, 2009, 2019) [18–20], Torra et al. (2014) [21], and Zong et al. (2016) [14]. A natural question is whether or not such a Borel–Cantelli lemma could be extended to the case where the probability measure is non-additive.

According to the property of the first Borel–Cantelli lemma, we can easily extend the lemma to the case where the probability is no longer additive. In fact, the first Borel–Cantelli lemma holds for all set functions that are of countable subadditivity and monotonicity; see Billingsley (1995) [22]. However, for the second Borel–Cantelli lemma, it is not easy to do so because this lemma depends on the assumption of independence. Therefore, many concepts of independence under nonadditive probability/expectation have been introduced, for example, Peng's independence in Peng (2006, 2009, 2019) [18–20], Marinacci pre-independence in Maccheroni and Marinacci (2005) [23], and Puhalskii independence (2001) [24], as well as the Fubini-Like Theorem for Choquet Integrals, in Zong et al. (2016) [14]. A natural question is whether we could investigate the second Borel–Cantelli lemma for capacities without the assumption of independence. In this paper, we obtain a sufficient condition under which the second Borel–Cantelli lemma for capacity holds. It turns out that our results are natural extensions of the classical Borel–Cantelli lemma. However, the proofs are different from the existing literature.

This paper is organized as follows: In Section 2, we show some basic definitions and propositions with respect to capacity and present some preparatory lemmas. In Section 3, we provide a sufficient condition under which the second Borel–Cantelli lemma for capacities holds. In Section 4, we consider the case where random variables are independent under non-additive expectations or non-additive probabilities.

2. Preliminaries

Assume that $(\Omega, \mathcal{F})$ is a measurable space; we define capacity, V, as follows.

Definition 1. *A set-function, V, on $\mathcal{F}$ is called a* capacity *if it satisfies*

(i) $V(\emptyset) = 0,\ V(\Omega) = 1.$
(ii) $V(A) \leq V(B),\ A \subset B,\ A, B \in \mathcal{F}.$
(iii) $V(A \bigcup B) \leq V(A) + V(B), \quad A, B \in \mathcal{F}.$

Given a capacity, V, let the $\mathcal{F}$-measurable function $X : \Omega \to R$ be a random variable defined on $(\Omega, \mathcal{F})$. We focus on Choquet expectation, $\mathbb{E}$, denoted as

Definition 2. *Given a capacity, V, a Choquet (integral) expectation is denoted as*

$$\mathbb{E}[X] := \int_0^\infty V(X \geq t)dt + \int_{-\infty}^0 [V(X > t) - 1]dt.$$

We assume that $\mathcal{H}$ is the set of all random variables, X, with $\mathbb{E}[|X|] < \infty$.

Definition 3. *Two random variables, $\xi, \eta \in \mathcal{H}$, are comonotone if, almost surely,*

$$(\xi(\omega) - \xi(\omega'))(\eta(\omega) - \eta(\omega')) \geq 0.$$

For more knowledge about comonotonicity, see, for instance, Dhaene et al. (2002) [25].

The basic properties of Choquet expectations are given in the following proposition (see, e.g., Denneberg (1992) [16]).

Lemma 1.

(a) *Monotonicity: $X, Y \in \mathcal{H}$, if $X \geq Y$, then $\mathbb{E}[X] > \mathbb{E}[Y]$.*
(b) *Constant preserving: $\mathbb{E}[c] = c, \forall c \in \mathbb{R}$.*
(c) *Translation invariance: $\mathbb{E}[c + X] = c + \mathbb{E}[X], \forall c \in \mathbb{R}$.*
(d) *Positive homogeneity: $\mathbb{E}[\lambda X] = \lambda \mathbb{E}[X], \forall \lambda \geq 0$.*
(e) *Lower–upper Choquet expectations: $-\mathbb{E}[-X] \leq \mathbb{E}[X]$.*
(f) *Comonotonic additivity: if X, Y are comonotonic random variables, then*

$$\mathbb{E}[X + Y] = \mathbb{E}[X] + \mathbb{E}[Y].$$

Remark 1. *Usually, a Choquet expectation does not satisfy the following sub-linearity:*

$$\mathbb{E}[X+Y] \leq \mathbb{E}[X] + \mathbb{E}[Y].$$

However, it has been proven that a Choquet expectation satisfies sub-linearity if and only if the corresponding capacity, V, is 2−alternating in the sense of

$$V(A \cup B) \leq V(A) + V(B) - V(A \cap B), \quad A, B \in \mathcal{F}.$$

Proposition 1. *Let φ on $\mathbb{R}$ be a positively convex function. Then, the Jensen inequality under Choquet expectation holds:*

$$\varphi(\mathbb{E}[X]) \leq \mathbb{E}[\varphi(X)].$$

Proof. First, it is easy to check that a Choquet expectation has the following property:

$$\lambda\mathbb{E}[X] \leq \mathbb{E}[\lambda X], \ \lambda \in \mathbb{R}.$$

In fact, obviously, the above inequality becomes equality if $\lambda \geq 0$, by the definition of Choquet expectation. We now prove the case where $\lambda \leq 0$. In fact,

$$\lambda\mathbb{E}[X] = -|\lambda|\mathbb{E}[X] = -\mathbb{E}[|\lambda|X] = -\mathbb{E}[-\lambda X] \leq \mathbb{E}[\lambda X].$$

The last inequality is due to Lemma 1(e).

Using the above inequality, we can easily prove this lemma. Indeed, because the function $\varphi : \mathbb{R} \to \mathbb{R}$ is convex, there exists a countable set, D, in $\mathbb{R}^2$, such that $\varphi(x) = \sup_{(a,b)\in D} (ax+b)$. Via the translation invariance of the Choquet expectation in Lemma 1(c), we have

$$\begin{aligned} \varphi(\mathbb{E}[X]) &= \sup_{(a,b)\in D} (a\mathbb{E}[X]+b) \\ &\leq \sup_{(a,b)\in D} (\mathbb{E}[aX+b]) \\ &\leq \mathbb{E}[\sup_{(a,b)\in D} (aX+b)] \\ &= \mathbb{E}[\varphi(X)]. \end{aligned}$$

The proof is complete. □

Because the probability measure in probability theory is assumed to be continuous in the sense that $P(A_n) \to P(A)$ whenever $A_n \to A, n \to \infty$, Fatou's lemma is naturally true. However, for capacities, Fatou's lemma is usually not true because the capacity in the nonlinear case is no longer continuous. Thus, we need the following concept.

Definition 4. *A capacity, V, is called a Fatou-like capacity if*

$$V\left(\limsup_{n\to\infty} A_n\right) \geq \limsup_{n\to\infty} V(A_n), \ A_n \in \mathcal{F}. \tag{1}$$

It is easy to show that the following capacities are Fatou-like capacities:

Example 1. *Let B_n, $B \in \mathcal{F}$ and $\lim_{n\to\infty} V(B_n) = V(B)$ whenever $B_n \downarrow B$, and then V is a Fatou-like capacity.*

Example 2. *Let $\mathcal{P}$ be a weakly compact set of probability measures defined on $(\Omega, \mathcal{F})$; then, the upper probability, V, defined by*

$$V(A) = \sup_{Q \in \mathcal{P}} Q(A),$$

is a Fatou-like capacity.

The following lemma is an important lemma that we use in this paper. The main idea is from Yan (2006) [12].

Lemma 2. *Let X be a random variable, such that $\mathbb{E}[e^X] > e^\alpha$ for a constant, α, and then*

$$V(X > \alpha) \geq \frac{\left(\mathbb{E}\left[e^X\right] - e^\alpha\right)^2}{\mathbb{E}\left[\left(e^X - e^\alpha\right)^2\right]}.$$

Proof. It is easy to check that, for any $x, \alpha \in R$,

$$(e^x - e^\alpha) I_{\{x > \alpha\}} \geq e^x - e^\alpha,$$

here and in the sequel, I_A represents the indicator function of set A.

Therefore,

$$\mathbb{E}\left[(e^X - e^\alpha) I_{\{X > \alpha\}}\right] \geq \mathbb{E}\left[e^X\right] - e^\alpha \geq 0. \tag{2}$$

For convenience, we denote

$$\xi := (e^X - e^\alpha) I_{\{X > \alpha\}} \quad \text{and} \quad \eta := I_{\{X > \alpha\}}.$$

It then follows the elementary inequality $|ab| \leq \frac{1}{2}a^2 + \frac{1}{2}b^2$ that

$$\frac{|\xi\eta|}{(\mathbb{E}[|\xi|^2])^{\frac{1}{2}} (\mathbb{E}[|\eta|^2])^{\frac{1}{2}}} \leq \frac{1}{2}\frac{|\xi|^2}{\mathbb{E}[|\xi|^2]} + \frac{1}{2}\frac{|\eta|^2}{\mathbb{E}[|\eta|^2]}, \tag{3}$$

Taking the Choquet integration $\mathbb{E}[\cdot]$ on both sides in inequality (3), according to the monotonicity of Choquet integration in Lemma 1(a), we have

$$\mathbb{E}\left[\frac{|\xi\eta|}{(\mathbb{E}[|\xi|^2])^{\frac{1}{2}} (\mathbb{E}[|\eta|^2])^{\frac{1}{2}}}\right] \leq \mathbb{E}\left[\frac{1}{2}\frac{|\xi|^2}{\mathbb{E}[|\xi|^2]} + \frac{1}{2}\frac{|\eta|^2}{\mathbb{E}[|\eta|^2]}\right]. \tag{4}$$

Furthermore, it is easy to check that both $|\xi|^2 = (e^X - e^\alpha)^2 I_{\{X > \alpha\}}$ and $|\eta|^2 = I_{\{X > \alpha\}}$ are co-monotonic; hence, via the comonotonic additivity of the Choquet expectation, we get

$$\mathbb{E}\left[\frac{1}{2}\frac{|\xi|^2}{\mathbb{E}[|\xi|^2]} + \frac{1}{2}\frac{|\eta|^2}{\mathbb{E}[|\eta|^2]}\right] = \mathbb{E}\left[\frac{1}{2}\frac{|\xi|^2}{\mathbb{E}[|\xi|^2]}\right] + \mathbb{E}\left[\frac{1}{2}\frac{|\eta|^2}{\mathbb{E}[|\eta|^2]}\right] = 1$$

This, with (4), implies that

$$(\mathbb{E}[|\xi\eta|])^2 \leq \mathbb{E}[|\xi|^2]\mathbb{E}[|\eta|^2].$$

That is

$$\begin{aligned} \left(\mathbb{E}\left[\left|(e^X - e^\alpha) I_{\{X > \alpha\}}\right|\right]\right)^2 &\leq \mathbb{E}[|(e^X - e^\alpha) I_{\{X > \alpha\}}|^2]\mathbb{E}[|I_{\{X > \alpha\}}|^2] \\ &\leq \mathbb{E}[|(e^X - e^\alpha)|^2] V(X > \alpha), \end{aligned}$$

which, with (2), implies the desired result. □

Lemma 3. *Suppose that* $\{A_i\}_{i=1}^{\infty}$ *is a sequence of events; set* $X_i := I_{A_i}$. *Assume that*

$$a_n := \sum_{i=1}^{n} V(A_i) \to \infty, \quad n \to \infty,$$

and for any sequence of real numbers, $\{k_n\}$ *with* $k_n > 0$,

$$\limsup_{n\to\infty} \frac{\mathbb{E}\left[e^{k_n \sum_{i=1}^{n} X_i}\right]}{\prod_{i=1}^{n} \mathbb{E}\left[e^{k_n X_i}\right]} < \infty.$$

Then,

(I) *For any constant,* $\alpha > 0$, *and any sequence,* $\{b_n\}$ *with* $b_n \geq \sqrt{a_n}$,

$$\sup_{n\geq 1} \mathbb{E}\left[e^{\frac{\alpha}{b_n}\sum_{i=1}^{n}(X_i - \mathbb{E}[X_i])}\right] < \infty. \tag{5}$$

(II) *For any* $\epsilon > 0$,

$$\lim_{n\to\infty} V\left(\frac{1}{a_n}\sum_{i=1}^{n} X_i > 1+\epsilon\right) = 0. \tag{6}$$

(III) *For any constant* $\alpha > 0$,

$$\lim_{n\to\infty} \mathbb{E}\left[e^{\frac{\alpha}{a_n}\sum_{i=1}^{n} X_i} I_{\{\frac{1}{a_n}\sum_{i=1}^{n} X_i \geq 1+\varepsilon\}}\right] = 0. \tag{7}$$

Proof. The proof of (I):

A trite calculation of a double integral, the following elementary equality can be obtained easily:

$$e^x = 1 + x + x^2 \int_0^1 r dr \int_0^1 e^{rxy} dy, \quad x \in (-\infty, +\infty).$$

Immediately, we get

$$e^x \leq 1 + x + \frac{x^2}{2} e^{|x|}, \quad x \in (-\infty, +\infty). \tag{8}$$

Choosing $x = \frac{\alpha}{b_n}(X_i - \mathbb{E}[X_i])$ in (8).

Since $|X_i - \mathbb{E}[X_i]| = |I_{A_i} - V(A_i)| \leq 2$ and $b_n \geq \sqrt{a_n} \to \infty$ as $n \to \infty$, thus, for a sufficiently large n, we have $b_n \geq 1$

$$\frac{\alpha}{b_n}|X_i - \mathbb{E}[X_i]| \leq \frac{2\alpha}{b_n} \leq 2\alpha.$$

Note the fact that $X_i^2 = X_i$. Thus,

$$\begin{aligned}
e^{\frac{\alpha}{b_n}(X_i - \mathbb{E}[X_i])} &\leq 1 + \frac{\alpha}{b_n}(X_i - \mathbb{E}[X_i]) + \frac{\alpha^2 |X_i - \mathbb{E}[X_i]|^2}{2b_n^2} e^{\frac{\alpha}{b_n}|X_i - \mathbb{E}[X_i]|} \\
&\leq 1 + \frac{\alpha}{b_n}(X_i - \mathbb{E}[X_i]) + \frac{\alpha^2 |X_i - \mathbb{E}[X_i]|^2}{2a_n} e^{2\alpha} \\
&\leq 1 + \frac{\alpha}{b_n}(X_i - \mathbb{E}[X_i]) + \frac{\alpha^2 e^{2\alpha}}{2a_n}\left((1 + 2\mathbb{E}[X_i]) + \mathbb{E}[X_i]^2\right) X_i \\
&= 1 + \left(\frac{\alpha}{b_n} + \frac{\alpha^2 e^{2\alpha}}{2a_n}(1 + 2\mathbb{E}[X_i])\right) X_i - \frac{\alpha}{b_n}\mathbb{E}[X_i] + \frac{\alpha^2 e^{2\alpha}}{2a_n}\mathbb{E}[X_i]^2
\end{aligned}$$

Set expectation $\mathbb{E}[\cdot]$ on both sides of the inequality above; given the translation invariance in Lemma 1 and $\mathbb{E}[X_i] = V(A_i) \leq 1$, immediately,

$$\begin{aligned}\mathbb{E}\left[e^{\frac{\alpha}{b_n}(X_i-\mathbb{E}[X_i])}\right] &\leq 1+\Big(\frac{\alpha^2e^{2\alpha}}{2a_n}(1+2\mathbb{E}[X_i])\Big)\mathbb{E}[X_i]+\frac{\alpha^2e^{2\alpha}}{2a_n}(\mathbb{E}[X_i])^2 \\ &\leq 1+\frac{4\alpha^2e^{2\alpha}}{2a_n}V(A_i) \\ &\leq e^{\left(\frac{2\alpha^2e^{2\alpha}}{a_n}V(A_i)\right)},\end{aligned}$$

The last inequality follows from the fact that, for $x \geq 0, 1+x \leq e^x$.

Therefore, for a sufficiently large n, we have

$$\begin{aligned}\mathbb{E}\left[e^{\frac{\alpha}{b_n}\sum_{i=1}^n(X_i-\mathbb{E}[X_i])}\right] &= \frac{\mathbb{E}\left[e^{\frac{\alpha}{b_n}\sum_{i=1}^n X_i}\right]}{\prod_{i=1}^n \mathbb{E}\left[e^{\frac{\alpha}{b_n}X_i}\right]}\prod_{i=1}^n \mathbb{E}\left[e^{\frac{\alpha}{b_n}(X_i-\mathbb{E}[X_i])}\right] \\ &\leq \frac{\mathbb{E}\left[e^{\frac{\alpha}{b_n}\sum_{i=1}^n X_i}\right]}{\prod_{i=1}^n \mathbb{E}\left[e^{\frac{\alpha}{b_n}X_i}\right]}e^{\left(\frac{4\alpha^2e^{2\alpha}}{a_n}\sum_{i=1}^n V(A_i)\right)} \\ &= e^{4\alpha^2e^{2\alpha}}\sup_{n\geq 1}\frac{\mathbb{E}\left[e^{\frac{\alpha}{b_n}\sum_{i=1}^n X_i}\right]}{\prod_{i=1}^n \mathbb{E}\left[e^{\frac{\alpha}{b_n}X_i}\right]} < \infty.\end{aligned}$$

The proof of (I) is complete.

The proof of (II): For any $\epsilon > 0$, via Markov's inequality, we get

$$\begin{aligned}& V\Big(\tfrac{1}{a_n}\sum_{i=1}^n X_i \geq 1+\epsilon\Big) \\ =\ & V\Big(\tfrac{1}{a_n}\sum_{i=1}^n (X_i-\mathbb{E}[X_i]) \geq \epsilon\Big) \\ =\ & V\Big(\tfrac{1}{\sqrt{a_n}}\sum_{i=1}^n (X_i-\mathbb{E}[X_i]) \geq \epsilon\sqrt{a_n}\Big) \\ \leq\ & e^{-\epsilon\sqrt{a_n}}\mathbb{E}\left[\exp\Big(\tfrac{1}{\sqrt{a_n}}\sum_{i=1}^n (X_i-\mathbb{E}[X_i])\Big)\right] \to 0, \quad n\to\infty\end{aligned}$$

due to (I) and $a_n \to \infty$, $n \to \infty$.

The proof of (III): Let $\xi := e^{\frac{\alpha}{a_n}\sum_{i=1}^n X_i}$ and $\eta := I_{\{\frac{1}{a_n}\sum_{i=1}^n X_i \geq 1+\varepsilon\}}$. It is easy to obtain confirmation that ξ and η are comonotonic. Similarly to (3), we have

$$\mathbb{E}\left[\frac{|\xi\eta|}{(\mathbb{E}[|\xi|^2])^{\frac{1}{2}}(\mathbb{E}[|\eta|^2])^{\frac{1}{2}}}\right] \leq \mathbb{E}\left[\frac{1}{2}\frac{|\xi|^2}{\mathbb{E}[|\xi|^2]}+\frac{1}{2}\frac{|\eta|^2}{\mathbb{E}[|\eta|^2]}\right]=1,$$

due to the comonotonic additivity of Choquet integration. Thereby, we obtain

$$\begin{aligned}& \left(\mathbb{E}\left[e^{\frac{\alpha}{a_n}\sum_{i=1}^n X_i}I_{\{\frac{1}{a_n}\sum_{i=1}^n X_i>1+\varepsilon\}}\right]\right)^2 \\ \leq\ & \mathbb{E}\left[e^{\frac{2\alpha}{a_n}\sum_{i=1}^n X_i}\right]V\Big(\frac{1}{a_n}\sum_{i=1}^n X_i \geq 1+\varepsilon\Big) \\ =\ & e^{2\alpha}\mathbb{E}\left[e^{\frac{2\alpha}{a_n}\sum_{i=1}^n(X_i-\mathbb{E}[X_i])}\right]V\Big(\frac{1}{a_n}\sum_{i=1}^n X_i \geq 1+\varepsilon\Big) \to 0\end{aligned}$$

due to (I) and (II). □

3. The Second Borel–Cantelli Lemma for Capacities

We now begin to prove the second Borel–Cantelli lemma for capacities:

Theorem 1. *Let V be a Fatou-like capacity, and let $\{A_n\}_{n=1}^{\infty}$ be a sequence of events, such that*

$$\sum_{i=1}^{\infty} V(A_i) = \infty.$$

If, for any sequence $k_n > 0$,

$$1 \leq \liminf_{n\to\infty} \frac{\mathbb{E}\left[e^{k_n \sum_{i=1}^{n} I_{A_i}}\right]}{\prod_{i=1}^{n} \mathbb{E}\left[e^{k_n I_{A_i}}\right]} \leq \limsup_{n\to\infty} \frac{\mathbb{E}\left[e^{k_n \sum_{i=1}^{n} I_{A_i}}\right]}{\prod_{i=1}^{n} \mathbb{E}\left[e^{k_n I_{A_i}}\right]} < \infty, \tag{9}$$

then

$$V(A_n \ i.o.) = 1.$$

Proof. Set $X_i = I_{A_i}$ and $a_n := \sum_{i=1}^{n} \mathbb{E}[X_i]$. Immediately, $\mathbb{E}[X_i] = V(A_i)$, and

$$a_n = \sum_{i=1}^{n} \mathbb{E}[X_i] = \sum_{i=1}^{n} V(A_i) \to \infty.$$

Now, we consider the following two events:

$$\{\omega : \limsup_{n\to\infty} A_n\} \quad \text{and} \quad \{\omega : \limsup_{n\to\infty} \frac{1}{a_n} \sum_{i=1}^{n} X_i > \varepsilon\},$$

and here, $\varepsilon \in (0,1)$.

If $\omega \notin \{\limsup_{n\to\infty} A_n\}$ holds, then $\lim_{n\to\infty} \sum_{i=1}^{n} X_i = \lim_{n\to\infty} \sum_{i=1}^{n} I_{A_i}$ is a finite number. Hence,

$$\frac{1}{a_n} \sum_{i=1}^{n} X_i \to 0 \quad \text{as } n \to \infty$$

because of $a_n \to \infty$. This implies $\omega \notin \{\limsup_{n\to\infty} \frac{1}{a_n} \sum_{i=1}^{n} X_i > \varepsilon\}$. Therefore, we have the following inclusion relation:

$$\{\omega : \limsup_{n\to\infty} A_n\} \supseteq \{\omega : \limsup_{n\to\infty} \frac{1}{a_n} \sum_{i=1}^{n} X_i > \varepsilon\}.$$

The monotonicity of the capacity V and the definition of Fatou-like capacity (1) imply that

$$V(\limsup_{n\to\infty} A_n) \geq V\Big(\limsup_{n\to\infty} \frac{1}{a_n} \sum_{i=1}^{n} X_i > \varepsilon\Big) \geq \limsup_{n\to\infty} V\Big(\frac{1}{a_n} \sum_{i=1}^{n} X_i > \varepsilon\Big). \tag{10}$$

In order to apply Lemma 2, we need to check the conditions of Lemma 2.
Given the assumption of Theorem that

$$\liminf_{n\to\infty} \frac{\mathbb{E}\left[e^{\frac{1}{a_n} \sum_{i=1}^{n} X_i}\right]}{\prod_{i=1}^{n} \mathbb{E}\left[e^{\frac{1}{a_n} X_i}\right]} \geq 1$$

and Jensen's inequality, we have, for $\varepsilon \in (0,1)$,

$$\begin{aligned}\mathbb{E}\left[e^{\frac{1}{a_n}\sum_{i=1}^n X_i}\right]-e^{\varepsilon} &= \frac{\mathbb{E}\left[e^{\frac{1}{a_n}\sum_{i=1}^n X_i}\right]}{\prod_{i=1}^n \mathbb{E}\left[e^{\frac{1}{a_n}X_i}\right]}\prod_{i=1}^n \mathbb{E}\left[e^{\frac{1}{a_n}X_i}\right]-e^{\varepsilon}\\ &\geq \prod_{i=1}^n e^{\frac{1}{a_n}\mathbb{E}[X_i]}-e^{\varepsilon}=e-e^{\varepsilon}>0.\end{aligned}$$

Thanks to Lemma 2, we thus have

$$V\Big(\frac{1}{a_n}\sum_{i=1}^n X_i>\varepsilon\Big)\geq\frac{\left(\mathbb{E}\left[e^{\frac{1}{a_n}\sum_{i=1}^n X_i}\right]-e^{\varepsilon}\right)^2}{\mathbb{E}\left[\left(e^{\frac{1}{a_n}\sum_{i=1}^n X_i}-e^{\varepsilon}\right)^2\right]}. \tag{11}$$

For the numerator in fraction (11), we see that

$$\left(\mathbb{E}\left[e^{\frac{1}{a_n}\sum_{i=1}^n X_i}\right]-e^{\varepsilon}\right)^2\geq(e-e^{\varepsilon})^2. \tag{12}$$

On the other hand, for the denominator in fraction (11), note that $X_i\geq 0$, and we have

$$\begin{aligned}&\mathbb{E}\left[\left(e^{\frac{1}{a_n}\sum_{i=1}^n X_i}-e^{\varepsilon}\right)^2\right]\\ =\ &\mathbb{E}\left[\left(e^{\frac{1}{a_n}\sum_{i=1}^n X_i}-e^{\varepsilon}\right)^2 I_{\left\{\frac{1}{a_n}\sum_{i=1}^n X_i\leq 1+\varepsilon\right\}}+\left(e^{\frac{1}{a_n}\sum_{i=1}^n X_i}-e^{\varepsilon}\right)^2 I_{\left\{\frac{1}{a_n}\sum_{i=1}^n X_i>1+\varepsilon\right\}}\right]\\ \leq\ &\left(e^{1+\varepsilon}-e^{\varepsilon}\right)^2+\mathbb{E}\left[\left(e^{\frac{1}{a_n}\sum_{i=1}^n X_i}-e^{\varepsilon}\right)^2 I_{\left\{\frac{1}{a_n}\sum_{i=1}^n X_i>1+\varepsilon\right\}}\right].\end{aligned}$$

For the second term, for simplicity, we write $B_n:=\{\frac{1}{a_n}\sum_{i=1}^n X_i>1+\varepsilon\}$; via the comonotonic additivity of Choquet expectation, we have

$$\begin{aligned}&\mathbb{E}\left[\left(e^{\frac{1}{a_n}\sum_{i=1}^n X_i}-e^{\varepsilon}\right)^2 I_{B_n}\right]\\ \leq\ &\mathbb{E}\left[e^{\frac{2}{a_n}\sum_{i=1}^n X_i}I_{B_n}+2e^{\varepsilon}e^{\frac{1}{a_n}\sum_{i=1}^n X_i}I_{B_n}+e^{2\varepsilon}I_{B_n}\right]\\ =\ &\mathbb{E}\left[e^{\frac{2}{a_n}\sum_{i=1}^n X_i}I_{B_n}\right]+2e^{\varepsilon}\mathbb{E}\left[e^{\frac{1}{a_n}\sum_{i=1}^n X_i}I_{B_n}\right]+e^{2\varepsilon}V\left(\frac{1}{a_n}\sum_{i=1}^n X_i>1+\varepsilon\right).\end{aligned}$$

According to (III) in Lemma 3, the first term and the second term on the right-hand side go to zero as $n\to\infty$. The last term on the right-hand side also goes to zero as $n\to\infty$, according to (II) in Lemma 3.

This, with (11) and (12), implies that

$$\limsup_{n\to\infty}V\left(\frac{1}{a_n}\sum_{i=1}^n X_i>0\right)\geq\limsup_{n\to\infty}V\Big(\frac{1}{a_n}\sum_{i=1}^n X_i>\varepsilon\Big)\geq\frac{(e-e^{\varepsilon})^2}{\left(e^{1+\varepsilon}-e^{\varepsilon}\right)^2}. \tag{13}$$

Letting $\varepsilon\to 0$, we arrive at

$$\limsup_{n\to\infty}V\left(\frac{1}{a_n}\sum_{i=1}^n X_i>0\right)=1. \tag{14}$$

According to (10) and (14), we have

$$V\left(\limsup_{n\to\infty} A_n\right) = 1.$$

Therefore, we complete the proof of this theorem. □

By this theorem, immediately, we have

Corollary 1. *Assume that a sequence of events, $\{A_i\}$, is exponentially independent under a Choquet expectation, $\mathbb{E}$, in the sense that*

$$\mathbb{E}\left[e^{k_n \sum_{i=1}^n I_{A_i}}\right] = \prod_{i=1}^n \mathbb{E}\left[e^{k_n I_{A_i}}\right], \quad \forall n \geq 1, \quad \forall k_n \in R_+.$$

Then, Condition 9 in Theorem 1 holds.

4. Independence Cases

The notion of independence for random variables under non-additive expectation or non-additive probability is important. Motivated by mathematical finance and robust statistics, various different notions of independence have been investigated, for example, Peng's independence, Marinacci pre-independence, and Puhalskii independence. It can be proven that all notions mentioned above satisfy Condition 9 in Theorem 1.

We now check that Condition 9 in Theorem 1 holds if event $\{A_i\}$ is Puhalskii-independent. The remaining cases can be verified in a similar manner. As defined below, Puhalskii independence implies the following:

Definition 5. *A sequence, $\{A_i\}$, of events is said to be Puhalskii -independent if*

$$V\Big(\bigcap_{i=1}^n A_i\Big) = \prod_{i=1}^n V(A_i).$$

This leads to the following lemma.

Lemma 4. *Let $\{A_i\}$ be a sequence of Puhalskii-independent events. Then, for any $a_n \in R^+$,*

$$\mathbb{E}\left[e^{a_n \sum_{i=1}^n I_{A_i}}\right] = \prod_{i=1}^n \mathbb{E}\left[e^{a_n I_{A_i}}\right].$$

Proof. Let $\varphi_i(x) = e^{a_i x}, i = 1, \cdots, n$

$$\begin{aligned}
\mathbb{E}\left[\prod_{i=1}^n \varphi_i(X_i)\right] &= \mathbb{E}\Big[\int_0^\infty \cdots \int_0^\infty \prod_{i=1}^n I_{\{\varphi_i(X_i)>x_i\}} \prod_{i=1}^n dx_i\Big] \\
&= \int_0^\infty \cdots \int_0^\infty \mathbb{E}\Big[\prod_{i=1}^n I_{\{\varphi_i(X_i)>x_i\}}\Big] \prod_{i=1}^n dx_i \\
&= \int_0^\infty \cdots \int_0^\infty V\Big(\bigcap_{i=1}^n \{\varphi_i(X_i) > x_i\}\Big) \prod_{i=1}^n dx_i \\
&= \int_0^\infty \cdots \int_0^\infty \prod_{i=1}^n V(\{\varphi_i(X_i) > x_i\}) dx_i \\
&= \prod_{i=1}^n \mathbb{E}[\varphi_i(X_i)],
\end{aligned}$$

Here, we have used Fubini's theorem for Choquet expectation (see Ghirardato (1997) [26] or Chateauneuf and Lefort (2008) [27]). □

Author Contributions: Writing—original draft, C.K.; Writing—review & editing, G.Z. All authors have read and agreed to the published version of the manuscript.

Funding: This research received no external funding.

Data Availability Statement: Data are contained within the article.

Conflicts of Interest: The authors declare no conflicts of interest.

References

1. Borel, E. Les probabilités dénombrables et leurs applications arith-métiq-ues. *Rend. Circ. Mat. Palermo* **1909**, *27*, 247–271. [CrossRef]
2. Borel, E. Sur un probléme de probabilités relatif aux fractions continues. *Math. Ann.* **1912**, *77*, 578–587. [CrossRef]
3. Cantelli, P. Sulla probabilitiá come limite della frequenza. *Rend. Accad. Lincai Ser. 5* **1917**, *24*, 39–45.
4. Chandra, K. *The Borel-Cantelli Lemma*; Springer: Berlin/Heidelberg, Germany, 2012.
5. Barndorff-Nielsen, E. On the rate of growth of the partial maxima of a sequence of independent and identically distributed random variables. *Math. Scand.* **1961**, *9*, 383–394. [CrossRef]
6. Martikainen, A.I.; Petrov, V.V. On the Borel–Cantelli lemma. *Zap. Nauch. Semin. Leningr. Otd. Steklov Mat. Inst.* **1990**, *184*, 200–207. (In Russian); English translation in: *J. Math. Sci.* **1994**, *63*, 540–544. [CrossRef]
7. Balakrishnan, N.; Stepanov, A. A generalization of the Borel-Cantelli lemma. *Math. Sci.* **2010**, *35*, 61–62.
8. Erdös, P.; Rényi, A. On Cantor's series with convergent $\sum 1/q_n$. *Ann. Univ. Sci. Budapest Eötvós. Sect. Math.* **1959**, *2*, 93–109.
9. Kochen, S.; Stone, C. A note on the Borel-Cantelli lemma. *Ill. J. Math.* **1964**, *8*, 248–251. [CrossRef]
10. Petrov, V. A note on the Borel-Cantelli lemma. *Stat. Probab. Lett.* **2002**, *58*, 283–286. [CrossRef]
11. Petrov, V. A generalization of the Borel-Cantelli lemma. *Stat. Probab. Lett.* **2004**, *67*, 233–239. [CrossRef]
12. Yan, J. A simple proof of two generalized Borel-Cantelli lemmas. In *Memorian Paul-Andre Meyer: Seminaire de Probabilitiés XXXIX*; Lecture Notes in Mathematics No. 1874; Springer: Berlin/Heidelberg, Germany, 2006.
13. Xie, Y.Q. A bilateral inequality on nonnegative bounded random sequence. *Stat. Probab. Lett.* **2009**, *79*, 1577–1580. [CrossRef]
14. Zong, G.; Chen, Z.; Lan, Y. Fubini-Like Theorem of Real-Valued Choquet Integrals for Set-Valued Mappings. *Int. J. Uncertain. Fuzziness Knowl.-Based Syst.* **2016**, *24*, 387–403. [CrossRef]
15. Huber, P. The use of Choquet capacities in statistics. *Bull. Int. Stat. Inst.* **1973**, *45*, 181–191.
16. Denneberg, D. *Non-Additive Measure and Integral*; Kluwer: Alphen aan den Rijn, The Netherlands, 1994.
17. Wang, Z.; Klir, G. *Generalized Measure Theory*; Springer: Berlin/Heidelberg, Germany, 2009.
18. Peng, S. G-expectation, G-Brownian Motion and Related Stochastic Calculus of Ito type. In Proceedings of the 2005 Abel Symposium, Oslo, Norway, 29 July–4 August 2006.
19. Peng, S. Survey on normal distributions, central limit theorem, Brownian motion and the related stochastic calculus under sublinear expectations. *Sci. China Ser. A Math.* **2009**, *52*, 1391–1411. [CrossRef]
20. Peng, S. *Nonlinear Expectations and Stochastic Calculus under Uncertainty: With Robust CLT and G-Brownian Motion*; Springer: Berlin/Heidelberg, Germany, 2019.
21. Torra, V.; Narukawa, Y.; Sugeno, M. *Non-Additive Measures: Theory and Applications*; Springer: Berlin/Heidelberg, Germany, 2014.
22. Billingsley, P. *Probability and Measure*, 3rd ed.; Wiley: New York, NY, USA, 1995.
23. Maccheroni, F.; Marinacci, M. A strong law of large numbers for capacities. *Ann. Probab.* **2005**, *33*, 1171–1178. [CrossRef]
24. Puhalskii, A. *Large Deviations and Idempotent Probability*; Chapman and Hall/CRC: Boca Raton, FL, USA, 2001.
25. Dhaene, J.; Denuit, M.; Goovaerts, M.J.; Kaas, R.; Vyncke, D. The concept of comonotonicity in actuarial science and finance: Theory. *Insur. Math. Econ.* **2002**, *31*, 3–33. [CrossRef]
26. Ghirardato, P. On independence for non-additive measures with a Fubini theorem. *J. Econom. Theory* **1997**, *73*, 261–291. [CrossRef]
27. Chateauneuf, A.; Lefort, J. Some Fubini theorems on product σ-algebras for non-additive measures. *Int. J. Approx. Reason.* **2008**, *48*, 686–696. [CrossRef]

mathematics

Article

Self-Weighted Quantile Estimation for Drift Coefficients of Ornstein–Uhlenbeck Processes with Jumps and Its Application to Statistical Arbitrage

Yuping Song [1], Ruiqiu Chen [2], Chunchun Cai [1], Yuetong Zhang [3] and Min Zhu [1,*]

1 School of Finance and Business, Shanghai Normal University, Shanghai 200234, China; songyuping@shnu.edu.cn (Y.S.); 1000510746@smail.shnu.edu.cn (C.C.)
2 Institute of Applied Economics, Shanghai Academy of Social Sciences, Shanghai 200020, China; chenrq@mail.ustc.edu.cn
3 School of Mathematics, Shandong University, Jinan 250100, China; 202311857@mail.sdu.edu.cn
* Correspondence: zhum@shnu.edu.cn; Tel.: +86-021-64323363

Abstract: The estimation of drift parameters in the Ornstein–Uhlenbeck (O-U) process with jumps primarily employs methods such as maximum likelihood estimation, least squares estimation, and least absolute deviation estimation. These methods generally assume specific error distributions and finite variances. However, with the increasing uncertainty in financial markets, asset prices exhibit characteristics such as skewness and heavy tails, which lead to biases in traditional estimators. This paper proposes a self-weighted quantile estimator for the drift parameters of the O-U process with jumps and verifies its asymptotic normality under large samples, given certain assumptions. Furthermore, through Monte Carlo simulations, the proposed self-weighted quantile estimator is compared with least squares, quantile, and power variation estimators. The estimation performance is evaluated using metrics such as mean, standard deviation, and mean squared error (MSE). The simulation results show that the self-weighted quantile estimator proposed in this paper performs well across different metrics, such as 8.21% and 8.15% reduction of MSE at the 0.9 quantile for drift parameter γ and κ compared with the traditional quantile estimator. Finally, the proposed estimator is applied to inter-period statistical arbitrage of the CSI 300 Index Futures. The backtesting results indicate that the self-weighted quantile method proposed in this paper performs well in empirical applications.

Keywords: self-weighted quantile estimation; drift coefficients; O-U process with jumps; heavy-tailed distributions; statistical arbitrage; asymptotic normality; Monte Carlo simulations

MSC: 62M05; 60J75; 62P20

1. Introduction

The Ornstein–Uhlenbeck (O-U) process is a stochastic process that exhibits mean-reverting characteristics, and its parameter estimation problem is an important research area in the statistical inference of stochastic processes. In the 21st century, the parameter estimation problem of the O-U process has been widely developed, with the main research achievements including the following:

1. MCMC methods (Griffin, Steel [1], Roberts, Papaspiliopoulos [2]) that use Markov chain Monte Carlo simulation to estimate parameters;
2. Nonparametric methods (Jongbloed [3]);

3. Parametric methods (Valdivieso [4], Valdivieso [5]). The main estimation methods focus on the maximum likelihood estimation (MLE) and least squares estimation (LSE).

As the driving process of the O-U process evolves from continuous to discrete, from Wiener process to Lévy-driven, and from Gaussian to non-Gaussian, the O-U-type process gradually becomes more precise in describing actual market data. However, the early statistical inference methods and conclusions face certain difficulties and resistance when extended to these new O-U processes, and are less effective in the statistical inference of new O-U processes. Therefore, there are relatively few theories and methods that can be directly applied to these new O-U processes. The Lévy-driven O-U process was first proposed by Barndorff-Nielsen and Shephard [6] and has been widely used in the modeling of financial asset return volatility. In the parameter estimation problem of the Lévy-driven O-U process, most previous work has focused on special types of Lévy processes driving the O-U process, such as non-negative Lévy processes (Jongbloed et al. [3], Jongbloed and Van Der Meulen [7], Zhang et al. [8], Brockwell et al. [9], Leonenko et al. [10]), compound Poisson processes (Zhang [11], Wu et al. [12]), α-stable Lévy processes (Hu and Long [13], Zhang [14]), Lévy processes composed of Wiener process and α-stable Lévy process (Long [15]), heavy-tailed symmetric Lévy processes (Masuda [16]), and Lévy processes without Brownian motion component (Taufer and Leonenko [17], Valdivieso et al. [17]). For the parameter estimation methods of these special types of Lévy–O-U processes, they mainly still focus on least squares and maximum likelihood methods. Hu and Long [18] used a combination of trajectory fitting method and weighted least squares method to discuss the consistency and asymptotic distribution of the estimators of the O-U equation driven by α-stable Lévy motion in both ergodic and non-ergodic cases. Subsequently, Hu and Long [13] studied the parameter estimation problem of the generalized O-U equation driven by α-stable noise at discrete time points. Masuda [16] introduced LAD estimation into the drift parameter estimation of general Lévy–O-U processes, and then found that the SLAD estimator has a limit distribution, satisfies asymptotic properties, and is robust to large "jumps" in the driving process. Mai [19] developed an estimator based on the maximum likelihood estimation method for the drift parameter. Spiliopoulos [20] derived the estimators of the drift parameter and other parameters related to the Lévy process for the O-U process driven by a general Lévy process based on the moment estimation method. Wu and Hu [21] proposed a moment estimator for the drift parameter of the O-U process driven by a general Lévy process, derived the asymptotic variance, and proved the central limit theorem. Shu [22] et al. proposed a trajectory fitting estimator for the drift parameter of the O-U process driven by small Lévy noise and proved its consistency and asymptotic distribution. Wang [23] et al. constructed a fractional Ornstein–Uhlenbeck model driven by tempered fractional Brownian motion. They derived the least squares estimator for the drift parameter based on discrete observations and proved its consistency and asymptotic distribution. Han [24] proposed a modified least squares estimator for estimating the drift parameter of the Ornstein–Uhlenbeck process from low-frequency observations and proved the strong consistency and joint asymptotic normality. Fares [25] investigated the strong consistency and asymptotic normality of the least squares estimator for the drift coefficient of complex-valued Ornstein–Uhlenbeck processes driven by fractional Brownian motion. Zhang [26] proposed the modified least squares estimators (MLSEs) for the drift parameters and a modified quadratic variation estimator (MQVE) for the diffusion parameter. The study leverages the ergodic properties of the O-U process to prove the asymptotic unbiasedness and normality of these estimators, and validates their effectiveness through Monte Carlo simulations.

Statistical arbitrage is a strategy that uses statistical methods and mathematical models to find inconsistencies in market price fluctuations, identify pricing errors or price deviations from normal levels in the market, and thus implement arbitrage operations in investment portfolios. Board [27] used cointegration techniques to arbitrage the price spread of the Nikkei 225 Index Futures across markets such as Singapore and Osaka, Japan, and found that there was indeed arbitrage space. Bondarenko [28] was the first to propose the concept of statistical arbitrage, and subsequently Hogan [29] summarized the definition of statistical arbitrage based on the definition of risk-free arbitrage, which has been widely used. Alexander [30] applied the statistical arbitrage strategy based on cointegration methods to the study of index tracking portfolios, and their empirical results showed that the arbitrage strategy based on cointegration methods had low volatility, low correlation with the market, and nearly normally distributed characteristics. Elliot [31] et al. proposed that due to the mean-reverting characteristics of the O-U process, it can be used to describe the mean-reverting nature of the spread sequence in statistical arbitrage. Bertram [32] gave the optimal solution of the trading signal when the stock price follows the O-U process. Rudy et al. [33] used high-frequency minute data for statistical arbitrage and found that the cointegration degree of the paired assets was positively correlated with arbitrage opportunities and returns. Wale conducted statistical arbitrage research on the US Treasury futures market and obtained significant excess returns, indicating that the US Treasury market had phenomena such as incomplete market efficiency and information asymmetry. Fang Hao [34] simulated and tested with Chinese closed-end funds, and discussed the possible situations of statistical arbitrage in practice according to the steps of selecting arbitrage objects, establishing arbitrage signal mechanisms, and establishing trading portfolios, proving that statistical arbitrage strategies are effective in the Chinese closed-end fund market. Calderia [35] constructed a cross-period arbitrage model combining cointegration theory for futures contracts with different maturities, and found that the price spread sequence of the same futures had a cointegration relationship and there was a large arbitrage space. Zhu Lirong et al. [36] designed a statistical arbitrage strategy for the domestic futures market, and the empirical results showed that stable returns could be obtained during the trading test period. Fan [37] found that the error obtained by the traditional cointegration model was non-stationary when looking for arbitrage opportunities between soybean oil and palm oil futures, so the Bayesian method was added to estimate the error, making the estimated parameters more sensitive and thus obtaining a larger expected return. Wang Jianhua, Cui Wenjing et al. [38] used the time-varying coefficient cointegration regression model to detect the structural breakpoints of financial time series, and established a cointegration statistical arbitrage model based on high-frequency data for IF1707 and IF1706 futures contracts. The results showed that the model was significantly better than the arbitrage performance of the ordinary cointegration model. Liu Yang, Lu Yi [39] selected the daily closing prices of the financial stock index futures of the Shanghai Stock Index 50 and the 50ETF to establish a dynamic statistical arbitrage model based on the O-U process, and determined the optimal trading signal and arbitrage interval under the goal of maximizing the expected return function. According to the performance of the arbitrage strategy, the O-U process is suitable for describing financial time series. Zhang Long [40] introduced the O-U process into the cross-commodity arbitrage of futures, taking palm oil and soybean oil as the modeling targets. Wu et al. [41] and Piergiacomo [42] showed that the simple O-U process has certain limitations in fitting the stock market spread sequence data, and cannot accurately fit the jump phenomena in the data sequence. The use of double exponential discrete jumps in the O-U process can significantly improve this deficiency. Zhao Hua, Luo Pan et al. [43] studied the high-frequency paired trading strategy in the Chinese stock market based on the Lévy–O-U process, and screened out stock pairs by estimating the mean reversion rate and realized volatility.

This paper systematically combs and reviews the literature on jump behavior, parameter estimation of jump O-U process, and statistical arbitrage. This literature has great inspirational significance for the development of this paper, but it cannot be denied that there are still some shortcomings in these studies.

1. In the research on parameter estimation of jump O-U process, the least squares estimation method based on the square loss function and maximum likelihood estimation method have good estimation performance under the assumption of specific error distribution and finite variance. Under the finite variance scenario, the LSE based on the assumption of normal distribution of errors has asymptotic normality and optimal convergence rate but is sensitive to outliers. The maximum likelihood estimation also possesses large-sample asymptotic properties under the assumptions of distribution and finite variance. However, when the assumption conditions are relaxed to infinite variance, these estimators have problems that the asymptotic properties cannot be proved and the estimation is not robust. Under the premise of infinite variance, some scholars have proposed the self-weighted least absolute deviation estimator of the drift parameter and proved its good properties. It is found that the weighted least absolute deviation estimator is more robust to outliers. As a special case of the self-weighted quantile estimation 0.5 quantile, it can be further extended to various quantiles of self-weighted quantile, which can further improve the estimation accuracy and has large room for improvement.
2. In the research on statistical arbitrage, many scholars have designed arbitrage strategies based on cointegration theory, GARCH, and O-U process, and the estimation methods used are mainly OLS and MLE. With the development of high-frequency trading, the data used gradually turns to high-frequency. However, existing research lacks consideration of the possible jumps and heavy tails in the price spread sequence of paired assets, and still uses traditional estimation methods to estimate and construct trading signals, which will cause the trading signals to deviate greatly, miss potential arbitrage opportunities, and weaken the overall performance of the strategy. Therefore, considering jumps and corresponding robust estimation methods to establish statistical arbitrage models, so that the models are closer to the real situation, is an issue worth paying attention to and improving in the design of statistical arbitrage strategies.

Based on these considerations, this paper proposes a self-weighted quantile estimation method for the O-U process with jumps under both finite and infinite variance scenarios, estimating the drift parameters for the pure jump structure O-U process. On one hand, the self-weighted quantile estimator does not rely on assumptions about the data distribution and provides a more comprehensive description of the distribution characteristics by offering confidence intervals and probability distributions at different quantiles, thus providing more complete uncertainty information. On the other hand, it further reduces the impact of outliers through weighting while being insensitive to them. Finally, by proving its asymptotic normality under the infinite variance scenario, the excellent properties of the self-weighted quantile estimator are demonstrated.

The structure of the paper is organized as follows. Section 2 proposes a self-weighted quantile estimator for the drift parameters, laying the groundwork for the proof of the conclusion. Section 3 proves its asymptotic normality and conducts Monte Carlo simulations to evaluate the performance of the proposed estimator. Section 4 applies the method to statistical arbitrage on the CSI 300 Index Futures and presents backtesting results. Section 5 concludes the paper.

2. Preliminaries

2.1. The O-U Process with Jump and Estimation Methods

The Ornstein–Uhlenbeck process is a type of diffusion process in physics, which is an odd-order Markov process with mean-reverting characteristics, suitable for capturing typical features of financial data, including mean reversion, volatility clustering, drift, and jumps.

The O-U process is defined by the following stochastic differential equation:

$$dX_t = (\gamma - \kappa X_t)dt + \sigma dZ_t, \tag{1}$$

where γ represents the instantaneous drift parameter, κ represents the mean reversion strength, σ is the diffusion parameter, $dZ_t = dW_t + dJ_t$, W_t is a standard Brownian motion, and J_t is a jump component. The jump structure is diverse, mainly including Gaussian and Poisson structures, etc. It is commonly represented by a compound Poisson process with a jump intensity λ, where the jump size follows a normal distribution $\left(\mu_\xi, \sigma_\xi^2\right)$ and is independent of W_t. dZ_t is a Lévy process. Typically, we estimate the unknown parameters $\theta := (\gamma, \kappa)$ based on discrete-time samples $(X_{t_i})_{i=0}^n$, where t_i is the time interval between adjacent samples, also denoted as $t_i = ih$, with h being the fixed sampling grid. Parameters γ and κ are both drift parameters, describing the overall trend of the random variables in the stochastic process, representing the average growth rate or average drift speed of the stochastic process.

For the estimation of unknown parameters $\theta := (\gamma, \kappa)$, the simplest and most common method is to use the approximate least squares estimator (LSE), by minimizing the following squared loss function:

$$\theta \mapsto \sum_{i=1}^{n} \left\{X_{t_i} - X_{t_{i-1}} - h(\gamma - \kappa X_{t_{i-1}})\right\}^2 \tag{2}$$

The LSE estimator is obtained. Under the squared loss function, the difference between normal values and abnormal values will be amplified, making the model more sensitive to abnormal values, and abnormal values will receive more attention. The estimator satisfies asymptotic normality when Z has finite variance and its convergence rate is $\sqrt{nh}$, which is the optimal convergence rate in the estimation of diffusion drift with Poisson jumps. However, when Z has infinite variance, the premise assumption that the error obeys a normal distribution is broken, and the situation is no longer the case.

In addition, the least absolute deviation estimator (LAD) can be used, by minimizing the following absolute value loss function:

$$\theta \mapsto \sum_{i=1}^{n} \left|X_{t_i} - X_{t_{i-1}} - h(\gamma - \kappa X_{t_{i-1}})\right| \tag{3}$$

The LAD estimator is obtained. Compared with the squared loss function, the absolute value loss function does not amplify the difference between normal values and outliers, so the impact of outliers on the model is smaller, and the model is more robust. The estimator converges to the normal distribution at a rate of $\sqrt{n}$ when the error term has sufficiently high-order finite moments, but it is difficult to derive the specific form of its asymptotic normal distribution in the case of infinite variance. In addition to estimating parameters by minimizing the loss function, the maximum likelihood estimation method based on the probability distribution of data can also be used, which is usually maximized by numerical optimization algorithms to maximize the likelihood function of the observed data. Usually, the above common estimators can estimate the unknown parameters under the asymptotic properties of large samples, but their estimation effects are limited by the structure of the jump term. When it is a pure jump, its estimation effect is proved to be not as good as the case of simple distribution jumps, especially the appearance of large jumps, which makes the robustness of simple estimators impacted.

2.2. Optimal Trading Trigger Points

First, let us clarify that the trading objective of this paper is to maximize the expected return per unit time. Let the time interval of a trading cycle be T, which is a random variable. a and m (assuming $a < m$) are the trading signal trigger points. When the spread is equal to a, enter the trade; when it is equal to m, reverse the trade. The spread sequence is equal to a again, then the process from a to m and back to a constitutes a trading cycle τ. Assume the profit function within a trading cycle is $r(a,m,c) = m - a - c$, where c is the transaction cost, then the objective function is expressed as

$$\max_{a,m} \frac{r(a,m,c)}{E(T)}. \tag{4}$$

Assume that the spread sequence of the paired assets follows the following O-U process:

$$dX_t = -\theta X_t dt + \sigma dW_t. \tag{5}$$

At this time, according to the state of the transaction, it is divided into T_1 and T_2, where T_1 represents the holding time from a to m, and T_2 represents the time from m to a. Since X_t is a Markov process, T_1 and T_2 are independent of each other, therefore, in a complete trading process, we have

$$E(T) = E(T_1) + E(T_2). \tag{6}$$

According to Itô's lemma, after variable substitution for X_t, the mean time interval of a trading cycle can be expressed as

$$E(T) = \frac{\pi}{\theta}\left(Erfi\left(\frac{m\sqrt{\theta}}{\sigma}\right) - Erfi\left(\frac{a\sqrt{\theta}}{\sigma}\right)\right), \tag{7}$$

where $Erfi(x) = -i \cdot Erfi(i \cdot x)$ is the imaginary error function, and its derivative is $\frac{d}{dx}Erfi(x) = \frac{2}{\sqrt{\pi}}e^{x^2}$.The target function for the unit time return within a trading cycle is

$$\mu(a,m,c) = \frac{\theta(m-a-c)}{\pi\left(Erfi\left(\frac{m\sqrt{\theta}}{\sigma}\right) - Erfi\left(\frac{a\sqrt{\theta}}{\sigma}\right)\right)}. \tag{8}$$

To find the maximum value of Equation (8), we take partial derivatives with respect to a and m, respectively:

$$\sqrt{\frac{4\pi}{\theta\sigma^2}}e^{\frac{\theta a^2}{\sigma^2}}(m-a-c) - \frac{\pi}{\theta}\left(Erfi\left(\frac{m\sqrt{\theta}}{\sigma}\right) - Erfi\left(\frac{a\sqrt{\theta}}{\sigma}\right)\right) = 0, \tag{9}$$

$$\sqrt{\frac{4\pi}{\theta\sigma^2}}e^{\frac{\theta m^2}{\sigma^2}}(m-a-c) - \frac{\pi}{\theta}\left(Erfi\left(\frac{m\sqrt{\theta}}{\sigma}\right) - Erfi\left(\frac{a\sqrt{\theta}}{\sigma}\right)\right) = 0. \tag{10}$$

Solving the above equations yields

$$a = -\frac{c}{4} - \frac{c^2\theta}{4\left(c^3\theta^3 + 24c\theta^2\sigma^2 - 4\sqrt{3c^4\theta^5\sigma^2 + 36c^2\theta^4\sigma^4}\right)^{1/3}} \tag{11}$$

$$-\frac{\left(c^3\theta^3 + 24c\theta^2\sigma^2 - 4\sqrt{3c^4\theta^5\sigma^2 + 36c^2\theta^4\sigma^4}\right)^{1/3}}{4\theta} \tag{12}$$

$$m = -a \tag{13}$$

2.3. Construction of the Self-Weighted Quantile Estimator of Drift Parameters for the O-U Process with Jumps

Assume $X = (X_t)_{t\in\mathbb{R}_+}$ is a univariate O-U process with jumps given by the following stochastic differential equation:

$$dX_t = (\gamma - \kappa X_t)dt + dZ_t, \tag{14}$$

where γ is the instantaneous drift parameter, κ is the mean reversion strength, and Z_t is a Lévy process independent of X_t. We denote the Lévy measure and Gaussian variance of Z_t by ν and σ^2, respectively, and assume $\nu(\mathbb{R}) > 0, \sigma^2 > 0$ to exclude trivial cases. Referring to Sato [44] for a systematic description of Lévy processes, we define the activity index β to measure the degree of small jump fluctuations:

$$\beta := \begin{cases} 2, & if\ \sigma^2 > 0 \\ \inf\left\{r > 0 : \int_{|z|\leq 1} |z|^r v(dz) < \infty\right\}, & if\ \sigma^2 = 0. \end{cases} \tag{15}$$

Compared to specific distribution structures such as Gaussian or Poisson structures, this structure is more general, and its specific characteristics are seen in Assumption 6. Let P_0 represent the true distribution of X related to $\theta_0 := (\gamma_0, \kappa_0)$, and E_0 be the corresponding expectation. Under the distribution P_0, Equation (14) has the following autoregressive representation:

$$X_{t_i} = \frac{\gamma_0}{\kappa_0}\left(1 - e^{-\kappa_0 h}\right) + e^{-\kappa_0 h}X_{t_{i-1}} + \int_{t_{i-1}}^{t_i} e^{-\kappa_0(t_i - s)}dZ_s. \tag{16}$$

For convenience, let

$$\varepsilon_{ni} = h^{-1/\beta}\int_{t_{i-1}}^{t_i} e^{-\kappa_0(t_i-s)}dZ_s, \tag{17}$$

$$\varepsilon'_{n,i-1} = h^{-1/\beta}\left(X_{t_{i-1}} - \frac{\gamma_0}{\kappa_0}\right)\left(e^{-\kappa_0 h} - 1 + \kappa_0 h\right), \tag{18}$$

$$x_{i-1} = \left(-X_{t_{i-1}}, 1\right)^T. \tag{19}$$

To derive the conditional quantile function, assume that for any $n \in \mathbb{N}$ and $i < n$, ε_{ni} has a positive smooth Lebesgue density P_h on $\mathbb{R}$, is independent of i, and is symmetric about 0. Then, the distribution of ε_{ni} is $F_h(dz) = p_h(z)dz$. For any $0 < \tau < 1$, given $\varepsilon_{n,i-1}$, we require that the τ conditional quantile function $Q(\tau)$ of ε_{ni} satisfies $P(\varepsilon_{ni} < Q(\tau)) = \tau$. Then for any $0 < \tau < 1$, we define the quantile loss function for the O-U process with jumps as

$$M_n(\theta) = \sum_{i=1}^{n} w(X_{t_{i-1}})\rho_\tau\left(X_{t_i} - X_{t_{i-1}} - h(\gamma - \kappa X_{t_{i-1}}) - h^{1/\beta}Q_{\varepsilon_{ni}}(\tau)\right), \tag{20}$$

where $\rho_\tau(x) = x(\tau - I(x < 0))$ is the quantile loss function, and $w(\cdot)$ is the weight function, whose specific form is seen in Assumption 7. Based on the goal of minimizing the loss function, the τ quantile estimator for the drift parameter $\theta_0 := (\gamma_0, \kappa_0)$ is

$$\hat{\theta}_n(\tau) = \arg\min_{\gamma,\kappa} \sum_{i=1}^{n} w(X_{t_{i-1}})\rho_\tau\left(X_{t_i} - X_{t_{i-1}} - h(\gamma - \kappa X_{t_{i-1}}) - h^{1/\beta} Q_{\varepsilon_{ni}}(\tau)\right). \tag{21}$$

Self-weighted quantile estimation is an advanced statistical technique that adjusts the traditional quantile estimation process by incorporating observation-specific weights. These weights are typically derived from the data itself, often reflecting the relative importance, reliability, or inverse variance of each observation. The method is particularly useful in contexts where data points are heteroskedastic (exhibit non-constant variance) or when certain observations should influence the quantile estimates more than others due to domain-specific considerations.

Traditional quantile estimation assumes homoskedasticity (constant variance). In financial or risk modeling, volatility clustering is common, and self-weighted methods adapt by down-weighting high-volatility periods. Self-weighting can reduce the influence of outliers by assigning them lower weights (e.g., based on Mahalanobis distance or residual analysis). Weights can evolve over time (e.g., time-decaying weights for older data), enabling the estimator to prioritize recent observations without discarding older data entirely. Moreover, the weights can incorporate domain knowledge (e.g., higher weights for liquid assets in portfolio risk models) or model confidence (e.g., inverse prediction error).

2.4. Assumptions

Let X be given by Equation (14), and let η represent the initial distribution of X. Assume the following:

1. There exists a constant $q > 0$ such that $\int |x|^q \eta(dx) < \infty$;
2. Assume Θ is a bounded convex set, whose closure $\Theta^- \subset (0, \infty) \times \mathbb{R}$;
3. As $n \to \infty$, the time interval $h_n \to 0$ and $nh_n \to \infty$;
4. $nh_n^{4-2/\beta} \to 0$, given Assumption 3 that $\beta > 2/3$;
5. π_0 is the unique invariant distribution of X independent of θ_0, which is exponentially absolutely regular under P_0, and satisfies $\int |x|^q \pi_0(dx) < \infty$ and $\sup_{t\in\mathbb{R}_+} E_0\left[|X_t|^q\right] < \infty$. The characteristic function of π_0 is

$$u \mapsto \exp\left\{i\left(\frac{\gamma_0}{\kappa_0}\right)u - \frac{1}{2}\left(\frac{\sigma^2}{2\kappa_0}\right)u^2 + \int (\cos(uz) - 1) \int_0^\infty v(e^{\kappa_0 s} dz) ds\right\};$$

6. The structure of Z_t is the following:
   (a) v is symmetric about the origin, and there exists a constant $q > 0$ such that $\int_{|z|>1} |z|^q v(dz) < \infty$. The characteristic function of Z_t is

   $$\varphi_{Z_t}(u) := \exp\left\{t\left(-\frac{\sigma^2}{2}u^2 + \int (\cos(uz) - 1)v(dz)\right)\right\},\ u \in \mathbb{R}$$

   (b) If $\sigma^2 = 0$, then $v = v' + v''$ can be represented by two Lévy measures v' and v'', which satisfy the following conditions:
      i. v' has a symmetric density function $g(z) = c|z|^{-1-\beta}\{1 + \tilde{g}(z)\}$ on $U/\{0\}$, where $\beta \in (0,2), c > 0$, and as $|z| \to 0$, $\tilde{g}(z) = O(|z|^\delta), \delta > 0$
      ii. $\beta'' := \inf\left\{r \geq 0 : \int_{|z|\leq 1} |z|^r v''(dz)\right\} \in [0, \beta)$;
7. The structure of the weight w is described as follows:

(a) w is a bounded and uniformly continuous function;

(b) $\limsup_{|x|\to\infty} w(x)|x|^{4-q} < \infty$, in particular, if for any $q' > 2$ $\int_{|z|>1} |z|^{q'}\nu(dz) = \infty$, then the weight function $x \mapsto w(x)x^2$ is uniformly continuous.

Remark 1. *Assumptions 1 and 2 are the same assumptions for X be given by Equation (14) used in Masuda [16]. Assumptions 3 and 4 on sample size and bandwidth are sufficient. Note that it suffices that $nh_n^3 \to 0$ when $\sigma^2 > 0$, while a faster decay of h_n, i.e., $nh_n^2 \to 0$, is required when $\sigma^2 = 0$. Assumption 5 is some facts concerning the O-U processes; see Masuda [45] for more details. Assumption 6 entails that small fluctuations of Z should be like that of a β-stable Lévy process. In the self-weighting method, Assumption 7 is usually a necessary condition, which can reduce the impact of outliers by selecting appropriate weights. Inspired by Ling [46], we consider the following weight function:*

$$w_i = \begin{cases} 1, & \text{if } a_i = 0 \\ \frac{C_{0.95}^3}{a_i^3}, & \text{if } a_i \neq 0, \end{cases} \tag{22}$$

where $a_i = \left|X_{t_{i-1}^n}\right| \mathbf{1}\left(\left|X_{t_{i-1}^n}\right| \geq C_{0.95}\right)$, $C_{0.95}$ is the 0.95 quantile of $X_{t_{i-1}^n}$. This weight satisfies the requirements of Assumption 7, with a value range from 0 to 1, which can reduce the weight of estimators with outliers and has no effect on estimators without outliers. It implies that this weight can down-weight covariance matrices with outliers, and at the same time, it has no effect on the estimation results when there is no outlier.

2.5. Lemmas and Theorems

Let $N_r(\mu, U)$ denote the r-dimensional normal distribution with mean vector μ and covariance matrix U, and let ϕ_β denote the symmetric β-stable density function corresponding to $N_1(0,\sigma^2)$ when $\beta = 2$, and the Lévy density $z \mapsto c|z|^{-1-\beta}$ when $\beta < 2$. This implies

$$\phi_\beta(0) = \begin{cases} \frac{1}{\sqrt{2\pi\sigma^2}}, & \text{if } \beta = 2 \\ \frac{1}{\pi}\Gamma\left(1+\frac{1}{\beta}\right)\left\{\frac{2c}{\beta}\Gamma(1-\beta)\cos\left(\frac{\beta\pi}{2}\right)\right\}, & \text{if } \beta < 2. \end{cases} \tag{23}$$

Lemma 1 (Hjørt and Pollard [47]). *Let A_n be a real-valued convex random function defined on a convex domain $S \subset \mathbb{R}^p$, and assume A_n can be expressed as $A_n(s) = s^T U_n + \frac{1}{2}s^T V_n s + r_n(s)$, where U_n converges weakly to a random variable $U \subset \mathbb{R}^p$, V_n converges in probability to a positive definite matrix $V \subset \mathbb{R}^p \otimes \mathbb{R}^p$, and for any $s \in S$, $r_n(s)$ converges in probability to 0. Then the minimum value α_n of $s \mapsto A_n(s)$ converges weakly to $-V^{-1}U$.*

Lemma 2 (Masuda [16]). *Under Assumption 6, we have a uniform estimate $\sup_{z\in\mathbb{R}} |p_h(z) - \phi_\beta(z)| \leq h^d$, where ϕ_β is the symmetric stable density of β, d is a positive constant, and the values of d are as follows:*

1. *When $\sigma^2 > 0, \nu(\mathbb{R}) < \infty$ or $\sigma^2 = 0, \tilde{g} \equiv 0, \nu''(\mathbb{R}) < \infty, d = 1$;*
2. *For any $\beta'_+ > \beta'$, if $\sigma^2 > 0, \nu(\mathbb{R}) = \infty$, then $d = 1 - \beta'_+/2$;*
3. *For any $\beta''_+ > \beta''$, if $\sigma^2 = 0, \tilde{g} \equiv 0, \nu''(\mathbb{R}) = \infty$, then $d = 1 - \beta''_+/\beta$;*
4. *For any $\delta' \in (0,\beta) \cap (0,\delta]$, if $\sigma^2 = 0, \delta > 0, \nu''(\mathbb{R}) < \infty$, then $d = \delta'/\beta$;*
5. *For any $\delta' \in (0,\beta) \cap (0,\delta]$ and $\beta''_+ > \beta''$, if $\sigma^2 = 0, \delta > 0, \nu''(\mathbb{R}) = \infty$, then $d = (\delta'/\beta) \vee (1 - \beta''_+/\beta)$.*

Lemma 3 (Masuda [16]). *If Assumption 7 holds, and for some $q > 0$, $\int_{|z|>1} |z|^q \nu(dz) < \infty$, then for $k \in \{0,1,2\}$ and $l \in \{1,2\}$, let*

$$g_{k,l}(x) := x^k w(x)^l,$$

$$\delta_n(g_{k,l}) := \left| \frac{1}{nh} \int_0^{nh} g_{k,l}(X_s) ds - \frac{1}{n} \sum_{i=1}^{n} g_{k,l}(X_{t_{i-1}}) \right|,$$

then $\delta_n(g_{k,l}) \xrightarrow{p} 0$.

Theorem 1. *Under the Assumption 2.4, for any* $0 < \tau < 1$*, as* $h_n \to 0, nh_n \to \infty$*,*

$$\sqrt{n} h_n^{1-1/\beta} (\hat{\theta}_n - \theta_0) \xrightarrow{d} N_2 \left(0, \frac{\tau(1-\tau)}{\phi_\beta^2(Q_{\varepsilon_{ni}}(\tau))} V_0 \right), \tag{24}$$

where $V_0 := \Gamma_0^{-1} \Sigma_0 \Gamma_0^{-1}$*,* Γ_0 *and* Σ_0 *are positive definite symmetric matrices, defined as follows:*

$$\Sigma_0 := \int w(x)^2 \begin{pmatrix} x^2 & -x \\ -x & 1 \end{pmatrix} \pi_0(dx),$$
$$\Gamma_0 := \int w(x) \begin{pmatrix} x^2 & -x \\ -x & 1 \end{pmatrix} \pi_0(dx).$$

Remark 2. *To make Theorem 1 applicable in practice, we must estimate* Σ_0*,* Γ_0*, and* $\phi_\beta(Q_{\varepsilon_{ni}}(\tau))$*. Since* Σ_0 *and* Γ_0 *are represented by* $\int x^k w(x)^l \pi_0(dx)$*, according to Lemma 3, it is easy to obtain the uniform estimators for* Σ_0 *and* Γ_0 *as* $\frac{1}{n}\sum_{i=1}^{n} w_{i-1}^k X_{t_{i-1}}^l$*. For* $\phi_\beta(Q_{\varepsilon_{ni}}(\tau))$*, since the density function* p_h *of* ε_{ni} *is symmetric, we can shift the* τ *quantile of* ε_{ni} *to 0 such that* $P(\varepsilon''_{ni} < 0) = \tau$*, where* $\varepsilon''_{ni} = \varepsilon_{ni} - Q_{\varepsilon_{ni}}(\tau)$*. According to Lemma 2, the estimation of* $\phi_\beta(Q_{\varepsilon_{ni}}(\tau))$ *is transformed into the estimation of* $\phi_\beta(0)$*. According to Equation (23),* $\phi_\beta(0)$ *depends only on the two parameters* β *and* c*. Using the uniform estimator of* $\phi_\beta(0)$ *demonstrated in Theorem 1 of Masuda [16], we can use this uniform estimator without directly estimating* β *and* c*, thus obtaining all the estimators needed for the normal distribution.*

Corollary 1. *Under the Assumption 2.4, for any* $0 < \tau < 1$*, as* $n \to \infty, \hat{\gamma}_n(\tau) \xrightarrow{p} \gamma_0$*,* $\hat{\kappa}_n(\tau) \xrightarrow{p} \kappa_0$*.*

3. Main Results

3.1. Theoretical Proofs

For the drift parameter self-weighted quantile estimator, this paper considers the proof of its asymptotic normality.

Proof of Theorem 1. Let $\hat{u}_n = \sqrt{n} h_n^{1-1/\beta} (\hat{\theta}_n - \theta_0)$, according to Lemma 1, we construct a function $f(u)$ about u. According to Equations (16)–(19), we have

$$h^{-1/\beta} \left\{ \Delta_i X - h(\gamma - \kappa X_{t_{i-1}}) - h^{1/\beta} Q_{\varepsilon_{ni}}(\tau) \right\} = (\varepsilon'_{n,i-1} + \varepsilon_{ni}) - (\theta - \theta_0)^T x_{i-1} h^{1-1/\beta} - Q_{\varepsilon_{ni}}(\tau). \tag{25}$$

According to the definition of the loss function, for any $\theta \in \Theta$, we have

$$\begin{aligned} &h^{-1/\beta}\{M_n(\theta) - M_n(\theta_0)\} \\ &= \sum_{i=1}^{n} w_{i-1} \left\{ \rho_\tau \left((\varepsilon'_{n,i-1} + \varepsilon_{ni}) - (\theta - \theta_0)^T x_{i-1} h^{1-1/\beta} - Q_{\varepsilon_{ni}}(\tau) \right) - \rho_\tau ((\varepsilon'_{n,i-1} + \varepsilon_{ni}) - Q_{\varepsilon_{ni}}(\tau)) \right\}. \end{aligned} \tag{26}$$

Let $U_n(\theta_0) := \{ u \in \mathbb{R}^2 : \theta_0 + a_n u \in \Theta \}$, where $a_n = a_n(\beta) := \left(\sqrt{n} h_n^{1-1/\beta} \right)^{-1}$. Define the function $\mathbb{Z}_n(u; \theta_0) : U_n(\theta_0) \times \Omega \to (0, \infty)$:

$$\log \mathbb{Z}_n(u; \theta_0) = -h^{-1/\beta} \{ M_n(\theta_0 + a_n u) - M_n(\theta_0) \}. \tag{27}$$

Then $f(u) = -\log \mathbb{Z}_n(u;\theta_0)$, and we will prove that its minimum value is $\hat{u}_n = a_n^{-1}(\hat{\theta}_n - \theta_0)$.

First, we provide the asymptotic local quadratic structure of $\log \mathbb{Z}_n(u;\theta_0)$. For any $u \in U_n(\theta_0)$, we have

$$\log \mathbb{Z}_n(u;\theta_0) = u^T \Delta_n - \frac{1}{2} u^T \Gamma_n u^T + o_p(1). \tag{28}$$

According to Lemma 1, we need to prove that $\Delta_n \xrightarrow{d} N(0, \tau(1-\tau)\Sigma_0)$ and $\Gamma_n \xrightarrow{p} \phi_\beta(Q_{\varepsilon_{ni}}(\tau))\Gamma_0$.

Next, we infer the specific local quadratic structure of Equation (28). For any K-function of the form $K(x) = \int_0^x k(y)dy$, we have $K(x-y) - K(x) = -yk(x) + \int_0^y \{k(x) - k(x-s)\}ds$. Referring to Knight [48], taking $k(y) = I(y \geq 0) - I(y \leq 0)$, we have the formula

$$\rho_\tau(x-y) - \rho_\tau(x) = -y\{\tau - I(x<0)\} + \int_0^y [I(x \leq s) - I(x \leq 0)]ds. \tag{29}$$

By Lemma 2, for any $n \in \mathbb{N}$ and $i \leq n$, $P[\varepsilon_{ni} \neq 0] = 1$. Combining Equations (26), (27) and (29), we get $\log \mathbb{Z}_n(u;\theta_0) = L_n(u) + Q_n(u)$, where

$$L_n(u) := u^T \sum_{i=1}^n \frac{1}{\sqrt{n}} w_{i-1} x_{i-1} \left\{ \tau - I_{(\varepsilon'_{n,i-1} + \varepsilon_{ni} - Q_{\varepsilon_{ni}}(\tau) < 0)} \right\}, \tag{30}$$

$$Q_n(u) := -\sum_{i=1}^n w_{i-1} \int_0^{u^T x_{i-1}/\sqrt{n}} \left\{ I_{(\varepsilon'_{n,i-1} + \varepsilon_{ni} - Q_{\varepsilon_{ni}}(\tau) \leq s)} - I_{(\varepsilon'_{n,i-1} + \varepsilon_{ni} - Q_{\varepsilon_{ni}}(\tau) \leq 0)} \right\} ds. \tag{31}$$

Let $L_n(u) := u^T \sum_{i=1}^n l_{ni}$, $Q_n(u) := \sum_{i=1}^n q_{ni}(u)$, then we examine the asymptotic behavior of $L_n(u)$. Decompose $L_n(u)$ as follows:

$$L_n(u) := u^T \sum_{i=1}^n \left(l_{ni} - E_0^{i-1}[l_{ni}] \right) + u^T \sum_{i=1}^n E_0^{i-1}[l_{ni}] =: u^T \sum_{i=1}^n \Delta_{ni} + R_n^1(u). \tag{32}$$

Denote $A^{\otimes 2} = AA^T$ for any matrix A, then

$$\begin{aligned}
&E_0^{i-1}\left[\Delta_{ni}^{\otimes 2}\right] \\
=&E_0^{i-1} l_{ni}^2 - \left(E_0^{i-1}[l_{ni}]\right)^2 \\
=&\frac{1}{n} w_{i-1}^2 x_{i-1}^{\otimes 2} \left\{ E_0^{i-1}\left(\tau - I_{(\varepsilon'_{n,i-1} + \varepsilon_{ni} - Q_{\varepsilon_{ni}}(\tau) < 0)}\right)^2 - \left(E_0^{i-1}\left(\tau - I_{(\varepsilon'_{n,i-1} + \varepsilon_{ni} - Q_{\varepsilon_{ni}}(\tau) < 0)}\right)\right)^2 \right\} \\
=&\frac{1}{n} w_{i-1}^2 x_{i-1}^{\otimes 2} \left\{ E_0^{i-1}\left(I_{(\varepsilon'_{n,i-1} + \varepsilon_{ni} - Q_{\varepsilon_{ni}}(\tau) < 0)}\right) - \left(E_0^{i-1}\left(I_{(\varepsilon'_{n,i-1} + \varepsilon_{ni} - Q_{\varepsilon_{ni}}(\tau) < 0)}\right)\right)^2 \right\} \\
=&\frac{1}{n} w_{i-1}^2 x_{i-1}^{\otimes 2} \left\{ P_0^{i-1}(\varepsilon_{ni} < Q_{\varepsilon_{ni}}(\tau) - \varepsilon'_{n,i-1}) - \left(P_0^{i-1}(\varepsilon_{ni} < Q_{\varepsilon_{ni}}(\tau) - \varepsilon'_{n,i-1})\right)^2 \right\}.
\end{aligned} \tag{33}$$

Since p_h is bounded, and

$$|\varepsilon'_{n,i-1}| \lesssim h^{2-1/\beta}(1 + |X_{t_{i-1}}|), \tag{34}$$

we have

$$\begin{aligned}
&\frac{1}{n}w_{i-1}^2x_{i-1}^{\otimes 2}P_0^{i-1}(\varepsilon_{ni}<Q_{\varepsilon_{ni}}(\tau)-\varepsilon'_{n,i-1})\\
=&\tau\frac{1}{n}w_{i-1}^2x_{i-1}^{\otimes 2}+\frac{1}{n}w_{i-1}^2x_{i-1}^{\otimes 2}\left[P_0^{i-1}(\varepsilon_{ni}<Q_{\varepsilon_{ni}}(\tau)-\varepsilon'_{n,i-1})-\tau\right]\\
=&\tau\frac{1}{n}w_{i-1}^2x_{i-1}^{\otimes 2}+\frac{1}{n}w_{i-1}^2x_{i-1}^{\otimes 2}\left[P_0^{i-1}(\varepsilon_{ni}<Q_{\varepsilon_{ni}}(\tau)-\varepsilon'_{n,i-1})-P_0^{i-1}(\varepsilon_{ni}<Q_{\varepsilon_{ni}}(\tau))\right]\\
=&\tau\frac{1}{n}w_{i-1}^2x_{i-1}^{\otimes 2}+\frac{1}{n}w_{i-1}^2x_{i-1}^{\otimes 2}\int_{Q_{\varepsilon_{ni}}(\tau)-\varepsilon'_{n,i-1}}^{Q_{\varepsilon_{ni}}(\tau)}p_h(z)\,dz\\
\le&\tau\frac{1}{n}w_{i-1}^2x_{i-1}^{\otimes 2}+\frac{1}{n}w_{i-1}^2x_{i-1}^{\otimes 2}|\varepsilon'_{n,i-1}|\\
=&\tau\frac{1}{n}w_{i-1}^2x_{i-1}^{\otimes 2}+o_p(1).
\end{aligned}\tag{35}$$

Then, Equation (33) can be written as

$$E_0^{i-1}\left[\Delta_{ni}^{\otimes 2}\right]=\tau(1-\tau)\frac{1}{n}w_{i-1}^2x_{i-1}^{\otimes 2}+o_p(1),\tag{36}$$

therefore,

$$\left|\sum_{i=1}^{n}E_0^{i-1}\left[\Delta_{ni}^{\otimes 2}\right]-\tau(1-\tau)\frac{1}{n}\sum_{i=1}^{n}w_{i-1}^2x_{i-1}^{\otimes 2}\right|=o_p(1).\tag{37}$$

Now we note that the mixing property of X under the distribution P_0 leads to the ergodic theorem, that is, for each π_0 integrable function F, $(nh)^{-1}\int_0^{nh}F(X_s)\,ds\xrightarrow{p}\int F(x)\pi_0(dx)$. Combining Lemma 3, we get $\frac{1}{n}\sum_{i=1}^{n}w_{i-1}^2x_{i-1}^{\otimes 2}\xrightarrow{p}\tau(1-\tau)\Sigma_0$, therefore,

$$\sum_{i=1}^{n}E_0^{i-1}\left[\Delta_{n,i}^{\otimes 2}\right]\xrightarrow{p}\tau(1-\tau)\Sigma_0.\tag{38}$$

Similarly, under these assumptions, it is easy to see that for any $a\in(0,2]$,

$$\begin{aligned}
\sum_{i=1}^{n}E_0\left[|\Delta_{n,i}|^{2+a}\right]\lesssim&n^{-a/2}\sup_t E_0\left[\{w(X_t)(1+|X_t|)\}^{2+a}\right]\\
\lesssim&n^{-a/2}\sup_t E_0\left[w(X_t)(1+|X_t|)^4\right]\\
=&O\left(n^{-a/2}\right)\\
=&o(1).
\end{aligned}\tag{39}$$

From Equations (38) and (39), applying the Martingale central limit theorem to $\Delta_n:=\sum_{i=1}^{n}\Delta_{ni}$, we get $\Delta_n\xrightarrow{d}N_1(0,\tau(1-\tau)\Sigma_0)$. According to Equation (35), it is clear that $|R_n^1(u)|=\left|u^T\sum_{i=1}^{n}E_0^{i-1}[l_{ni}]\right|=o_p(1)$. Therefore, $L_n(u)=u^T\Delta_n+o_p(1)$, and for any u, $\Delta_n\xrightarrow{d}N_1(0,\tau(1-\tau)\Sigma_0)$.

Next, we examine the asymptotic behavior of $Q_n(u)$. We separate the Martingale term of $Q_n(u)$ to get

$$Q_n(u)=\sum_{i=1}^{n}E_0^{i-1}[q_{ni}(u)]+\sum_{i=1}^{n}\left\{q_{ni}(u)-E_0^{i-1}[q_{ni}(u)]\right\}.\tag{40}$$

For the first term on the right-hand side, according to Taylor's formula, we have

$$
\begin{aligned}
&\sum_{i=1}^{n} E_0^{i-1}[q_{ni}(u)] \\
=&-\sum_{i=1}^{n} w_{i-1}\int_0^{u^T x_{i-1}/\sqrt{n}} \{F_h(s+Q_{\varepsilon_{ni}}(\tau)-\varepsilon'_{n,i-1})-F_h(Q_{\varepsilon_{ni}}(\tau)-\varepsilon'_{n,i-1})\}ds \\
=&-\sum_{i=1}^{n} w_{i-1}\int_0^{u^T x_{i-1}/\sqrt{n}} \left\{s\cdot p_h(Q_{\varepsilon_{ni}}(\tau)-\varepsilon'_{n,i-1})+\frac{1}{2}s^2 p'_h(Q_{\varepsilon_{ni}}(\tau)-\varepsilon'_{n,i-1})\right\}ds \\
=&-\sum_{i=1}^{n} w_{i-1}p_h(Q_{\varepsilon_{ni}}(\tau)-\varepsilon'_{n,i-1})\frac{(u^T x_{i-1})^2}{2n}-\frac{1}{2}\sum_{i=1}^{n} w_{i-1}\int_0^{u^T x_{i-1}/\sqrt{n}} s^2 p'_h(Q_{\varepsilon_{ni}}(\tau)-\varepsilon'_{n,i-1})ds \\
=&-\frac{1}{2}u^T\left\{p_h(Q_{\varepsilon_{ni}}(\tau))\frac{1}{n}\sum_{i=1}^{n} w_{i-1}x_{i-1}^{\otimes 2}\right\}u+\left[-\frac{1}{2n}\sum_{i=1}^{n} w_{i-1}\left(u^T x_{i-1}\right)^2\{p_h(Q_{\varepsilon_{ni}}(\tau)-\varepsilon'_{n,i-1})-p_h(Q_{\varepsilon_{ni}}(\tau))\}\right. \\
&\left.-\frac{1}{2}\sum_{i=1}^{n} w_{i-1}\int_0^{u^T x_{i-1}/\sqrt{n}} s^2 p'_h(Q_{\varepsilon_{ni}}(\tau)-\varepsilon'_{n,i-1})ds\right] \\
=:&-\frac{1}{2}u^T\Gamma_n u+R_n^2(u).
\end{aligned}
\tag{41}
$$

Therefore, with the help of Lemmas 2 and 3, we have $\Gamma_n \xrightarrow{P} \phi_\beta(Q_{\varepsilon_{ni}}(\tau))\Gamma_0$. For the term $R_n^2(u)$, first, according to Lemma 2, we have $|\partial p_h(z)| = |\partial p_h(z)-\partial p_h(0)| \lesssim |z|$. Second, for any $x \in \mathbb{R}$ and $g:\mathbb{R}\to\mathbb{R}$, $|\int_0^x g(y)\,dy| \le \int_0^{|x|}\{|g(y)|\vee|g(-y)|\}\,dy$, we can obtain the following estimate:

$$
\begin{aligned}
&\left|R_n^2(u)\right| \\
=&\left|\frac{1}{2n}\sum_{i=1}^{n} w_{i-1}\left(u^T x_{i-1}\right)^2\{p_h(Q_{\varepsilon_{ni}}(\tau)-\varepsilon'_{n,i-1})-p_h(Q_{\varepsilon_{ni}}(\tau))\}+\frac{1}{2}\sum_{i=1}^{n} w_{i-1}\int_0^{u^T x_{i-1}/\sqrt{n}} s^2 p'_h(Q_{\varepsilon_{ni}}(\tau)-\varepsilon'_{n,i-1})ds\right| \\
\lesssim&|u|^2\frac{1}{2n}\sum_{i=1}^{n} w_{i-1}|x_{i-1}|^2\left|Q_{\varepsilon_{ni}}(\tau)\varepsilon'_{n,i-1}-\frac{1}{2}(\varepsilon'_{n,i-1})^2\right|+\frac{1}{2}\sum_{i=1}^{n} w_{i-1}\int_0^{u^T x_{i-1}/\sqrt{n}} s^2|Q_{\varepsilon_{ni}}(\tau)-\varepsilon'_{n,i-1}|ds \\
\lesssim&h^{2-1/\beta}Q_{\varepsilon_{ni}}(\tau)|u|^2\frac{1}{n}\sum_{i=1}^{n} w_{i-1}(1+|X_{t_{i-1}}|)^3+h^{2(2-1/\beta)}|u|^2\frac{1}{n}\sum_{i=1}^{n} w_{i-1}(1+|X_{t_{i-1}}|)^4 \\
&+\frac{|u|^3}{\sqrt{n}}Q_{\varepsilon_{ni}}(\tau)\frac{1}{n}\sum_{i=1}^{n} w_{i-1}(1+|X_{t_{i-1}}|)^3+\frac{h^{2-1/\beta}|u|^3}{\sqrt{n}}\frac{1}{n}\sum_{i=1}^{n} w_{i-1}(1+|X_{t_{i-1}}|)^4 \\
\lesssim&\left(h^{2-1/\beta}Q_{\varepsilon_{ni}}(\tau)|u|^2+h^{2(2-1/\beta)}|u|^2+\frac{|u|^3}{\sqrt{n}}Q_{\varepsilon_{ni}}(\tau)+\frac{h^{2-1/\beta}|u|^3}{\sqrt{n}}\right)\frac{1}{n}\sum_{i=1}^{n} w_{i-1}(1+|X_{t_{i-1}}|)^4 \\
=&O_p\left(h^{2-1/\beta}Q_{\varepsilon_{ni}}(\tau)|u|^2+h^{2(2-1/\beta)}|u|^2+\frac{|u|^3}{\sqrt{n}}Q_{\varepsilon_{ni}}(\tau)+\frac{h^{2-1/\beta}|u|^3}{\sqrt{n}}\right)=o_p(1).
\end{aligned}
\tag{42}
$$

Therefore, for any u, $\sum_{i=1}^{n} E_0^{i-1}[q_{ni}(u)] \xrightarrow{p} -u^T\phi_\beta(Q_{\varepsilon_{ni}}(\tau))\Gamma_0 u/2$. For the second term of $Q_n(u)$, let

$$
R_n^3(u)=\sum_{i=1}^{n}\left\{q_{ni}(u)-E_0^{i-1}[q_{ni}(u)]\right\}. \tag{43}
$$

Using Burkholder's inequality and Schwarz's inequality, we have

$$
\begin{aligned}
&E_0\left[\left\{R_n^3(u)\right\}^2\right] \\
=&\sum_{i=1}^n E_0\left[\left\{q_{ni}(u)-E_0^{i-1}[q_{ni}(u)]\right\}^2\right] \\
\lesssim&\sum_{i=1}^n E_0\left[w_{i-1}^2\left\{\int_0^{u^T x_{i-1}/\sqrt{n}}\left(I_{(\varepsilon'_{n,i-1}+\varepsilon_{ni}-Q_{\varepsilon_{ni}}(\tau)\le s)}-I_{(\varepsilon'_{n,i-1}+\varepsilon_{ni}-Q_{\varepsilon_{ni}}(\tau)\le 0)}\right)ds\right\}^2\right] \\
\le&\sum_{i=1}^n E_0\left[w_{i-1}^2\left\{\int_0^{|u^T x_{i-1}|/\sqrt{n}}\left(I_{(|\varepsilon'_{n,i-1}+\varepsilon_{ni}-Q_{\varepsilon_{ni}}(\tau)|\le s)}\right)ds\right\}^2\right] \\
\le&\sum_{i=1}^n E_0\left[w_{i-1}^2\frac{|u^T x_{i-1}|}{\sqrt{n}}\int_0^{|u^T x_{i-1}|/\sqrt{n}}\left(I_{(|\varepsilon'_{n,i-1}+\varepsilon_{ni}-Q_{\varepsilon_{ni}}(\tau)|\le s)}\right)ds\right] \\
=&\sum_{i=1}^n E_0\left[w_{i-1}^2\frac{|u^T x_{i-1}|}{\sqrt{n}}\int_0^{|u^T x_{i-1}|/\sqrt{n}}\left(\int_{-s+Q_{\varepsilon_{ni}}(\tau)-\varepsilon'_{n,i-1}}^{s+Q_{\varepsilon_{ni}}(\tau)-\varepsilon'_{n,i-1}}p_h(z)dz\right)ds\right] \\
\lesssim&\frac{|u|^3}{\sqrt{n}}\sup_{t\in\mathbb{R}^+}E_0\left[w(X_t)^2(1+|X_t|)^3\right]\lesssim\frac{|u|^3}{\sqrt{n}}\to 0.
\end{aligned}
\tag{44}
$$

Therefore, for any u, $Q_n(u)=-u^T\Gamma_n u/2+o_p(1)$ and $\Gamma_n\xrightarrow{p}\phi_\beta(Q_{\varepsilon_{ni}}(\tau))\Gamma_0$.

In summary, combining the asymptotic behaviors of $L_n(u)$ and $Q_n(u)$, we obtain Equation (28), and Theorem 1 is proved. □

Proof of Corollary 1. Based on Theorem 1 and continuous mapping theorem, it is known that when $n\to\infty$, we have

$$\sqrt{n}h_n^{1-1/\beta}(\hat{\kappa}_n-\kappa_0)\xrightarrow{d}N(0,\sigma^2(\theta))$$

That is, for every real number x, it holds that

$$\lim_{n\to\infty}P\left(\sqrt{n}h_n^{1-1/\beta}(\hat{\kappa}_n-\kappa_0)\le x\right)=\Psi(x). \tag{45}$$

Here, $\Psi(\cdot)$ represents the distribution function of the normal distribution $N(0,\sigma^2(\theta))$:

$$\Psi(x)=\int_{-\infty}^{x}\frac{1}{\sqrt{2\pi}\sigma(\theta)}e^{-\frac{t^2}{2\sigma^2(\theta)}}dt. \tag{46}$$

It is known that for any positive number $\varepsilon>0$, it holds that

$$\lim_{n\to\infty}P(|\hat{\kappa}_n-\kappa_0|>\varepsilon)=0. \tag{47}$$

Consider

$$
\begin{aligned}
&P(|\hat{\kappa}_n-\kappa_0|>\varepsilon) \\
=&P(\hat{\kappa}_n-\kappa_0>\varepsilon)+P(\hat{\kappa}_n-\kappa_0<-\varepsilon) \\
=&P\left(\sqrt{n}h_n^{1-1/\beta}(\hat{\kappa}_n-\kappa_0)>\sqrt{n}h_n^{1-1/\beta}\varepsilon\right)+P\left(\sqrt{n}h_n^{1-1/\beta}(\hat{\kappa}_n-\kappa_0)<-\sqrt{n}h_n^{1-1/\beta}\varepsilon\right),
\end{aligned}
\tag{48}
$$

thus,

$$\begin{aligned}
&\overline{\lim_{n\to\infty}} P(|\hat{\kappa}_n - \kappa_0| > \varepsilon) \\
\leq &\overline{\lim_{n\to\infty}} P\Big(\sqrt{n}h_n^{1-1/\beta}(\hat{\kappa}_n - \kappa_0) > \sqrt{n}h_n^{1-1/\beta}\varepsilon\Big) + \overline{\lim_{n\to\infty}} P\Big(\sqrt{n}h_n^{1-1/\beta}(\hat{\kappa}_n - \kappa_0) < -\sqrt{n}h_n^{1-1/\beta}\varepsilon\Big)
\end{aligned} \tag{49}$$

It can be seen that it is only necessary to prove

$$\overline{\lim_{n\to\infty}} P\Big(\sqrt{n}h_n^{1-1/\beta}(\hat{\kappa}_n - \kappa_0) > \sqrt{n}h_n^{1-1/\beta}\varepsilon\Big) = 0, \tag{50}$$

and

$$\overline{\lim_{n\to\infty}} P\Big(\sqrt{n}h_n^{1-1/\beta}(\hat{\kappa}_n - \kappa_0) < -\sqrt{n}h_n^{1-1/\beta}\varepsilon\Big) = 0. \tag{51}$$

For any positive number $\tau > 0$, since

$$\lim_{x\to\infty} \Psi(x) = 1, \tag{52}$$

take a sufficiently large real number $M > 0$ such that

$$\Psi(M) > 1 - \tau, \tag{53}$$

obviously such M exists, the larger the better. For the chosen $M > 0$, there naturally exists a positive integer n_0, such that when $n > n_0$, it holds that $\sqrt{n}h_n^{1-1/\beta}\varepsilon > M$. Thus, when $n > n_0$,

$$P\Big(\sqrt{n}h_n^{1-1/\beta}(\hat{\kappa}_n - \kappa_0) > \sqrt{n}h_n^{1-1/\beta}\varepsilon\Big) \leq P\Big(\sqrt{n}h_n^{1-1/\beta}(\hat{\kappa}_n - \kappa_0) > M\Big). \tag{54}$$

Furthermore,

$$\begin{aligned}
\overline{\lim_{n\to\infty}} P\Big(\sqrt{n}h_n^{1-1/\beta}(\hat{\kappa}_n - \kappa_0) > \sqrt{n}h_n^{1-1/\beta}\varepsilon\Big) &\leq \overline{\lim_{n\to\infty}} P\Big(\sqrt{n}h_n^{1-1/\beta}(\hat{\kappa}_n - \kappa_0) > M\Big) \\
&= \overline{\lim_{n\to\infty}} \Big[1 - P\Big(\sqrt{n}h_n^{1-1/\beta}(\hat{\kappa}_n - \kappa_0) \leq M\Big)\Big] \\
&= \lim_{n\to\infty} \Big[1 - P\Big(\sqrt{n}h_n^{1-1/\beta}(\hat{\kappa}_n - \kappa_0) \leq M\Big)\Big] \\
&= 1 - \Psi(M) < \tau.
\end{aligned} \tag{55}$$

Additionally, due to the arbitrariness of $\tau > 0$, it is known that

$$\overline{\lim_{n\to\infty}} P\Big(\sqrt{n}h_n^{1-1/\beta}(\hat{\kappa}_n - \kappa_0) > \sqrt{n}h_n^{1-1/\beta}\varepsilon\Big) = 0. \tag{56}$$

By the same reasoning,

$$\overline{\lim_{n\to\infty}} P\Big(\sqrt{n}h_n^{1-1/\beta}(\hat{\kappa}_n - \kappa_0) < -\sqrt{n}h_n^{1-1/\beta}\varepsilon\Big) = 0. \tag{57}$$

□

Similarly, it can be proven that $\hat{\gamma}_n(\tau) \xrightarrow{p} \gamma_0$.

3.2. Monte Carlo Numerical Simulation

Based on the proof of the self-weighted quantile estimation method for the O-U process with jumps in the previous chapter, this chapter discusses the simulation and implementation of the fitting estimation algorithm for the O-U process with jumps. The simulation results are an important tool for subsequent evaluation of the quality of the estimators. We use Monte Carlo numerical simulations to study the properties of the weighted quantile estimators for the O-U process with jumps and compare them with the estimators obtained from quantile estimation methods, power variation estimation methods, and least squares estimation. In the simulation process, the O-U process with jumps is first discretized using the Euler method to generate a discrete O-U process with known parameters. Based on the simulated data, the drift parameters are estimated, and then the differences between the estimated values and the true values are compared. The accuracy and efficiency of the algorithm are evaluated using indicators such as mean, standard deviation, and mean squared error.

3.2.1. Sample Path Simulation

The sample path simulation equation for the O-U process with jumps is defined as follows:

$$dX_t = (\gamma - \kappa X_t)dt + \sigma dZ_t. \tag{58}$$

When estimating the drift parameter, according to the assumption of the jump term Z_t structure in Section 2.3, take this distribution as $NIG(1,0,1,0)$, whose density is $x \mapsto \frac{e}{\pi}K_1\left(\sqrt{1+x^2}\right)/\sqrt{1+x^2}, x \in \mathbb{R}$. Set the true parameter values as $(\gamma, \kappa) = (10, 4)$, the time interval $h_n = \frac{1}{48}$, perform $N = 500$ Monte Carlo simulations of sample paths, and each path contains $n = 10,000$ observations. According to the Euler iteration, the simulated path of the random array X_t following the above NIG jump structure O-U process is shown below:

As shown in Figure 1, the random array generated by model (58) exhibits certain fluctuation characteristics and obvious jump phenomena. In the actual financial market, when encountering information shocks or policy impacts, there are indeed significant jumps in intra-day high-frequency data, so our simulated paths can reflect the true characteristics of financial market data.

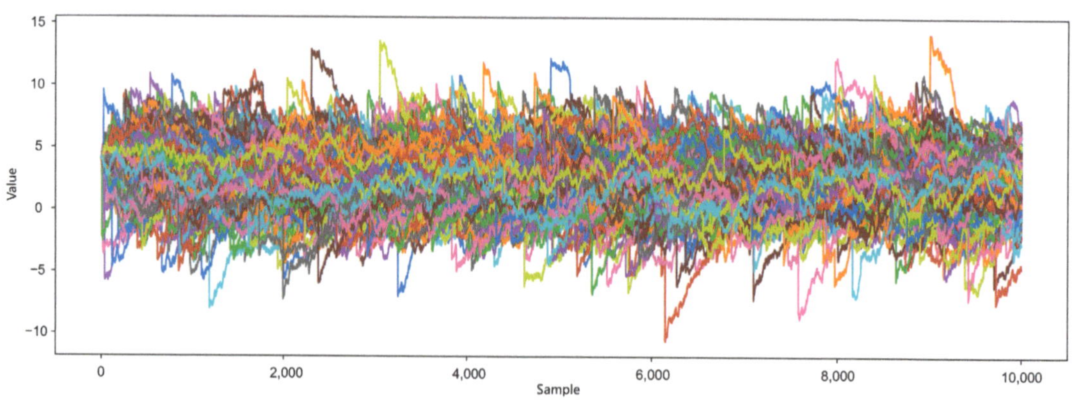

Figure 1. Simulated path of O-U process with NIG jumps.

3.2.2. Method Comparison and Result Evaluation

Unlike other estimators, quantile estimation divides the data into several parts, each containing a certain proportion of data points, and focuses on describing the location and distribution of the data by estimating the quantiles. Therefore, we select $\tau = 0.1, 0.25, 0.45, 0.55, 0.78, 0.9$ as six quantile points to observe the data distribution. Based on the assumption of the weight structure, we choose an appropriate weight function to reduce the impact of abnormal observations on the estimation results, and it has no effect on the estimation of normal observations. Referring to Ling [46], consider the following weight function:

$$w_i = \begin{cases} 1 & \text{if } a_i = 0 \\ \frac{C_{0.95}^3}{a_i^3} & \text{if } a_i \neq 0, \end{cases} \tag{59}$$

where $a_i = \left|X_{t_{i-1}^n}\right| \mathbf{1}\left(\left|X_{t_{i-1}^n}\right| \geq C_{0.95}\right)$, $C_{0.95}$ is the 0.95 quantile of $X_{t_{i-1}^n}$. Combining settings of the path parameter and the estimator, perform self-weighted quantile estimation for each simulated path, and calculate the mean, standard deviation, and MSE of the estimated values for evaluation.

3.2.3. Comparison of Estimation Results for Drift Parameters

For the finite sample estimation effect of the drift parameters, consider the quantile estimation and least squares estimation as comparative estimation methods. Compared with the quantile and least squares estimators, the self-weighted quantile estimator can better estimate the drift parameters of the O-U process with specific jump structures. The Monte Carlo simulation results for the two drift parameters to be estimated are given in Tables 1–4, and visualized by drawing box plots, as shown in Figures 2 and 3.

Table 1. Monte Carlo simulation results for drift parameter γ.

τ	Method	Mean	Std	MSE
0.9	SQR	9.8661	0.8492	0.7391
	QR	9.8551	0.8855	0.8052
	LSE	68.6390	23.9942	4048.1622
0.75	SQR	10.0000	0.0005	2.48259×10^{-7}
	QR	9.9994	0.0102	0.0001
	LSE	68.6390	23.9942	4048.1622
0.25	SQR	9.9672	0.4224	0.1795
	QR	9.9670	0.4248	0.1816
	LSE	68.6390	23.9942	4048.1622
0.1	SQR	10.0109	0.4037	0.1631
	QR	9.9897	0.2151	0.0464
	LSE	68.6390	23.9942	4048.1622

Table 2. Monte Carlo simulation results for drift parameter κ.

τ	Method	Mean	Std	MSE
0.9	SQR	3.9464	0.3397	0.1183
	QR	3.9420	0.3542	0.1288
	LSE	26.5142	9.2131	596.7796
0.75	SQR	4.0000	0.0002	3.97185×10^{-8}
	QR	3.9998	0.0041	1.6868
	LSE	26.5142	9.2131	596.7796
0.25	SQR	3.9869	0.1690	0.0287
	QR	3.9868	0.1699	0.0291
	LSE	26.5142	9.2131	596.7796
0.1	SQR	4.0045	0.1621	0.0263
	QR	3.9965	0.0829	0.0069
	LSE	26.5142	9.2131	596.7796

Table 3. Monte Carlo simulation results for drift parameter γ via SQR method across various quantiles of weight function (59).

τ	Quantile	Mean	Std	MSE
	0.99	9.8735	0.9867	0.9685
0.9	0.95	9.8661	0.8492	0.7391
	0.9	9.9999	0.8584	0.9768
	0.99	9.9998	0.0018	3.3657×10^{-6}
0.75	0.95	10.0000	0.0005	2.48259×10^{-7}
	0.9	9.9998	0.0059	4.9852×10^{-6}
	0.99	10.0789	0.5916	0.6987
0.25	0.95	9.9672	0.4224	0.1795
	0.9	10.0123	0.4792	0.2967
	0.99	9.9789	0.4817	0.2457
0.1	0.95	10.0109	0.4037	0.1631
	0.9	10.0234	0.6489	0.1967

Table 4. Monte Carlo simulation results for drift parameter κ via SQR method across various quantiles of weight function (59).

τ	Quantile	Mean	Std	MSE
	0.99	4.0345	1.3658	0.9897
0.9	0.95	3.9464	0.3397	0.1183
	0.9	4.0997	1.8894	1.1547
	0.99	3.9123	0.0015	7.254×10^{-7}
0.75	0.95	4.0000	0.0002	3.97185×10^{-8}
	0.9	4.0789	0.0024	9.9451×10^{-7}
	0.99	3.9654	0.2647	0.1645
0.25	0.95	3.9869	0.1690	0.0287
	0.9	3.9876	0.3489	0.2654
	0.99	4.0515	0.2545	0.1564
0.1	0.95	4.0045	0.1621	0.0263
	0.9	3.9124	0.4287	0.1147

From the overall estimation of the drift parameters in Tables 1 and 2, it can be seen that regardless of the quantile, the self-weighted quantile estimator and the quantile estimator significantly outperform the least squares estimator in terms of mean, standard deviation, and mean squared error. Under the premise that the true parameter values are $\theta_0 = (\gamma_0, \kappa_0) = (10, 4)$, it can be seen from the mean indicator that the estimated values of the self-weighted quantile estimator and the quantile estimator are very close to the true values, with the best performance at the 0.75 quantile and the self-weighted quantile estimation effect being better than the quantile estimation. The estimated values of the two parameters to be estimated for the sample path are shown below, and box plots are drawn for visualization, as shown in Figures 2 and 3. It can be seen that the median of the LSE estimated values is significantly different from the estimated results of SQR and QR at the 0.75 quantile. The median of the SQR and QR estimated values is very close, but the right box plot shows that the QR estimated values have more outliers.

Monte Carlo simulation results for drift parameters γ and κ via SQR method across various quantiles of weight Function (59) are displayed in Tables 3 and 4, which show how the different choices of w_i can influence the properties of the estimator. It is found the 0.95 quantile of weight Function (59) possesses the smaller bias and MSE.

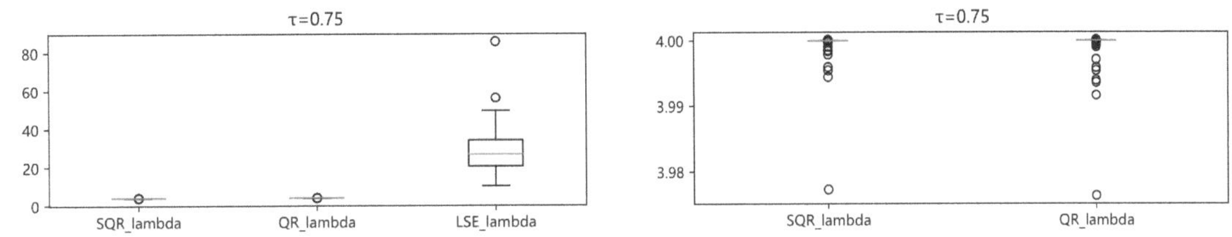

Figure 2. Boxplot comparison of the estimated values of drift parameter κ.

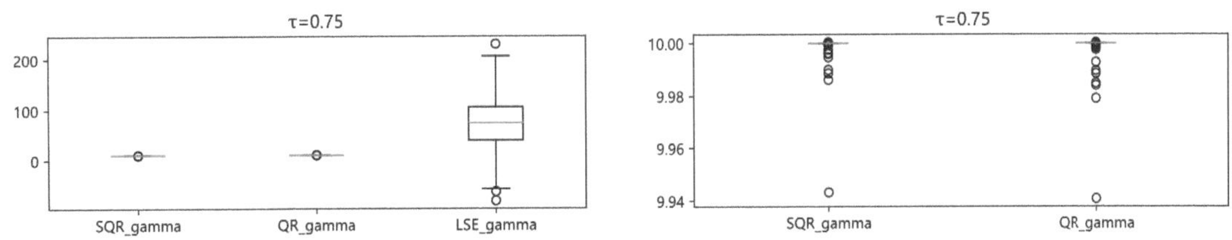

Figure 3. Boxplot comparison of the estimated values of drift parameter γ.

4. Statistical Arbitrage Strategy Based on Self-Weighted Quantile Estimation of Jump O-U Process

In cross-period arbitrage trading, considering that the futures market has night trading, and for the same trading rules, overnight strategies may lead to large fluctuations in the price spread of different futures contracts at the opening of the next day when facing major policy changes or large fluctuations in the external market at night, thereby increasing the risk. Therefore, in order to avoid the adverse impact of such fluctuations on the performance of cross-period arbitrage, it is more reasonable to choose intra-day trading for cross-period arbitrage strategies, and at the same time, in order to increase potential arbitrage opportunities, high-frequency data is chosen for modeling, pursuing higher returns under low risk.

4.1. Data Sources and Descriptive Statistics

This paper selects the CSI 300 stock index futures contract of the China Financial Futures Exchange as the research object for empirical analysis, and the main terms of the contract are listed in the following Table 5.

Table 5. China Financial Futures Exchange CSI 300 stock index futures contract.

Element	Clause
Contract underlying	CSI 300 Index
Contract multiplier	300 CNY/point
Pricing unit	Index point
Minimum price fluctuation	0.2 points
Contract months	Current month, next month, and the following two quarterly months
Trading hours	Morning: 9:30–11:30, Afternoon: 13:00–15:00
Trading direction	Buy open, sell close, sell open, buy close
Daily price limit	±10% of the previous trading day's settlement price
Minimum trading margin	8% of the contract value
Last trading day	The third Friday of the contract month, extended for national holidays
Delivery date	Same as the last trading day
Delivery method	Cash settlement
Trading code	IF
Trading type	Real-time transaction and order transaction

Select the 5 min closing prices of the current month and next month contracts of the CSI 300 stock index futures as the samples for this trading strategy, with contract codes IF00 and IF01, respectively. The time span is from 12 April 2021 to 5 December 2023, with a total of 30,905 data points. Among them, the data from 12 April 2021 to 31 December 2022 is used as the in-sample data for fitting the jump O-U process and parameter estimation, and the data from 1 January 2023 to 5 December 2023 is used as the out-of-sample backtesting data to evaluate the strategy performance. The data is sourced from the Wind Financial Data Platform, and data processing is carried out using Python version 3.8 and R version 4.1.

The descriptive statistics of the 5 min high-frequency closing prices of the two contracts are as follows Table 6.

Table 6. Descriptive statistics of CSI 300 stock index futures current month and next month contracts.

Contract Code	Mean	Std	Min	Max	Kurt	Skew
IF00	4284.12	505.9124	3412.2	5366	−1.1684	0.4495
IF01	4277.24	498.7956	3413.6	5334.6	−1.1869	0.4456

Sliced data from April 2021 is extracted to show the local trend chart of the current month and next month contracts as follows.

As shown in Figure 4, the current month and next month contracts of the CSI 300 stock index futures have a trend of rising and falling together, and there is a close correlation between the contracts. Since the variety is the same, the price trend is highly correlated and affected by similar factors. However, the simultaneous rise and fall does not necessarily mean that there is a stable correlation. It is still necessary to calculate the correlation coefficient and conduct sufficient market analysis to choose this pair of contracts for arbitrage, ensuring the stability of the statistical arbitrage strategy and reducing the strategy risk.

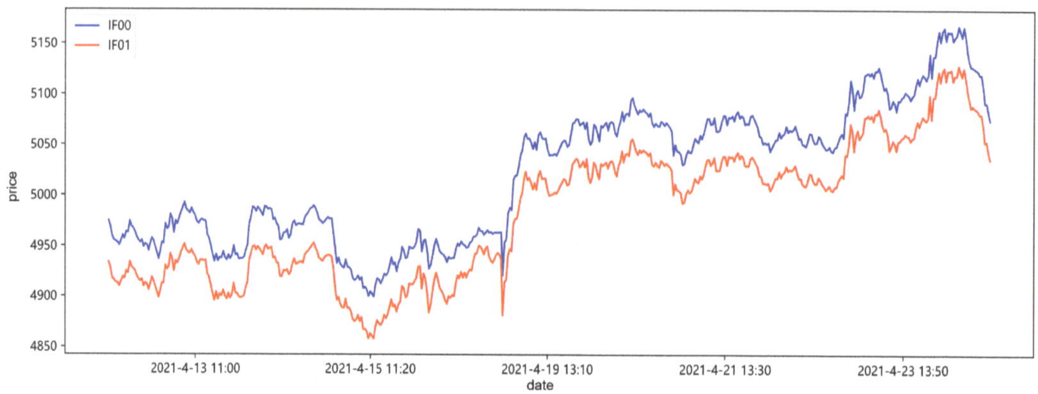

Figure 4. The local trend of the CSI 300 stock index futures contracts for the current and next month.

4.2. Data Processing and Sample Testing

4.2.1. Correlation Test

The Pearson correlation coefficient between the two contract asset prices and the t-statistic of the Fisher correlation coefficient significance test can be calculated to determine whether they have correlation. The Pearson correlation coefficient is a statistical measure of the degree of linear correlation between two variables, with a range of −1 to 1. When the correlation coefficient is close to 1, it indicates that the two variables are positively correlated; when it is close to −1, it indicates that the two variables are negatively correlated; when it is close to 0, it indicates that there is no linear correlation between the two variables.

The Fisher significance statistic is used to test whether the Pearson correlation coefficient is significantly different from 0, thereby determining whether there is a significant linear correlation between the two variables. Statistically, if the p-value of the Fisher significance statistic is less than the set significance level (usually 0.05), the original hypothesis can be rejected, that is, it is considered that there is a significant linear correlation between the two variables. The test results are as follows.

From the Table 7, it can be seen that at the 5% significance level, the original hypothesis is rejected, that is, it can be considered that there is a significant correlation between the current month and next month contracts of the CSI 300 stock index futures.

Table 7. Correlation coefficient and significance test between IF00 and IF01.

Variety		IF01
IF00	Pearson correlation coefficient	0.999695
	Significance test	0.000000

4.2.2. Stationarity Test

Before conducting the cointegration test on the 5 min quotation time series of the current month and next month contracts of the CSI 300 stock index futures, it is first necessary to determine that these two time series have the same order of integration, so it is necessary to conduct the unit root test on the series first. In order to ensure that there is no spurious regression between the paired two contract price sequences, this paper uses Python software to conduct the ADF test on them, respectively, and judges whether the p-value is less than 0.01 at the 99% confidence level to reject the original hypothesis (that is, when the p-value is less than 0.01, the original hypothesis is rejected). If the original hypothesis is not rejected, the corresponding sequence is differenced and the above process is repeated until a stationary sequence is tested. The test results are shown in the following Table 8.

Table 8. ADF unit root test results.

Series	**Test Form (c, t, k)**	**ADF Value**	**Critical Values**		
			1%	**5%**	**10%**
IF00	(c, t, 0)	−0.8815	−3.4306	−2.8616	−2.5668
IF01	(c, t, 0)	−0.8656			
ΔIF00	(0, 0, 0)	−124.1978	−3.4306	−2.8616	−2.5668
ΔIF01	(0, 0, 0)	−124.0170			

In Table 8, the test form c indicates that the test equation has an intercept term, t indicates the existence of a trend term, and k indicates the lag order. The ADF values of the price sequences and their first differences of CSI 300 IF00 futures contract and CSI 300 IF01 futures contract per hand are calculated, respectively. The test results show that at the 1%, 5%, and 10% significance levels, the absolute values of the ADF values of IF00 and IF01 are less than the absolute values of the critical values, so the original hypothesis is accepted, and it is considered that they are non-stationary sequences. Therefore, further test the stationarity of the difference sequences ΔIF00, ΔIF01. The test results show that at the 1%, 5%, and 10% significance levels, the absolute values of the ADF values of the difference sequences are greater than the absolute values of the critical values, and the original hypothesis is rejected, and it is considered that the price difference sequences of CSI 300 IF00 futures contract and CSI 300 IF01 futures contract per hand are stationary sequences. Therefore, the price time sequences of CSI 300 IF00 futures contract and CSI 300 IF01 futures contract per hand are all first-order integrated, that is, they are $I(1)$ processes.

4.3. Cointegration Test

Futures price sequences are generally non-stationary time series, but there may be a long-term equilibrium relationship between futures with high correlation. In order to effectively measure this relationship, Engle and Granger proposed the concept of cointegration. If the price sequences of two futures themselves are not stationary, but become stationary after differencing, then it is very necessary to determine the long-term equilibrium relationship between futures through cointegration test. Through the ADF unit root test, we concluded that the price sequences of the current month and next month contracts of the CSI 300 stock index futures are all first-order integrated, so the Engle–Granger two-step method can be used for testing. First, estimate the cointegration regression equation with the least squares method to obtain the following cointegration relationship:

$$IF00_t = 1.0140 \times IF01_t + e_t, \tag{60}$$

where the coefficient 1.0140 is the weight for buying and selling contracts during backtesting, that is the β, indicating that for every 1 hand of IF00 contract bought, the corresponding 1.0140 hands of IF01 contract are sold. The goodness of fit R^2 is 0.99939.

Secondly, test whether the residual term e_t is stationary. Based on the ADF test, the ADF value is -3.85414, its absolute value is greater than the absolute values of each critical value; the p-value is 0.00239, less than 0.05, rejecting the original hypothesis, it can be considered that there is a long-term equilibrium relationship between IF00 and IF01, and the next step of verification and testing can be carried out.

4.3.1. Descriptive Statistics of Spread Sequence

After the above tests, we define the spread of the paired futures contracts. Assuming that the price sequences of the current month contract A and the next month contract B of the CSI 300 stock index futures are $S_A(t)$ and $S_B(t)$, respectively, then the spread sequence $Price_t$ is expressed as

$$Price_t = \ln\left(\frac{S_A(t)}{S_A(0)}\right) - \ln\left(\frac{S_B(t)}{S_B(0)}\right), t \geq 0. \tag{61}$$

Its overall trend is shown in Figure 5.

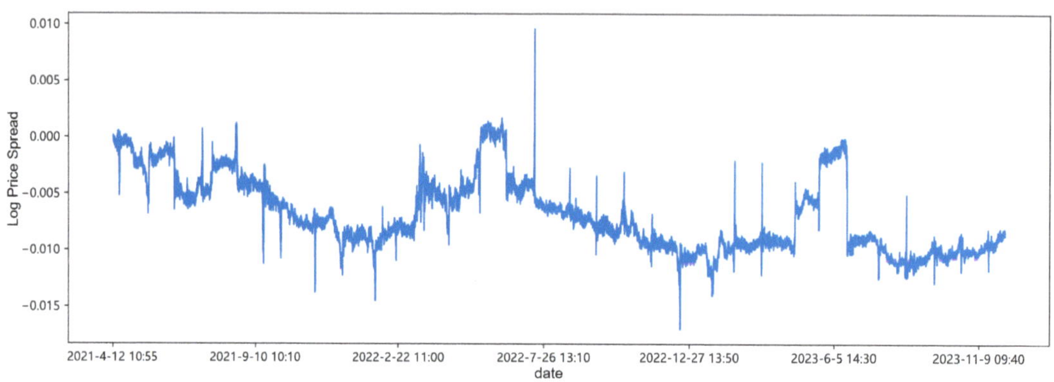

Figure 5. Overall trend of spread sequence.

Descriptive statistics were performed on the spread sequence, and the results are as follows.

From Table 9, it can be seen that the standard deviation of the data is large, indicating a high degree of dispersion. The skewness and kurtosis indicate that the data distribution is roughly symmetrical, slightly skewed to the left, and slightly flatter relative to the normal distribution. The p-value is the p-value of the ADF stationarity test, less than 0.05, indicating that the spread sequence has stationarity.

Table 9. Descriptive statistics of spread sequence.

Spread Sequence	Mean	Std	Min	Max	Kurt	Skew	p-Value
Price	6.88	14.29	−34.40	76.00	−0.5189	0.6886	0.011825

4.3.2. Jump Test

Since this paper uses the jump O-U process to fit and estimate the spread sequence, compared with the ordinary O-U process, this process adds a jump term to describe the phenomenon of large fluctuations in prices in a short time, better capturing extreme fluctuations or non-mean properties in the market. Therefore, we use the LM test proposed by Lee and Mykland [49] to test the data for jumps point-by-point and calculate the amplitude of the jumps. The jump amplitude is visualized and plotted as shown in Figure 6.

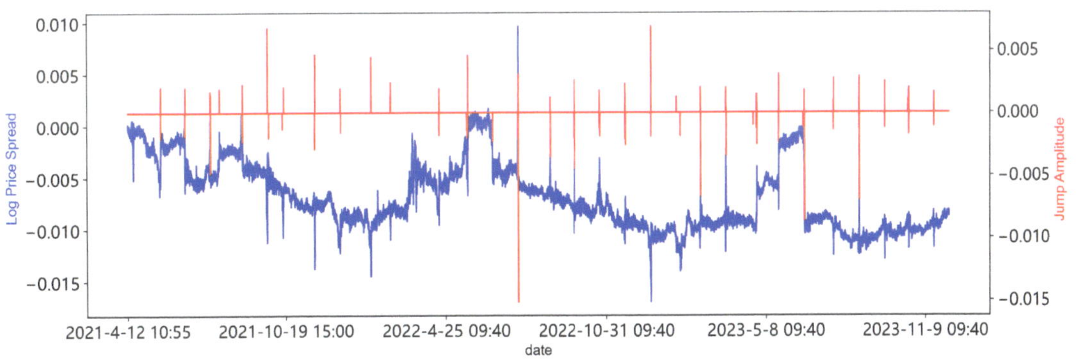

Figure 6. Jump detection of spread sequence.

4.4. Design of Statistical Arbitrage Strategy Scheme

4.4.1. Trading Rule Settings

In a statistical arbitrage strategy, screening targets and strategy timing are both very important key factors, which have a decisive effect on whether the strategy has good performance. In the strategy scheme design of this paper, we do not screen targets through a target pool, but test the targets that have been seen well, and use the self-weighted quantile estimation results of this paper to conduct technical analysis for strategy timing, determine when to make buying and selling decisions, and reasonably set the trigger levels of trading signals.

In the traditional cointegration timing strategy, the standard deviation multiple method is usually used for timing, that is, for the spread sequence of paired targets, calculate its historical equilibrium level and standard deviation, and determine whether to open or close positions according to the multiple of the spread sequence exceeding or less than the historical equilibrium level. However, such a threshold set relying on a simple multiple for timing may miss many potential profitable trading opportunities. For example, a high threshold leads to too few trades, reducing the total statistical arbitrage profit, while a low threshold may lead to frequent trading, and the high transaction costs will erode a lot of profit and may even lead to losses, and cannot obtain the statistical arbitrage returns brought by deviations. Therefore, this paper uses the target of maximizing the expected return per unit time, calculates the probability distribution and density function of the average duration of a trading cycle, and uses the opening and closing trading points obtained for trading.

The opening and closing trading rules are shown in Table 10. When the spread sequence crosses down through the lower trigger point a, buy 1 contract of the current month and sell β times the next month's contract, where β is the cointegration coefficient of the two contracts. If β is not an integer, round it to the nearest whole number. When the spread sequence crosses up through the mean line, close the position. When the spread sequence crosses up through the upper trigger point m, open a position to sell 1 contract of the current month and buy β times the next month's contract. When the spread sequence crosses down through the mean line, reverse close the position. This trading rule aims to ensure the market neutrality of the investment portfolio, enabling the portfolio to achieve the expected return regardless of whether the future market trend is upward or downward.

Table 10. Trading rules for opening and closing positions.

Process	Condition for Positioning	Operation
$o \to a$	Crossing down the lower trigger point	Buy current month contract, sell β times the next month contract
$a \to o$	Crossing up the mean line	Close position
$o \to m$	Crossing up the upper trigger point	Sell current month contract, buy β times the next month contract
$m \to o$	Crossing down the mean line	Close position

During the arbitrage process, the next opening position can only be triggered after the spread sequence is closed; otherwise, the original position is held until it is closed. Secondly, rolling over positions from one contract month to the next is a common operation in futures trading. As the contract expiration date approaches, investors close their futures positions and open new futures positions in the next expiration month to avoid the risks and costs associated with actual delivery, while extending the holding period of their positions. However, this paper does not perform rolling operations, i.e., it closes positions on the contract expiration date and does not open positions for the next month of the same contract after delivery. Finally, the cost settings for strategic simulated trading are as follows: the opening and closing fees are six ten-thousandths, without calculating the costs of price impact and slippage. The initial capital is set at one unit, and the returns for each time point are calculated using the rate of return. The weight ratio for buying and selling contracts is set through the cointegration coefficient.

4.4.2. Parameter Estimation and Trading Signal Determination

Within the backtesting framework, the dataset is initially segmented with 2023 as the pivot point. The dataset from 2021 to 2022 is primarily used for fitting and parameter estimation, while the 2023 dataset is used for out-of-sample simulation trading and backtesting to calculate strategy returns and other metrics. Subsequently, during the backtesting period, we dynamically estimate and adjust the calculations for parameter estimation and trading signals. By promptly incorporating the sample data from the previous time point into the historical spread sequence, we obtain the historical spread sequence closest to the point to be estimated. Parameter estimation is conducted based on this spread sequence, and the different parameter estimates at each time point are used to calculate the trading signal thresholds by substituting into Equations (11) and (13). As out-of-sample data is continuously updated and added, our strategy can better adapt to price changes.

To achieve the optimal result, we employed a grid search approach to determine the optimal quantile levels for calculating the lower and upper thresholds, a and m, using the self-weighted method. Specifically, we evaluated quantile levels in increments of 0.25 and computed the corresponding threshold values. An arbitrage strategy was then executed based on trading signals generated when the spread exceeded these thresholds.

After establishing the trading rules, fitting estimation, and trading signal calculations, we select the self-weighted quantile estimation results at the 0.25, 0.75, and 0.9 quantiles to observe whether there are any patterns in the trading trigger threshold lines obtained based on different quantile estimates, whether they have a significant impact on strategy returns, and whether layered investment strategies based on different quantiles can be developed. The parameter estimation results and thresholds for the 0.75 quantile are shown in Table 11, and the trading thresholds for each quantile are visualized in Figures 7–11.

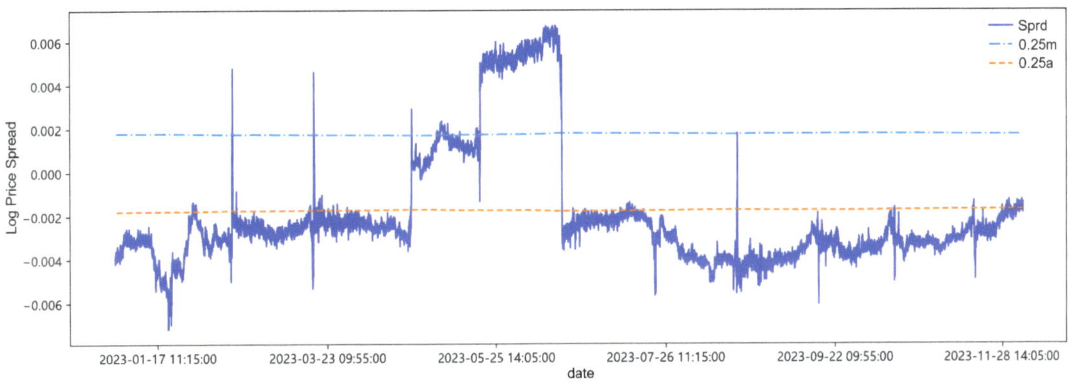

Figure 7. Trading threshold at 0.25 quantile.

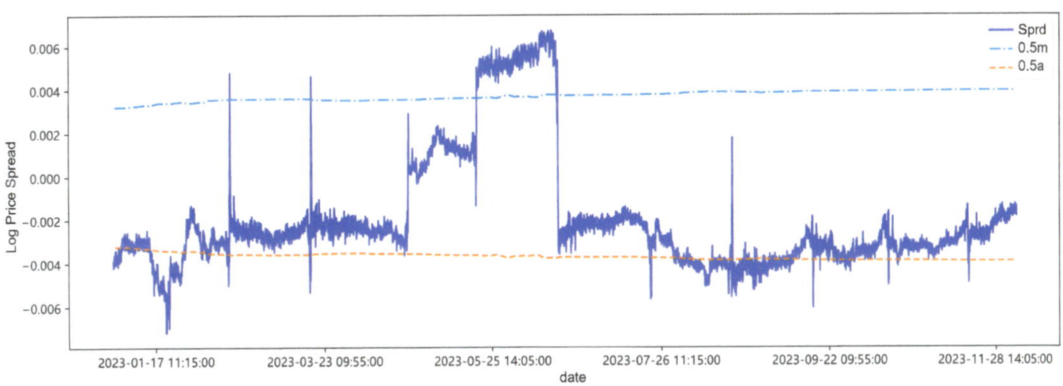

Figure 8. Trading threshold at 0.5 quantile.

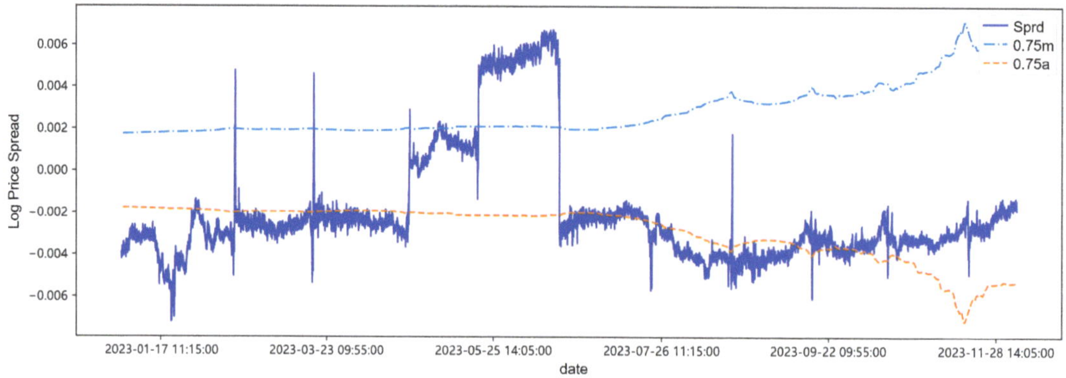

Figure 9. Trading threshold at 0.75 quantile.

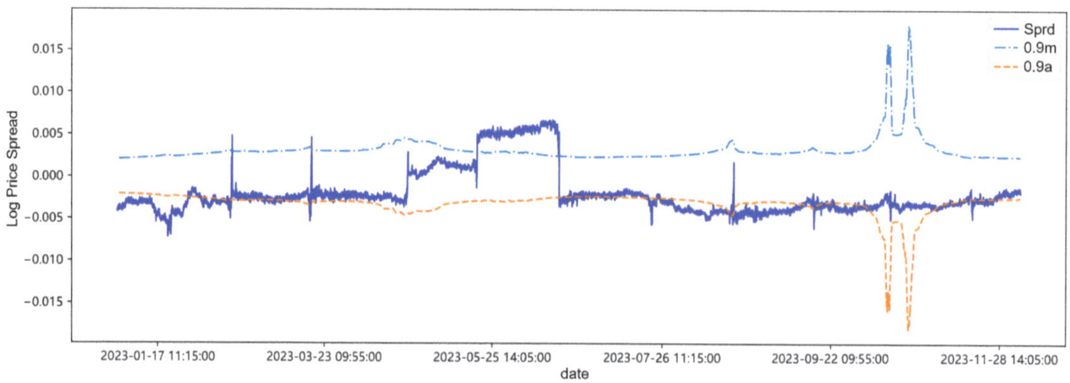

Figure 10. Trading threshold at 0.9 quantile.

Table 11. Time series data example.

Date	γ ($\times 10^{-2}$)	κ	σ ($\times 10^{-3}$)	m ($\times 10^{-3}$)	a ($\times 10^{-3}$)
3-Jan-2023 09:35	4.7696	1.2712	4.3102	2.0810	−2.0810
3-Jan-2023 09:40	4.7688	1.2700	4.3067	2.0811	−2.0811
3-Jan-2023 09:45	4.7680	1.2690	4.3102	2.0811	−2.0811
3-Jan-2023 09:50	4.7680	1.2688	4.3067	2.0813	−2.0813
3-Jan-2023 09:55	4.7694	1.2717	4.3076	2.0815	−2.0815
3-Jan-2023 10:00	4.7695	1.2711	4.3067	2.0818	−2.0818
3-Jan-2023 10:05	4.7689	1.2703	4.3102	2.0822	−2.0822
3-Jan-2023 10:10	4.7681	1.2688	4.3067	2.0827	−2.0827
3-Jan-2023 10:15	4.7679	1.2685	4.3076	2.0834	−2.0834
3-Jan-2023 10:20	4.7674	1.2677	4.3084	2.0843	−2.0843
3-Jan-2023 10:25	4.7666	1.2666	4.3102	2.0854	−2.0854
3-Jan-2023 10:30	4.7666	1.2666	4.3067	2.0867	−2.0867
3-Jan-2023 10:35	4.7680	1.2687	4.3102	2.0883	−2.0883
3-Jan-2023 10:40	4.7678	1.2685	4.3067	2.0900	−2.0900
3-Jan-2023 10:45	4.7665	1.2669	4.3102	2.0919	−2.0919
3-Jan-2023 10:50	4.7679	1.2693	4.3067	2.0939	−2.0939
3-Jan-2023 10:55	4.7679	1.2686	4.3076	2.0959	−2.0959
3-Jan-2023 11:00	4.7676	1.2681	4.3084	2.0980	−2.0980
3-Jan-2023 11:05	4.7687	1.2697	4.3102	2.1001	−2.1001
3-Jan-2023 11:10	4.7679	1.2690	4.3067	2.1020	−2.1020

Table 11. *Cont.*

Date	γ ($\times 10^{-2}$)	κ	σ ($\times 10^{-3}$)	m ($\times 10^{-3}$)	a ($\times 10^{-3}$)
3-Jan-2023 11:15	4.7680	1.2687	4.3076	2.1038	−2.1038
3-Jan-2023 11:20	4.7692	1.2706	4.3084	2.1054	−2.1054
3-Jan-2023 11:25	4.7679	1.2693	4.3084	2.1068	−2.1068
3-Jan-2023 11:30	4.7680	1.2688	4.3076	2.1078	−2.1078
3-Jan-2023 13:05	4.7680	1.2690	4.3076	2.1086	−2.1086
3-Jan-2023 13:10	4.7675	1.2679	4.3084	2.1089	−2.1089
3-Jan-2023 13:15	4.7666	1.2667	4.3102	2.1089	−2.1089
3-Jan-2023 13:20	4.7666	1.2666	4.3067	2.1086	−2.1086
3-Jan-2023 13:25	4.7666	1.2665	4.3076	2.1079	−2.1079
3-Jan-2023 13:30	4.7666	1.2665	4.3067	2.1069	−2.1069
3-Jan-2023 09:35	4.7666	1.2665	4.3102	2.1058	−2.1058
3-Jan-2023 09:40	4.7666	1.2665	4.3067	2.1046	−2.1046
3-Jan-2023 09:45	4.7666	1.2665	4.3102	2.1033	−2.1033
3-Jan-2023 09:50	4.7665	1.2664	4.3067	2.1021	−2.1021
3-Jan-2023 09:55	4.7665	1.2664	4.3076	2.1010	−2.1010
3-Jan-2023 10:00	4.7663	1.2660	4.3067	2.1000	−2.1000
3-Jan-2023 10:05	4.7660	1.2655	4.3102	2.0992	−2.0992
3-Jan-2023 10:10	4.7660	1.2655	4.3067	2.0986	−2.0986
3-Jan-2023 10:15	4.7660	1.2655	4.3076	2.0981	−2.0981
3-Jan-2023 10:20	4.7655	1.2647	4.3084	2.0977	−2.0977
3-Jan-2023 10:25	4.7654	1.2647	4.3102	2.0975	−2.0975
3-Jan-2023 10:30	4.7654	1.2646	4.3067	2.0975	−2.0975
3-Jan-2023 10:35	4.7650	1.2640	4.3102	2.0975	−2.0975
3-Jan-2023 10:40	4.7648	1.2630	4.3067	2.0976	−2.0976
3-Jan-2023 10:45	4.7655	1.2647	4.3102	2.0977	−2.0977
3-Jan-2023 10:50	4.7651	1.2641	4.3067	2.0976	−2.0976
3-Jan-2023 10:55	4.7649	1.2637	4.3076	2.0975	−2.0975
3-Jan-2023 11:00	4.7647	1.2633	4.3084	2.0971	−2.0971
3-Jan-2023 11:05	4.7656	1.2649	4.3102	2.0966	−2.0966
3-Jan-2023 11:10	4.7655	1.2647	4.3067	2.0960	−2.0960

After centering the spread sequence, the mean is 0, the upper trigger threshold line is m, and the lower trigger threshold line is a. Observing and analyzing in combination with Table 11 and Figure 11, first of all, it can be found in Table 11 and Figure 11 that with the continuous addition of the latest out-of-sample data in the backtesting process, the parameter estimation values and trading thresholds change accordingly. Secondly, at low quantiles such as 0.25 quantile and 0.5 quantile, the changes in the threshold lines are small, while with the increase of the quantile, it may be affected by the sudden change of the spread from April to June in 2023. The sudden increase of the spread in this period leads to an increase in the amount of high quantile data, changing the data structure of the high quantile, causing the corresponding changes in the volatility and drift parameters, and thus the fluctuation of the threshold line increases. Finally, from the overall spread sequence, the threshold lines of each quantile have little impact on the triggering of trading time points, which may be attributed to the data structure distribution of the target.

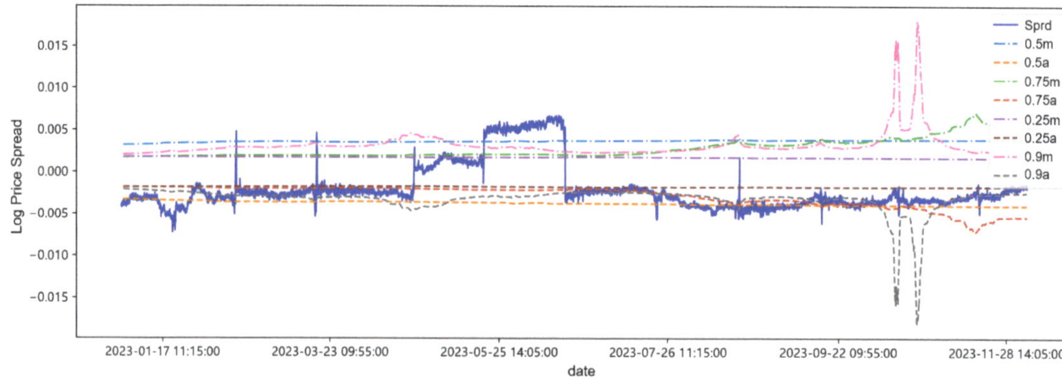

Figure 11. Trading thresholds at various quantiles.

4.4.3. Arbitrage Strategy Return Statistics and Indicator Assessment

Based on the trading rules outlined in Section 4.4.1, we perform a backtesting analysis of the pair trading strategy. To evaluate profitability, we use metrics total return rate and annualized return, while annualized volatility and the Sharpe ratio are employed to assess the associated risk. The results of the strategy implemented at each quantile are shown in the following Table 12.

Table 12. Strategy return statistics at different quantiles.

Indicator	0.25 Quantile	0.5 Quantile	0.75 Quantile	0.9 Quantile
Total Return Rate (%)	1.147	1.310	1.056	1.177
Annualized Return Rate (%)	0.027	0.031	0.025	0.028
Annualized Volatility (%)	0.228	0.184	0.223	0.215
Sharpe Ratio	0.118	0.167	0.111	0.129

As the simulation trading progresses, by the end of the strategy, there are a total of 5 trading cycles and 20 buy/sell transactions. During 2023, the strategy returns are positive at all quantiles, but the return rate and Sharpe ratio are not high. On one hand, this is due to the limited number of transactions, and on the other hand, we did not set a stop-loss line, which led to the consumption of previous gains during the long holding period. The strategy's net value curve is shown in Figure 12. It can be observed that the strategy at the 0.5 quantile has the highest net value, and regardless of the quantile, the overall net value of the strategy shows a step-like upward trend, with some drawdowns at a few points and intervals. This is partly because the trading decisions triggered are not 100% correct, and partly due to the long-term holding without a stop-loss line, which consumes the gains.

As shown in Table 12, the annualized volatility is relatively high, but the drawdowns in the net value curve of Figure 12 are not significant. It can be judged that the strategy has a relatively high risk compared to the return, but the drawdown risk is controllable. This indicates that by increasing the number of transactions or setting a stop-loss line, the strategy's returns can be increased, thereby improving the overall Sharpe ratio of the strategy to a more desirable level.

Next, we compare the performance of pair trading strategies triggered by thresholds derived from self-weighted quantile estimation and the variance multiplier method. The variance multiplier approach serves as a benchmark due to its widespread use in practice. Given that the residuals from the regression between the prices of two paired equities follow a normal distribution, the variance multiplier is commonly used to determine trading thresholds. To adapt to changing market conditions, we implement a rolling window approach, re-estimating the variance at each window and dynamically adjusting the thresholds for the pair trading strategy. The rolling window length is set to match that of the self-weighted quantile estimation to ensure consistency in threshold updates. The performance of the variance multiplier-based strategy is reported in Table 13.

Table 13. Strategy return statistics at different variance multipliers.

Variance Multipliers	4.8	5.0	5.2	5.4
Total Return Rate (%)	0.002	0.002	0.003	0.001
Annualized Return Rate ($\times 10^{-5}$%)	3.874	5.508	6.085	3.108
Annualized Volatility (%)	0.001	0.001	0.001	0.001
Sharpe Ratio	0.032	0.046	0.052	0.027

In terms of return performance, the self-weighted quantile estimation method significantly outperforms the variance multiplier-based strategy. The former achieves total return rates between 1.056% and 1.310%, whereas the latter yields a maximum of only 0.003%. Similarly, the annualized return rate for the self-weighted quantile approach remains consistently higher (0.025% to 0.031%) compared to the variance-based strategy, which produces returns on the order of 10^{-5}%. These results indicate that self-weighted quantile estimation is far more effective in generating cumulative and annualized returns, making it a superior choice for return maximization.

On the risk side, the self-weighted quantile estimation strategy exhibits an annualized volatility range of 0.184% to 0.228%, significantly higher than the near-zero volatility observed in the variance multiplier-based approach. While the lower volatility in the latter suggests greater stability, it may also indicate overly conservative risk constraints, which limit return potential. The Sharpe ratio comparison further highlights this contrast: the self-weighted quantile estimation method achieves Sharpe ratios between 0.111 and 0.167, whereas the variance-based strategy reaches a maximum of just 0.052. Given that a higher Sharpe ratio signifies better risk-adjusted returns, the self-weighted quantile estimation method emerges as the more attractive option, offering a better balance between risk and return.

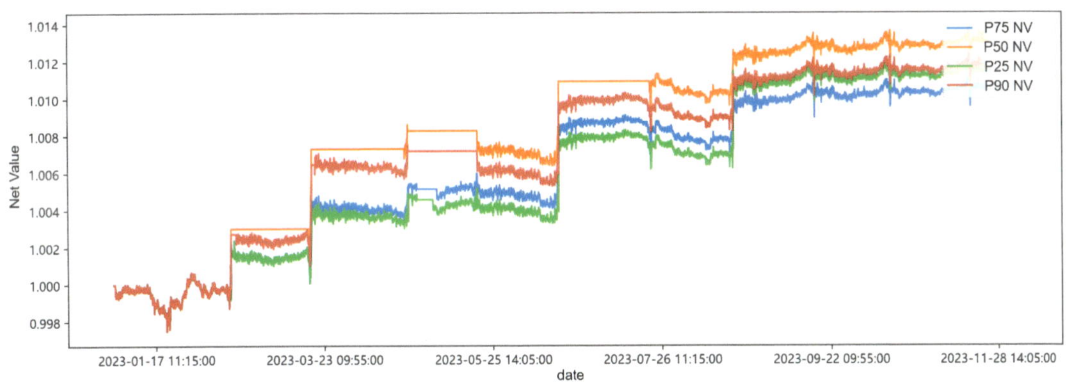

Figure 12. Net value of statistical arbitrage strategy in backtesting period.

5. Conclusions

On the theoretical front, this paper introduces self-weighted quantile estimation into the estimation of the drift parameters of the jump Ornstein–Uhlenbeck process, and proves the asymptotic normality of the estimator under large sample properties in a statistical sense. At the same time, through Monte Carlo simulation experiments, it verifies that compared to other estimators under this stochastic process, the self-weighted quantile estimator has better stability and accuracy in estimation performance.

In the empirical part, this paper first verifies the existence of jumps in asset prices (spreads) in the financial market, detects the direction and magnitude of asset price jumps through the LM test, and then matches them with the jump Ornstein–Uhlenbeck process, proving that the stochastic process with a jump term can better fit the jumps and other phenomena existing in the actual financial market. Secondly, under the premise of being as close as possible to the real market rules, this paper studies the statistical arbitrage strategy under the high-frequency data of CSI 300 stock index futures, conducts multiple tests on the related asset price sequences, sets reasonable trading trigger thresholds based on the goal of maximizing the expected return per unit time of the trading cycle, and conducts strategy backtesting at multiple quantiles. The backtesting results prove that the jump Ornstein–Uhlenbeck process and self-weighted quantile method adopted in this paper perform well in empirical tests. In the out-of-sample backtesting period of 2023, the number of trading cycles for each strategy is 5, and all quantiles have achieved positive returns, with an average total return rate of 1.17%. Thirdly, the net value curves of the strategies at each quantile are similar, all showing a step-like upward trend, with no obvious drawdowns, and the highest net value at the 0.5 quantile. Finally, due to the limited number of trading times and the absence of a stop-loss line, the annualized return rate of the strategy is relatively low compared to the annualized volatility, resulting in a lower Sharpe ratio, but the drawdown risk is controllable. This indicates that by adjusting the number of trades and setting a stop-loss line, the returns can be increased to some extent, thereby improving the Sharpe ratio and achieving a more desirable level.

However, due to the focus and depth of our research, this paper has certain limitations and potential directions for future study. As this paper focuses on methodology rather than practical implementation, our empirical study does not take into account factors such as capital constraints and liquidity issues in high-frequency pair trading, even though they are crucial to trading performance. We plan to explore these aspects further in future research.

Author Contributions: Conceptualization, Y.S.; methodology, Y.S.; software, C.C.; validation, R.C.; formal analysis, C.C.; investigation, Y.Z.; resources, M.Z.; data curation, C.C.; writing—original draft preparation, R.C.; writing—review and editing, M.Z.; visualization, Y.Z.; supervision, M.Z.; project administration, Y.S.; funding acquisition, Y.S. All authors have read and agreed to the published version of the manuscript.

Funding: This research work is supported by National Natural Science Foundation of China (11901397).

Data Availability Statement: The dataset for the empirical analysis can be derived from the following resource available in the public domain: https://www.joinquant.com/data/ (accessed on 1 January 2024).

Conflicts of Interest: The authors declare no conflicts of interest.

References

1. Griffin, J.E.; Steel, M.F. Inference with non-Gaussian Ornstein–Uhlenbeck processes for stochastic volatility. *J. Econom.* **2006**, *134*, 605–644. [CrossRef]
2. Roberts, G.O.; Papaspiliopoulos, O.; Dellaportas, P. Bayesian inference for non-Gaussian Ornstein–Uhlenbeck stochastic volatility processes. *J. R. Stat. Soc. Ser. B Stat. Methodol.* **2004**, *66*, 369–393. [CrossRef]
3. Jongbloed, G.; Van Der Meulen, F.H.; Van Der Vaart, A.W. Nonparametric inference for Lévy-driven Ornstein-Uhlenbeck processes. *Bernoulli* **2005**, *11*, 759–791. [CrossRef]
4. Valdivieso, L. Parameter estimation for an IG-OU stochastic volatility model. *Math. Day* **2005**, 95.
5. Valdivieso, L.; Schoutens, W.; Tuerlinckx, F. Maximum likelihood estimation in processes of Ornstein-Uhlenbeck type. *Stat. Inference Stoch. Process.* **2009**, *12*, 1–19. [CrossRef]

6. Barndorff-Nielsen, O.E.; Shephard, N. Non-Gaussian Ornstein–Uhlenbeck-based models and some of their uses in financial economics. *J. R. Stat. Soc. Ser. B (Stat. Methodol.)* **2001**, *63*, 167–241. [CrossRef]
7. Jongbloed, G.; Van Der Meulen, F.H. Parametric estimation for subordinators and induced OU processes. *Scand. J. Stat.* **2006**, *33*, 825–847. [CrossRef]
8. Zhang, S.; Zhang, X.; Sun, S. Parametric estimation of discretely sampled Gamma-OU processes. *Sci. China Ser. A Math.* **2006**, *49*, 1231–1257. [CrossRef]
9. Brockwell, P.J.; Davis, R.A.; Yang, Y. Estimation for nonnegative Lévy-driven Ornstein-Uhlenbeck processes. *J. Appl. Probab.* **2007**, *44*, 977–989. [CrossRef]
10. Leonenko, N.; Sakhno, L.; Šuvak, N. Parameter estimation for reciprocal gamma Ornstein–Uhlenbeck type processes. *Theory Probab. Math. Stat.* **2013**, *86*, 137–154. [CrossRef]
11. Zhang, S.; Zhang, X. Moment estimation of parameters for discretely sampled OU-compound Poisson processes. *Chin. J. Appl. Probab. Stat.* **2010**, *26*, 384–398.
12. Wu, Y.; Hu, J.; Zhang, X. Moment estimators for the parameters of Ornstein-Uhlenbeck processes driven by compound Poisson processes. *Discret. Event Dyn. Syst.* **2019**, *29*, 57–77. [CrossRef]
13. Hu, Y.; Long, H. Least squares estimator for Ornstein–Uhlenbeck processes driven by α-stable motions. *Stoch. Process. Their Appl.* **2009**, *119*, 2465–2480. [CrossRef]
14. Zhang, S.; Zhang, X. A least squares estimator for discretely observed Ornstein–Uhlenbeck processes driven by symmetric α-stable motions. *Ann. Inst. Stat. Math.* **2013**, *65*, 89–103. [CrossRef]
15. Long, H. Least squares estimator for discretely observed Ornstein–Uhlenbeck processes with small Lévy noises. *Stat. Probab. Lett.* **2009**, *79*, 2076–2085. [CrossRef]
16. Masuda, H. Approximate self-weighted LAD estimation of discretely observed ergodic Ornstein-Uhlenbeck processes. *Electron. J. Stat.* **2010**, *4*, 525–565. [CrossRef]
17. Taufer, E.; Leonenko, N. Characteristic function estimation of non-Gaussian Ornstein–Uhlenbeck processes. *J. Stat. Plan. Inference* **2009**, *139*, 3050–3063. [CrossRef]
18. Hu, Y.; Long, H. Parameter estimation for Ornstein-Uhlenbeck processes driven by α-stable Lévy motions. *Commun. Stoch. Anal.* **2007**, *1*, 1. [CrossRef]
19. Mai, H. Efficient maximum likelihood estimation for Lévy-driven Ornstein–Uhlenbeck processes. *Bernoulli* **2014**, *20*, 919–957. [CrossRef]
20. Spiliopoulos, K.V. Method of moments estimation of Ornstein-Uhlenbeck processes driven by general Lévy process. In *Annales de l'ISUP*; LSTA: Paris, France, 2009; Volume 53, pp. 3–18.
21. Wu, Y.; Hu, J.; Yang, X. Moment estimators for parameters of Lévy-driven Ornstein–Uhlenbeck processes. *J. Time Ser. Anal.* **2022**, *43*, 610–639. [CrossRef]
22. Shu, H.; Jiang, Z.; Zhang, X. Parameter estimation for integrated Ornstein–Uhlenbeck processes with small Lévy noises. *Stat. Probab. Lett.* **2023**, *199*, 109851. [CrossRef]
23. Wang, J.; Wang, L.; Li, H. Parameter Estimation for the Harmonic Fractional Ornstein-Uhlenbeck Financial Model. *J. Henan Norm. Univ. (Nat. Sci. Ed.)* **2025**, *53*, 75–81. [CrossRef]
24. Han, Y.; Hu, Y.; Zhang, D. Modified least squares estimators for Ornstein–Uhlenbeck processes from low-frequency observations. *Appl. Math. Lett.* **2024**, *156*, 109143. [CrossRef]
25. Alazemi, F.; Alsenafi, A.; Chen, Y.; Zhou, H. Parameter estimation for the complex fractional Ornstein–Uhlenbeck processes with Hurst parameter $H \in (0, 12)$. *Chaos Solitons Fractals* **2024**, *188*, 115556. [CrossRef]
26. Zhang, D. Statistical inference for Ornstein–Uhlenbeck processes based on low-frequency observations. *Stat. Probab. Lett.* **2025**, *216*, 110286. [CrossRef]
27. Sutcliffe, C.; Board, J. *The Effects of Spot Transparency on Bid-Ask Spreads and Volume of Traded Share Options*; University of Southampton: Southampton, UK, 1996.
28. Bondarenko, O. Statistical arbitrage and securities prices. *Rev. Financ. Stud.* **2003**, *16*, 875–919. [CrossRef]
29. Hogan, S.; Jarrow, R.; Teo, M.; Warachka, M. Testing market efficiency using statistical arbitrage with applications to momentum and value strategies. *J. Financ. Econ.* **2004**, *73*, 525–565. [CrossRef]
30. Alexander, C.; Dimitriu, A. A comparison of cointegration and tracking error models for mutual funds and hedge funds. *ISMA Cent. Discuss. Pap. Financ.* **2004**, *4*, 1–26.
31. Elliott, R.J.; Van Der Hoek, J.; Malcolm, W.P. Pairs trading. *Quant. Financ.* **2005**, *5*, 271–276. [CrossRef]
32. Bertram, W.K. Analytic solutions for optimal statistical arbitrage trading. *Phys. A Stat. Mech. Its Appl.* **2010**, *389*, 2234–2243. [CrossRef]
33. Rudy, J.; Dunis, C.; Giorgioni, G.; Laws, J. Statistical Arbitrage and High-Frequency Data with an Application to Eurostoxx 50 Equities. 2010. Available online: https://ssrn.com/abstract=2272605 (accessed on 1 January 2024).

34. Fang, H. Empirical Research on the Theoretical Model and Application Analysis of Statistical Arbitrage Based on China's Closed-end Fund Market. *Stat. Decis.* **2005**, 3.
35. Caldeira, J.F.; Moura, G.V. Selection of a portfolio of pairs based on cointegration: A statistical arbitrage strategy. *Rev. Bras. Financ.* **2013**, *11*, 49–80. [CrossRef]
36. Zhu, L.r.; Su, X.; Zhou, Y. Research on Statistical Arbitrage Based on China's Futures Market. *J. Appl. Stat. Manag.* **2015**, *34*, 11.
37. Fan, B.T. Futures arbitrage of different varieties and based on the cointegration which is under the framework of bayesian-in the case of soy oil and palm oil. *DEStech Trans. Econ. Bus. Manag.* **2018**. [CrossRef]
38. Wang, J.; Cui, W.; Wang, C. Research on Statistical Arbitrage of Stock Index Futures Based on Time-Varying Coefficient Cointegration. *Wuhan Financ.* **2017**, 29–33.
39. Liu, Y.; Lu, Y. Empirical Study on Statistical Arbitrage of Options and Futures Based on the O-U Process. *Mod. Bus. Trade Ind.* **2016**, *37*, 2.
40. Zhang, L. Application Research on the Cross-Breed Arbitrage of O-U Model in Agricultural Futures Market. Ph.D. Thesis, Anhui University, Hefei, China, 2018.
41. Wu, L.; Zang, X.; Zhao, H. Analytic value function for a pairs trading strategy with a Lévy-driven Ornstein–Uhlenbeck process. *Quant. Financ.* **2020**, *20*, 1285–1306. [CrossRef]
42. Sabino, P. Exact simulation of variance gamma-related ou processes: Application to the pricing of energy derivatives. *Appl. Math. Financ.* **2020**, *27*, 207–227. [CrossRef]
43. Zhao, H.; Luo, P.; Wang, S. High-frequency pairs trading in Chinese stock market: Based on Lévy-OU processes. *Syst. Eng.-Theory Pract.* **2023**, *43*, 2251–2265.
44. Ken-Iti, S. *Lévy Processes and Infinitely Divisible Distributions*; Cambridge University Press: Cambridge, UK, 1999; Volume 68.
45. Masuda, H. Ergodicity and exponential β-mixing bounds for multidimensional diffusions with jumps. *Stoch. Process. Their Appl.* **2007**, *117*, 35–56. [CrossRef]
46. Ling, S. Self-weighted least absolute deviation estimation for infinite variance autoregressive models. *J. R. Stat. Soc. Ser. B Stat. Methodol.* **2005**, *67*, 381–393. [CrossRef]
47. Hjort, N.L.; Pollard, D. Asymptotics for minimisers of convex processes. *arXiv* **2011**, arXiv:1107.3806.
48. Knight, K. Limiting distributions for L1 regression estimators under general conditions. *Ann. Stat.* **1998**, *26*, 755–770. [CrossRef]
49. Lee, S.S.; Mykland, P.A. Jumps in financial markets: A new nonparametric test and jump dynamics. *Rev. Financ. Stud.* **2008**, *21*, 2535–2563. [CrossRef]

MDPI AG
Grosspeteranlage 5
4052 Basel
Switzerland
Tel.: +41 61 683 77 34

Mathematics Editorial Office
E-mail: mathematics@mdpi.com
www.mdpi.com/journal/mathematics

www.ingramcontent.com/pod-product-compliance
Lightning Source LLC
Chambersburg PA
CBHW041351210926
51850CB00013B/3052